DENBY & DISTRICT II

From Landed Lords to Inspired Industrialists

Above: Wakefield Road, Denby Dale, 1907. The letter box in the wall identifies the Post Office. Next door, to the right was Dyson's cobblers. The Co-operative buildings are to the left.

Below: Taken from the viaduct, this early twentieth century view of Denby Dale includes the mills of Brownhills and Kenyons, Norman Road and Sunny Bank. Miller or 'Ranter' Hill leads away in the top middle part of the picture. The roof of the old tin church, built in 1893, on land donated by Walter Norton, is to the bottom right of the picture. *Old Barnsley*

Denby & District II

FROM LANDED LORDS TO INSPIRED INDUSTRIALISTS

CHRIS HEATH

Wharncliffe Books

By the same author:

Denebi – Farmstead of the Danes
(Richard Netherwood 1997)

The History of the Denby Dale Pies
(J R Nicholls, 1998)

Denby & District – From Prehistory to the Present
(Wharncliffe Books 2001)

First edition published in Great Britain in 2004 by
Wharncliffe Books
an imprint of
Pen & Sword Books Ltd
47 Church Street
Barnsley
South Yorkshire S70 2AS

ISBN: 1-903425-66-2

Printed in the United Kingdom by
CPI UK

For up-too-date information on other titles produced under
the Wharncliffe imprint, please contact:
WHARNCLIFFE BOOKS
47 Church Street, Barnsley, South Yorkshire, S70 2AS, England
Telephone: (24 hours) 01226 734555
E-mail: enquiries@wharncliffebooks.co.uk
Website: www.wharncliffebooks.co.uk

Contents

✧

Dedication

For my Grandmother, Ava,

my Great Aunt Annie 'Nan' who would have been one of my greatest fans

and for Zara Jade who is one of my youngest.

Acknowledgements

As is usual when compiling books of this sort I have a number of individuals to thank.

Without the services of Richard Samways and Celia Parker I would not have been in a position to relate much of the material focusing on the medieval period. With only photocopies from which to work, some of them very poor! They came up trumps every time.

The chapter on Industry, aside from being a pleasure to research, was supported, encouraged and endowed by:

James Hinchliffe, George Wilby, Audrey & Bill Kenyon, Charles & Mary Brownhill, John Hall, Edward Naylor, Liz Hudston, Mr & Mrs Braithwaite and Judy at Bagden Hall and my brother, Paul, for finding an inexpensive way to produce pictures from 80 year old negatives!

Other grateful thanks are due to:

Sheila Wiseman, for allowing me access to her late husband, Bob Wiseman's research. John Goodchild for his help with copying medieval documents relating to Denby housed in his archive, Wendy Hawkins at Barnsley Local Studies Library, Winifred Wheable Archer for the details on the New Inn, Jacey Bedford and Beryl Smith - for information and photographs of Birdsedge, High Flatts and Denby, Chris Sharp for allowing me to use his archive of photographs to help illustrate the book, all of which are available to buy at his 'Old Barnsley' stall on Barnsley market, Wilf and Julie Charlton, Professor David Hey, Dr George Redmonds, Tom Scargill, Ava Newby, Bryan Heath, Peter Beaumont, Audrey Tyas, Tony Turton, Frank Burdett, Guy Hirst; also the staff of Nottingham Archives, Huddersfield Archives and the Borthwick Institute of Historical Research, York.

Whilst every effort has been made to contact the copyright holders of the illustrations within this book, the author apologises to anyone who has not been acknowledged.

Introduction

✿

Never say never again! It was never in my mind to write another book on the district – at least – not so soon after the last one. New material always comes to my attention upon the publication of a new book, so it was with Denby and District. I was approached in October 2002, via the bookshop in Denby Dale by a lady from Kirby Moorside who had obtained a copy after reading an article in which the book was featured in *Yorkshire Life Magazine*. Her late husband had pursued the history of the Burdet family for some years and asked, would I like to see his work. This was the 'kick start' for this work, which is a companion to Denby & District, From Pre-History to the Present, which has now become Volume 1, though I have tried to write this book in such a way that read singly it still tells the history of the district. There have been times when a short resume of the facts have been necessary in order to keep the reader in touch with the story but this has been kept to the bare minimum in order to allow for all the new research.

The emphasis within these pages is slightly more upon Denby Dale, though Ingbirchworth, High Flatts and Birdsedge and to a lesser extent High Hoyland, Clayton and Cumberworth are included. As usual I have had to undertake large cuts in the manuscript in order to make publishing a realistic possibility and to try and keep down the price of the book.

The translation of a number of ancient documents has brought to light much that was previously unknown, not only for Denby but all the other villages that came under its banner throughout the various different historical epochs. These translations have barely touched the surface of the vast quantity now known to have survived the ravages of time, but the heavy cost of translation has meant only a very selective few have been possible. At least this gives scope for further work to be undertaken in the future – who knows what still lies unknown in a dusty archive awaiting modern understanding.

I have tried to let some of the documents speak for themselves. In the centuries before the census returns were undertaken manorial documents list a great many individuals and their property. For reasons of space no whole single document has been included, family historians take note, there is no substitute for the original.

The chapter on the Industrial Revolution, centres very much upon Denby Dale. There have been times during the compilation of the manuscript that I considered that this chapter and its accompanying illustrations would make a good read if published on their own. In the end I wanted to tell a tale of a thousand years and decided to leave it in.

In this work I have tried to feature more of the people who lived in the district and follow the transition from tenant to freeholder, though, of course, not every local family could be included. Every individual has a tale to tell, be it from the twelfth or twentieth centuries and it is sometimes difficult to distinguish where genealogy and local history meet. Being in full time employment I am unable to research all that I would like and can only apologise to those who are disappointed that a family member or name has been omitted.

By late Autumn, 2003 this book was written. In just over a year I have doubled my understanding of the district in which I live. I hope that by reading this work, others can achieve the same goal.

Chris Heath, October 2003.

Aerial view of Denby Dale taken in 1973. Although the picture was taken only 31 years ago, it is only recently that the village has expanded to the size it is today. In the top left corner are the mills of the Hinchliffe family and their home, Strathdearne. To the right of them is the Naylors site. Below them are Kitsons works and towards the bottom left are Kenyons buildings which are adjacent to Brownhills site. To the bottom right are the old corn mill buildings. Note the numerous chimney's and small reservoirs and ponds which at one time supplied the mills. *Simmons Aerofilms Ltd., copies of this picture can be obtained by calling 01934 745820*

Chapter One

Early Lords of the Manor and their Tenants, 1066–1485

The descent of the first 'de Denby' family is a complicated and difficult thread to follow. In the first volume of this work we examined the Norman conquest and its effects upon the people in the area. New information has now come to light which may give an indication of the origin of the family. We will therefore, begin this book with an overview of the sub-infeuded Saxon family of Alric (Ailric) and their dealings with the all powerful de Lacy family.

At the time of the Domesday survey the 42 townships in the Staincross wapentake were held by 28 Saxon thanes (Lords), only 7 of whom survived the conquest. One of the most important of these was Ailric, son of Ashenbald, whom Eli Hoyle suggests was Lord of Pontefract as well as the Denby area and who may have been responsible for a castle here before the arrival of the Norman de Lacy family. The 'ric' element of his name, was a Royal patronymic contracted from 'Aethel-ric' which meant a prince over a district, an element we find in other names from the period, most notably, Godric who was supplanted in Denby after the conquest by Ailric. Legend has it that Ailric was a person of such note and rank that he was carried to France in the train of King William the Conqueror on his first return to Normandy after his victory in England.

Ailric had a dwelling at Cawthorne and also one in Cumberland, and besides his many manors in Staincross, including Denby, he also owned Culgaith, Kirklands, part of Keswick, Edenhall and other places in Cumberland. The reason for his holdings so far North of Staincross would seem to lay with the policy of planting reliable Englishmen in this buffer zone between Scotland and England to help police the area.

From the Saxon Chronicle 1092:

This year King William II went northward to Carlisle with a large army and he repaired the city and built the castle. Having placed a garrison in the castle he returned to the south and sent a great number of rustic Englishmen thither with their wives and cattle that they might settle here and cultivate the land.

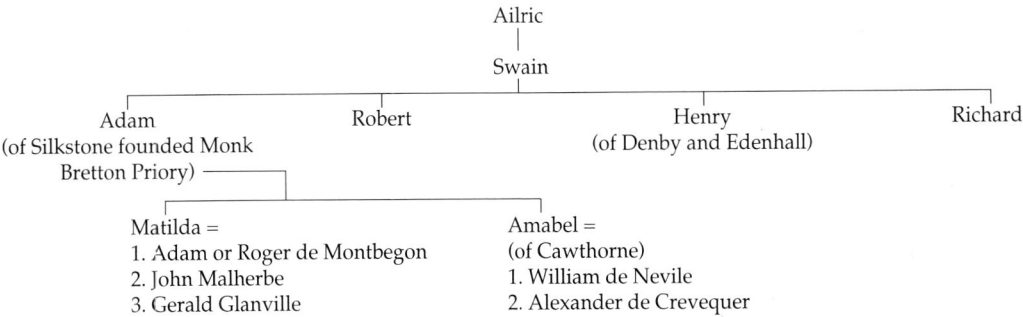

Ailric died around 1087, coincidentally the same year as William the Conqueror and the first Ilbert de Lacy. They were succeeded, respectively, by Swain, King William II and Robert de Lacy. Robert de Lacy was a younger son of Ilbert de Lacy and his wife Hadruda, his elder brother, Hugh pre-deceased his parents and was buried within a monastery at Rouen in France, endowed by Ilbert and his wife. Robert was born around 1066 and was in full possession of his father's estates by 1089. One of his first acts was to resume possession of Dodworth from Swain fitz Ailric. His inheritance was vast and was later valued at 60 knights fees. On the death of King William II (1100) he supported the cause of Robert of Normandy over that of the eventual monarch, Henry I, who deprived him of his estates for this, only restoring them in 1107. He offended King Henry a second time in 1121 and was again dispossessed of his estates. He founded the Carmelite monastery of St. John's at Pontefract in 1090 soon after which Swain fitz Ailric endowed it with the church at Silkstone, the chapel at Cawthorne and other possessions. Swain's charter relating to this continues:

> To his spiritual father T (homas) Archbishop and to all the sons of the Holy church, Swain, the son of Ailric sends greeting. I will that all men know both now and hereafter that I in remission for all my sins and for the salvation of my soul and of all my kindred who have passed from this world and for the souls of my heirs, have given, by this my charter and seal to the church of St. John at Pontefract and the monks who serve God there, the church of Silkstone and six bovates of land in the same vill and with all things which belong to the same anywhere; and the chapel of Cawthorne with two bovates of land in the same vill with two parts of the titles of all my Lordships, viz., of sheaves in pure and perpetual alms, so that in the aforesaid church and chapel I have retained nothing to myself or any of my heirs and if anyone who holds of me shall have wished to make them any alms from my fee I admit it freely. I invoke God as witness of this gift.

NB: the Archbishop Thomas mentioned above was Archbishop of York 1070–1100.

It seems likely that Swain was responsible for the first church at Silkstone as there was no church mentioned here in 1086. The gift was twice confirmed by Robert de Lacy in 1090 and 1114, by the King, Hugh de la Val and by Theobald, Archbishop of Canterbury.

Robert de Lacy died before 1130. In 1112 he had married, late in life, to a woman we know only as Matilda who bore him four sons, Albreda, Ilbert, Henry and Walter. On the death of Henry I (1135) the honour of Pontefract was held by William Maltravers who was murdered by his servant, Peganus, soon afterwards. Ilbert, Roberts heir, was restored to his family estates after this by King Stephen, though Ilbert disappears after the Battle of Lincoln in 1141. The name Ilbert or Gilbert de Lacy appears a few years later fighting with the Crusaders in Palestine alongside Robert Mansel where they were involved in the victory over Nur-Ed-Din, the Saracen leader prior to Saladin. Robert's second son, Henry, obtained possession of the Pontefract inheritance but his right was disputed by Gilbert de Gaunt, who claimed the inheritance through his wife. The two were soon involved in a war which lasted ten years. Gilbert de Gaunt burnt down the monastery at Pontefract (1151/2) but Henry seems to have got the better of the affair, before King Stephen died he sought and was granted a charter of forgiveness from the Empress Matilda, daughter of Henry I and mother of Henry II (1153), and order was restored.

Returning to Swain fitz Ailric, as we know, he had at least four sons, Adam, Robert, Henry and Richard. In volume I of this work we saw how Adam founded Monk Bretton Priory, and that the churches of High Hoyland and Penistone had been founded during his time. It is interesting to note that Monk Bretton Priory should more correctly be called The Priory of Lund, as it stood at the edge of Lund forest from which the later village of Lundwood takes its name. Adam also founded Felkirk church which he donated to Nostell Priory. A charter of Robert de Laci dated 1112 was witnessed by Swain fitz Ailric who must by now have been around 70 years old. Adam must have inherited his estates soon after this, it is interesting to note that Swain died at his father's Cumbrian residence.

The Pipe Rolls of 1130 tell us that Adam, the son of Swain, owed 20 silver marks for land in Cumberland. Adam fitz Swain is charged a death duty of 5 marks on the decease of his mother, which shows that Adam's father must have pre-deceased his mother. The entry copied above shows that he was still holding his lands in 1158 and although the money was owing for his Cumbrian estate this entry proves that he was living in Yorkshire.

Adam was an old man when he founded Monk Bretton Priory and by using the Pipe Rolls we can deduce the year of his death. Amongst his many possessions, he farmed from the King the Royal town of Doncaster, paying a yearly rent of £60 for it. A return was made by the Sheriff on this account. In the Pipe Roll for the year ending September 1158 Adam was recorded as having settled his account for the rent of Doncaster. The following year ending September 1159, it is recorded that:

Alan and his friends rendered an account of £15 for the rent of Doncaster.

This was for the last quarter. The document goes on to state that the heirs of Adam fitz Swain owe £45 for the rent of the previous three quarters. Therefore Adam had died sometime during the third quarter of 1159.

Adam's heirs were mentioned in the following charter, relating to Monk Bretton Priory as Adam Montbegon and Matilda (Adam's daughter):

1158 – I Adam fitz Swain have given, etc., for the religion, the house of St. Mary Magdalen of Lund, which I have founded on my patrimony … there is granted to me an obit yearly in their mother church of Charite and an obit in the house of Pontefract and my anniversary each year there and in all their houses a trental, but in others as much as for a Clugniac monk. And Adam the prior and founder when he shall depart from Pontefract shall dwell in that same house at Lund as long as he shall live as keeper and prior. After his decease the prior and monks with my advice or my heirs shall put in his place others who may be suitable and if any brother from Pontefract come to me in a suitable season on the business of his house he shall eat with me. In gratitude for this there ought to be paid every year a silver mark from the house of Lund to the church of St. John, etc.

It is difficult to tell how Adam divided his estates between his daughters. Amabel (Mabel), whose first husband was Thomas de Burgh, though she remarried to Alexander Crevequer, appears to have settled at the family home in Cawthorne. Matilda or Maud, as she is better known, although still holding lands around Cawthorne, settled at Brierley. The family genealogy becomes very complicated at this point with each daughter making a number of marriages and producing offspring. As the Lords of Denby held their manor, directly from the Lord's of Brierley, it might be useful to list the Lords of this place:

1086 – Ailric (all of Staincross)	1335–1347 – Robert Nevile
1087–1112 app. - Swain fitz Ailric	1347–1403 – Sir Robert Nevile
1112–1158 – Adam fitz Swain	1403–1438 – Sir William Harrington
1158 – John Malherb	1438–1460 – Sir Thomas Harrington
1232 – Hugo Longvilliers	1460–1485 – Sir James Harrington
1254–1279 – John Longvilliers	1485–1489 – Thomas Stanley
1279–1284 – Geofrey Nevile	1489–1523 – Sir Edward Stanley, Lord Mounteagle
1284–1289 – Margaret Nevile	1523–1560 – Sir Thomas Stanley, Lord Mounteagle
1289–1335 – John Nevile	1560–1580 – Sir William Stanley, Lord Mounteagle

Amabil and Matilda and their respective husbands were involved in deeds a little closer to home. Matilda and her husband, John de Malherbe, by deed, granted 12 bovates at Penistone and all liberties in field, wood, mill, water, meadow and pasture to John de Penistone, clerk, to hold by knight service of Phillip, son of William de Wlvelai (Woolley) in the time of Henry III (1216–72). Following this, John de Penistone gave to Henry, son of Roger del Rodes of Penistone, an assart containing 8 acres of land and wood in Penistone called 'Longherste'.

Amabel and her husband appeared in York on 2 November 1208 regarding lands distant to their manor but the case was very similar to one which took place in 1202 during the reign of King John. In this, she proved that she had inherited the right of presentation to a moiety (a half) of the church at High Hoyland against Adam de Hoyland.

This case proves the growing power and influence of the de Hoyland family. Though records are incomplete, Adam appears to have been the son of Hugh de Hoyland in this period before the manor became united with that of Denby. The following dating from the thirteenth century illustrates the family's growth:

Grant, by John son of Mathew de Boleholes to Adam de Holand of the service of 2s 0d annually and homage of John de Sindelesache, in return for 1 silver mark and an annual payment of 12d.

Grant by Robert de Wetel to Adam de Holande of 1 assart in return for his homage and service on account of which he is to pay 6d annually and a payment of half a silver mark.

Grant by Robert de Wetelai to Adam de Holande of one bovate of land and the service of Hugo de Turnstal and his heirs in return for his homage and service on account of which he is to pay 6d annually and do forensic service and a payment of 10s 0d.
NB: forensic service was a duty to attend a court of law or a manorial court.

Grant by Robert de Wetelei to Adam de Holanda of 9 bovates, the homage and service of Hugo de Tunstal, John de Byrkethwait and Adam son of Roger de Scandclive and their heirs, and 1 assart in return for 5 marks of silver and his service and homage on account of which he is to pay one pound of cummin annually and do forensic service.

Warranty by Robert de Schelflay to Adam de Holand of 9 bovates given to Adam by Robert de Wetelay and one meadow quit claimed to him by Henry son of Robert de Wetelay in return for his service and homage on account of which he is to pay one pound of cummin annually and forensic service.

Grant by John de Byrweytt to Robert son of Adam de Holand of the service of Roger Capellanus of all the land he held of John in Clayton and of 2 perches and the homage of Roger Capellanus on them in return for 10s sterling.

Grant by John, son of Roger the chaplain to Adam de Holand of 6 acres of land in return for 18s and his homage and service on account of which he is to pay 2s annually.

Grant, by Simon le Vilur to Robert son of Adam de Holand of the service of a bovate of land, namely 5d annually, in return for 4s and his service on account of which he is to render a pair of white gloves annually and homage.

Grant by Hugo de Denton to Michael de Brenethwisel of all his land in Clayton, that is to say 2 bovates held of him by Adam de Holand at 4s annually, 1 bovate held of him by Henry de Tunstal at 12d annually, and 1 bovate held of him by Osbert de Branskroft at 12d annually, with all homages and services; also the site of the demesne mill with all its suit. In return Michael gives 14 silver marks and will do forensic service for 6 bovates.

Grant by Robert de Wetelei to Adam de Holanda of the homage and service owned by Robert son of Gillian on land in Clayton and Crossland and that of Alan de Dentun and Alice his wife, on land in Clayton and Crossland and that of Alan, son of William on land in Clayton and that of Mathew de Sepelei on meadow land in Langley, and that of Norman, the smith (Faber) on land in Wheatley, and that of Alexander son of Symon on land in Wheatley and that of John de Weledun on land in Wheatley and that of John son of Helias de Wluelei on land in Crossland in return for his homage and service on 28 bovates of land (Clayton, Crossland, Wheatley, Langley).

An early grant for the neighbouring manor of Clayton shows that the Lords of this place too had begun to develop their autonomy:

Grant by Adam son of Robert de Claitun to Thorald son of Aissolf de Tunstall of 1 bovate of land in return for his homage and service on account of which he is to pay 2s 6d in silver annually Thorald to do forensic service.

Returning to the Pipe Rolls, which were introduced in 1130, the most complete is dated 1156 but the following details have survived from the period 1130 to 1165:

Henry fitz Swain of Denby (1160) paid £10 for Langworthy & Edenhall an added note shows that this was £6 7s 9d more than he ought to have been received from him.

Mathew de Denby (1165) owed 100s.

Dolfinus de Denby paid 4s into the treasury the same year.

Alan, son of Dolfin (of Tankersley) paid 1 mark (1165).
This Alan or Alanus is supposed by Hunter to have been progenitor of the Wortley family. Nicholas, son of Alan is one of the witnesses to the foundation deed of Kirklees nunnery.

NB: There is some confusion as to who held the Lordship of Denby during the fourteenth century. The above document seems to imply that Dolfin of Denby was the father of the progenitor of the de Wortley family. This would explain why in 1304 Robert Balliol and his wife came to an agreement whereby they conceded that the manors were 'of the right' of Nicholas de Wortley but he in turn granted them to Balliol and after de Wortley's death they were to be held by any issue of Robert Burdet and Idonea Balliol, namely, Aymer Burdet. We will shortly return to Dolfin of Denby.

Bernard de Silcheston (1165) owed 20s which sum was paid the following year and a quittance given.

This same Bernard in 1160 leased Dodworth from the monks of which deed Henry fitz Swain was one of the witnesses. He is thought to have been a man of great influence and in some way connected with the fitz Swain family.

The latter set of records may, in part, lead us to a conclusion as to the origins of the 'de Denby' family of Lords.

As we have noted, Swain fitz Ailric had at least four sons, Adam, who we have already cited, Robert, Henry and Richard.

Henry is styled as of Denby, Yorkshire and Edenhall in Cumbria, but in the above document he is called Henry fitz Swain of Denby. In the original document he would have been called Henry fitz Swain de Denby, or for short, Henry de Denby. The power of the Lords of Denby had to come from somewhere, they did not just spring up and take control! Henry was the grandson of the renowned Ailric. His brother was one of the most powerful men of his time in the Staincross wapentake and elsewhere.

Of Henry we know only a little, he was a benefactor to Byland Abbey although he made donations to other places. As we have seen, he seems to have inherited some of his Grandfather's lands near Penrith in Cumbria. Several of his charters survive in the British Museum, though these have never been translated. To be described as of Denby suggests that he lived in the village as it stood at that time. His brother, Richard, may also have adopted the surname 'de Denby'. A fellow historian discovered that a Richard de Denby was acting as a 'member of parliament' in 1113. At this early stage in the country's development the role involved the King summoning, infrequently, an assembly of his representatives from various areas and ascribing administrative, judicial and advisory tasks to them. The Richard referred to may be just a little too old to be Henry's younger brother, but it is not impossible, providing that he was a young man when he gained the position.

Knowing that Henry's elder brother, Adam, died in 1158 and that the pipe roll dates to 1160 it is likely that Henry died soon afterwards – who were his heirs?

The herald's visitation during the sixteenth century began the descent of the 'de Denby' family with Robert de Denby, we are now able to go a little further back:

> *Quitclaim by Simon son of Mathew de Denby in favour of Robert son of Robert son of Dolfin of all his right in a wood at Denebi in return for two and a half silver marks.*

The original Robert de Denby was the son of Dolfin de Denby, named in the above pipe rolls of 1160, along with Matthew de Denby whom I speculated about in the first volume of this work. If Henry fitz Swain lived at Denby, his heir would almost certainly inherit his father's home and estates. As the succession seems to run through Dolfin to Robert and then Sir Robert de Denby the reason for the families wealth and status might now be explained.

The following abbreviated documents, though all undated, have surfaced since V1 and can only add to our knowledge and understanding of this period in Denby's history. They appear to date from the late twelfth century through to the thirteenth century:

> *Grant by the Prior and convent of Watton to William son of Robert de Deneby of land beside the River Calder at an annual rent of 5s 0d sterling.*

> *Grant by Thomas son of Mathew de Rilay to Thomas son of William de Denby of the mill of Melteham with suit of service belonging there to.*

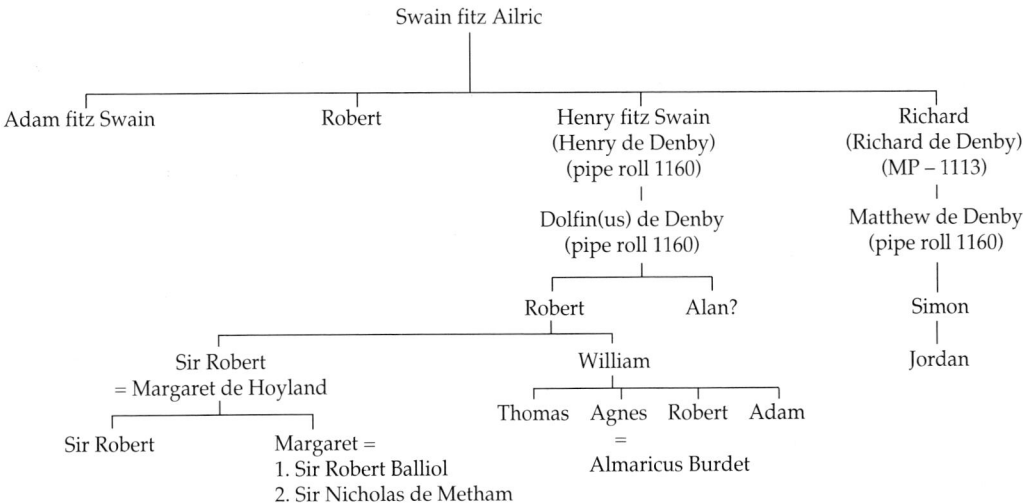

Grant, for a consideration of 5s by Jordan son of Simon de Deneby to Sir Robert de Holand, for his service of a farthing yearly (excluding foreign service due to the King for a bovate in Denby), of 2 acres of land in Deneby and an annual rent of 3d which the said Robert is accustomed to pay to the grantor.

Grant for a consideration of 3s of silver by William, son of Robert de Denebi inferiori (Robert of Lower Denby) to John Cusin for his homage and service of 4d yearly of a piece of land in Denebi.

Release by Thomas de Dronefeld to Robert de Denebi of homage and service on half a bovate of land which Thomas had sold to Sir Robert de Holaund, saving forensic service to the King.

The following documents finally give us the names of some of the other occupants of Denby during the thirteenth century:

Grant by William son of Alan de Neutona to William son of John Knyth de Over Deneby in frank marriage with Juliana his daughter of one assart of land called 'Le Rye Rode' with its meadow and wood for an annual rent of 12d during William son of Alan's life.

The de Denby family can also be found in a deed involving Henry de Portbref:

I Henry, son of William Portbref have … confirmed William, son of Hugh my man and my native with all his goods and all his following etc. Witnesses, Alano de Rand tunc allivio, Willelmo filio Ade, Roberto de Deneby, Ade Holanda, Ade de Oldefelda et allis.
(Note the Alan mentioned here is Alan Smeaton).

Witnesses to Henry de Portbref's confirmation of a bovate of land in Barnsley included, Roberto de Deneby, Ade de Holand, Roberto filio Williami de Deneby.
    As regards the Portbref family, all we know is that William de Portbref had two sons, Henry and Andrew. Andrew, the dyer, appears in conjunction with Henry in almost every deed where the latter is mentioned, therefore it is probable that it is the brother, Andrew.

1259 11th Nov – *Lease for ten years, for a consideration of 12d of silver by Robert de Holand to Edmund son of Peter de Denby of land in Birchewod sometime held by Adam Dun at an annual rent of 3s 2d*

A writ dated 9th January 1284 was issued to enquire into the possessions of John, son of Thomas of Norland who was an outlaw. The inquisition sat the next day and was presided over by the Sheriff of Yorkshire, John Lythegrins, among the jurors was Adam de Deneby.

By the time of the dates of the last two documents Denby had long been endowed with its first chapel. The following charter was made by William de Denby, who was a priest of sorts, possibly at one time in Cumberworth. It is possible that he was the same man mentioned in the family tree above as the brother of the first Sir Robert de Denby. The charter refers to William giving land to the church in order to build a chapel and licensing his own home for use as a religious house without prejudice to the chapel at Denby or the church at Penistone:

May present and future people know that I William de Deneby have given and granted, and by this my present charter confirmed, to God and the church of Saint John the Baptist of Penigeston in pure and perpetual alms, a toft with a croft and meadow with all appurtenances, which Thomas Leuenath once held. Moreover I William, and my heirs, guarentee the said land with all its appurtenances to the said church in perpetuity against all people. And let it be known that Godfrey de Ludham, then the parson of the said church, permitted me the said William to build a certain oratory in my house and there to celebrate mass, ensuring only that the mother church of Penigeston and Deneby chapel are not disadvantaged, both during visitations, festival days, and concerning the fabric of the same, and in all things, as I have sworn upon the altar of Saint John the Baptist at Penigeston. On condition that it may be permitted to the parsons, for the time being, to suspend the said chapel or oratory, or to remove totally the chantry. On condition that if they destroy the said oratory, then it may be permitted to me, William, to take over the said land again. And for greater certainty I have appended my seal to this present writing before the whole parish of Penigeston. With these witnesses: Master W de Ludham, then Steward of Pontefract, Richard de Locspring, William de Penigeston, William de Gunildthuait, William de Deneby, John de Holdefeld and others.

Though the latter is proof that a chapel existed at Denby long before the petition was raised by the villagers to Archbishop Toby Mathew in 1627 to erect a chapel of ease it is difficult to determine the length of time it was in operation. One suspects that it was not for long, it is not referred to in any other extant document and by the late fourteenth and fifteenth centuries the Burdet Lord's of the Manor were making bequests and leaving money to High Hoyland and Penistone churches, not Denby. It would be easy to suggest reasons for its discontinuation, the effects of the Black Death may have caused such a reduced number of villagers and a lack of religious direction that the chapel was abandoned, but we could speculate forever. Its location must also remain a mystery. Professor David Hey suggests that it may have been sited on the same ground as the present Denby church. This is possible as an ancient memory of the edifice may have persisted through the centuries. It is also tempting to speculate that it could have been sited near 'Butcroft' in Upper Denby, at the back of Denroyd farm. During the thirteenth century every person earning less than 100 pence a year was to have a bow in his possession, so to be ready for a call to arms. Practising was made compulsory, after service on a Sunday at the village 'butts' which were usually sited near to the church. Alternatively, the term 'butt' also described an irregular shaped field and this is probably the case in the latter instance.

The document dates from the period when Godfrey de Ludham (Loudham) was parson of Penistone church, 1229–1232. Godfrey became a clerk to a mediety of Penistone church on 26th August 1228 after a lapse and he went on to unite the living of Penistone in himself. A mediety was a half share in the living, therefore prior to Godfrey uniting the living there were two vicars at Penistone, as at High Hoyland. De Ludham moved on from Penistone, later becoming Archbishop of York in 1258. He founded two chapels in York Minster and was himself buried in a tomb there when he died in 1264.

A possible relative was Eustace de Ludham (Loudham) who was Sheriff of Yorkshire 1225/6, at a time when other records recall the name of Robert Hood – fugitive! Eustace was also Sheriff of Nottinghamshire and Derbyshire in 1233/4 and Under Sheriff to Cokefeld, his successor in Yorkshire. He was probably a Royal servant sent into Yorkshire by the government of King Henry III.

Another set of documents regarding a de Denby family has survived, though they are difficult to tie in with the latter mentioned clan. Largely regarding land at Cawthorne, they begin in 1250, when a William de Denby son of Robert signed a deed. Along with others, a William de Denby can be found, again as a witness to documents in 1252/3 and 1280, alongside a William de Penistone. In circa 1300, William de Denby along with his brothers, John and Adam were witnesses to a feoffment at Cawthorne.

In 1315, John, son of Robert de Denby was involved in a quitclaim with Robert de Barnby and his wife, Margaret, who held land at Cawthorne called 'Steuarderode' which had belonged to Johanna de Denby, the mother of the aforementioned John.

It is probable that these 'de Denby' people were kin of a man we noted in V1. William de Denby was the son of Adam Canun of Cawthorne and was one of the progenitors of the Barnby family. William's surname almost certainly implies a strong link to the Denby family though the details of this are currently unknown.

We have now reached the period when the Burdet family arrived in Denby. We will briefly re-cap these events. The de Denby line of descent probably began, as we have discussed, with Henry fitz Swain followed by Dolfin, Robert, Sir Robert and Sir Robert II. Sir Robert de Denby II died around 1302/3 without an heir and so the manor of Denby passed to his sister, Margaret. Her marriage to Sir Robert Balliol produced one daughter and heir, Idonea. After the death of Balliol, Margaret remarried to Sir Nicholas de Metham and bore two more children, Alice, who married William de la Sancery and Elizabeth who married John Feckleton. Idonea Balliol married Robert Burdet, son of Almaricus Burdet of Rande in Lincolnshire. The Burdet's had been tenants on land at Rande and Fulnetby which was used as the dower of Aubreye de Harcourt when she married William Trussebutt around 1150. The Harcourt family had been brought into Leicestershire from France by the Earl of Leicester to help him control the area. Family ties seem to have been strengthened in around 1210 when a marriage took place between John de Harcourt and Hawise Burdet. The mother of Robert Burdet was Agnes de Denby, probably the daughter of the William de Denby who founded Denby chapel (1229–32), and was the cousin of Margaret Balliol nee de Denby. During 1303/4 Idonea and Robert Burdet inherited the manors of Denby and Nether (High) Hoyland and it was also around this time that their son was born, christened Aymer.

It is unclear as to how long the Burdet family had been associating with the Denby area and its Lords. As we have seen, successive Kings had endeavoured to plant loyal supporters on the northern borders to act as a buffer zone since the days of Ailric. In 1291, during the reign of Edward

I, a Peter Burdet can be found acting as Constable of Berwick on Tweed. These were very disturbed times for England as a whole. Edward I had conquered Wales during two campaigns dated, 1276–7 and 1282–3 but the Scottish question was still very open. Border raids were common place and it was only when Edward told the Scots that if they wanted to oppose his overlord-ship that they would have to do so by force that he was asked to settle the 'Great cause' as to the matter of the Scottish succession. John Balliol was chosen by King Edward and a later mandate was issued, dated 18th November 1292 to Peter Burdet which commanded him to hand over Berwick castle to John Balliol. John Balliol, under extreme provocation from Edward I soon threw off his allegiance to the English King, the immediate result of which was the storming of Berwick and the battle of Dunbar in 1296 which led to a submission of the Scottish towns. It also led to the rise of Scottish resistance under leaders such as Andrew Moray and William Wallace. The battle of Stirling Bridge took place in 1297 followed by a Scottish reverse in 1298 at Falkirk. The wars of independence continued through the reign of Edward II and up until the defeat of Edward Balliol, John's son at Halidon Hill in 1333 when Edward III took revenge for Bannockburn.

In 1332 Edward III had moved his government to York which became, for the next five years the administrative capital of England. Large forces were raised and trained under his personal supervision and at the end of the year he invested Berwick.

On 4th July 1333, in readiness for Halidon Hill, Edward III commanded Robert Burdet and others to array the men of Leicestershire in order to fight the Scots. This branch of the Burdet family is of a more ancient derivation than that which came from Rande to Denby. It is certain that Staincross men were involved in the battle, probably veterans from Denby but to date their names elude me. The well disciplined English using large numbers of rapid firing bowmen destroyed the Scots who were more used to travelling light and avoiding battle on any ground not of their own choosing.

Edward's desire to re-claim his lands in France led to a reduction in his interest in Scotland and gradually it slid from his grasp leaving the borders as a very dangerous place for some two centuries or more. It is interesting to note that on 1st October 1297, only 20 days after the English defeat at Stirling Bridge by Wallace and others, a William Burdet was given letters of protection by King Edward to travel through Scotland with the elder Robert de Bruce. Later, in 1308, the same William Burdet, whilst in Scotland, gave letters of protection and powers of attorney to Edmund Hastings.

Quite how involved Robert Balliol was in these momentous events touching on his country and his families Kingdom is unknown. What does seem to be clear is that the de Denby family were very involved in wars with the Scots before, during and, after this period. New sources show the reason for Balliol's sojourn in Denby, as an important scion of the Scottish Royal house he was deemed too important to be allowed back into Scotland and was held as a political prisoner by the de Denby family. They were trusted so much by King, Edward I, as to act as his jailers. This was at the time that the third Robert de Denby held the manor. Whether Balliol had been caught after a battle is unknown – he fought for Edward I in the Welsh wars and may have been on the King's payroll and placed in a secure environment to dispel the possibilities of treason. Balliol's incarceration did not last, and the implications for an inter family marriage with the heiress of the de Denby family were fully realised. When Robert Balliol married Margaret de Denby he would appear to have been much older then she. As a result of the marriage a dispute arose concerning the manor of High Hoyland which was in the possession of Sir Nicholas de Wortley:

> 1304 12th April – *Fine made in the King's court at York between Robert de Balliol and Margaret his wife, complainants and Nicholas de Wortley, deforciant, concerning the manors of Denby and High Holland: Robert and Margaret admit the manors to be the right of Nicholas as of their gift and in return he grants them to Robert and Margaret for their lives, with remainders.*

The result of this saw that de Wortley held the manor for life, if he outlived Balliol and his wife the manor was to descend to Robert Burdet, whose wife, Idonea was the heiress to Balliol. Sir Nicholas died in 1357 when the manor came into the possession of Aymer Burdet, son of Robert and Idonea. We know that the latter manor's are unlikely to have been all encompassing as inter family marriage between the de Denby and de Hoyland families in the previous two centuries had already seen some parts of the two manors united. We know that Aymer Burdet considered himself to be Lord of the Manor of Denby from surviving documents of this time which would seem to suggest that the two manors referred to were only a part of the Burdet families possessions. Aymer seems to have been very friendly with the de Wortley Lords and may, as we have seen, have held some of his manor's as of their gift.

Another man noted to be a Lord of a portion of Denby at this time was John de Vavsour who held his lands of the King in 1309. Quite what his relationship to Denby was is unknown, probably an absentee Lord, he was most likely a member of the great Vavasour family of whom William was one of the most famous. William fought in the vanguard of the army of Edward I at the battle of Falkirk (1298), at the siege of Caerlaverock in 1300 and was keeper of Pontefract castle until May 1311. The Burdet, de Denby and Vavasour families had all been involved in the wars of Scottish independence and it is most likely that the John de Vavsour had gained his lands at Denby as a result of these operations. A Henry le Vavasour received an order from Edward II to prepare for the defence of York proving the families links with the county at this time. It is also worth noting that an effigy of one of the members of this family is cut into the stone work at the great west door of York Minster. Vavasour is derived from Valvassor, in feudal society a knight or noble with vassals under him, though he was a subject or vassal of a greater noble, a vassal of vassal's.

Another 'Lord' of a portion of Denby can be found in the following agreement:

> 1321 – *Agreement for the demise by Richard, son of Sir John de Thornhill to William Danyel de Thurgerland and John de Bretton of his manor of Deneby etc., with certain chattels, for 12 years at an annual rent of 44s in silver.*

A further Lord of a portion of Denby, around 1325, was the Abbot of Byland who proved this to the satisfaction of parliament. So, by this date, there would have been surviving members of the de Denby family still holding land, the relatively new, Lord of the Manor, Aymer Burdet, the Lords of Wortley, the Vavasour family and the Abbot, all claiming Lordship of part of Denby. It should be remembered that a 'manor' was not a single geographical entity, it could involve only parts of the title district and include lands in other villages and townships spread over a wide area. Land which was retained by the Lord for his own use was known as 'demesne' whilst the rest was tenanted or else used for common or waste.

War was not exclusively located in Scotland during this early part of the fourteenth century. The battle of Boroughbridge in 1322 took place between the rebel Earl of Lancaster and Edward II. Lancaster, largely deserted by his forces, was routed by Andrew de Harclay and taken prisoner to Pontefract castle. Along with him went the following men, Sir Nicholas de

Wortley, Sir Robert de Hoyland and Sir Richard de Hoyland. Nicholas de Wortley bought his freedom for £40, Richard de Hoyland was set free due to his age without ransom, Robert de Hoyland was ordered to be delivered by his captor to the King and he was presumably beheaded along with the beaten Earl. It is unlikely that the Robert de Hoyland mentioned was the son of Adam of High Hoyland, already noted. He was a knight in 1247 and though we know he had a family only the name of his son William has so far come to light. The Nicholas de Wortley is probably the same man who had granted the Burdet Lords of Denby their manor as of his right, though he may also have been one of his sons.

The Scottish borders continued to cause trouble for a number of years and the following order, signed by Edward III himself was issued on 22nd January 1335 to his Yorkshire knights, one of whom was Emery (Aymer) Burdet giving them directions for raising and equipping horse and foot. By 1st February, Aymer had arrived with his forces at the King's headquarters, then at Newcastle upon Tyne, though he and others had the Kings license to return home. The tradition of the people of Denby fighting for their King in Scotland was thus continued by the Burdet dynasty.

A similar levy was called for by the King in 1338. Before he set sail for France on his mission to become King of that country, a title he assumed in 1340, he had taken measures for the protection of the North from the Scots. On 2nd May, Emericus (Aymer) Burdet of Denby, John de Gunnelthwayt and Thomas de Ranmull, amongst others, were ordered to supply 20 men each, properly furnished with horses and arms. On this occasion the men of Staincross and Osgoldcross wapentakes were also ordered to raise 70 archers, strong and suitable men with bows, arrows and the implements of war. In Staincross alone, 160 men at arms were also equipped. The troops were to be sent to:

> our faithful Richard, Count of Arundel, who is already with our army in those parts.

Four years later, 1342, the requirement was for 6 men at arms and 220 archers, but this time they were to be raised by knights not resident in Denby, though it is certain that Denby veterans would have been recruited. King Edward's soldiers had regular rates of pay, a record dating to 1346, (around the time of the battle of Crecy), records the following. Bannerets were paid 4s a day (a banneret was a knight entitled to carry a banner, each banneret was expected to find an archer for each man at arms he provided), 136 knights at 2s a day, 143 esquires (rank and file men at arms) at 1s a day, 900 mounted archers at 6d a day and foot archers who received sums ranging from 2d to 4d a day. Of course, all this recruiting and raising men and arms did not occur without some expense. In 1340 parliament allowed King Edward III, the ninth lamb, sheep and fleece and the fifteenth part of the stock of each merchant. This grant was for two years and Francis Barnetby and the Prior of St Oswalds, Nostell, were commissioned to levy it throughout the West Riding. Among them men called before the commissioners were John de Denby and Roger de Denby, who each, after arranging about the amount of money to be paid for the ninths, declared that there was no merchant in their part of the parish (of Penistone), living otherwise than by agriculture. Another tax levied in 1340 was collected by William de Scargill and Brian de Thornhill, for the Liberty of Tickhill for Staincross wapentake:

> Denby 20s, Clayton West 16s, Wortley 28s, Skelmanthorpe 12s, Penistone 14s, Hoyland 21s, Silkstone 25s and Cawthorne 47s.

Returning to the year 1335, as we have seen, Aymer Burdet led his men to Newcastle upon Tyne in person before returning home. His reasons for taking them himself have previously been a mystery but the following document explains his actions:

1335 – At York, Edward III sat in person trying cases/prisoners. Aldemar (Aymer) Burdet, Elias the Clerk and John de Wortelay of Denby for diseisin William de Metham of his free tenement at Denby.

In another case, Ademan (Aymer) Burdet and John de Wortelay were brought before the King, again at York, in a case where they had unjustly diseised Nicholas de Metham of his free tenement at Darton:

1331 July 4th – A judgement in the King's Court at York of Hilary, 7 Edw III concerning a plea of trespass and disseisin brought against Adomarus, son and heir of Robert Burdett and of Idonia his wife, Ellis le Clerk, John de Wortelay of Denbye, and Mathew Daniell by Nicholas de Metham, chivaler, who married Margaret widow of Robert de Bailliolo, in respect of tenements and lands which were parcels of the manors of Deneby and Heghholand.

So, Aymer was having a family feud with his grandmother's second husband and presumably one of his children. Diseisin was unlawful dispossession of a persons dwelling or land. Whether there was more to the dispute than the de Methams being of lesser status than Aymer we can only wonder. What is certain is that he was serious enough about it to travel to York, on his way to or on the way back from Newcastle and stand before the King of England to plead his cause. Taking John de Wortley with him, he had a solid and able companion of high status to back him up, of course, de Wortley would also have had an interest in the land. Nicholas de Metham may have tried to pursue a claim to Burdet lands at Denby, after all, he was a close relative of Aymer, if only by marriage:

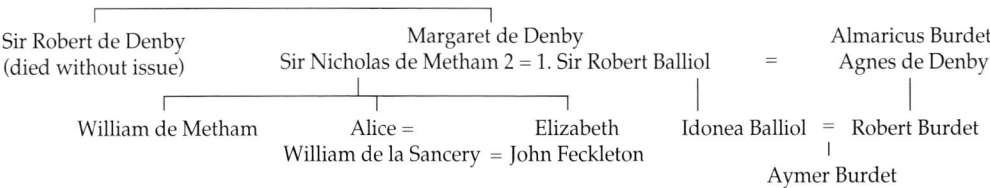

It is possible that the name 'de Metham' could be derived from the place name Meltham. We have noted that Thomas de Denby bought a mill at Meltham during the thirteenth century, and as an aside, the poll tax returns of 1379 for Meltham contain the following individuals: John de Dendby and his wife Isabella, Adam de Dendby, and John de Dendby – pure coincidence? Without further research we must leave this for now.

It might now be interesting to see some of the names of the people who rented their lands and homes from Lord Aymer Burdet. As we have seen, Aymer Burdet appears to have been one of the most important and influential people ever to have lived at Denby. Indeed, the family was perhaps never more powerful. To achieve this power and status and to supply men to the King to fight in his wars Aymer had to have a large number of tenant farmers and labourers to work his lands. Individual documents have survived which list a few individuals:

1325–6 – Quitclaim by John, son of Thomas de Shepelay in favour of Brian son of John de Thornhill of his claim to lands, tenements etc in Thurlestone, Deneby and Over Whitelay.

1327 25th June – Grant, fore various considerations by Sir Nicholas (de Denby) and Margaret, his wife to Robert Leghfote of Mhellay (?Shelley/Methley?) and Adam de Breythwayt of their forge in Deneby and of timber, charcoal and ore.

This document supplies proof that a blacksmiths shop was operating in Denby in 1327.

1344 25th Sep – *Grant by Robert son and heir of Adam de Deneby to Adoman son of Robert Burdet of a place called Stubbings of 15 acres, paying the chief lords of the fee their due of 12d annually.*

1395 10th October – *Lease for 20 years by Robert de Barneby, Thos Marryk, vicar of Bolton and John del Roydes to John, son of Henry de Denby of all those messuages, lands, rents, etc. which the said Robert, Thos and John formerly held by gift of the said John son of Henry in Overdenby, Netherdenby, Cumbirworth, Huland and Shelley; the lesee rendering yearly service of a rose to the lessors.*

Prior to recent translation work, the Poll Tax of 1379 was the first document to list a substantial number of the tenants in Denby. Before this, information concerning individuals has been slim and scanty. Thankfully, the survival of a number of court rolls and manorial surveys will finally provide new information to flesh out the earlier years of the fourteenth century; indeed, we will be able to learn a little about some of the individuals mentioned in the Poll Tax returns. Written in medieval, abbreviated Latin, the documents have been professionally translated for the first time ever. Due to the fragile nature of the documents not all the words are legible and in some cases not all the document has survived, therefore we are sometimes left with fragmentary and tantalising glimpses.

Court Rolls were really only concerned with transfers and grants of land, sometimes they would record details of minor offences, such as firewood theft or trespass in woods or perhaps animals impounded at the local pinfold. Depending on how complete the roll is they usually start with a list of tenants who were due to come to the court and swear fealty or answer any questions or make payments. These documents give us a record of the tenants living within the manor, or, holding land within it. The one thing to remember with Denby is that it was coupled with High Hoyland and included parts of Cumberworth, Clayton and other areas. Unless stated, there is no way of knowing which person came from which locale though they do illustrate how many people were living in the district at that time. It will also be noticed that some of the rolls and the court itself appear to have taken place at High Hoyland, this is not to suggest that High Hoyland was of paramount importance within the manor at this time. The present Denby Hall Farm lies on the edge of High Hoyland and it is known that lands now within the High Hoyland parish boundary were once a part of the demesne of Denby Hall. What is certain is that Lord Burdet still showed allegiance to Penistone church and was in most cases buried there. Each village within the manor would have held its own court, it is due to chance alone that more records have survived from High Hoyland than from Denby. The Burdet family would still have been the Lords of the Manor though they do not seem to have regarded High Hoyland as a place of burial, though they did make bequests to the fabric of the church. The site of the court at High Hoyland was the manor house of John Appleyard which was rebuilt between 1710 and 1720 and is now known as Hoyland Hall. The site seems to overly a much more ancient edifice and appears likely to be the site of the court meeting from its earliest days, perhaps even back as far as the time of Adam de Hoyland in the thirteenth century. A hall dating to the middle ages was replaced by a Tudor house of plaster and brick, though it is unknown as to when the Appleyard family first came to live here. The Appleyards got into financial difficulties during the early eighteenth century and sold the building to the Wentworths who undertook the rebuilding work by demolishing everything but the cellars of the Tudor house. The building has been let to tenant farmers since 1722.

If the Lord of the manor was not present the steward took his place, others present would be the reeve who acted as go between in relations between the Lord and his tenants, the bailiff, who decided farming policy, a constable, and a pinder. There was also a jury of 12 men who heard evidence and advised accordingly, these men had knowledge of local tradition and custom and in time tended to be drawn from the same families as we shall see.

Before we dive into these records it might be useful to examine a simple glossary in order to understand a number of the archaic terms within the text.

Assart	A piece of woodland which has been cleared, enclosed and adapted for arable land.
Bovate	Also known as an Oxgang. Variable measure related to soil quality and the amount an ox could plough in a year, an eighth of a carucate.
Butland	Waste land.
Butt	A piece of land in an open arable field which, because of the irregular shape of the field was shorter than the normal strip.
Carucate	From 'caruca' meaning a plough. Variously estimated to be 60, 80, 100 or 120 acres depending upon the quality of the land. It was a term used to describe the amount of land that could be ploughed by an 8 ox team in one year.
Chain	Once standardised, it was a measure of 22 yards.
Close	An enclosure from the open fields.
Commons	The right of pasturing beasts on the common land.
Croft	Enclosed meadow or arable land, usually next to a dwelling.
Demesne	Land retained by the Lord for his own use and upon which tenants gave free service according to the customs of the manor. Land which was once part of the main farm of the manor.
Demise	To convey a property by lease.
Disseisin	Unlawful dispossession of a persons dwelling or land.
Fardel	A group of Selions
Fine	A payment of money made to the manorial Lord by an incoming tenant.
Freehold	A tenure which was not subject to the customs of the manor or the will of the Lord and which could be disposed of without restriction.
Knights Fee	In an agricultural context – a variable measure of land depending upon the quality of the soil. Considered to be the amount of land needed to support a knight and his family for a year. Anything from 4 to 48 carucates. A knights fee obliged the holder to provide military assistance to the Crown, usually he and his servants for 40 days a year. This was quite often commuted to a payment of money.
Livery of Seisin	The infant heir of a tenant in chief of the Crown had to sue Livery of Seisin to obtain possession of his fathers estate.
Moiety	Usually a half portion of an estate.
Nonage	Being under age.
Perch	Originally a variable measure between 9 and 26 feet but when standardised $16\frac{1}{2}$ feet. Also a rod or pole.
Relief	A payment of money made to the manorial Lord by an incoming tenant.
Royd	A clearing in a wood.

Selion	A cultivated strip in an open field. It was ploughed in such a manner that the strip became a ridge with furrows on either side acting as a drain.	
Severalty	A portion of common assigned for a period to a particular occupier.	
Slade	A valley	
Stubbing	A clearing, land from which tree stumps have been removed, land which can still be covered by tree stumps.	
Tenement	A farm held of a superior Lord, a holding of land.	
Toft	A plot of land on which a building stood or had formerly stood. Common rights might still attach to the house even though the building might be gone.	

Tenants of Denby and, probably, Skelmanthorpe who paid homage or were fined 2d for not doing so, at a Court at High Hoyland dated Friday after the feast of St (?) in the 18th year of King Edward III – 1344/45:

The term 'essoin' meant that the individual concerned had an excuse for not coming to court and was not fined. Words in Italics are probable modern equivalent spellings.

John of Denby	William of Bulhols *(Bullhouse?)*	Henry son of Thomas
Robert Marierison	Robert of the same	John Sponv …
John, son of Robert of Denby	Thomas of Hasilheued *(Hazlehead)*	Thomas Crappar
William, brother of above	John son of Roger of Bilcliff (because he did not come 2d)	William son of Stephen
John Clareson	William son of Robert of Smalschagh (because he did not come 2d) *(Smallshaw)*	William Bollot
Robert of Schelmerthorpe	Richard of Penistonrodes	John son of H … (because he did not come 2d)
Amice daughter of Adcok	Robert son of John of Birchworth	…….. S…hill
Simon, the Lady's servant	William Ward, (because he did not come 2d)	Richard Br….r
William Not…. (2d)	John Wicher, (because he did not come 2d)	John of Gren…
John Wortlay	Adam of Leghe	William of W….telay (because he did not come 2d)
Robert of Thorpe (because he did not come 2d)	Ralph of Scelmerthorpe	John Ken…
Hugh Horn	Emma Nailer	John of Burnscros (because he did not come 2d)
Robert of Walton	John Horn	Thomas Laynde
Alice of Bretton	Walter of the Brom (because he did not come 2d)	Thomas of Bilham
Margery, daughter of William	Matilda Ward (Essoin)	Thomas Hug…het (because he did not come 2d)
Adam son of Robert	Alice daughter of Matilda (Essoin)	John of Lathes
Robert son of Robert	Gilbert Newill' (Essoin)	Robert Jonotson
Roger son of Richard B…ar	Henry son of Simon	Thomas Kent (because he did not come 2d)
Robert Carter	Thomas of Brumton	Thomas Cha….ll *(Charell)*, (because he did not come 2d)

Richard of T(re)ton?	William Belamy	William of Pillay
William of Smalschagh, (*Smallshaw*)	Elias Graver (Grauer)	William of the Rodes
William Flosshe	Richard Lertam	William Dyatt
William Bulle..	Adam Uppeden	Roger Do
Richard Caynok (because he did not come 2d)	Iuo of Mapplewell	Thomas Spink (because he did not come 2d)
Laurence Textor (*weaver or the weaver*)	John Batty (because he did not come 2d)	William of Keueresforth (*Keresforth*)
William R....ner	Adam of the Lone (Longe)	Thomas Haliday (because he did not come 2d)
Thomas the chaplain of Oldten' (because he did not come 2d)	John of the Moor in Dritker	John Isold

All the latter were sworn and did homage for their tenements, held of Lord Burdet. Pleas proceeding in the court were adjourned until the next court left in their current state. The total sum of the court was 2s 11d. The people that were fined for not paying homage could, most likely, afford the fine and had better things to do elsewhere.

Of the 81 people named above it might seem a little surprising that the document lists six women, these, in part, may have been widows and, or, daughters of deceased men, still holding and doing homage for family homes and lands.

'Simon' the Lady's servant (serviens) is also interesting. The obvious question is, to which lady does the document refer? The wife of Aymer Burdet, Isabel Langton would have been the Lady to the Lord of the Manor and she remains the most promising option.

It is also interesting to note the infancy of the development of the surname and the number of villages to which people were associated somewhat more distant to Denby than one would expect.

The Adam of Leghe (a clearing in a wood) noted above can also be found mentioned in 1371 on the feast of St Thomas the Martyr:

William de la Legh, son of Adam de la Legh gave to William Turton and Alice his wife a messuage called Magot-House in Over Cumberworth, which I have of the gift of the said William with remainder to Margaret, daughter of William and Alice, with remainder to Joan, daughter of Margaret de la Legh, daughter of Adam de la Legh. If she die without issue, one half to the light of St Nicholas in the chapel of over Cumberworth for ever; and the other half to the sustentation of the chaplain in the said chapel, performing divine offices.

The above is certainly clear documentation of an early chapel in Cumberworth though Hunter could find no mention of it during Henry VIII's time.

The following court roll, made at High Hoyland, dates to the same period, although the document does not possess a date, it is certainly no more than a few years either side of the latter tenant roll.

As can be seen, a detailed translation has been difficult to produce due to the quality of the original but the roll mentions the following:

Line Number 4		Roger (?) de Kirk (*burton?*)
5		Thomas (?) Erk..
8		From Robert Long…
9	Amerced 4d	
11 & 12		Adam of Leghe complains of Alan Chapmon in a plea of trespass, pledge for prosecution William Horn who was not summonsed therefore, and c.
13 & 14		….of Irlond complains of Matilda of the Brom in a plea of………pledge for prosecution William Horn
15 & 16		Matilda of the Brom complains of John of Irlond in a plea ….., pledge for prosecution, John Wolf
17		William of M(ic)kelthayt complains of Robert son of William (inserted above this line is : Thomas of B….ton and Robert son of Roger in a plea….
18		Adam of Leghe…..John son…..in a plea of trespass, pledge for prosecution William Horn
18a		………..John H….land and on the part….
19		Court held at Holand Monday next after the feast of St Hilary in the year ….
20	Amerced 3d	From Agnes Day for 3 animals taken in….
21	Amerced 4d	Thomas of Bosseuill (*Bosville*) for 4 oxen taken there..
22		William of Hacforth
23	Amerced 6d	From Robert the Longe for 6 animals taken there, pledge Ro….. of Bilham
24, 25, 26, 27 & 28	Respited until…	John Wicher who was distrained…….for meadows and ….pasture and certain…five……in Colyar oxgang to the Lords damage of half a mark and … by letters of Sir Nicholas de Wortlay was distrained…………until the Lords coming to then give satisfaction to the Lord. The said John has done nothing yet, therefore distrained.
29 & 30	Amerced 2d	Alan Chapmon for pasturing his animals in the meadow and …. Of Colyar oxgang in the aforesaid year
31	Distraint	It was ordered to distrain Adam of Holm and Emma his wife to reply to Adam……..and ……
32 & 33	Essoin	John Spink against Nicholas son of Henry in a plea of debt by Elias…….. of Bilham, pledge Elias Grauer (Graver)
34 & 35	Respite	A day was given to John of Irlond, plaintiff and Matilda of the Brom in a plea of trespass to the next……..essoin
36 & 37	Respite	A day was given to Matilda of the Brom plaintif and John of Irlond in a plea of trespass to the next…essoin.
38 & 39	Amerced 3d	William of Mikelthwayt and Robert son of William are agreed and Robert is amerced, pledge Thomas of Bilham
40	Distraint	It was ordered to distrain Alan Chapmon to reply to Adam of Leghe in a plea…..
41	Amerced 3d	From John son of Matilda against ….Adam of Leghe amerced…
42, 43 & 44		Adam of Leghe……against John son of Alan…..his oats……to the damage &c of 2(s)?
45		Adam of Leghe…..against John son of Matilda….his…..in the aforesaid croft to the damage…..he came and contradicted…..therefore he…

NB: lines 17 and 18 eighteen were inserted later.

Entry numbers 24 to 28 seem to confirm my earlier assumption that Nicholas de Wortley was still an overlord of at least some portion of Denby, though Aymer Burdet styled himself as Lord of the Manor. Adam of the Leghe can be found in the poll tax returns of 1379 in Cumberworth as can the del Brome family and others.

The following court roll again dates from this period and includes a number of names recounted above:

> **Court of Holand held there and Denby also on Monday next after Easter.**
> *Fine 12d – Elias Graver (Grauer), Thomas Bretyng, William son of Stephen and Alan Graver for digging a ditch in the......of the Lord without licence.*
> *Fine 4s 6d – Master William de Hide for cutting the Lords wood (he promised 2s) grass and meadow (6s) for breaking the Lords hedges (12d), by a plea of Thomas de Bilham and Elias Graver and also for cutting the Lords ash trees (12d).*
> *Fine 4d - Hugh Horn for his animals taken in severalty.*
> *Fine 4d – Thomas de Bilham for his oxen taken in the Lords cornfield.*
> *Fine 4d – William de Whetelay for his oxen taken in the same place.*
>
> *William de Rodes for cutting the Lords wood everywhere and the Lords grass and pasture – he denies it.*
>
> *John de Mosley … of Robert King in a plea of debt (made at the request) of Henry de Whetlay.*
>
> *Thomas de Bilham … of William de Whetley in a plea of debt (made at the request of) Robert de H … .*
>
> *William de Seyvill … of William de Whetley made at the request of Robert de H … .*
>
> *Richard Bercar … of John Spink in a plea of debt (made at the request of) Thomas de Brampton.*
>
> *John Wither finds John Nailor his pledge for paying compensation to the Lord for pasture which he holds against the will of the Lord, and moreover he came and objected and required his right (acquitted).*
>
> *Nicholas son of Henry, and John Spink for permission (for a sheepfold) and John is in mercy on a plea of Elias Graver (3d).*
>
> *John son of Alan in mercy for default of law against Adam of Leght (Leghe) in a plea of trespass. It is decided that Adam shall recover 2s damages, pledge is John de Irland (4d).*
>
> *Action between Thomas Hunt, complainant, and William de Hatford …*
>
> *Robert Kyng against John de Mosley by John Wortley and John … (he makes his excuse).*
>
> *Richard Bercar speaks against John Spink that he owes him 2 … of bread which he granted … plea of Elias Graver.*
>
> *Richard Bercar speaks against John Spink that he owes him … and ploughland … he denies it and is at law on a plea of Elias Graver.*
>
> *John de Irland speaks against Matilda de Brom that she took three of his animals…in the pasture of the said John and took animals of other men…without licence, damages to him of 6s 8d.*

(This would seem to be a continuation from the last document of the trouble between these two when a day was given over to them – this at least proves that the documents are all of a similar date).

It is fortunate that the latter have survived to record the years around 1334–44, we can only wonder as to which of all the above named people survived the Black Death, which struck in 1348/9. The disease certainly visited the area, the Vicar of Darton, William Addy died from the disease in 1349 after only a year's incumbency. The family of Elias Graver do not appear in 1379, he is mentioned in all the above documents along with an Alan Graver but does not appear in the story again. The surname could also be spelt Grauer as the Latin is difficult but a Graver was usually associated with engraving, perhaps in copper. Alternatively, Graver could derive from the old English 'greyve' which meant a 'steward'. It would seem that the plague may well have taken them both . The Spink family also disappears but others, such as the Horns, and Mosleys were here to stay.

Matilda de Brom is also prominent on the court rolls, probably a widow and looking after her late husbands lands with the help of her offspring it is tempting to speculate as to their location.

A further survey, this time of tenants lands in Cumberworth who owed homage to Lord Burdet, mentions a number of areas described variously as:

'2 selions in Fisshedore', 1¹/2 rods and 2¹/2 acres in Alynrod', 5 selions and 1 fardel or land lying in nether est Halghes', '3 rods lying on oueresthalges', '1 butt containing ¹/2 rod ... on stokwoderods' and '1 acre 1 rod lying in Bromyleye and in Brendbrom'.
NB: (a fardel was a fourth part of a selion).

It is likely that Matilda de Brom lived and farmed at Bromley, between Denby Dale and Cumberworth, a part of which was much later to become the site of Naylor Brothers. As 'lea' simply meant a meadow and Brom can be identified with the old English 'gorse' the implication is that the land was not the best in the district. In 1379 Walter del Brom paid 4d Poll Tax and was recorded in the Agbrigg wapentake.

One man not mentioned in the latter is Roger Dycson, whose son, John and grandson, John junior, both paid Poll Tax in 1379. Roger Dycson can be found, along with his wife in the Denby court rolls of 1357/8, when a note was made regarding their homage.

From a surviving rental of 'Aldoman' (Aymer) Burdet, dated 1 Feb 1354 we find the following places listed:

Over Denby, Birchworth, Small Shaw, Bullhols, Rough Birchworth, Penistone, Billcliff, Nethircum Birworth, Overcum Birworth, Skelmanthorpe.

Aymer Burdet was probably dead by 1360, the last document to refer to him dates to 1359, he was around 55 years old. His wife, Isabel, re-married to Ralph Hyde but had provided Aymer with an heir. His son, Nicholas Burdet took over as Lord of the Manor though he was to remain childless till his death around 1407/8 which left his younger brother Richard as his heir. The name of a further brother has also survived, William, who seems to have made his home at Darton. Previously unknown save for his short entry in the Poll Tax returns of 1379 his will has now been translated:

Will of William Burdet 1391
In the name of God, Amen: the 4th day of July Anno Domini 1391, I William Burdet of good sound memory make my will in the following form:

Firstly: I bequeath my soul to God Almighty, to our Blessed Mary His Mother, and to all His Saints, and my body to be buried in the chapel of St. Mary of Derton (Darton).

Item: I bequeath to Frances my wife half of all my goods, equally divided and I give and bequeath the other half of the said goods to Nicholas and Richard my brothers to be used and disposed of for my soul according to their will and pleasure; and moreover I ordain, make and constitute Nicholas and Richard executors of this will.

Probate of this will was granted on the 15th of July in the year above said to the executors named who have been sworn in the proper form of law.

NB: Probate was granted by the Probate Court when it was satisfied with the will presented and which enabled the executors to proceed with carrying out the provisions of the will. A will was proven when probate was granted.

Aymer Burdet probably had a number of daughters as well, but as is usual their names have not survived as at this time their sex rendered them irrelevant to inheritance of property, wealth and estate.

Richard Burdet was married to Joan Storpe of Worcestershire, which again illustrates the mobility of people within the country at this early date. The following document dating from his time describes a raid on the church of Woolley by one of the rectors of High Hoyland:

Tourn held at Barnsley 2nd April 1410 (Henry IV).
'the jurors say that David, rector of a moiety of the church of High Hoyland in the 5th year of Henry IV (1404) entered Wooley church and there brake (open) a certain chest and took thereout oblations and tithes and carried the same away against the peace, thereafter, let him be attached'.

To be attached meant that your goods were seized by a legal procedure it is unclear who this 'David' was, in the early 1400's the two livings of the church were held by John de Crosland and Thomas de Mathersey.

We have examined the details of the life of Richard Burdet in V1 but the following court roll gives us an insight into the people who owed him their loyalty:

The Great Court of the Lord of Denby held on the Feast of All Souls ….(undated but probably around 1419).
Enquiry was made on the oaths of Richard Horn, William Hengeclyff, John Prist, Robert … , Ranworth, William Bellamy, William the Herle, Thomas of D … who say on oath that:

William Waturhill (3d), John of the Appulyherd (3d), … … , John Smyth of Mappulwell (3d) … … William Pogin (2d) … … (these were tenants who did not come to the court and were fined or amerced for non-attendance).

The jurors say that Robert of Whiclay entered the lands … and so is ordered to be distrained for the next court … .

It is ordered that Richard Oxpringe be distrained for the next court …

It is ordered that John Hudson be distrained for the next court … .

William de Hengeclyff came into court and is … … For the homage and for his services, all his land with buildings and all appurtenances which Adam of Holande … … son of Adam of Smalschogh within the bounds of Rilclyff, to have and to hold from me and my heirs … In fee and free inheritance, quietly, peacefully and fully, with all commons, liberties and easements … in meadows, in woods, in turbaries, in waters, in marshes, and in all other parts, which belong to such land within ... ... of Langesyde (Langsett?), except for the annual rent to me and my heirs of 4s 6d at Easter for all services, fees, customs and demands which belong to such land ... .

It is ordered that there be distraint upon that messuage and 25 acres of land at Bretton (W)yhouse now in the hands of Thomas Dron ... of a hood for his arrears of service owed to the Lord.

John of Whetelay accepts liability for 1 capon to be paid to the Lord before Christmas next ... so that Katherine of Clayton shall not be distrained for any services made to the Lord before the next court.

The court assessors: Thomas of Denby, William the Herle.

The sum total from this court = 6s 9d.

Court of Richard Burdet, Lord of Denby, held at Heghholande 6th August 7 Henry V (1419). Enquiry was made on the oaths of:

John Marschal, Richard Horn, William of Turton, John Robynson, Richard Nichols, Thomas Hyne, John Raworth, Thomas Nottson, John Bartrem, Robert Westhall, William the Herle, John Naylor, who say on oath that:

John Appulyherd (6d), William Hyngeclyff (4d), John Prist (4d), Thomas Walkur (4d), John Smyth of M. (4d), Simon Hannelay (2d), owe suit of court and did not come and so are in mercy.

Item: they say that Robert Luppishede is a trespasser since the last court with 18 animals on the pasture of the Lord of Denby (8d)
NB: the de Lipheued family are recorded in 1379 in the Agbrigg wapentake at Cumberworth.

Item: they say that the house of John Stock has deteriorated because of a damaged roof and it is ordered that the whole of the lean-to should be repaired, under a penalty of 40d paid to the Lord.

Item: they say that another messuage in his tenure is badly deteriorated because of a defective roof and that it should be repaired (40d).

It is ordered that Abraham of Bolande be distrained for the next court for arrears of services to the Lord for half a bovate of land in Banscroft.

It is ordered that Richard Oxpringe be distrained for arrears of services to the Lord for lands and tenements in Darton, late belonging to Thomas Bell.

They order that William of Rilleston be distrained for arrears of services to the Lord for lands he holds in Bykedon. (Probably Bagden)

They order that the said Richard Oxspringe be distrained for 4d arrears owed to the Lord for the last 11 years from his lands in Darton.

Richard of Nichols in person in court took from the Lord 1 messuage and half a bovate, late in the tenure of John Almonbery, and a long time ago in the tenure of William Kitson, in Nethyrcumburworth, to be held by him at the will of the Lord, according to the custom of the manor, from the feast of St Martin in Winter (11th Nov.) 1420, for the term of 12 years, paying to the Lord for it annually and to his heirs, 18s at the usual terms, in equal portions, and 2 boon days in Autumn in Sygilbone and to make 2 appearances at the Great Court at Michaelmas and Easter – and he gives to the Lord for his admission 13s 4d, to be paid at the feast of St Martin, and he made his fealty.

NB: Feast of St. Martin – Martinmas – was once of great significance, traditionally farm workers and servants were hired for the ensuing year amidst great feasting. After the end of the first world war the 11th November became better known as armistice day.

Joan Bartrem came to court and surrendered into the Lord's hands 2 bovates in Mappulwell, which she formerly held of the Lord.

Roger Grubbar came to court and took land called Falgrove in Darton to be held from 11 Nov. 1420 for 12 years. Rent 2s per annum, with boon days and two court appearances.

Agnes of Rilay came to court and took Payntkerre to hold from 11 Nov. for 12 years. Rent 2s per annum.

Katherine of Clayton came to court and made fealty for lands and tenements she holds in Clayton, a long time ago belonging to Thomas Doggeson. Rent is 2s per annum and 2d for the farm of the castle. and 2 appearances at the Great Court.
(farm = form of annual rent).

John Hudson came to court and agreed to pay 8d withheld from his tenure at the feast of St Martin next, unless he shows sufficient evidence why not.

John Thompson and Thomas Walker of Crigilston came and made fealty for 1 croft with 2 bovates adjoining which they hold freely of the Lord in Crigilston, in the right of John and his wife Alice. Rent is 8s per annum, and to appear once at the next court held at Holande after Michaelmas.

John Hudson came to court and acknowledged that he held of the Lord half a bovate in Overcumburworth called Fyshelande. Rent 16d per annum.

Total sum of money from this court 16s 10d

The court of Richard Burdet, Lord of Denby, held at Heghholande on the morrow of St Luke the Evangelist 7 Henry V (19th October 1419)

Inquiry was made on the oaths of John Marschall, Richard Horn, John Robynson, Richard Nichols, John the Herle, Thomas Hyne, Thomas Nottson, John Rauworth, John Bartrem, John Stoke, William the Herle, who say on oath that:

John Herrison (4d), Emma Robinson (2d), William of Lynlay (2d), John Pristson (by infirmity), John Prist of Rikliff (4d), William Hengeclyff (4d), William of Waturhall (4d), John Appulyherd (8d), Richard Wortley of Thurleston (2d), John Hudson (6d), owe suit of court and have not come, and so are in mercy, and John Smyth of Mappulwell for the same (4d).

Item: they say that Robert of Whitlay who freely held of the Lord lands and tenements in Clayton and also half a bovate at the will of the Lord, annual rent for the bovate being 12s 1d, is dead and it is ordered that the heirs of the said Robert shall be distrained to appear at the next court to make their services to the Lord.

Robert Luppishede came to the court and acknowledged that he had alienated lands and tenements which he held of the Lord in Cumburworth, to Robert of Rokelay and others, to be held in fee simple of the Lord and that he had received these lands and tenements from the said Robert Rokelay to be held at will etc.

The said Robert Luppishede says that when the Lord asks of him the 8d per annum which are in arrears for the past three years, that he used to pay the Lord 2s rent per annum for the lands and tenements called Pridkenlande, lately belonging to Adam of the Leghe, which lands and tenements he held only at the will of the heirs of the said Adam and that John Hudson, as kinsman and heir of the said Adam expelled him from them and holds them, and by right he should pay the said rent of 2s, and he says that 8d of the same, the Lord had allowed him was part of the said rents of 2s, and this he asks the twelve jurors of the court to verify, and so enquiry shall be made, and the said John warned to be present at the next court.

It is ordered that the said Robert Luppishede be distrained for the said 8d, which he should pay each year for 2 acres of land which he holds of the Lord, in addition to the lands and tenements which he has previously acknowledged he holds of the Lord as formerly a court held on the morrow of the Purification of the Blessed Virgin Mary in 6th year of Edward III (3rd Feb 1329).

Item: the jurors say that Richard of Wodhous has trespassed with his beasts within the township of Holande in the Lord's pasture and so in mercy (6d).

Item: that the said Richard cut down green wood in Holandbanke and in other places there, to mend fences, without licence, and is in mercy (2d).

Item: that Thomas of Whitlay and John Wiget cut down green wood there and so are in mercy (2d each).

Item: that Robert of Mosselay with 20 sheep (4d), Robert (Scheres) with 8 sheep (2d), William of Bery with 10 sheep, also with one (horse) and a foal, also with 3 cows and mares (8d), also Robert of Mosselay with 3 cows (4d), also Richard of le Rodes with 2 horses (4d), also William Wills with 1 horse and a foal (2d), also Agnes of Rolay with 2 horses and 12 cows and a mare (4d), also Richard of le Rodes with 10 cows and a mare (4d), also Thomas Heyne with his draught animals (4d), also John Rauworth with his draught animals (6d), Thomas Nottson for the same (6d), trespassed on the demesne lands of Holande and in the pastures and in the woods there and so are in mercy.

Item: the jurors say that Thomas Gosyllinge, a miller, holds … of pasture of the Lord, called … schotclyff.

Item: they say that Robert (Happishode), John Helays and John Robinson trespassed with their draught animals upon Hegh …

Richard Smyth, clerk, in his own person, came to court and took from the Lord that tenement and those two bovates of land with appurtenances, which Thomas of the Hall formerly held and which William Way since held within … of (Keresforth) in Barneslay, to be held by him and his heirs from the Feast of St Martin in the Winter next (11 Nov) for the term of 30 years, paying for it annually for the said term for the Lord for his lands and tenements in Keresforth, to the Lord of Barneslay, 6s 8d, at the usual terms by equal portions, and paying annually during the said term to the said Lord of Denby and his heirs 16d … and to make two appearances in the court of the said Lord of Denby, held at Heghholande aforesaid after Easter and Michaelmas, and paying nothing for admission, since the Lord had exempted him, and he makes fealty.

Thomas of Whitlay (Wheatley), in his own person, came to court and made fealty to the Lord for lands and tenements which he claims to hold of the Lord in Clayton, and on this day made acknowledgement until the next court.

William Pogin came to court in his own person and presented himself to take that messuage and that bovate of land, which he formerly held in Keresford.

Court Assessors: Thomas of Denby, Richard Horn, John the Herle, William the Herle.
Sum total from this court 11s 1d

Court of Richard Burdet, Lord of Denby, held at Heghholande the 6th February, 7 Henry V (1420)

Enquiry was made on the oaths of, John Marschall, Thomas of Denby, Richard Horn, John Robinson, Richard Nichols, John the Herle, Thomas Hyne, John Ranworth, Thomas Nottson, John Bartre, Robert Westhall and William Herle, who say on oath that:

William Hengeclyff (3d), William Waturhall (3d), John Appulyherd (3d), Richard Wortelay of Thurleston (3d), John Harrison (4d), Robert Luppishede (2d), and Thomas Walker (2d), owe suit of court and did not come and so they are in mercy.

It is ordered with the consent of the tenants that for any of their mares without iron nose-rings, to prevent them wandering in the fields, they shall pay to the Lord 2d.

William Rery for 5 animals caught in the Lord's pasture in Les Rodes, and is in mercy (1d).

Robert Henschoghe, because he took away les holyncroppis from the common of Holande near to Holynyhate without licence and so is in mercy (4d).

Richard of le Rodes for 12 animals which trespassed on the Lord's pasture in Les Rodes, and is in mercy (4d).

Richard of Mosselay for trespass with 5 animals (2d).
Agnes of Rilay for trespass with 12 animals (3d).
William Wills for trespass with 8 animals (3d).
Thomas Hyne for trespass with 6 animals (2d).
Robert Schires for trespass with 2 cows (1d).
John the Herle for the same (1d).
John Marschall for some cows in Doncroft (2d).
John the Rector of Holande for trespass in le Halleyherdes(1d). (Possibly John Bettison.)
John Seygmyhs for trespass (2d).
William Bellamy for trespass (2d).
John Ranworth because he cut down (willows) unseasonably in the Molderode (4d).

Item: the jurors say that John of Birton and his son Richard hold in severalty during the winter Les Scalpyres, contrary to the right of the tenants, and so are to be distrained.

Item: they say that the said John and Richard have enclosed by estimation 4 acres of land in Welegrove in the said township, which used not to be enclosed with the Falghfolde.

It is presented that John Hudson is distrained to acknowledge the lands and tenements which he claims to hold of the Lord.

It is presented that the said John is distrained for his arrears of services to the Lord, and for 8d rent held back for 11 years.

It is presented that the said John is distrained for 40d for arrears of penalties, as in the court in the 14th year of King Henry IV (1412/13), because he did not acknowledge it.

William Stringar in person took from the Lord a messuage with lands and appurtenances adjoining, which he formerly held in Nothirbretton, to be held at the will of the Lord, according to the custom of the manor, from the Feast of St Martin in the Winter next (11 Nov.) for the term of 12 years, paying for it yearly, to the Lord, at the said terms, 10s in equal portions and 2 boon days in Autumn, and he gives for his admission 12 hens and chickens, and makes his fealty.

William Lynelay, in person, took from the Lord that messuage with land adjoining, late in the tenure of Thomas Stokelay, formerly held by John Barynge, in Denby, to hold from the Lord from the Feast of St Martin in the Winter (11 Nov.), at the will of the Lord, according to the custom of the manor, for twelve years – rent is 10s per annum, and 2 boon days in Autumn, fine for admission is 40d, which the Lord pardons him, because the house is not built.

Robert of (Hamur) in person took from the Lord that messuage long ago held by John Radclyffe called le Nothirbretton, with land adjoining, lately held by Richard of le (Wode), to be held at the will of the Lord according to the custom of the manor from 11 November for 12 years, rent is 13s per annum and 2 boon days in Autumn, fine for admission is 40d and he makes his fealty.

John the Herle took from the Lord a messuage with land adjoining in Clayton he formerly held, to hold for 12 years. Rent is 3s 4d per annum and 2 boon days in Autumn. Admission fine is 40d, pardoned by the Lord.

William the Herle took from the Lord a messuage with land adjoining in Holande, formerly held of Geoffrey of (Reston), to hold for 12 years from 11 November. Rent is 12s per annum and 2 boon days in Autumn. Admission fine is 4s.

William Bellamy took from the Lord a messuage and 16 acres of land (formerly held by) William Seygmyhe in Holande, to be held for 12 years.

At this point the original document becomes impossible to translate any further.

We can see from the latter just how extensive Richard Burdet's lands had become as a result of inter family marriage and acquisition by earlier members of his family. Richard died in 1436 leaving his son, Robert as Lord of the manor of Denby. His will, never before translated gives us the following details:

Will of Richard Burdet 1436 – Lord of the Manor of Denby
In the name of God Amen: the 21st of June Anno Domini 1436, I Richard Burdet of Denby, esquire, of sound mind and perfect memory, do make my will in this manner:

Firstly: I bequeath and commend my soul to God Almighty, to the Blessed Mary and to all the Saints and my body for burial according to church law wherever it may please God.

Item: I bequeath what is customary as my mortuary.

Item: I bequeath to a suitable priest for celebrating mass for the salvation of my soul for a year, as soon as is fitting after my death, £4 13s 4d.

Item: I bequeath for the adornment of the high altar in the choir of Penistone, 6s 8d.

Item: I bequeath for the adornment of the high altar in the church of Holand, 6s 8d.

Item: I bequeath to the fabric of the cathedral church of St Peter of York, 6s 8d.

Item: I bequeath to the brothers/friars of the order of St Robert of Knaresborough, 6s 8d.

Item: I bequeath as the marriage portion of Margaret my daughter, £20.

Item: I bequeath to Alice my daughter what is due to her according to the discretion of her mother.

Item: I bequeath to Master Robert Pullayne, the Vicar of Penistone, 6s 8d.

I give and bequeath the residue of all my goods not disposed of to Joan, my wife, and I constitute her my executrix.

In witness whereof I attach my seal to this my will.

With these witnesses: Sir Henry Faldewe, Rector of half of the church of Holand, Henry del Storthes, Richard Smyth of Barneslay and others.

Given at Denby the day and year abovesaid.

This will was proved on the 9th of July in the abovesaid year and administration was granted to the executrix named in it and she was sworn according to the form of law.

NB: Robert Pullayne remained vicar of Penistone until his death around 1458.

Mortuary was a payment due to the church on death. Usually the deceased was required to leave his second best chattel (personal property) in recompense for tithes and other debts supposedly unpaid during their lifetime. In 1529 Parliament limited mortuaries to moderate payments according to the value of the estate involved. Richard probably left an ox. He appears to have divided his religious loyalties between High Hoyland and Penistone though he makes a separate payment to the vicar of Penistone, Robert Pullayne. Why might he do this and ignore Henry Faldewe? The payment to the friars at Knaresborough and the family name Pullayne are very good clues.

Burdet family of Fulnetby

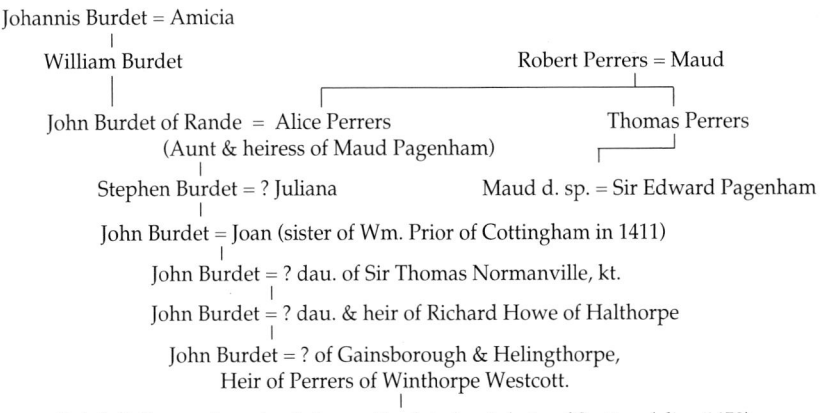

The latter pedigree concerns the Burdet family originating from Fulnetby, the next village to Rand in Lincolnshire. As we know, the Burdet family which became Lords of Denby emanated from Rande. Robert Burdet, the first of the name in Denby left his brother Sir Nicholas behind in Rande, Nicholas had a son but the line seems to fail after this. By the 14th century both lines had failed in their respective villages of origin but the line from Fulnetby continued elsewhere, notably around Knaresborough with Joanne or Jennet Burdet eventually marrying the Pulleyn heir and moving north west of Knaresborough to Scotton. Robert Pulleyn was therefore related by marriage to the Burdet's of Denby albeit distantly. The latter evidence seems to suggest that the two branches of the Burdet family kept in touch and did not forget that they were tied by blood a number of generations ago.

It is interesting to note the name of Alice Perrers, I am currently unable to track down the Perrers family lineage but there was a very famous lady by this name who became the mistress of Edward III. This Alice Perrers was born around 1345 and entered the service of the Queen of Edward III, Phillipa of Hainaut. Alice married Sir William de Windsor but became Edwards mistress possibly as early as 1366, though due to her interference in lawsuits and other matters she was impeached in 1374 and later banished from the royal household in 1376 by the 'Good Parliament'. The King recalled her in 1377, the year of his death though the story goes that Alice stole the rings from his fingers as he breathed his last. She later gained favour at the court of Richard II and became very wealthy. It is likely that she came from the same family mentioned above which is suggestive in linking the Burdet family even closer to the King than has previously been thought.

It was also in the year of Richard Burdet's death that the following document was created. In it we find that John Bosville of Newhall and his wife are pursuing claims to lands as of their manor of Gunthwaite.

HENRY VI (1436)

Fine between Maud, Countess of Cambridge, Percival Cresacre Esq., and James Cressacre, complainents and John Bosville of Newhall Esq., and Isabell his wife, doforciants. (Amongst other places, land at Denby and Gunthwaite and High Hoyland).

The said Countess granted to the aforesaid John and Isabella the aforesaid lands and the heirs of Isabella of the chief lord.

(there were many other lands and appurtenances mentioned including Ingbirchworth and Cumberworth.)

Robert Burdet became Lord of Denby after his father's death in 1436. The following manorial/rental survey would appear to date from soon after this. Although incomplete it may have been produced for Lord Robert to allow him to see how much he was worth in the various places mentioned within it:

… Hamlet, part in manor of Denby, namely 1 bovate in Denby bought by the ancestors of the Lord, which are in the fee of Donning.

Robert, Lord of Denby, bought 1 bovate in Denby from John Harper worth 5s per annum, and is in demesne.

There is in Denby 1 bovate bought by the ancestors of the said Robert, and half a bovate worth per annum 2s 6d in demesne, and another half bovate of the same is in the hands of a freeman, rent is 2s 6d per annum.

In Birchworth there are 1 and a half bovates in demesne worth 6s 6d per annum.

Item: there are there in the hands of freeholders 2 and a half bovates, rent is 4s 3d per annum.

Item: there is in Schelmerthorpe 1 assart containing 10 acres which is called Tithwayt, bought by the ancestors of Robert of Denby, it is in demesne and worth 18d per annum.

Item: there is there 1 assart in Schelmerthorpe called Westrode in the hands of freeholders, bought by the ancestors of Robert of Denby, rent is 6d per annum.

Item: Gilbert of Schelmerthorpe holds freely in the same place half a bovate, rent is 2s per annum.

Item: there are in Penistone in the hands of freeholders, 6s 6d annual rents coming from assarts, these rents were bought by Lord Robert of Denby, and are pardoned.

Item: in the same place in the demesne is an assart worth 6d per annum, bought by the said Lord Robert.

Item: in Denby there are in demesne (125) acres of arable land belonging to the manor.

Item: there are there in the demesne 2 acres of meadow with additional pieces of meadow and land adjoining.

Item: there are in the same place 2 bovates in the hands of the Parson of Penistone, of the Lord's fee, and are a gift of the ancestors of the Lord of Denby, no rent due to the Lord.

NB: The parson was Robert Pulleyn – again family ties explain the free rent.

Item: there are in the same place of the fee of the Lord of Denby in the hands of freeholders 5 bovates, rent is 17s 8d per annum.

Item: in the same place there are in demesne 3 bovates worth 14s per annum.

Item: in the same place there are 2 water mills in demesne worth 66s 8d per annum.

Item: John of Denby holds in demesne 12 bovates by knights service.

Item: John Wyth holds freely 1 meadow worth 12d per annum.

Item: the Lord holds in demesne an annual rent of 8d in Overdenby coming from 4 acres in Tillerset in the hands of freeholders.

A rent of 2s per annum which Lord Robert of Holand bought of Roger son of Beta in Denby of the fee of Donning and belongs to the manor of Holand.

Item: in Thurleston there are 2 acres enclosed by a fence for a cow pasture, it is in demesne, worth 2d per annum, bought by Adam of Holand, for 20 cows and offspring for 3 years.

Item: in Thurleston there are 20 acres in 1 assart, rent is 6s per annum, which was bought by the said Adam of Holand.

Item: in Langeside (Langsett) at Rilclif 12s annual rent in the hands of freeholders, which the said Adam bought.

Item: in Smalrehagh in the hands of freeholders is 5s annual rent, purchased by the said Lord Adam of Holand.

Item: in Bircheworth are in the hands of freeholders in demesne 5 bovates worth 20s per annum.

Item: in the same demesne are 2 assarts and half an acre worth 18d per annum.

Item: a water mill worth 6s per annum.

Item: in the hands of freeholders 3 bovates, rent is 2s 8d per annum.

Item: Robert of Irland holds 2 bovates for which he pays nothing per annum, but 1 knight's service, and which the said Lord Adam bought.

Item: in Clayton in the hands of John of Lathes from his freeholder, 6s 7d, of ancient tenure.

John of Irland 2 bovates in fee, 12d per annum rent, of ancient tenure.

Thomas son of Hugh of Lathes holds freely half a bovate and 2 pieces of meadow, rent is 3s 6d per annum, of ancient tenure.

Item: Scheplayeag 1d per annum of ancient tenure.

Item: in the same township the Lord has an assart called ryding in the demesne, worth per annum 18d of ancient tenure.

Item: in the same an assart called (No)rmanrode, worth 5s 6d per annum of ancient tenure.

Item: in the demesne the Lord has in the same Payntker, worth per annum 6d, of ancient tenure.

Elias son of Erkin (holds) land at will of the demesne, worth 5s per annum, of ancient tenure.

Thomas son of William (holds) of the Lord at will half a bovate worth per annum (2s 6d) of ancient tenure.

The Lord has in Clayton in demesne 1 meadow called Brodker, worth per annum 6s 8d of ancient tenure.

Item: in Cumburworth, Adam of Legh of Holande holds freely 1 assart of Power, rent is half a mark (6s 8d) per annum, of ancient tenure.

John Witber holds freely in the same place 1 bovate and a half, rent is 3s 10d per annum, of ancient tenure.

Emma (Miller) holds freely $^3/_4$ of a bovate, rent is 2s per annum. The same Emma holds of the demesne of the Lord land worth 6s 8d per annum, of ancient tenure.

John (W)ath the younger holds freely 1 bovate, rent is 12d per annum.

Richard of (Birker) holds freely half a bovate, rent is 2s per annum of ancient tenure.

Adam of le Gy holds a quarter bovate.

John son of Stephen holds freely half a bovate, rent is 3s per annum.

John of Legh holds freely 1 assart, rent is 12d per annum.

Robert Carp holds freely a quarter bovate, rent is 18d per annum.

Hugh son of Stephen holds freely half a bovate, rent is 3s per annum.

John Wolf holds of the Lord at will 1 bovate and a quarter.

Adam (Perdran) holds freely half a bovate, rent 2s per annum.

William son of Mathilda holds freely 1 bovate, rent is (4s) per annum.

John of Hathiley holds freely 20 acres of land with appurtenances, rent is 6s 8d per annum.

Idonia daughter of Henry the smith holds freely half a bovate …

NB: the blacksmith was a very important part of the manor at this time and performed a crucial service.

In demesne the Lord has half a bovate of Co …

Item: in Mepilwelle he has in the hands of the free holders 4 bovates, 2 messuages, 11 acres of land, rent is (23s) per annum.

Item: in demesne he has in the same place 5 bovates worth (30s) per annum.

Item: in demesne 6 acres of land worth per annum …

In Kesseburgof (Kexborough) 1 assart freely, 14d per annum, of ancient tenure.

In Kenessmill there are in the hands of Henry of Roklay for 1 tenement 6d annual rent.

Robert was also involved in the following lease in 1441:

1441 20th Oct – Lease for 38 years by Robert Burdett of Denby, esq., to William Turton the elder and John his son of 7 oxgangs of land in Yngbyrcheworth lately held by the said William of Richard Burdett father of the said Robert at an annual rent of 32s.

Robert did not long out live his father as only fifteen years after his death he followed him to the grave:

Will of Robert Burdet 1451 – Lord of the Manor of Denby
The Will of Robert Birdded formerly of Penistone.
In the name of God Amen. In the year 1451 on the Friday before the feast of St. Peter's Chair I Robert Birdded of sound mind and memory make my will. Firstly I leave my soul to God, blessed Mary and all the Saints and my body to be buried in the church of St. John the Baptist at Penyston.

Item: I leave as mortuary my best draught animal.

Item: For the expenses on the day of my burial 20s for bread, ale and cheese.

Item: To the Vicar 6s 8d for commemoration in the church and in his prayers.

Item: For the Lord's alms 6s 8d to be paid on Sundays and the aforesaid sum is confirmed.

Item: To making a cross 6s 8d.

The residue of all my goods whatsoever I give and bequeath to Amery (my) son and ordain and constitute him my executor.
And the same Robert owes £20 and it was his will that each of his daughters should have 24s namely Joan, Agnes and Elizabeth.
Witnesse Robert Normanville, John Birkes and others.
This will was proved 19th August in the year aforesaid by the aforesaid witnesses and administration granted to the executor named in the will and sworn in due form.

The first point to note regarding the latter is that Robert overlooked his debts and forgot to make provision for his daughters, either Aymer, his eldest son, who would almost certainly have been present, or one of the other witnesses must have added this in. Perhaps it was written whilst Robert was laying on his death bed, finally unable to speak and reliant on others around him. The mortuary payment would most likely have been an Ox. At least he made provision for the funeral wake! His funeral would have been performed by his kinsman, Robert Pulleyn. One thing the wills do allow us to do is add more leaves to the tree of the family and finally include some of the daughters, previously unrecorded.

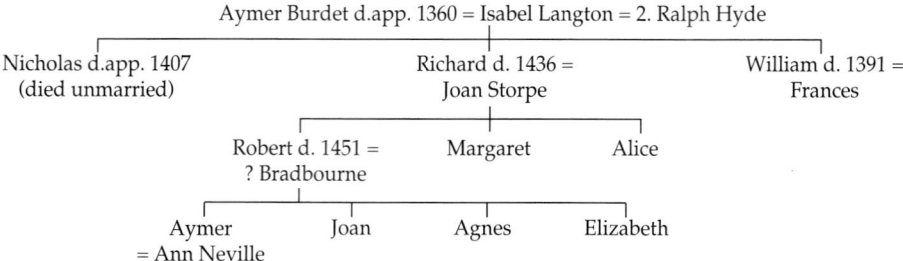

Robert Burdet's son, Aymer now became Lord of the Manor. Aymer, according to the Heralds of Elizabeth I, who were privy to an indenture, the whereabouts of which are now unknown, was married in 1447/8 to Anne Nevile of Liversedge We find him in the following lease. The assart is one of the earliest references to High Flatts.

> 1453 13th Dec – *Lease for 40 years by Amer ('Adamarus') Burdet of Denby to John Parkynson of the same of a bovate of land in Overdenby called 'Mortenlande' and an assart called 'Heghflatt' at an annual rent of 5s.*

A further document dated to approximately 1473 tells us,

> *… that William Turton and Thomas Walton without the consent of Robert Burdet demised their own and Robert's lands in Byrcheworth; that William Turton erased the boundaries between his lands and the said Robert's; that in 1473 Thomas Walton claimed certain lands against Hemer (Aymer), son and heir of Robert Burdet and Thomas Turton'.*

These are probably the same lands we have noted above as being leased by Robert Burdet to William Turton in 1441, perhaps the death of Robert, ten years later had led the Turtons to chance their arm and try to acquire access to more land than was their due.

It is likely that he is the same man mentioned by the historian Eli Hoyle:

> *Edward IV (1475). Adrain Burdet witness to deed conveying lands at Monk Bretton to John Genne of Workesburgh (Worsbrough).*

The medieval scribes certainly seem to have had a problem recording the name Aymer, which was obviously very unfamiliar to them. Variously written, Ademan, Almaricus, Amarius, Adomar, Aymericus, Eymer, Emery, Edmund. Historian, George Redmonds has investigated the origin of the name. He concluded that it was of Germanic origin, brought into England by the Norman's, a good example of which was Adomar, derived from Eadmaer. The name prospered within the Burdet family although the best known use of it was the individual known as Adomar or Aymar de Valence, Count of Pembroke. Other families began to use the name, the earliest example of which was Haymer Kirshawe of Birstall parish (1450). Redmonds goes on to say that though there is currently no evidence to suggest a link to the Burdet family it might be significant that Aymer Burdet witnessed Birstall deeds in 1465.

Chapter Two

A Period of Transition – From Burdet to Savile, 1485–1666

Aymer Burdet was succeeded by his son Nicholas who we can find in a document dated 1485/6,

Grant for life by Richard Burdet to his father Nicholas Burdet of all his lands etc. in Mapilwell, Penyston and Yngbrychworth.

The feud between Aymer Burdet and the Turtons at Ingbirchworth continued during Nicholas's tenure as Lord, a memoranda has survived which concerns the dispute, now between Richard Turton and Nicholas Burdet over 2 messuages and 2 oxgangs, in wardship of Thomas Turton of Wakefield, deceased.

We know that Nicholas certainly held court at High Hoyland, but again it begs the question as to where. As previously stated, central to the family possessions was the site of Denby Hall, the most likely place to hold the court. On 1st December 1500 Nicholas granted Richard Oxle a piece of land for 12 years at an annual rent of 14d in Clayton. The record for 1501 is much more complete and gives us an insight into the size of the community at this time and some of the minor offences they committed.

Court held at Holand 1 December 17 Henry VII (1501)
Enquiry held on the oaths of John Jenkyson, Henry Wodcok, John Denys, William Walton, Robert Wynburne, John Walton, Richard Walton, Richard Oxle, Aymer Benyon, John … , … Holde, James Stayley, Edward H(orne), Robert Denton, John Hy(nch)lyff, William Parson, Robert Walton, John Mekyltwett(Micklethwaite), Thomas Hoyle, Walter Byegod, Thomas Adde, John … , who say on their oaths that Richard Wod … ofte, knight, did not come to court to make his homage.

Matthew Wyntworth, esquire, did not come.
Thomas Wytley for the same did not make homage… is admitted at request of William (Arne).
John for the same and Robert for the same(5d).
They present Robert Baynby (Barnby) for the same (4d).
Thomas Tinton (Turton?) for the same (4d).
Peter de Monkbretton for the same (4d).
Thomas (Brist)wytt for the same (6d).
Richard Kerrforth (Keresforth?) for the same (4d).
John Rebys for the same and for a relief if he makes his homage (2s).
William Symys did not come and did not make homage for land in Cumbryworth late Robert Lupsett's and is distrained 6s.

John Denton did not come.

Ralph Eyre for the same (2s).

John Hagh (Haigh) *for the same (6d).*

The heirs of Robert Peck for the same (6d).

John Hagh for not coming to court (4d).

Executors of John Benson for the same (2d).

Robert Walton for the same (2d).

Thomas Dyconson (Dickinson) *for not coming for his relief (4d).*

William Jacson for the same.

Mistress Foth(eringham) *of Aldwarke for the same and for her service for her land in Skelmanthorpe (6d).*

Abbot of Byland for not coming and making homage for his lands in Clayton.

John Wolfe for not coming to do service for his lands late belonging to Robert (Iretene) *in Barnsley (3d).*

Robert … for not coming for his relief.

John Peyteler for not coming to do his homage.

John Clayton of Clayton for not coming (8d).

Thomas Jenkynson for trespass made in the Lords wood.

John Jenkynson for the same trespass.

William Burton for the same (2d).

Thomas Hole for breaking fences and …

John Denys for the same and so is in mercy (2d).

Agnes Lyntwell for trespass in the Lord's wood and for buying and selling services …

Richard Schampney for trespass in the Lord's wood (2d).

William Fernley for the same.

Nicholas Bylclyff for … distrained.

William Walton for the same and is in mercy (2d).

Henry Wodcok for the same.

Robert Swynburns for the same and for trespass and fined (4d).

John (Walton) *for the same … (6d).*

John Godard for the same (2d).

William Byn(feld) *for the same (2d).*

Nicholas (Parkyn) *for the same (2d).*

Richard Walton for the same (2d).

Richard Oxle for the same (6d).

Richard Hyrst …

Thomas Paslew … (2d).

John Wodcok of Cumburworth, Peter Aprestroyd, John (Normanwryg), *are in mercy … for trespass in the Lord's wood.*

Thomas H…d for a tenement.

John Dughtyman, Rector of the church for ….(probably High Hoyland – he was here in 1497).

Edmund Clayton for the same.

NB: The latter list includes the Abbot of Byland. The dissolution of the monastery's took place between 1536 and 1539, the lands owned by the Abbey in Denby, Flockton, Whitley and Emley were sold by the Court of Augmentation to Arthur Kaye, a member of the family that had long associations with Denby Grange and Woodsome. Arthur Kaye was also instrumental in the settlement of the brothers, Aymer and Thomas Burdet upon the dispute of their inheritance after the death of their father, Richard in 1546 considered in V1.

The following deeds have also survived for the sixteenth century:

1502 16th December – *Receipt by Nicholas Burdett of Denby, for money paid to him by Richard his son and heir, being the rent of lands held by James Bray and William Royds of Yngbrychworth on a six year lease.*

1519 25th June – *Indented agreement between Richard Burdet and Amer Denton, guardian of Jennet, wife of William Denton, concerning their right to hold certain lands and messuages in Yngbyrchworth during the nonage of the said Jennet.*

1519–20 – *Demise by Richard Burdett of Paneston, esq., to William More of Holland of 2 parcels of wood in Paneston and a close in Holand for 7 years at a rent of £3.*

1547 24th Sep – *Grant, by Amer Burdett of Denby,esq, to Henry his eldest son of his manor of Denby with lands and appurtenances in Denby, Clayton, Skelmanthorp, Inglebyrchworth, Langside, Thurleston and Peniston.*

1549 1st Nov – *Grant, by Amer Burdett, esq, to Martin Anne, esq., Ric Pek, Hugh Seybeth and Thos Burdett, gents, of a messuage and divers lands and rents in Clayton in the parish of Hughlaunde and in Birchworthe to the use of himself for life and there after to his son Richard and his heirs male.*

1553 9th June. – *Lease for 21 years by Henry Burdett of Denbie, gent., to Richard Streyt of Rowley, miller, of a dwelling house and water mill known as 'Denbie Milne' and 2 closes known as 'Ynge' and 'Martyn Royd' in the parish of Penistone; at an annual rent of £7.*

1572/73 18th March – *Grant, with warranty by Robert Savile of Pullam, Co. Lincs, esq., Thomas Watterton of Walton, esq., Coton Gargrave of Nostell esq., John Lacye of Brereley, esq., Almer Burdett of Denby, esq., and Henry Burdett, son and heir apparent of the same Almer (in performance of an award dated 23 Jan 15 Eliz) to John Burdett, one of the younger sons of the aforesaid Almer, and the heirs male of his body, of an annual rent of 46s and 8 pence issuing out of the manor of Denby and the lands etc. limited by the above award to Henry Burdett and his heirs male after the decease of the aforesaid Almer in Denby, Clayton, Ingbirchworth, Skelmanthorpe, Langsett, Penystone, Thurleston and Barmebye – the first payment of the annuity not to be made until after the death of the aforesaid Almer.*

1572 – *Indenture of a Fine between Robt Savile, Thos Watterton, Coton Gargrave and John Lacye, esqs, querents, and Almer Burdett, esq, and Hen Ric Nich and John Burdett, deforciants, concerning the manor of Denbye and lands etc in Denbye, Clayton, Ingburchworth, Skelmanthorppe, Langsett, Penyston, Thurleston and Barmebye. Consideration - £280.*

NB: The inclusion of Thomas Waterton in the latter two documents might imply that Henry Burdet was on friendly terms with him. Waterton lived at Walton, where Henry Burdet eventually moved with his illegitimate family leaving Denby in the hands of his son, Richard.

1573–4 – *Certificate to the effect that two and a half carucates of land late belonging to Nicholas Burdhead and afterwards to Amarius Burdhead are now leased to Henry Burdheadd at an annual* rent of 2s. A relief of 3s on the land has already been answered for by Richard Bunny, feodary at Pontefract, who signs the document (Clayton).

1573/4 January 20th – *Award, supplementary to that of 23 Jan 15 Eliz, by Thomas Gargrave of Nostell, Kt, and John Lacye of Brereley, esq. The arbitrators declare that Nicholas Burdett, younger son of Aylmer Burdett, shall have and enjoy the lands stated in the earlier Award to be in the tenure of Gilbert (wrongly called Richard) Wood and a yearly rent of 46s giving forth out of lands in Bagden, and that Henry Burdett shall peaceably suffer the said Nicholas and the heirs male of his body to hold the said lands.*

1575 July 11th – *Exemplification of a Recovery suffered by Robt Savile, esq and Thos Savile, gent against Hen Burdett alias Burdhede, esq in respect of the manor of Denbie with lands etc in Denbie, Clayton, Comberworthe, Yugburcheworthe, Cawthorne, Skelmanthorp, Langsett and Carlecotes.*

10th July 1584 – *Bond in £20 for the payment of £10 by John Blagburne (Blackburn) and Nicholas Armytage, yeoman, to Henry Burdet of Denibie Hall.*

1585 – *Voucher to the account of Brian Stapleton, Esq., Sheriff of York, viz a receipt for fines paid by Henry Burdet, Esq., a juror in the Court of Common Pleas.*

1585 1st Oct. – *Bond in 200 marks by John Moore of North Leverton, Co. Notts to Henry Burdett of Denby Hall in the parish of Penniston, esq., for the performance of covenants contained in a pair of indentures dated the same day, being a bargain and sale by the said John Moore of his lands and tenements in Ingburchworthe and Thurleston*

The document dated 1553 regards the water mill at Denby Dale, in fact a number of mills have operated over the years. Hartcliffe mills will be considered in a later chapter. The oldest mill was the 'Lower Mill', to the right of Miller Hill in Denby Dale just before one crosses the road bridge, to which the 1553 document refers. It was mentioned in 1546 when the two brothers, Aymer and Thomas Burdet were thrashing out the details of their fathers will – see V1. By 1637 John Lynley alias Wilde of Denby appears to have been the miller here, as we find him in the following document:

1637 August 21st – *Lease for 31 years by Geo Burdett of Denbie Hall, esq, to John Lynley alias Wilde of Denbie, miller, of land in Denbie; the lessee paying an annual rent of £9.*

He was later supplanted by George Green who paid a half yearly rent of £4 in 1701 and 1704 for the mill. Joshua Moseley, a Denby yeoman paid annually £10 10s for the lease of the mill and its associated buildings in 1736. In around 1790 the old pack horse bridge and ford which crossed the Dearne at the bottom of Miller Hill were replaced by a road bridge which considerably enhanced the trade routes. Competition increased from the 'Upper Mill' which was re-built between 1813 and 1815 and though we find the miller Joseph Dalton here in 1822 and 1833, by 1839 it seems that the site had been abandoned. These ruins were later buried by industrial waste from Kenyon's woollen mill and by tons of soil which were excavated in order to build a mill chimney. The mill pond was filled in and now lies buried under the Youth club and children's play area on Sunny Bank.

The 'Upper Mill' was the one to the left of the junction of Miller Hill and Wakefield Road and which was only demolished in 1974. In 1746 Nathaniel Shirt was described as 'corn miller of Denby Dale', this relates to the Upper Mill, he was the tenant of the Bosvilles of Gunthwaite. He died prior to the major re-building which took place, as noted above between 1813 and 1815. This work cost £1785 and was far above the amount estimated causing Mr Bosville to comment that had he known this in advance he would not have undertaken the work. The first tenants were the Senior's, though by 1822 Joshua Moxon was here. The mill was offered for sale by Godfrey Bosville in 1830 (probably to help finance his improvements to Thorpe Hall, owned by the family since 1773 and now the main place of residence as much of Gunthwaite Hall had been demolished), though it remained unsold at auction in Barnsley. The miller was Thomas Senior at this time. By 1833 and until 1852 Joshua Moxon was the miller, he was recorded from 1857 until 1861/2 as being in partnership with Joseph Moxon. They were followed by John Wood and Charles Holmes from 1867 to 1871. The Denby estate was finally sold by the Bosvilles in 1870 to Walter Norton, the following were the subsequent tenant millers:

1877 & 1881 Charles Holmes, 1892 & 1897 Fred Horn, 1901 & 1904 William Chilton, 1908 & 1910 Richard Chumley, 1912 Mr Wooley.

In 1908 the mill used steam and water power but by 1910 had installed a turbine. In the 1920's the water wheel was replaced by a high speed turbine which generated electricity for the mill owners as well as the Wesleyan chapel and Salvation Army Hall. The mill was disused by 1929, the premises were later used by a concrete manufacturers until 1960, and I remember a cotton/wool/sewing equipment shop here in the 1970's. By 1974 the buildings had become something of an eyesore and were demolished this year, making way for the Brookside housing estate. The mill pond also underlies this modern development.

One other mill worthy of mention is Lower Putting Mill, almost opposite to Highfield House and the Travellers Inn (now Argrar Indian restaurant). It seems to have been built by 1818 when it was mentioned on a map and could be identified with Ward and Haywood, scribbling millers. In 1830 a paper maker, Thomas Hartley, occupied the site, though he was declared insolvent in 1834. By 1841 the buildings had become private homes and a document of 1851 relates that there were four cottages, 3 of which were formerly a fulling mill called Pudding or Putting Mill.

The Upper Corn Mill buildings, prior to demolition in 1974. *W H Senior.*

Many of the documents latterly examined involve Aymer Burdet and his son and heir, Henry. Slightly distant from their affairs was Aymer's third son, Nicholas who lived at Darton and can be found at the muster of the militia in Barnsley, bearing a pike, this in response to the threat of the Spanish invasion in 1587. The following document also relates to him:

> 1597 December 3rd – ... *vicar or curate or churchwardens of the parish of Peniston a yearly rent of 12s 22/3d towards the maintenance of the Free Grammar School there, and to pay annual rents as specified to Nicholas Burdett of Swanwell, gent, and his heirs male, the Lord of the Manor of Breareley, and sundry tithes and lay assessments.*

He is also, probably the man noted as follows:

> *In Darton church there are six old monumental stones, 4 in the North chapel, 2 in the south, each bearing an inscribed cross, supposed to have covered the remains of former monks of Bretton. One bears the name of Nicholas Burdet.*

Though Nicholas was never destined to be Lord of the Manor like his father or brother, his will, made at Swawell, Darton in 1598, proves that he was still a man of substance and standing:-

> *In the name of God, Amen: the 13th of March in the year of our Lord God 1597 and in the fortieth year of our Sovereign Lady Elizabeth by the Grace of God Queen of England, France and Ireland, Defender of the Faith etc., I Nicholas Burdett of Swawell in the parish of Darton in the diocese of York, being sick in body but of good and perfect remembrance, praised be God therefore, do make, constitute and ordain this my last will and testament in manner and form following etc. And first and principally I commit my soul unto the hands of Almighty God, my creator and maker, trusting to be saved by the death, passion and blood shedding of Jesus Christ, my only redeemer and sanctifier, and by no other ways whatsoever; and my body to be buried within the parish church of Darton aforesaid, or elsewhere it shall please God to call me to his mercy; and for my worldly goods, I do give and bequeath them in manner and form as hereafter followeth:*
>
> *And first I do give and bequeath to Anne my wife the third part of all my goods and chattels, moveable and unmoveable, of what kind and sort or property the same shall be of, according to the laws of this realm, as in the name of her thirds.*

> *Item: I give and bequeath to the poor people of Darton, 20 shillings.*

> *Item: I give and bequeath unto Sir George Brooke my best corn wain and wheels and my best cart wain and wheels, to be delivered unto him at the Turn Bridge Inn directly after my decease.*

> *Item: I give to Matthew Burdett's son one black filly.*

> *Item: I do give unto my son, Richard Burdett, the sum of one hundred marks of lawful English money, the which I did covenant by indenture at the day of his marriage, to him to be paid by executors hereafter written, at such days and times, and according to the covenants therein contained in full due and satisfaction of all the said covenants, having also of my own good will further given unto him already, by surrender, certain copyhold land as may appear (in) the same surrender thereof made as aforesaid, all which he is likewise to have in due satisfaction and discharge of all his childs part and portion of my goods.*

> *Item: whereas I have given by copy of court roll, according to the custom of the manor of Wakefield, to Beatrix my daughter and her heirs for ever in full contentation of her filial or childs portion that*

she may claim to my goods and chattels, certain copyhold lands lying and being in Cartworth within the graveship of Holme, called the Hill House, now my will is that the said Beatrix shall within the time and space of three years next coming after the day of my decease pay unto William Goodart, otherwise called Burdett, my base begotten son, his executors or assigns the sum of £20 that is to say in manner and form following, £6 13s 4d yearly during the said three years in equal portions at Whitsunday and Martinmas, and the first payment to begin at whether of the said feasts shall chance the sooner after my death and so to continue (until such) time as the said sum of twenty pounds be fully contented, satisfied and paid.

Item: I give unto the Right Worshipful Sir John Savile, knight, my very good master, one black … called Brode, desiring him as my special trust is in him to be good unto my wife and children; and also it is my full will and mind that Anne, my wife shall have the government, tuition and bringing up of my said children, until such time as they shall accomplish their several full ages.

Item: I do make, constitute and ordain Nicholas Burdet, Daniel Burdett and Arthur Burdett, my sons, my full and sole executors of this my last will and testament.

Item: I do make and appoint Ralph Burdett, Thomas Burdett, Thomas Cutler of (Fawthwait…) and Thomas Cutler of Fieldhead, supervisors of this my said will and testament, to see that … according to the true intent and meaning of the same.

   In witness whereof, I the said Nicholas Burdett unto this my said last will and testament I have set my hand and seal the day and year first above written. In the presence of Thomas Cutler the elder, John Alleth, Thomas Cutler, the younger.

Administration of the will was granted to Nicholas and Daniel Burdett since Arthur was still a minor.

Richard's son, Arthur, later of Cawthorne was born in 1581, and was named as a Roman Catholic Recusant in 1604. Recusants were Roman Catholics who refused to attend the Church of England when it was legally compulsory. They became known as dissenters.

The list survives in the Bodleian Library and includes Arthur Burdet, gent., Mary, his wife, Frances Tyngle and Michael, servants to the said Arthur. There were more Romanists given at Cawthorne than any other place locally. Also mentioned were Thomas Savile of Kexborough, 3rd son of Nicholas Savile of New Hall and the Haigh in Kexborough. This Thomas married Mary, daughter of Thomas Burdet of Birthwaite. Mary's sister, Beatrix Burdett had married Thomas Barnby and had a son, Sir Charles Barnby, knt. Charles married Hestor Disney, daughter of Daniel Disney of Norton Disney, who was also a Romanist.

The deeds at Denby continue.

1597 3rd Dec – Bargain and sale for a consideration of £125 5s 8d by William Claiton of NewBagden alias OverBagden or Bygden within the township of Denby, yeoman to Thomas Claiton of NetherBagden within the same township, tanner, his heir apparent, of the entire moiety of a messuage (inherited from his father Ralph Clayton, deceased) now being used as 2 messuages and known as Bagden alias Bygden in Denby the moiety of the other houses, edifices, foulds etc., belonging there to, half a garden; an orchard and various lands, watercourses, woods, etc.

1598 August 2nd – Bond in £20 by William Claiton, late of Over Bagden within the town of Denline, yeoman, to George Burdett, son of Richard Burdett of Denbie, gent, for the performance within 3 years of any additional assurances conveyances etc demanded by George Burdett in respect of the Bargain and Sale described below.

1598 2 Aug – Bargain and sale for a consideration of £5 by William Claiton to George Burdett, his heir apparent, of all his lands, tenements, waters, streams etc., in Denbie. Endorsement of livery of seisin.

1598 20th August – Bond in £20 by Peter Hawksworth of Wheatley Hill, yeoman, to William Claiton of Barmbie on the Donne, yeoman, for the observance of an undertaking not to divert from its course one 'becke brooke' or stream running through lands in Denbie conveyed to the aforesaid Peter Hawksworth by William Claiton.

The documents span the sixteenth century and in so doing encompass the lives of Richard, Aymer, Henry and Richard Burdet, successive Lords of Denby. We have examined the lives of these people in V1 and the latter are supplementary to the documents used in that book. To add to these we have the following:

The Charter of Sir Aymer Burdet

Know all men, now and hereafter, that I, Aymer Burdet, knight, have given, granted and confirmed to John Nevile, knight, Thomas Nevile, son of the same John, Robert Frost, rector of the church and parish of Thornhill, William Nevile, Ralph Normanvill, knight, Richard Burdet and William Burdet, my manor of Denby and Holand (High Hoyland) with its appurtenances and all my messuages, lands, tenements, pastures, woods, and farms with all their appurtenances in Denby, Holand, Nether Bretton, Mappylwelle, Clayton, Dyrtcar, Derton, Kexborough, Barnesley and Keresforth. Warrant. Witnesses, Henry Everingham, Mathew Wyntworth, knight, John Pasters, William Burton, William Jenkinson and others. Dated at Denby, 24th day of January, anno regis (year missing) Henry VII.

Unfortunately the date is missing but we know that it was written during the reign of Henry VII, 1485–1509. Aymer was born in 1497 and was obviously a minor when the charter was written. This means that it was his father, Richard who was responsible for it. The grant was in trust,

for by his will and settlement Aymer Burdet directs that the above named Sir John Nevile and his co-feoffee's should after the decease of the said Aymer, raise money for 'the helping of my daughters and for Elizabeth, wife of Richard Burdet, the daughter of John Rockley of Rockley.

John Rockley had three children, Sir Thomas, Elizabeth and Gracia. Sir Thomas conveyed lands at Keresforth Hill, Kexborough and Wooley to Sir George Meverill and Richard Burdet in 1507.

Evidently Richard was trying to make sure that the family estates were kept together and that after his death his wife was looked after, a common procedure at this time. Considering how the future worked out with the splitting of the manors of Denby and High Hoyland due to Aymer's accusations of treason against his father, the document takes on an ironic quality.

Richard Burdet was also mentioned during the Reformation at the time Monk Bretton Priory was closed down in 1538. He had been receiving 4s 10d from them annually for lands in Worshburdhall (probably Worsbrough) and Pennyston.

One other very important, though tantalising document we have omitted from the latter list concerns a 'felon' from Denby.

WRIT OF HABEUS CORPUS 1555/6

Philip and Mary by the grace of God, etc., to the Sheriff of Nottingham:
Whereas Leonard Longsden alias Wadsworth formerly of Denby in the County of York, yeoman was indicted before our Justices of the Peace for the West Riding of Yorkshire for various felonies and

was arrested by you on suspicion of felony and remains in your custody; he is to be handed over to the bearer (of the writ) for removal to York Castle immediately and kept in prison there until the next gaol delivery at York Castle.

Issued by Francis, Earl of Shrewsbury, Lord President of the Council of the North, Sir Thomas Chaloner, Sir Thomas Gargrave and Francis Frobisher, esq., Justices of the Peace at Sheffield 26th January 2 and 3 Philip and Mary (1555/6).

Unfortunately the document does not specify what Leonard's offences were. 'Felon' was a term ascribed to a criminal who had committed a serious crime, ranging from murder to theft. Prior to the nineteenth century a felon could be sentenced to death and before 1870 forfeit all their lands and possessions. Whatever he had done he would certainly have paid for it by languishing in the dungeons at York before his trial.

By now the Burdet family had become two distinct branches, one in Denby and one at Birthwaite. During the thirteenth century Birthwaite was held by Peter de Birthwaite, he was the last member of the family to draw his surname from the village. Peter had a daughter, Juliana who married John de Rockley. John appears to have died not long after the marriage for his father witnessed a deed of Juliana during her widowhood. In 1258 in an accord between Peter de Perry, the King's justice, Juliana for concord and good peace in her widowhood quit claimed to William, son of Peter de Rockley her manor of Birthwaite which came to her by hereditary right. Peter de Rockley was Juliana's son. This is how the Rockley family were endowed with the manor of Birthwaite which was the dowry of Elizabeth Rockley when she married Richard Burdet around 1496/7. In 1573, their descendent, Francis Burdett of Birthwaite, sold to Henry Burdet and his son Richard, lands in Barnsley, Keresforth and Mapplewell. In 1575 Francis bought the manor of High Hoyland from Henry Burdet with lands at Mapplewell, he made further purchases of land in Mapplewell in 1578 and 1587. In 1599 Francis Burdet was appointed by his brother in law Thomas Savile as supervisor to his will. The estates of the Saviles at West Haigh and Kexborough seem to have passed to Francis between 1634 and 1642. It is at least evident from two rent rolls of Burdet of those years that there had been a considerable acquisition of lands in that interval and in the inquisition of Francis Burdet in 1643 there are extensive lands mentioned at West Haigh which must previously have been those of Savile. The last Francis Burdet of Birthwaite died in 1718, his affluent lifestyle had cost him most of his estates in his lifetime and after his death the Hall passed to John Sylvester. Sylvester was a blacksmith who plied his trade in Barnsley, but, according to Eli Hoyle, to escape his cantankerous wife he ran away to London before 1664 where he found employment. He had three sons, John, Thomas and Edward who all followed their father to London. The family were employed by the Admiralty at Portsmouth and Gosport and in the Calendar of State Papers 1664, Edward Sylvester is noted to have been employed to make a chain across the mouth of the river at Portsmouth. In 1666 Edward petitioned for money owed to him by the government with which he was supposed to make 30 or 40 anchors, then urgently required at Portsmouth. In the same year he complained that he could not get any men to work for him on account of the plague and therefore he would not be able to complete the chain by Michaelmas. The chain was, however, completed and was even commented upon by Samuel Pepys who made references to it in his diary. Thomas Sylvester evidently returned to Darton where he died, though he and his sons are described as of 'the Tower of London'. His eldest son, John, now took up residence at Birthwaite, he died in 1722 and was succeeded by his nephew, Edward Sylvester, described of 'Birthwaite', who died in 1727, the diarist, John Hobson attended his funeral:

He had been married about a year ago to Miss Wentworth and soon after he was married the Countess of Strafford went to pay him a visit and he handed her Ladyship out of the coach. Up the steps his foot slipped and he fell upon his back and was never right well after. He was bred a clergyman and was minister at Winckersley, near Rotherham which he quitted when his Uncle left him the estate. He died without issue.

Birthwaite now passed to John Smith of the parish of Ecclesfield whose mother, Priscilla had been a Sylvester before marriage. Smith died in 1746 and was succeeded by Sir J S Smith, though at this time the Hall was abandoned to tenants by the name of Child. The Hall and estates were afterwards purchased by Colonel Beaumont of Bretton Hall.

Back at Denby, Henry Burdet had died in 1601/2 and been succeeded by his son, Richard, though Richard had been running the manor for a good while, after his father's removal to Walton near Wakefield where he brought up his illegitimate family. Richard and his heir, George appear in the following:

1610 2nd May – *Lease for a consideration of £10 for thirteen years by Richard Burdett of Denby Hall, esq., and George Burdett, gent, his son and heir apparent, of George More of High Hulland, clothier, of a messuage and lands within the demesne of Denbye Hall and in Claiton; the lessee paying an annual rent of £4.*

1611 27th July – *Bond in £24 by Mathew Burdet, of Denby, gent, son and heir of Nicholas Burdett late of Swawell, gent, deceased to George Burdett of Denby Hall, gent, son and heir apparent of Richard Burdett of Denby Hall, esq., for the performance of certain covenants etc., as described arising from the bargain and sale described below.*

1611 27th July – *Bargain and sale with warranty for a consideration of £12 by Mathew Burdett to George Burdett his son and heir apparent of an annual rent of 16s issuing from certain messuages and lands late in the inheritance of Robert Clayton and Ralph Bevett deceased in the town of Denby.*

1612 7th April – *Indented agreement between Richard Burdett of Denby Hall and George Burdett of the same, gent, son and heir apparent to the said Richard, and John Hawkesworth of Denby, yeoman, Richard and George Burdett for a consideration of £13 undertake to aquit John Hawksworth his heir apparent of all arrears of rents, services, etc., as are at were at any time due to the said Richard and George Burdett as to Henry Burdett, esq., deceased, father of the said Richard, for lands in Denby called 'Netheroodes' alias 'Roods' and any other lands which are the inheritance of John Hawksworth.*

1612 7th April – *Grant and quitclaim by Richard and George Burdett to John Hawksworth of lands in the town of Denby called 'Netheroodes' alias 'Roodes'.*

1616 27th Aug – *Grant, for consideration of £6 13s 4d by Richard and George Burdett to John Micklethwaite of Ingbirchworth and William Shirt of Cawthorne, yeoman, of the wardship and marriage of Richard Hawksworth, son and heir of John Hawksworth, deceased, and Josias and Jonas Hawksworth, his brethren, and the custody of a messuage in Denby holden in knights fee by the said Richard Hawksworth until the said John, Josias and Jonas shall attain the age of 21 years.*

1616 27th Aug – *Grant and confirmation by Richard and George Burdett to Elias Micklethwaite of the City of York, merchant, John Micklethwaite of Ingbirchworth, yeoman and Richard Hawksworth, son of John Hawksworth deceased, late of Denby of all those lands in Denby called 'the roydes' or 'netheroydes', the grantees paying suit of court to the manor of Denby.*

George Burdet, though heavily involved in the latter documents finally became Lord of the Manor of Denby in 1616 when his father died.

Will of Richard Burdett, Lord of Denby dated 1616.

In the name of God, Amen: the first day of March in the year of our Lord God one thousand six hundred and sixteen, I Richard Burdett of Denby Hall, esquire, whole of mind and of good remembrance, makes and ordains this my testament and latest will, in manner and form following:

First: I bequeath my soul to God Almighty, my maker and redeemer and my body to be buried in the parish church of Penistone in my choir.
Also I give my son Bosville Burdett 10 shillings.
Also I give my son-in-law Thomas Wheatley, 12d.
Also I give my daughter, Mary Greene 2s 6d.
Also I give to my wife, Mary Burdett and my daughters Joan Burdett and Arabella Burdett all the rest of my goods, equally divided amongst them.
Also I make and ordain Mary Burdett my wife, only executrix of this my last will and testament.
Also I make Francis Burdett of Birthwaite, esquire, and my son, George Burdett to be supervisors of this my testament and last will.
  These being witnesses of this my testament and last will: William Apleyearde, clerk, Thomas Ellis and Richard Brooke.

NB: probate grant given in Latin in which Mary Burdett is given administration of the will.

It was also in 1616 that the beginnings of a dispute arose between the Crown and the Burdet's of Denby concerning the manor of Clayton West, probably as a result of the death of Richard Burdet. This case would have been examined by the Council of the North though very few of this body's records have survived as Saint Mary's tower, York, where they were stored was blown up by a mine during the Civil War. Historian, John Addy discovered a fragment of a document in Bretton Hall (the whereabouts of which are now unknown) of this case concerning the ownership of the common lands in Clayton. The case was heard before the Council of the North in 1618. The dispute concerned George Burdet and Cotton Horne of Cumberworth who contested the claim of the Crown that these lands formed part of the Honour of Pontefract, part of the Duchy of Lancaster. The surviving fragment contains the depositions given to John Walter, attorney general to Prince Charles (later Charles I).

George Burdett said that the King was 'lawfully seised in his demesne as of his fee in right of His Majesties dutchie of Lancaster of the Honour of Pontefract with the rights and members thereof. He said that he hoped to prove that Clayton and its waste land were not part of the Honour of Pontefract but part of the manor of Denby, of which he was the Lord and claimed that he and his ancestors had owned Denby manor, 'of which Clayton is a part for tyme out of mind'. Evidence was brought into court to show that a case brought by Richard Wortley and William Clayton against Henry Burdett, his grandfather in 1583, again regarding the Burdett's rights to the wastes of Clayton, ended in a decision that Clayton and its wastes had always been part of the manor of Denby. Burdett went on to claim that the Prince of Wales had intruded into Clayton and that for time beyond the memory of any man he and his ancestors had owned one water corn mill in Clayton called Marshall Milne now in the tenure of John Dickinson. He also received rents of several cottages which had been built on the waste at Toppit but he had sunk no coal pit other than on waste. When asked by the attorney general if he sued any tenants of Clayton who had trespassed on the wastes he said none except two persons, namely Nicholas Hawksworth of Wheatley Hill and Leonard Tally of Clayton who had allowed their cattle to graze in Burdett's cornfield in Denby.

Cotton Horne said that George Burdett paid him a retaining fee to keep his Court Baron at Denby (Steward), and to perform the duty of presiding over it. He claims that the 'towne of Clayton and the Wastes and Commons belonging are part of the manor of Denby and not an independent manor'. Both plaintiffs ask that justice may be done.

At the same time claim was being made by the Crown to the common wastes in Cumberworth. Cotton Horne said that he had the right to waste lands at Hartcliff in Cumberworth parish and did mine coal there. This land had never formed part of the Honour of Pontefract and therefore the Prince of Wales had no title. George Burdett was doubtful about the ownership of wastes in Cumberworth but the reason he was so confident about his rights at Hartcliff was that this land had been conveyed to him by his kinsman, Francis Burdett of Birthwaite. He also stated that the tenants of Cumberworth had never been summoned to Denby court but those from Clayton had.

Marshall Mill mentioned above was the corn mill at Scissett which was demolished in 1928. The mill of Z. Hinchliffe & Sons in Denby Dale was built partly over the land in dispute at Hartcliff. Unfortunately the result of the above enquiry is lost.

A further example of similar trouble occurred during the reign of Elizabeth I.

1635 17th June – *Order of the Queen's council concerning a cause depending between the Queen and George Burdett and other defendants in respect of the title of certain lands and premises in Clayton and others alleged by the plaintiff to be in Cumberworth and by the defendants in Denby. The Council reserves judgement until George Burdett has brought an action of trespass in the common law against Francis Oglethorpe.*

George certainly began his tenure as Lord with problems, if only he knew how these were to multiply.

George was born in 1581 and was 35 when he took over responsibilities from his father. He can now be found acting alone in the following:

1619 24th Sep – *Grant, by William Clayton of Hymsworthe, yeoman to George Burdett of Denbye, esq., his heir apparent of a yearly rent of 9d payable out of the lands belonging to the tenement called Bagden in Over Denby, a yearly rent of 1d payable out of lands late of Richard Tyas and now of Henry Haigh, yeoman, in Nether Denby; a rent of 2d a year out of the lands of Robert Smyth, yeoman in Denby called Spring House and also a rent of 1d a year out of the lands of John Mosley, yeoman, in Over Denby.*

1620 – *Indenture of a Fine between Edmund Ogden, gent, querent, and Geo Burdett, Esq, deforciant concerning 80 acres of land, 28 acres of meadow and 60 acres of pasture and common pasture in Denbye.*

NB: Edward Ogden was either the father or brother of George's second wife, Anne Ogden.

1621 May 29th – *Award by Robert Rockly, John Kaye, Francis Burdet and Robert Snawsell, esqs, arbitrators in a dispute between George Burdet of Denbye Hall and Godfrey Bossevile of Gunthwaite, esqs, concerning land known as 'Gleadholte' and Long Greene' situate in the Lordships of Gunthwaite and Denbye, and land known as 'Ould feild' alias 'Swifte farme', 'Boothes farme',*

'Crowell hill' alia 'Colman Cliffe', 'Fearnehill Leiz', 'Pighells' and 'Hunger Hill' situate in Gunthwaite and Denbye.

1629 14th October – *Inquisition held at Barnsley before Francis Bellasse, gent, eschaetor, in consequence of the death of Thomas Copley late of Emsley who held lands in Clayton of George Burdett esq., of Denby.*

1629 4th Dec – *Letters patent under the seal of the Duchy of Lancaster being an exemplification (at the request of George Burdett esq.) of an Order in Council of the Duchy of Lancaster dated 13 Nov 1591 upholding the right of Richard Burdett, gent., to 2 water corn mills situate upon the river Dearne within the manors of Clayton and Denby respectively.*

1629/30 February 4th – *Voucher to the accounts of Thomas Fairfax, knight and Thomas Nortcliffe, knight, late Sheriffs of York viz: receipts for payments into the exchequer made in respect of Richard Burdett.*

1631/32 13th Jan – *Defeasance by Robert Earl of Kingston Upon Hull in respect of a Statute Merchant of even date by which George Burdett of Denby Hall, esq., Richard, his son and heir apparent and Edmund Ogden of Bullhouse in Penyston, Gent., stand bound to the said Earl for a sum of £400.*

1636 28th Jan – *Assignment, for a consideration of £20 by George Burdett of Denby Hall esq., to Joan Marshall of Over Denby, widow, of the wardship and marriage of Rychard Marshall, son and heir of Robert Marshall of Over Denby, yeoman, deceased, and the custody of a messuage and lands in Over Denby held by knights service of George Burdett.*

1636 20th May – *Bond in £200 by George Burdett of Denby, esq., and Richard his son and heir, gent., to Francis Nevile of Cheete (Chevet), esq.*

Sale of Denby Hall and Manor by George Burdett 1636/7
George Burdett of Denby Hall, Esquire, in consideration of a certain agreement as set out in indentures of the same date between himself of the one part and Walter Stonehouse of Darfield, clerk, and Nicholas Brodelay of Cawthorne, clerk, of the other, has granted to Robert Rockley of Rockley, Esquire, the said Walter and Nicholas and William Allen 'All that Capital Messuage or the Manor house the Denby Hall' with all buildings, barns, stables, folds, orchards and gardens belonging to it and all tofts, crofts, closes, meadows, pastures, arable.

Also the woods, coppices and waste called 'the Topett wood, Burne Bancke wood, Nether wood and the Glasingroide wood, the Sheappwood, Common Wood and the Sugdall wood'.

Also 'my two water mills for grinding corn commonly called the Denby Milnes and the Clayton Milnes and all constructed ponds, goits, waters, water courses', tolls, etc.

Also 'all my Manor of Denbye and all my other manors, Courts Baron, fees, rents, etc. in the several townships or hamlets of Denby, Clayton, Ingburchworth, Skelmanthorpe, Bullhouse, Smalshawe, Billcliffe, Thurlestone and elsewhere. Also all my messuages and lands in Denby, Clayton, Ingburchworth.

Also the common pastures in Clayton called 'Over Moore, the Nether Moore, the Clayton Greene, the Dunster Cliffe and Langeley Lane … and all the commons … in Denbie called Upper Common, the Crowellhill, the Longe Greene, the Sallage Hill, the Castle Hills, the Coale Pitt Hills, the

Bursedge, the nether common, the Cliffe and the Hartcliffe, the Pinfoudgreene and the Somerford and all the commons … in Ingburchworth lying on either side of the stream called Ingburchworth commons and all the commons … in Skelmanthorpe called the Skelmanthorpe Moore, with coal mines, roof tile and stone quarries on the said premises'.

And a fulling mill in Denby 'between the land of Thomas Burdett, Gentleman and the liberty within Denby for extracting iron for smelting or if preferred another water mill'.

To have and to hold for the uses set out in the indentures.

Signed and sealed George Burdett 7th January 1636/7.

Unfortunately the location of the indentures mentioned in the latter document are currently unknown. It would appear that George was trying to set up some form of trust, possibly as a way of evading death or inheritance duties or for providing for his wife and children. It would seam clear that at this time George was still in possession of Denby Hall and retained much of his ancestor's manor. He died soon after this document was prepared and only seven years later we find the manor of Denby in the hands of William Savile.

The latter document does seem to suggest that George Burdett had hit some kind of financial difficulty. Written just prior to the outbreak of the Civil War it could be a part of a grand scheme created by George to try and retain his family's ancestral estates. Questions had been raised, even by the Crown as to his right to be Lord of the Manor as in the style of his ancestors, and one gets the feeling that perhaps the Savile's were already influential in the area. He had already built or re-built Denby Hall Farm, on or close to the site of the original manor house, and had taken to leaving off the 'farm' part of his address for status reasons. He had a history of trouble and law suits with his tenants in Clayton who disputed his right as to being Lord of the Manor, perhaps he had already relinquished his rights here under some legal procedure, he was almost certainly feeling the effects of the large payment to the Birthwaite side of the family for his estates at Denby, and we know that he refused to attend his cousin, Francis, knighthood ceremony. We know that the manor of Denby was held by Sir William Savile by 1643 though the date of sale varies depending upon the source used. Some historians prefer 1600, but this seems unlikely as Richard Burdet who died in 1616, father of George styled himself Lord of Denby in his will. Of course, the Savile family could have become involved at this time as the death of Henry Burdett in 1601 and the fact that he left nothing for his legitimate children could have left Richard in a desperate financial position. There certainly seems to be some reason to doubt George's credentials to the title Lord of Denby though he styles himself one up until the period when he died, sometime between 1638 and 1643. It could be that it was his death and unifying presence that held the estates together and that his demise, coupled with the effects of the civil war caused Richard to cut his losses and sell out to the Savile's and move to new lands at Finningley and Hatfield Chase. As we have noted, George, Richard and Edmund Ogden were bound to the Earl of Hull for the sum of £400 in 1631/2, this might imply some sort of financial difficulty.

The Savile's seem to have arrived in England during the twelfth century, originally known as 'Sevilles'. The family was an off shoot from the Dukes of Sevelli in Italy who having settled in Anjou followed in the wake of the Normans to England. Indeed, one of them, Henry attended the coronation of Richard the Lionheart.

Another notable family in Denby at this time were the Blackburns. Noted Roman Catholics, they were responsible for some of the buildings still standing at Papist Hall in Lower Denby. In the wall of one of the barns is an inscription commemorating Robart Blackburn, dating to 1633. A relation, possibly a brother, was John Blackburn who made his will during the English Civil War and refers to his times within it.

John Blackburne of Denby, yeoman *'calling to minde the instabilitie of theise tymes and the seuerall troubles and distractions of this our Kingdome'*, he asked for Christian burial wherever he died. Amongst his bequests are a *'cottage at Swawellegreene with a barn, garden and croft in the tenure of Nicholas Wilkinson which I late purchased of one John Thornelee to my sister Dorothie Blackbunre of Denbye, widowe, for the term of her life'*. Reversion was left to John Blackburn's younger children, John, Joseph, Sara, Margaret and Martha. He left all his property in Denby to the latter children from 2nd February 1655 for 12 years as security for payment by Robert Blackburne, John's oldest son, of equal shares of £160 to each child as they reached 21 or got married. Any marriage was to be proved at the family home and payment was to be made at Cumberworth chapel. Once all payments had been made the property was to revert to Robert Blackburn:

> *All messuages in Denby (charged as aforesiad) to Elizabethe my lovinge wife until Robert reaches 21 in trust and to intent and purpose that the said Elizabethe….shall for the of the issues and profittes … well and orderlye educate and bring up the said Roberte … with all necessaries dureing his nonage.*

John's wife, Elizabeth was left with a third of his property, after his debts and funeral expenses had been paid, though on his death Robert was to receive *'three iron ranges, one in the halle, one in the kitchin and one other in the parlour with one paire of bedstockes in my loudginge parlour'*. Elizabeth was also committed to the tuition of the five younger children.

Hester Brooke, his niece, who was also left money for her education. John's servant's was not forgotten, 12d was left to any servant in his service at the time of his death though he made one exception, *'I give unto my olde servant John Gawberd, twentie shillings'*.

Elizabeth Blackburn was made sole executor though *'my trustye and lovinge frendes, Mr John Firthe of Cumberworth and John Shirles of Cumberworth'* were made supervisors.

The will was witnessed by John Firth, Edward Sanson, Roger Wordsworth, Joshua Horton, Richard Hawksworth, John Shirles, James Haighe and Mathew Lyndley. Probate was granted on 11th February 1645/6.

The John Blackburn who made the will could be the same man involved in the following:

> *12 April 1590. Assignment of Lease between Nicholas Armitage of Armitage, Yeoman and Mary, his wife, and John Blackborne of Over Denby, Yeoman, of the one part, and John Allott of Bentley Grange, Yeoman, of the other part; of a messuage with a croft called 'Jack Yard' in Wakefield.*

The will is a very long document and the latter is a very condensed version. This probably means that John was not on his deathbed when it was written. He was trying to make provision for his children and keep the family estate together by bequeathing it to his oldest son but ensuring that he does not neglect the interests of the others. The starting date of the trust, 1655, was most likely, the year that Robert would reach the age of 21.

The above mentioned Robert cannot have been the man who built Papist Hall in 1633, though he may well have been his nephew.

It is also known that Ralph, one of the sons of Henry Burdet, Lord of Denby, married a female member of the Blackburn family and that the brothers Thomas & Phillip Burdet married Elizabeth Blackburn and Mary Blackburn during the late seventeenth century.

The Blackburn family also became involved with a South Yorkshire glasshouse at Bolsterstone. Originally operated by the Fox brothers, John and George, on the event of George's death in 1692 a Richard Dixon of Worcester, took over the management of the concern but left in 1702 to found his own glass house. It was also in 1702 that Mary Fox, George's widow married Robert Blackburn, the extent of his activity here is unknown but we do know that Mary was not involved in petitions against the glass tax unlike neighbouring glass makers.

The diarist, John Hobson recorded that:

Robert Blackburn of the Glasshouse died 11th August 1727.

A later member of the family, Johannis Blackburn died in 1698, this could have been the man referred to in the latter will. Penistone parish registers also note that a Mary, wife of John Blackburn was a murderess together with Joseph, son of the same!

Returning to the manor of Denby, the following document is one of the earliest to record Sir George Savile's involvement:

1655

*(Copy) Indenture between Sir George Savile of Thornhill, Bart, Edmund Hoskins of Inner Temple, esq. And Robert Turner, gent and William Courtneye and Charles Bates of London, esqs., agreeing upon recoveries to be suffered to settle a good estate in fee simple upon Sir George of various manors etc., in Yorkshire and Lincolnshire (Thornhill, Emley, **Denby**, Clayton, Burchworth amongst many others)*

Although court rolls exist in abundance for the manor of Denby, the inhabitants still had to pay suit of court and offer their fealty at the superior manor court of Brierley. Denby had been held as of the Manor of Brierley since the Norman conquest and the following roll illustrates that although Denby inhabitants understood the requirement, very few of them made the journey and preferred to pay a fine, shown in brackets after the name. Aside from this, the roll follows closely the examples we have already examined.

Brierley Manor Court Roll 1655

Denby and Bagden: *Lionel Fanshaw, gent.,(2s)(George Savile's agent in Denby), Thomas Burdett, gent., (2s), Delarever Burdett, gent., (2s), Richard Clayton (1s), John Shaw, (1s), Francis West, Henry Hirst (2s), Clerk, Henry Hugh (1s), The heirs of the wife of Henry Boothroyd (1s), Robert Blackburn, John Mosley, (1s), Joseph Mosley, (1s), Henry Dickinson, (1s), Thomas Wormall (1s), Robert Ward (1s), The heirs of William Morehouse (1s), Joanna Marshall, widow (1s), Richard Marshall (1s), Thomas Haigh (excused), Godfrey Bosvile Esq., (3s 4d).*

Who:- present and say that Lionel Fanshaw is dead but do not know who is his heir or heirs, also that Thomas Burdett is dead and that Thomas Burdett is his heir, also that Richard Clayton is dead and that Thomas Morehouse enjoyeth the lands in right of his wife, also that Edward Burgess is dead, as for John Kay we know him not but William Kay we know possessed of an estate in Denby, also we find that Robert Ward is dead and that Robert Ward is his son and heir, as for Thomas Wormall, we know no such man.

Ingbirchworth: *John Micklethwaite the younger, Richard Micklethwaite (excused), John Nicholls (1s), John Waston (excused), George Shaw (1s), James Hinchcliffe (1s), John Micklethwaite (did fealty).*

Kexborough: *Francis Burdett Esq., appeared by attorney.*

Skelmanthorpe: *Hamlett or Hamnett Hide Esq., (3s 4d). (He was Savile's agent here, Robert Oxley took over soon after).*

LAW & ORDER

Matters of minor indiscretions were usually dealt with by the manorial courts, though it is interesting to note that in these days before the police force, parish constables were operating. Originally the constable was the representative of the Justices of the Peace in the parish at the Court Leet at Easter. Usually the position would be given to someone who had not turned up at court as the position was unpaid and therefore unpopular. The constables accounts from Cumberworth have survived and contain some interesting details. The holders of the office were, Thomas Jubbe and William Copley in 1652, George Pollard, 1654, Robert Oxley, 1656, Thomas Martin, 1658, Richard Littlewood 1660.

Details from 1657 include:

To searching with hue and cry for a man who has broken out of a house of correction 2d.
To 2 soldiers and 2 seamen taken at Dunkirk 2d.
I sent away a cripple with four men to bear hear on a barrow to the Constable of Shelley. His wife was with him 6d.
Paid for repairing the stocks 2d.

Thomas Martin, acting constable in 1658 appears to have been quite annoyed by the death of a woman at Denby Dale on the 5th January. He *wrote 'Cost us 3s 6d for that ould woman which dyed be axydent about Denby milne'*. In 1664 we find Joshua Shaw being paid 2d for repairing the stocks at Cumberworth and in 1674 Thomas Morton was paid $^1/_4$d for repairing the stocks at Skelmanthorpe. It was also in 1674 that James Batty was given the task of making a new 'cuckstole', or ducking stool for dealing with women who made a nuisance of themselves. In 1680 Joseph Norton had the difficult task of relieving 'two distracted women' taking four travellers to Denby, 'one being in labour' at a cost of 6d and keeping a woman one night then 'carrying her to Shepley with a horse and sledge at 6d'.

In 1662 an Act of Parliament laid down conditions for those who desired to move from one parish to another. Persons with an estate below £10 were not to be allowed to remain in a new parish for more than 40 days if they were liable to be a burden on the rates. Overseers and Churchwardens, being keen to keep the rates down moved on those who tried to obtain a settlement from another area. On 12th August 1662 the Churchwardens and inhabitants of Denby petitioned the court regarding Phoebe Slack whose husband had run away and left her. An order was given that the overseers remove Phoebe to Almondbury where her husband was last legally settled. The overseers at Almondbury were unwilling to accept her, they sent a petition to the court on 15th January 1663 stating that she had no legal settlement from her husband, Charles Slack, who was of Denby and never of Almondbury. The Justices made a new order which saw Phoebe moved back to Denby and there *'to be set on work by the overseers of the poor'*.

Enclosure of common land for pasture for erecting houses was often resisted since this meant the loss of arable land and pasture for animals. The usual way of protesting was to riot! In August 1662, Francis Walker, Mary Parker, George Burdett and John Haigh of Denby forcibly entered the Shepherds Ing and Denby Close to erect two bays of buildings to the loss of George and Elizabeth Exley who held their land of Sir George Savile.

A more serious riot was recorded in Cumberworth in January 1663. On 10th November 1662 Thomas Burdett, John Haigh, Joseph and Richard Hawksworth with seven other people assembled with shafts, swords, knives and hayforks to attack the cottage of William Slack then in the course of erection on Cumberworth common. The mob proceeded to demolish the property which they did with 'great glee' and with the support of the Lord of the Manor. House building required the Lord's consent and each house was to have 5 acres of land in order to support the occupying family, the latter case had involved an encroachment on common land, though the result of the inquiry saw both groups heavily fined.

Arrangements had been made within the manor of Denby for containing offenders as we can see from a note in the court rolls of 14 October 1627 when it was ordered that 'the inhabitants of Denby do repair their prison before the last day of May under the penalty of 3s 4d fine'. It is unusual to find evidence of a manorial prison, but as we continue to learn, there is much more to the township of Denby than has ever been thought. Perhaps the prison was used to contain Thomas Slack, housebuilder of Cumberworth who stole on the 13 November 1639, one stroke of wheat from Francis Boothroyd of Denby. Slack eventually pleaded guilty.

Slightly away from the manor of Denby but interesting nonetheless is a case which involves Francis Burdett of Birthwaite Hall. He brought charges of sheep stealing against Michael Wentworth of Wooley Hall on 5th June 1610 which were heard before the Council of the North. The Wentworth family had recently acquired Woolley manor from the Woodruff family. Burdett stated that on 22nd May he was the owner of 25 wether sheep valued at £13 6s 8d which were 'quietly depasturing in and upon one peece of common or more called Maplewelle moor lying and being in the district of Darton'. Burdett went on to relate that Wentworth had gone to the common with a number of armed men and 'with a strong hand did take and carry away the 25 wether sheep'. Wentworth hid the sheep but Burdett feared for their condition unless the court acted swiftly. Burdett had requested the return of his animals many times and was annoyed as he stood to lose £10 in dues for pasturing the sheep. Wentworth said that he owned Notton manor and also Staincross moor which extended to the boundaries of Mapplewell. He stated that Burdett's sheep had not been under proper control and had wandered into Mapplewell 'eating and destroying the grass where they had no right to go'. Wentworth had distrained the animals as compensation for damage to his pasture. When he had found that Burdett had commenced the suit against him he had immediately offered the return of the animals in the hope that the matter need go no further. The case seems to have been a part of a long running dispute between the pair regarding the title to Staincross common, in this case, Burdett got back his sheep and was awarded costs.

The Burdet Lord's of Denby were, by now, no more. As we have seen, Richard Burdett, son of George bought lands near Finingley from William Savile and was living there in 1643. The wealth of the family had reduced significantly, yet the will of Denby's last Burdet Lord indicates that he was still a man of healthy means, even though circumstances had caused the sale of the manor.

Last Will of Richard Burdett, Lord of Denby, dated 1661

In the name of God Amen, the 12th day of January Anno Domini 1660, I Richard Burdett of Austerfield in the county of Yorkshire, not well in body but of perfect remembrance (praise God for the same) and calling to mind my mortality and being desirous to settle my estate in my lifetime, do therefore constitute, ordain and make this my last will and testament in manner and form following:

Firstly: I commit my soul into the protection of him that gave it, and my body to the earth from whence it came and to be buried according to the discretion of my friends; and as touching my lands and temporal estate, which it hath pleased the Almighty to endue me withal I dispose thereof as followeth:

And first my will and mind is that my funeral expenses, debts and mortuary shall be paid and discharged out of my whole lands and goods, and then for my lands and goods which remain, I do hereby dispose thereof as followeth:

Firstly: I do give and bequeath unto Ellen Burdett, my now wife, threescore pounds yearly and every year during the term of her natural life to accrue and enue unto her out of my lands in the Level of Hatfield Chase which I purchased of Sir William Savile and others, to be paid out of my lands which I hereafter give to my three sons George, Richard and Henry Burdett, equally to be divided amongst them.

Item: I give unto Alice Pilkington, £6 13s 4d a year, every year for fifteen years next ensuing. (if she or her issue live so long).

Item: I give to Richard Pilkington, the son of Thomas £5.

Item: I give to Mary Benson £5.
(Richard's son, Robert married Jane Benson).

Item: I give and bequeath to Martha Burdett, my second daughter, the sum of £200, if it can be made and arise out of my lands before my son Henry shall accomplish the age of 21 years.

Item: I give to Sarah Burdett the sum of £200, if it can be made and arise out of my lands before my son Henry shall accomplish the age of 21 years.

Item: I give to Madam Mary Beaumont £5 to buy her a ring.

(Mary was Richard's sister, her first marriage was to Richard Pilkington, hence the latter mentions of the family).

Item: I give to John Poole of Thorne 40s if £50 be got of the participants and £4 a year if they only … pounds can be got of the participants, to be paid him yearly after my death.

Item: I give to Isabel Wood the relict of Thomas Wood of Thorne, the house (where) she now liveth for her life.

Item: I give to the poor of Denby, the sum of … pounds 6s 8d.

Item: I give to the poor of Hatfield the sum of … £3 6s 8d.

Item: I give to Sir Thomas Beaumont,(the second husband of Richard's sister, Mary), Thomas Ramsden, John Senior and George Senior, 10s apiece to buy every one of them a ring, which four I desire to be the supervisors of this my will and testament.

And for the rest of my goods and chattels undisposed of, I give and bequeath to my son Henry Burdett, whom I make sole executor of this my last will and testament.

In witness hereof I have hereunto set my hand and seal.

Richard Burdett

Signed and sealed in the presence of James Capper, Elizabeth Smith, Jane Shaw, Jane Bell, Hugh Shaw, clerk.

Chapter Three

Discovering Independence – From Tenants to Freeholders, 1666–1822

The Burdet Lords had been gone since at least 1643, with the death of Richard Burdet in Austerfield their last link with their past prestige was gone. Nevertheless, memories and pride remained as did many important and influential members of the family. Throughout the next century the influence of the Lord of the Manor began its long and slow decline. People still paid him rent for their properties but opportunities were opening up for smallholders and cottage weavers to make more money, and take more control over their lives.

DENBY CALL BOOK 1666

This was the year of the Great Fire of London and the plague. King Charles II ruled England after an end was made to the Commonwealth established by Oliver Cromwell whose son had not been up to the job. Civil war memories and hurts were still apparent in the minds of the populace and religion was riddled with division. The following, incomplete, call book, lists the names of the tenants who owed suit of court in the Denby district at this time and who would have heard the appalling news from southern England.

Free Tenants:

Thomas Wentworth Bt	Godfrey Bosvile Esq.	Thomas Barmby
Lionel Fanshawe, youth, Denby	Robert Blackburn, Denby	Francis West, now John Hatfield
Joseph Mosley, Denby	Richard Micklethwaite, Ingbirchworth	(Henry?) Swift, Bagden
Richard Clayton, Nether Bagden, now William Green of Barnsley	..?.. Shaw	Joseph Kay, Clayton
Peter Hawksworth, now John Wood	Robert Ward, now Godfrey Bosvile	Richard Marshall, Denby
Josias Wordsworth, Waterhall	..?.. Marshall	John Hinchliffe, fitz George, Ingbirchworth
Samuel Barber	Anthony Micklethwaite, now Godfrey Crossland	Richard Micklethwaite junior
John Micklethwaite of Town End	Richard Micklethwaite, now John Jessop	Thomas Clayton
Francis Pollard	..?.. Allott for Bryan Allott, infant	Titus Bottomley
John Mallinson	Mathew Exley	Dorothy Wentworth
Simon Lockwood, now Thomas ..?..	George Harpin, now Thomas ..?..	Maria Tinkler & Eliz. Tinkler, for George Tinkler, deceased now ..?.. Green
..?.. Marsden, Clayton	Edward Burgess, now ..?.. Micklethwaite	John Clayton of Bagden, now ..?.. Green
Edward Oxley, Clayton	(John?) Taylor	Ephraim Burdett for land in Denby

Tenants per indenture and voluntatem.

(John?) Burdett	George Burdett	(Richard?) Marshall
John Hepworth	Thomas Haigh	John Lindley
Joseph Hinchliffe	Robert Oxley	John Moore
John Nicholls	..?.. Brooke	Joanna Ellis
William (Story?)	George (Hirst?)	Thomas Naylor
William Wainwright	William Swift	

Another glimpse of the occupants of Denby has survived, this time in the form of a petition dated 1671 written to Lord Savile. Addressed *to 'The Most Noble Lord William, Marquis of Halifax from the freeholders, tenants and inhabitants within your Township of Denby'*. The petition concerned Elizabeth Worrall, a poor woman and late living in a cottage in Denby,

> *formerly the estate of the Burdett's but the now the Lordships inhabitants, which said cottage stands on the waste grounds commonly called Denby Green within the said township, the aforesaid Burdett's, or some of them have kept their courts for their manor at the said house as a part of the manor (word ?) within the memory of some now living and was always reputed the Lords and commons thereof some part whereof was (erected) by the aforesaid Elizabeth Worrall's husband, who was sometime the possessor there of, and a servant to the said Mr. Burdett's, these Elizabeth Worrall having a right in it from sons of their ancestors who had the same under the aforesaid Mr Burdett's.*

Since the Burdet's had sold the manor to the Savile's the cottage was now a part of their manor, initially at a rent of 6d which was raised to 1s around 35 years before the petition was created (1636) by Savile's agent, Robert Turner. The rent had risen again in around 1656 to 2s, again by Savile's agent, this time a Mr Whittaker who was now dead.

Elizabeth Worrall had died in 1669 and in her last will she had assigned part of the cottage to her son, John, and the other part to her daughter, Sarah. The pair were to pay the rent between them and were not to sell their part of the cottage to anybody other than family.

In approximately 1651 John Worrall enclosed a part of the *'common green or waste of Denby'* which contained about 2 roods of land. Four or five years before 1671 he bought a 'parcel of hay' from John Rich for 26s but an argument arose between them as Worrall had since fallen on hard times and was now poor. Rich and his attorney, James Dunford arrested Worrall who bought his liberty by conveying the cottage bequested to him by his mother, against the express instructions in her will. Worrall told Rich and Dunford that the property was freehold and solely his to convey. In 1670 John Worrall, his wife and two small children were thrown out of the cottage along with Sarah Worrall who had done nothing wrong, by Rich and Dunford and forcibly kept out. John Worrall was put in jail and only set free by an act for the relief of poor prisoners. The whole family became:

> *destitute of harbours….and now by poverty chargeable upon the inhabitants of the said town who are at great charge and expenses in hiring them houses and providing other maintenance for them.*

The people of Denby asked Lord Savile to:

> *commiserate their deplorable condition and grant to the petitioners, or some of them, azease of the said cottage for such terms of years and at what rent your Lordship please to appoint and under such other covenants as your other tenants and cottagers are obliged to, that they may thereby be enabled to provide them habitation at an easy rate under your Lordship's County and favour, which is not*

to be had of the before mentioned purchasers, Rich or Dunford who have already brought other poor people and placed them therein to be further burdensome to the inhabitants of the Township of Denby.

The petition was signed by the most prominent and influential people then living in Denby:

Thomas Burdett	James Beaumont	Simeon Firth
Robert Blackburn	John Priest	Elias Micklethwaite
Joseph Mosley	William Priest	(his mark)
Phillip Burdett	Joseph Blackburn	Christopher Firth
Thomas Haigh	Thomas Burdett Ju.	John Worrall
Jo. Hawksworth	Richard Ramsden	Joseph Bailey
Sam 'll Burdett	George Hirst	Charles Brownhill
Edward Dickinson	Sam 'll Clayton	Mathew Smith
Francis West	Richard Hanwell	
John Hanwell	Richard Hawksworth	
Richard Micklethwaite	Edward Ibotson	
Joshua Gaunt	John Robinson	(31 names)

Who was John Worrall? It is possible that he was a grandson of a former rector of High Hoyland church, Richard Worrall. Richard made his will in 1614. In it he mentions his wife, Marie and his children, Nathaniel, Samuel, John, Joshua, Marie, Elizabeth, Sara, Suzan and Martha, of whom the last three were aged under twenty one. Nathaniel, the eldest son, had evidently been a source of trouble to his parents as Richard made conditions in his will to prevent Nathaniel getting at his lands in order to pay his debts. Worrall's executors were Matthew Wentworth of Bretton Hall, John Clayton of Clayton Hall, Bartin Allott of Bilham Grange and Nicholas Hawksworth of Wheatley Hall. John Worrall may also be the same man mentioned in a record dating to 1664, when he was described as a clothier. The document tells us that Worrall of Upper Denby made affray on John Shaw, so breaking the King's peace, the fight seems to have been about the religious divisions prevalent in the country at that time.

The Worrall family look to have been servants of the Burdetts at some time. Thomas Burdett's name is first on the list of petitioners and the family is referred to in the document with some reverence. Perhaps Thomas led the group and utilised his family connections albeit much diluted. Maybe he was still a little aggrieved that he wasn't Lord of the Manor. His son, Thomas junior, is also mentioned. This Thomas was left £10 and a 'black nagg called Simond' in the will of Bartin Allott of Bilham Grange. The Allotts were once counted as country gentry but had fallen on hard times. Bartin surrendered his copyhold lands (lands held of the Lord which had to be surrendered to him when transferring the lands to a new tenant who then paid of a fine to be admitted) to Henry Wentworth and Thomas Burdett along with *'his ancient inheritance'* the ancestral home, Bilham Grange.

The cottage in question was used formerly by the Burdett family as a court house. It was sited close to Denby Green, where we already know that Thomas Burdett lived when he had his goose fair in 1647. The small green at the end of Smithy Hill, at the junction with Bank Lane may be all that is left of this. The word waste ground would imply a sight up on the common but there was an old route down into Gunthwaite very close to it as we know from Adam Eyre's diary. The houses now built in the triangle of land between Bank Lane and Smithy Hill are quite extensive, but this area was the centre of Upper Denby, and this was the green where they used to play bowls. In which case does the house in question still exist?

Rock House has a date stone of 1684, Manor Farm, one of 1677. It is unlikely that these were the first foundations on these sites. Could Rock House have been the cottage and Manor Farm the home of Thomas Burdett?, though we know Manor Farm cottage was built by Joseph Mosley in 1677 which implies this *family's* presence here. It is likely that both edifices have long since been demolished. There were also two cottages on Smithy Hill, which would have been close to Denby green, and were built in the seventeenth century and appear to have once been owned by Denby Township, possibly for poor relief. These were demolished in 1972 but could also be the property in question.

George Savile became 1st Marquis of Halifax (1633–95). He was the son of William Savile who was found to be in possession of Denby in 1643. George's son was another William Savile who became the 2nd Marquis (1665–1700) the line dying out with him. Therefore both George and William were alive at the time of the petition though it was addressed to William as Marquis not George who was not yet dead!

Another petition, dated 28 years later lists the following men from the Denby area who supported plans for the establishment of a market at Penistone:

1699 Supporters for a petition to establish a market at Penistone, amongst whom:
Ben Blackburn, Joseph Blackburne, Robert Blackburne, Amos Burdett, Samuel Burdett, Thomas Burdett, Thomas Burdett junior, Phillip Burdett, Benjamin Clayton, Elihu Dickinson, Francis Haigh, John Hanwell, Richard Hanwell, John Hawkesworth, Josias Hawkesworth, Richard Hawkesworth, Richard Hawksworth, John Mickelthwait, William Mickelthwait, Josias Mickelthwaite, Richard Mickelthwaite, Richard Mickelthwait, John Micklethwait, Elyas Micklethwaite, Joseph Mosley, William Norris (Curate of Denby), George Rigley, Walter Poole, Francis West.

Lord Savile was also interested in utilising his manor of Denby and its natural resources.

In 1684 an agreement was made for a bargain and sale between George Savile, Lord Marquis of Halifax to William Simpson of Babworth, Nottinghamshire, Francis Barlow of Shest, Yorkshire, and Dennis Hayford of Wortley Forges, Gent., of fallable woods in Denby. A similar agreement dated 1703 saw Sir George Savile, now of Rufford, Nottinghamshire, sell a fallable spring wood in Toppitt woods in Denby to John Spencer of Cannon Hall, Gent. and Dennis Staveley, Gent. of Derbyshire. Toppit is northeast of Bagden almost at the junction of Wheatley Hill and Hollin House Lane. In 1710 Sir George Savile sold to William Elmsall of Thornhill and Joseph Oates of Denby, tanner, the fallable part of *'a spinning wood, called New Park Spring'*, which amounted to about 40 acres at Brierley, payment to be made at £5 6s 8d per acre. Also in 1710 the fallable part of a spring wood called Hunsworth Wood (20 acres) and parcels of wood in Soothill, Penistone and Denby went up for sale. The Denby woodland costing £34.

In the case of the document regarding Wortley forges, the timber would be felled and turned into charcoal to fuel the furnaces of the iron making forges. As we know that the Oates family were involved with Barnby furnace and the Lords of Wortley, we may presume that the woods at Brierley were intended for a similar purpose.

The William Elmsall mentioned above was Lord Savile's agent for Denby and district, based at Thornhill. Savile was by now living at Rufford and needed someone to look after his affairs in manors more remote to his residence. The Savile's abandoned their hall at Thornhill after it was destroyed during the Civil War. This is also the reason why so many ancient documents regarding the manor of Denby have survived to be housed and preserved in Nottingham archives. When the Saviles purchased the manor of Denby from the Burdet's they also acquired all the old documents relating to ownership of the land which dated back to the twelfth century.

For the people of Denby, who once had their Lord living amongst them this must have taken some readjustment, although undoubtedly some would have taken great advantage of the situation. William Elmsall was, therefore, the first port of call when a resident had a grievance. For example, a letter from Jo. Micklethwaite of Denby was sent to William Elmsall at Thornhill, dated 21st September 1711. Micklethwaite had received a communication from Elmsall and begins his letter by telling Elmsall that he was in receipt of incorrect information regarding a George Wrigley, his neighbour. He goes on to leave Elmsall in no doubt whatsoever:

> *Geo. Wrigley, my good neighbour, is not such a Saint as he can appear, but the clear contrary, whose whole family is made up of Whores, Thieves and Bastards and as ill tongued people as is alive, and to come to our present case, most of what he has told you is false, only this I own to be but that some part of his encroachments I have pulled down, and am fully resolved to make him take down a great deal more of it; my reasons you shall have in as few words as I can.*

Micklethwaite was aggrieved that the Wrigley family home, previously a blacksmith's shop, had been extended by two or three rooms. He relates that another shop had been erected some distance from their home and a high wall built between the two:

> *so that now they can pass from one place to the other without being seen by their neighbours, for, give me leave to tell you, they are people that play least in sight and he that came to you dare not be seen nearer home.*

Micklethwaite also castigated George Wrigley's son:

> *Here is in this farmers family, a son, as they call him, yet born out of due time, who is grown to mans estate and mindful to do his endeavour to add to the number of this illustrious (I may better say spurious) family: and as am informed, this shop I spoke on before is designed for a nest for this young couple to breed in.*

Micklethwaite goes on to say that he and his cousin had pulled down the offending wall which had been built without the consent of the freeholders and affirmed his loyalty to Sir George Savile.

Jo. Micklethwaite followed this up with another letter. He describes that Mr. Bosville of Gunthwaite *'has been pleased to honour our poor little town with his being'*, and that, although he was himself absent, his neighbours had shown him the facts about the Wrigley family. He hoped, that when he was able to meet either Mr. Bosville or Lord Savile, that neither would blame him for what he had done. He even offered Lord Savile all of his freeholds, which, in his opinion were *'better than all the cottages in our township'*.

The John Micklethwaite involved with the latter would appear to be Jonas (John) 1661–1756, a descendent of Richard Micklethwaite born in 1490 at Ingbirchworth. His Grandmother was Elizabeth Sotwell of Catling Hall and his Great Grandfather was John, brother of Elias who became Lord Mayor of York. John certainly seems to have had a problem with the Wrigley family! This is the first mention of them that I have come across though they survived the onslaught of John Micklethwaite to appear in later court rolls and call books as we shall see. Their place of residence is difficult to pin down, we know that they were definitely in the Denby area though only one clue seems to exist. Still marked on modern maps is Rigley Hill which can be found off Miller Hill heading into Denby Dale just after Romb Pickle, the woods here are called Rigley Plantation.

Mr Elmsall was again asked to intervene in a matter regarding a Micklethwaite, though this is unlikely to be the same man, Mr William Elmsall had by now been succeeded by his son, Edward, as Savile's representative. A letter, dated 8th June 1759, was sent by William Fenton, who describes himself as 'your humble servant', to Edward Elmsall in Thornhill. In it he records the desire of the inhabitants of Denby to see a John Micklethwaite admitted to his, recently deceased, father's cottage in Denby. John was living in Hunshelf at the time and Fenton was trying to avoid him becoming a burden to the people of Hunshelf, one presumes that Micklethwaite was not a wealthy man. He asked Edward Elmsall to admit him to his father's property either solely or jointly with his mother. He finished his letter thus:

> *I devise my compliments to your father. I suppose he will produce you some testament of the inhabitants of Denby, desiring his admittance.*

Edward Elmsall was also appointed as gamekeeper to look after Denby and Thurlstone moors on behalf of Lords Savile and Foljambe on 26th September 1784.

Lord Savile was involved in the following grants and leases with his tenants at Denby:

1715 – To Mathew Ellis of Lower Denby, husbandman, of a cottage and croft containing 2 roods at Toppit in Denby at an annual rent of 5s 6d.

1715 – To Robert Shillitoe of Lower Denby, husbandman, of a messuage and lands amounting to 18 acres, 9 perches, together with the tithes or exemption from tithes; at an annual rent of £8.

1715 – To Joseph Robinson of Upper Denby, butcher, of a cottage and 3 acres, 2 roods, 36 perches of land at an annual rent of £2.

1715 – To Jonathan Ellis of Denby, husbandman, of a messuage and lands amounting to 11 acres 1 rood, 22 perches at Toppit in Denby, together with tithes, at an annual rent of £3 19s.

1715 – Jonathan Ellis of Denby, yeoman, messuage, closes, lands etc., £4 3s.

1715 – John Pool of Lower Denby, husbandman, messuage, closes, lands etc., £5 15s 6d.

1715 – Mary Micklethwaite of Lower Denby, widow, messuage, closes, lands, etc., £21 0s 0d.

1715 – Robert Shillitoe of Lower Denby, husbandman, messuage, closes, lands etc., £8 8s.

1736 – Ann Wolfinden of Lower Denby, widow, messuage, closes, lands etc., £13 16s 2d.

1736 – John Lockwood of Lower Denby, yeoman, 2 messuages, closes, lands etc., £51 9s.

1736 – Simeon Firth of Lower Denby, farmer and William Roebothom of the same, clothier, messuage, closes, lands, etc., £21 6s 4d.

1736 – Joshua Moseley of Denby, yeoman, dwelling house, mill, kiln etc., £10 10s.

1736 – Leonard Rusby of Denby, yeoman, stone or slate delves etc., £6 6s (Denby and Birchworth).

1737 – Joseph Robinson of Upper Denby, serge weaver, 2 cottages, lands etc., £2 2s.

COURT ROLLS AND CALL BOOKS

The court rolls and call books of the eighteenth century were created by and for Lord Savile's stewards in the district. Call Books or Suit Rolls contained the names of all the tenants who owed suit to the court and doubled up as court attendance registers. By means of them he controlled his estates here and was aware of his rents and land transactions. For the modern historian they read a little like a mini-census as they allow us to see who was living here and to trace the development of surnames. Of course, only the head of the family is listed but we are also able to see the gradual carving up, by rent at first, of the manor of Denby as the number of freeholders grew and became more important.

The following call book includes John Micklethwaite and George Wrigley, both previously mentioned, though it appears that Wrigley had died in the intervening years between the letters and 1719 as he had been succeeded by his son James, perhaps the man who occupied the 'nest' to 'breed in'! Underneath the tables are the names of other people who appeared in the actual court roll of this year who were not listed in the call book.

1719 – Callbook Denby

Freeholders:		
Sir William Wentworth	Bryan Allot, Gent.	Godfrey Bosville Esq.
Alexander Bottomley	Robert Blackburn, Gent.	Edward Oxley (crossed out)
Samuel Reddish, Gent.	Richard Greaves	Thomas Hirst (Mosley)
Thomas Beatson	John Hatfield, Gent.	John Hawksworth
Joseph Mosley	William Horn	Richard Micklethwaite (Ardsley)
Phillip Burdet	William Greene of Banks, Gent.	Jonathan Gaunt
John Shaw, found to reside here and at Barnsley	Joshua Horn	Edward Oxley
Thomas Haigh (for lands of Fanshaw's)	The heirs of Robert Oxley, Skelmanthorpe	Edward Dawson of Bagden
John Copley	Richard Marshall	William Oxley (Josias Mick?) (Skelmanthorpe)
John Wadsworth, Gent.	William Lockwood (Skelmanthorpe)	Arthur Hinchcliffe
Amor Rich (Thurlstone)	Godfrey Cropley	Richard Micklethwaite
Jonathan Gaunt	John Micklethwaite (Townend & Bovey)	Thomas Green (Skelmanthorpe)
William Rich (Roids, Thurlstone)	John Roebuck	Abraham Swallow
John Shaw (crossed out)	John Milnes (Thurlstone)	John Clayton of Bagden
Edward Dickinson (Marsden House)	Benjamin Micklethwaite	Ephraim Burdett (Birdsedge)

Edward Adamson of Bagden, Thomas Burdett, Godfrey Crosland, William Oxley (dead) in the right of his wife, Joshua Haigh for lands formerly his fathers, Samuel Shepley, Theophilus Shelton, esq., (dead), Thomas Townend (sold), Benjamin Barber of Birchworth, Thomas Burdett, gent., by right of his wife, Thomas Rhodes, clerk (sold), Godfrey Thurgarland, William Thurgarland (under age), Gervase Thurgarland (under age), the five sons of William Greene of Elmhirst, gent., by right unknown, Thomas Birkhead, gent., (sold), Daniel Clark (sold?), Emanuel Cockin, Edward Ellis, (dead), Jonathan Shaw, John Rhodes, Gent., Thomas Jubb.

Tenants at lease and at will:

Mr Thomas Burdett	John Roebuck	Elias Micklethwaite
Robert Shillitoe	Walter Pow	Jonathan Ellis
Symeon Firth	Joseph Robinson	Mathew (crossed out) Widow Sykes
Mathew Ellis	William Sykes	William Burdett.

Cottages

Thomas Addy	Jonas Arnold	Jonathan Lockwood
Thomas Oxley	Samuel Cawthorn	William Priest
William Dyson	Mary Beevers	Elkana Gawber
Thomas Eastwood	John Allot	John Hamilton
Arthur Ely	Thomas Ellis	Widow Eastwood
Richard Greaves	William Gilot	Jonathan Gaunt (Robert crossed out)
Abraham Horn	Mathew Haigh	John Ward
George Hobson	Nathaniel Robinson (now George)	John North
Thomas Robinson	Roger Rhodes	Martin Shaw
Mathew Slack	Thomas Blackburn	Thomas Wainwright
Mr Thomas Burdett's, Mr Robert Blackburn & wosseld?	Thomas Holden	Richard Mallinson
Sarah Swift	Mathew Walton	George Wrigley, now James
Daniel Roebottom	Mary Oxley	John Micklethwaite
Mathew Oxley	Thomas Burgess	John Robinson

Anthony Ellis, William Hobson, Mathew Robinson-now George, Martin Sheard, Robert Blackburn, Sara Priest, Martha Walton

The above gives us an excellent overview of the families living within the manor of Denby at this time, though do not forget that the 'Manor' included Clayton West and other smaller hamlets. In most cases, the names of the people omitted by the call book who were noted in the court roll can be explained. Aside from court documents being only irregularly updated, the death of the head of a family was followed by the inheritance of the heir, hence a name change. In the case of an heir being a minor, the widow was endowed with the inheritance until the heir became 21 and her name was listed.

The court itself differed little from the fourteenth and fifteenth century versions we examined earlier. By following the court rolls throughout the 18th century we can watch the changes in land ownership and see the establishment of family surnames. As some of these documents are quite extensive we will view only the more relevant findings of the court in regard to Denby/Denby Dykeside and the near area. This has led to the cutting of much material about Clayton West and elsewhere though perhaps this may be published at a later date.

Denby: Court Baron of George Savile Bart. Held 13th June 1719.

Inquest on the oath of: Richard Micklethwaite, gent., John Hawksworth, gent., Richard Greaves, gent., Philip Burdett, John Robinson, Jonathan Gant, Richard Marshall, John Roebuck, Elias Micklethwaite, Simeon Firth, Walter Pow and Jonathan Ellis, who say on oath:

Godfrey Bosvile, esq., who held several messuages, previously Fanshaws and another messuage called Wardham and a messuage called Marstin House and a water mill called Denby Mill is dead and William Bosvile esq., his nephew is his heir.

Edward Dickinson who held a messuage called Marstinhouse sold it to Godfrey Bosvile, esq., who has since died and William his nephew is his heir.

Thomas Rhodes, clerk, who held a capital messuage called Clayton Hall has conveyed it to Richard Greaves.

Thomas Birkhead who held a messuage at Upper Denby has conveyed it to Joshua Mosley and Joseph Parkinson.

Anyone not at the court should be summonsed in the sum of 6d.

Court Roll Denby - 1733

Denby, Court Baron of Sir George Savile, Baronet, Lord of the Manor, held there, 23rd June in the 7th year of King George II, before William Elmsall, Gentleman, steward there.

Freehold Tenants:

Sir William Wentworth Baronet	Jonathan Shaw (dead)	Thomas Haigh (dead)
Edward Oxley (dead)	Richard Marshall (sold)	Josias Wadsworth
Richard Micklethwaite (dead)	Jonathan Gaunt (dead)	John Micklethwaite- Townhead
Bryan Allott, Gentleman	Alexander Bottomley	Richard Greaves (dead)
Thomas Beatson (dead)	John Hawksworth (appears)	Widow Horne (dead)
Philip Burdit (dead)	Joshua Horne	George Allott, Gentleman
John Copley	William Lockwood	Thomas Green
John Roebuck (app)	William Allan	William Bosville, Esq., (dead)
Ephraim Burdet (sold)	Joshua Haigh	John Spencer Esq.,(dead)
Benjamin Barber (dead)	Thomas Burdit (dead)	Richard Greaves (dead)
Godfrey Thurgoland (sold)	William Thurgoland (sold)	Gervas Thurgoland (sold)
John Firth	Widow Hall,	Godphrey Thurgoland,
Joshua Moseley (app)	Joseph Parkinson (sold)	Daniel Clark (sold)
Emanuel Cockhill (dead)	John Ellis (dead)	John Roebuck (app)
Jonathan Shaw (dead)	John Rhodes, Gentleman (dead)	Edward Kennion (probably Kenyon)
Thomas Jubb	Samuel Cawthorne (dead)	John Woodhead (sold)

The jury comprised: John Hawksworth, Gentleman, Jonas Micklethwaite, Gentleman, Richard Greaves, Joshua Moseley, Jonathan Gaunt, Matthew Ellis, John Liversidge, Samuel Haigh, Thomas Haigh, Simeon Firth, Thomas Wolfenden, William Ellis and Joseph Robinson. Who said upon their oaths that:

1) *Thomas Haigh who held of the Lord by, fealty, suit of court and yearly rent of 2s one messuage and lands in Denby is dead and that Thomas Haigh (fealty) is his son and next heir.*

2) *Josias Wadsworth, Gentleman (fealty), holds of the Lord by fealty, suit of court and the yearly rent of ….. one messuage and lands in Upper Denby.*

3) *Richard Marshal who held of the Lord by the same services and the yearly rent of ….. one messuage and lands in Upper Denby hath conveyed the same to Samuel Haigh (fealty).*

4) *Jonathan Gaunt who held of the Lord by the same services and yearly rent of ….. one house and close in Upper Denby is dead and that Jonathan Gaunt is his son and next heir.*

5) *Richard Greaves who held by the same services and a yearly rent of 12s 4d one capital messuage and lands in Clayton called Clayton Hall, also one other messuage and lands called Lane End in Clayton, rent ….. Also one other messuage and lands at Park Mill in Clayton, rent ….. is dead, and that the above said capital messuage and lands called Clayton Hall descends unto his Grandson, Robert Greaves an infant, and that the said Richard Greaves devised by his last will the other two said messuages unto Richard Greaves (fealty) and Brice Greaves his sons and tenants in common, and the said Brice Greaves is since dead and the said Robert Greaves the infant is his son and next heir.*

6) *Ellen Horn, widow, who held by the same services and yearly rent of 5s 2d one house and croft near Denby Mill, is dead, and Abraham Horn (fealty) is her son and next heir.*

7) *Philip Burdit, who held by the same services and yearly rent 2s 10d one messuage and lands in Nether Denby, is dead and that Mathew Burdit is his son and next heir.*

8) *William Bosville Esquire who held by the same services and yearly rent of … one messuage and lands called Marsden House and also several other messuages and lands in Upper Denby, formerly Fanshaws, is dead and by his last will did devise the same unto Christopher Hodgson, Gentleman and Benjamin Blackburne, Gentleman and other trustees for the use of Godfrey Bosville, his son, who is under age.*

9) *Sarah, the wife of Thomas Burdit who held of the Lord by the same services and yearly rent of … one messuage and two closes of land in Lower Denby is dead, and that the said messuage and one of the closes descends unto Hannah Gawber and Sarah Gawber, daughters of Elkanah Gawber, and that the said Hannah Gawber is married to Joseph Pool (fealty) and the said Sarah Gawber is under age and the other close called Rodger Croft descends to Francis Wolfenden, an infant.*

10) *Joseph Parkinson who held of the Lord by the same services and yearly rent of 6d one messuage and lands in Upper Denby hath conveyed the same to Mathew Ellis (fealty).*

11) *Daniel Clark who held by the same services and yearly rent of … one messuage and lands at Toppit hath conveyed the same to William Radcliffe, Gentleman.*

12) *John Rhodes, Gentleman, who held of the Lord by the same services and yearly rent of … one messuage and lands in Clayton called Wheatley Hill, did convey the same to John Spencer Esq., who is since dead and by his last will did devise the same to William Spencer Esquire (fealty), his son and heir.*

13) *John Woodhead of Woodsats held of the Lord by the same services and yearly rent of 6d one messuage and lands formerly Wards, in Upper Denby did convey the same to*

14) *Godfrey Bosville Esquire who is dead and by his last will did devise the same unto William Bosville Esquire, his nephew who is also dead and by his last will did devise the same unto certain trustees for the use of Godfrey his son, an infant.*

The above mention of Clayton Hall is worth mentioning. The 'Clayton' family were of very ancient derivation taking their name from the village they occupied. Mentioned in the court rolls of 1501 are John and Edmund Clayton. In his will of 1559 William Turton of Denby gave to Ralph Clayton and his heirs a messuage, lands and tenements in Denby and Bagden with one half of the profits arising from the felling of spring woods or plantations growing on these lands, which were a part of Scissett woods. In addition to this he also left lands to William West of Bank End on condition that on Good Friday each year 12 strikes of rye (used to make bread) were distributed to the poor of Denby and Clayton West.

In his will of 1614, Richard Worrall, the rector of High Hoyland, named John Clayton of Clayton Hall as one of his executors.

In 1635, John Clayton of Clayton Hall held only half of this capital messuage, the other half being in the hands of his brother, Richard. When Richard died his daughters, Sara, aged 16 and Isabella aged 13 were his co-heirs and would share the property but not until they reached the age of twenty one. Re-building work of some kind took place around this time as the barn bears a date-stone of 1653.

On 16th October 1667, Thomas Clayton of Clayton Hall tried to bribe a juror after stealing a goose. The same Thomas offended again, against William Spencer of Canon Hall after slaying a joiner in High Hoyland.

During the reign of Charles II (1660–95) another member of the Clayton family became Recorder at Leeds and Dr Richard Clayton became Master of University College, Oxford. Before 1699 a Richard Carter of Flockton had come into possession of Clayton Hall, though he died in 1699. The Hall was later sold to a Dr Richard Greaves whose family had also long been resident in Clayton West.

The will of Anne Allott dated 1721 allows us to understand some of the important branches of the Greaves family. Anne had two daughters, one married John Allott of Bentley Grange, the other married Richard Greaves of Park Mill, Clayton West. Richard Greaves was a successful tanner, farmer and colliery owner who lived at Manor Farm in the village. He had five children, Richard, the eldest, followed by, Brice, Sarah, John and Mary. Sarah married into the Allott family of Bilham Grange. John inherited the corn mill at Marshall Mill and the land which was in the future to become Spring Grove Mills. Richard Greaves, junior, inherited Manor farm upon his fathers death in 1728, though fifty years later, when he died, he had no male heir left alive to inherit so it was his daughter Mary who became endowed with the farm and lands. She went on to marry Roger Hodson who had become vicar of High Hoyland in 1777 and they lived at Park Mill as the rectory at High Hoyland had been divided into cottages by 1790. The farm and lands were later sold and the family disappeared from the village. Clayton Hall was eventually sold to the Bretton Hall estate in 1831.

Court Roll Denby 1740
Denby, Court Baron of Sir George Savile, Baronet, Lord of the Manor held there 30th June in the 13th thirteenth year of the reign of our sovereign Lord King George II before William Elmsall, Gentleman, steward there.

Freehold Tenants:		
Sir William Wentworth, Baronet	Hannah Shaw, fealty (default)	Robin Shaw, to do fealty (default)
John Liversidge in right of his wife (both dead)	Thomas Haigh (app)	Samuel Haigh (app)
Josiah Wadsworth, Gentleman,	Jonas Micklethwaite (app)	Jonathan Gaunt (app)
John Micklethwaite, Townhead,	Bryan Allott, Gentleman	Alexander Bottomley (dead),

Robert Greaves (fealty)	Richard Greaves (app)	John Boatson,
John Hawksworth, Gentleman (app)	Abram Horne (app)	Mathew Burdet (app)
Joshua Horne	George Allott, Gentleman	John Copley
William Lockwood	Thomas Green,	John Roebuck (dead)
William Allan (default)	Godfrey Bosville Esq. (fealty)	John Clarkson
Joshua Haigh	William Senior, Esq. (default)	Barber Widow (sold)
Joseph Pool, in right of his wife (app)	Sarah Gawber (sold)	Francis Woofenden (NA)
Joseph Field (dead)	John Firth (default)	Hall widow
Godfrey Thurgoland, in right of his wife	Joshua Moseley (app)	Mathew Ellis
William Radcliffe, Gentleman	Sir William Rooks (dead)	Edward Ellis (default)
Edward Senior?(default)	Thomas Jubb	Samuel Cawthorn (fealty)
Richard Turner		

The jury comprised, John Hawksworth, Gentleman, Richard Greaves, Gentleman, Mathew Burdet, Gentleman, Joseph Swift, Robert Greaves, John Bottomley, Joseph Horsfall, Joshua Moseley, Jonas Micklethwaite, Samuel Haigh, Jonathan Gaunt, Joseph Pool and John Field.

1) *Sarah Gawber who held one moiety of a house and one close in Lower Denby hath conveyed the same to Joseph Pool (fealty) and the said Joseph Pool holds the other moiety in right of his wife, Hannah, sister to the said Sarah Gawber.*
2) *Joseph Field who held under the same tenure and yearly rent of 5s 6d one messuage and lands in Clayton is dead and that John Field (fealty) is his son and next heir.*
3) *George Bramhall of Skelmanthorpe for that he or his servant by his order, has broke into the Lords waste and got several loads of stones in a certain common called Stubbing Hill (or) Nether Common, within this manor and jurisdiction of this court and carried away the same to his premises in Skelmanthorpe (fined 10 shillings).*
4) *John Horne of Cumberworth Half for that he, or his servant by his order also has broke into the Lords waste and got several loads of stones in a certain common called Milner Hill within this manor and jurisdiction of this court and carried the same to his premises in Cumberworth Half (fined 10 shillings).*

Court Roll Denby 1751

DENBY Court Baron of Sir George Savile Baronet Lord of the Manor held there 8th July in the 25th year of the Reign of our Sovereign Lord King George, before William Wilcock, Deputy Steward there.

Freehold Tenants:		
Sir William Wentworth Baronet	Susannah Shaw (sold),	Robetta Shaw (sold)
Mrs Sarah Rhodes (NA)	Thomas Haigh (app)	Samuel Haigh (app)
Josiah Wadsworth, Gentleman (dead)	Jonas Micklethwaite (app)	Jonathan Gaunt (app)
John Micklethwaite, Comonhead	Bryan Allott, Gentleman	Shaunus and John Bottomley
Robert Greaves (dead)	Richard Greaves (app)	John Boatson
John Hawksworth, Gentleman (dead)	Abram Horne (sold)	Mathew Burdet (dead)
Joshua Horne	George Allott, Gentleman (dead)	John Copley

William Lockwood	Thomas Green	Jonathan Roebuck
William Allen (Toppit?)	Godfrey Bosville Esq.	John Clarkson
Joshua Haigh	William Spencer Esq.	Barber Widow
Joseph Pool (dead) in right of his wife	Francis Woffenden (fealty)	John Field (dead)
John Firth	Hall Widow	Godfrey Thurgoland (dead)
Joshua Moseley (app)	Mathew Ellis(app)	William Radcliffe, Gentleman
Sir William Rooks	Edward Ellis	Edward Rolman? (sold)
Samuel Cawthorne	Richard Turner	James Ellis

The jury comprised: Mr Jonas Micklethwaite, Mr Richard Greaves, Joshua Moseley, Joshua Swift, Samuel Haigh, Jonathan Gaunt, Charles Dransfield, Francis Horne, William Turner, Mathew Ellis, John Lockwood, Thomas Haigh, Mathew Sikes.

Who said upon their oaths that,

1) *John Hawksworth, Gentleman who late held by the same services and yearly rent of three shillings a messuage and lands in Lower Denby and three other messuages and lands there, is dead and by his last will and testament he devised the three messuages and lands to Elizabeth, the wife of William Hodgson and Mary Hawksworth his daughter and the messuage and lands in Lower Denby is now held by Mary Hawksworth widow of the said John Hawksworth.*
2) *Josias Wadsworth, Gentleman, who late held by the same services and a yearly rent of … a messuage and lands in Over Denby, is dead and Josias Wadsworth, Gentleman, is his eldest son and heir and hath hospited his fealty by John Wood his tenant.*
3) *Abram Horne who held by the same services and yearly rent of 5s 2d a house and croft near Denby Mill hath conveyed the same to Francis Horne his son who hath done his fealty.*
4) *Mathew Burdet who late held under the same services and yearly rent of 2s.10d a messuage and lands in Nether Denby, is dead and that Ann Burdet, his widow, now enjoys the same for her life and after her death the same by virtue of the marriage settlement of the said Mathew Burdet will descend to Thomas Burdet, his eldest son and the said Ann Burdet hath hospited her fealty by Francis Woofenden..*
5) *Joseph Pool who late held by the same services and yearly rent of … a house and close in Lower Denby, is dead, and that John Thicket, who has married his widow now enjoys the same.*

The following document reads a little like the survey undertaken by Robert Burdet in around 1451 though it is unfortunate that many of the entries do not state the name of the village involved with the property. As with the previous rolls I have largely omitted entries for Clayton and Skelmanthorpe for reasons of space. All the following owed their fealty and suit of court:

DENBY JURORS VERDICT 1784

The Court Baron of John Hewett Esq. Devise of Sir George Savile Bt. Deceased and the present Lord of the Manor aforesaid held there the 4th day of November in the 25th year of the reign of our Sovereign Lord George III, 1784, before David Baildon, Deputy Steward of the said Court.

The jury comprised: Mr Francis Horn, Mr Dan Dyson, Joshua Gaunt, John Ellis, Thomas Haigh, Mr Thomas Haigh, Joshua Robinson, Joseph Gaunt, Mr William Sykes, Mr John Priest, David Wrigley, James Hirst and Nathaniel Shirt. These men were sworn in and gave the following details regarding the people of the township of Denby, who all owed fealty and suit of court as well as a yearly rent.

David Wrigley holds a cottage and (freehold) by fealty, suit of court and yearly rent of 2/8 and also an encroachment at 1d.

Joseph Gaunt of Gunthwaite holds and cottage and encroachment at the yearly rent of 1/6.

John Wood holds a cottage, late Joshua Wood's, at Denby Dykeside, at the yearly rent of 3s.

William Mellor holds a cottage and croft at the yearly rent of 10s.

Mary the wife of James Abbott holds a cottage at the will of the Lord 2s 6d.

Nathaniel Shirt holds a cottage at the will of the Lord.

Henry Dickinson holds a cottage at Strines at the will of the Lord 2s 6d.

Thomas Hardy holds a messuage and lands in Nether Denby by the same services and yearly rent of 2/10.

Walter Spencer Stanhope Esq., Mr Taylor of Barnsley, William Day of the Hill in Barnsley, the rector of Clayton Jo. Moss and Jo. Laycock of Penistone hold a messuage and land at Bagden by the same services and yearly rent of 4/11.

Dan. Dyson holds two messuages and lands in Lower Denby by the same services and yearly rent of 4/2.

Miss Margaret Walker holds a messuage and lands in Denby by the same services and yearly rent of 4s.

Mr Mead holds a house in Birchworth, late Micklethwaites by the same services and yearly rent of £1.12.0, did his fealty.

Mr Wolfenden holds a cottage and Encroachment called Swift Crofte, by the same services and yearly rent of 18s.

Martha Wood holds a cottage at the yearly rent of 2s.

Denby Town (the Overseers of the Poor of Denby) holds a cottage on loan at the yearly rent of 2s.

John Marshall holds a cottage and croft on lease at the yearly rent of 1s 4d.

Mary the widow of John Shootes holds a cottage at the will of the Lord 1s 6d.

John Robinson holds a cottage at the will of the Lord 5s.

John Whitaker holds a cottage at the will of the Lord 1s 6d.

Weetman Dickinson and George Kaye hold a messuage and lands in Upper Denby late, Moseley and Ellis by the same services and yearly rent of … paid £2 fealty.

Tim Mortimer holds a house and lands at the lower end of town in trust by the same services and yearly rent of 2/9.

Thomas Haigh Junior, son of Thomas Haigh, holds a messuage and lands in Denby called Tenters 2s.

John Lockwood and John Armitage hold … late Burdett's in Denby by the same services and a yearly rent of 1s.

Mr Walton of Thurlstone, holds a house in Ingbirchworth by the same services and a yearly rent of 2/6.

Joseph Gaunt of Denby holds a cottage and encroachment at the yearly rent of 2s.

James Hirst holds a cottage at the yearly rent of 3s.

John Dyson holds a cottage at the yearly rent of 5/6.

Jo. Lockwood holds a cottage at Dykeside at the will of the Lord.

Joseph Healey holds a cottage called Dunkirk at the will of the Lord.

Hannah, the widow of Jonathan Burgess holds a cottage at the will of the Lord 1s 2d.

Francis Horn holds a cottage at Denby Dykeside at the will of the Lord 5s 2d.

William Bosville Esq. Holds by fealty suit and service only.

John Ellis holds a house and lands at Lane End by the same services and yearly rent of 4/2.

Sir Thomas Blackett holds his estate by the same tenure.

Mr Benson, of York, holds, late Burdett's, (land in Denby) by the same services and yearly rent of 1/6.

His Grace the Duke of Devonshire holds a messuage and lands in Ingbirchworth and one third of another, formerly Hinchcliffe's by the same services and yearly rent of 1s.

John Chapman holds 2 cottages at Moor Royd Nook, late Kennion by the same services and yearly rent of 5s.

William Kilner holds a cottage at the yearly rent of 2s.

William Rhodes holds a cottage at Ingbirchworth at the yearly rent of 2s.

Mr William Fenton of Underbank holds 2 messuages and lands at Ingbirchworth, late, Jonathan Shaw's by the same services and yearly rent of 8/ and did his fealty.

They also say that Edmund Eastwood did hold...?...which is burnt down, at the will of the Lord.

Thomas Dawson holds a moiety of ... ... with Sir Thomas Blackett at the will of the Lord, late Martin Sheards. **NB1**

John Senior holds a cottage at the yearly rent of 6d. And James Hirst another at the yearly rate of 1/6.

Jo. Hall holds a cottage at the will of the Lord.

William Sykes holds a dyehouse at the will of the Lord. And his freehold by fealty, suit of court and the yearly rent of 1s.

John Haigh holds a cottage, at Denby Dykeside, at the will of the Lord 1s 6d.

Mr Radcliffe of York, holds a messuage near Toppit, late Burdett's, in the occupation of Jonas Rowley by fealty, suit of court and yearly rent of 2s.

John Priest holds a cottage at Quaker Head Hill at the will of the Lord 3s 4d.

Martha Haigh, widow, holds a close called Milner Hill in Denby by fealty, suit of court and at the yearly rent of 2s.

John Peace holds a stable at bottom of Chapel Green at the will of the Lord 1s.

John Chapman and Daniel Broadhead hold 2 cottages at Moor Royd Nook at the will of the Lord 5s.

John Micklethwaite holds a cottage at Denby Green at the will of the Lord 1s. **NB2**

Mr John Senior holds a cottage at Exley Gate at the will of the Lord 1s 6d.

John Haigh, James Barraclough, Jo. Lockwood and John Shaw each hold a house in Upper Denby by fealty, suit and service and James Barraclough by his fealty.

John Ellis holds part of Tenters called Town Field, late (purchased of) Thomas Haigh's and did his fealty.

NB1: Thomas Blackett was the last in the line of Wentworth's of Bretton who changed his name to Blackett on inheriting property from his mothers family in Northumberland, his mother being a Blackett.

NB2: this could be the same cottage referred to in the letter from Fenton to Elmsall dated 1759 and could relate to one of the two cottages now demolished on Smithy Hill.

The Court Rolls & Verdicts of Denby 1787, add a few more interesting details, as some of the properties mentioned above had changed hands. John Howett Esq. was the acting devisee on behalf of the late Sir George Savile at the court which was held on Wednesday 16th May, Robert Parker was the Steward:

The names of the jury sworn to enquire & present for the Lord of the said manor:

Mr John Marshall
Amos Burdett, the elder
John Priest
Samuel Horn
Dally River Burdett
Leonard Rusby

James Beaumont
Daniel Dyson
Joseph Gaunt, the elder
Francis Horn
William Robinson
Joseph Healey, of Dunkirk

Tenants' Names	Yearly Rents	Description of Lands Tenements
David Rigley		A croft at Ingbirchworth
Mr John Marshall, late Wolfenden's	18/	A cottage and encroachments called Swift Croft
Jeremiah Marshall of Leeds	10/6	A cottage and croft
James Firth	3/2	A cottage
Ditto	2/2	Ditto
Joseph Eley (Healey ?)	1/10	Two cottages at Denby Dykeside
Benjamin Fretwell	1/6	A cottage at Denby Dykeside
Elihu Dickinson, tanner	6d	A tanyard
Elihu Dickinson, clothier	1/2	A cottage
John Ward	1/6	Ditto
William Robinson	3/	A cottage, dyehouse and croft
John Lockwood	1/6	Dykeside, a cottage, pays to Mr Thomas Blackett
(Mathew ?) Hirst	4d	A cottage, pays to Sir Thomas Blackett
Rev Mr Allott	2/1	Billham Grange
Mr Taylor of Barnsley		Ditto
William Day of Hill near Ardsley		Ditto
John & Joseph Moss		Ditto
The Rev Mr Hodgson		Ditto
Joseph Laycock of Penistone		Part of Bagden
Mr Richard Greaves		Clayton Hall, rent sold off
Sir Thomas Blackett, Bt		Rent sold off
Mr Copley	2/	Ditto – said to be Mr Radcliffe's
Ditto	2/	A messuage at Toppit
Mr Hardy	2/3	A house and lands in NetherEnd of Denby – late Burdett's
Thomas Stead Esq.	£1 12s	Ditto in Ingbirchworth
Ann Roebottom	1/2	Ditto at ditto
John Bilcliffe	2/	A cottage at Ingbirchworth
William Brook	1/4	Ditto
Joshua Lockwood	6d	A cottage at Denby Dyke
Thomas Haigh		Part of Lane End purchased of John Ellis
John Birkhead	1/6	A cottage at Birchworth
Samuel Kippax	6d	A cottage on Denby Moor
Richard Bottomley		A garden in Clayton
Thomas Senior		A smithy in Ingbirchworth
Dally River Burdett		A watering place on Nether Common
And we amerce each defaulter in 3d and 4d as usual.		

We have examined only a tiny part of a very extensive set of documents which survive and yet within them we can see so much of the development of the manor as its villages become more and more defined. In reading so many names in such a short space we must not forget that each of them had a full life, just like you or I and many spawned dynasty's which continue to this day. The culmination of those lives was death as for us all, we will now take a look at some of the wills left by these people though for reasons of space we can only include a small number. They follow, largely, the same format and give an indication of the status of some of these 'ordinary' citizens.

WILLS OF THE EIGHTEENTH CENTURY
Will of Anne Barrowby 1727

Anne was the sister of Samuel Burdett and daughter of Tobias Burdet and was a member of the once great family of the Lords of Denby. She had left the village because of her marriage but at her death did not forget her place of origin.

In the name of God, amen, I, Anne Barrowby of Thirsk in the County of York, widow, being weak in body but of sound and perfect memory, praised be God for the same, do make and publish this, my last will and testament in manner and form following. I commend my soul into the hands of Almighty God and I desire my body may be buried in the parish church of St. Nicholas, commonly called Belfrey's within the County of York.

The more interesting bequests included:

I give and bequeath to my brother, Samuel Burdett of Denby, 2 broads (a broad was a 17th century 20 shilling coin).

I give to my son in law, Richard Barrowby, 5 guineas and my silver watch.

Item, I give to my other nephew, George Burdett of Denby in the parish of Penistone £10.
Item, I give to John Burdett, his brother £5.
Item, I give to the poor of Denby, that have not assessment made for the poor there £2.

I give to the children of my late sister, Mary Smithson (word?), Richard, John, William and Anne, each of them £5 and I order the said £5 so given to Anne, be paid to her hands and her receipt to be a full discharge to my executrix for the same.
Item, I give 40 shillings to the elder daughter of the said Anne.
Item, I give to the children of my late sister Sarah (word ?), to Elizabeth £10, to George and James, 50 shillings a piece.
Item, I give to Joseph Morton of Denby, 20 shillings if he be living and if not, then I give the same to his daughter, if living.
Item, I give to the poor persons in York Castle, 10 shillings, to the poor persons in Ousebridge Gaol, 5 shillings, to the poor persons in (Peter?) gaol, 2s 6d, to be distributed by my executrix in bread.

All the rest and residue of my goods and chattels, plate and personal estate I give and bequeath the same unto Ellen Barrowby, jurat, of Elizabeth (Spindow?) House. I do hereby make sole executrix of this my last will and testament. Hereby revoking all former wills by me at any time heretofore made. In witness whereof, I the said Ann Barrowby have hereunto set my hand and seal this sixteenth day of February, Anno domini 1727.

The Samuel Burdet mentioned in the will as the brother of Anne died only five years later.

The last will of Samuel Burdett, 1660–1732, son of Tobias Burdett.

In the Name of God Amen *Samuel Burditt of Nether Denby in the Parish of Penistone and County of York, Clothier, being in reasonable good health of body and of sound and perfect mind and remembrance give praise to God for the same do make and appoint this my last will and testament in manner following, but first and principally I commend my soul into the hands of almighty God my heavenly father hoping by the merits death and passion of my saviour Jesus Christ to have full and free pardon and forgiveness of all my sins and to inherit everlasting life and my body I commit to the earth to be buried in decent and orderly manner at the discretion of my executrix whom I shall hereafter name and I dispose of all my temporal estate as followeth.*

First I do and appoint that my just debts and funeral charges be paid by my executrix out of my personal estate.

Item, my will and mind is that, Martha, my loving wife during the term of her natural life possess, hold and enjoy all my housing, lands and tenements and real estate that is in my possession in Denby, aforesaid.

Samuel, having catered for his wife also stated that after her death all his estate in Nether Denby was to be inherited by his eldest son, George Burdett. Out of this inheritance, George was to pay to his younger brothers, Tobias and James £5 within 12 months after their mother's death.

George was also to pay Amos Burdett, son of Matthew £5 when he reached the age of 21, further sums of money were also to be paid out to George's brothers, John and James of £15 each, within 12 months of Samuel's death.

The will finishes,

Item, I give Mary, the wife of Mathew Burdett the sum of twelve pence in full for their part and portion.

All the rest and residue of my goods, cattles, chattels, possessions and estates whatsoever, give, devise and bequeath unto Martha, my wife aforesaid and do make and appoint her full and soul executrix of this, my last will and testament and hereby revoke and make void all former wills and testaments here to for, by me made (2 words?) whereof I have hereunto set my hand and seal, the sixth day of September in the twelfth year of the reign of our sovereign Lord George, King of Britain, anno domini 1725, Samuel Burdett.

(William Priest, Joseph Morton, William Ellis and (?) Langley witnessed the will.)

The Hawksworth family were prominent in the Denby area from at least the sixteenth century. Various branches of the family being involved with Wheatley Hill farm, Clayton West, and Broad Oak Farm, Gunthwaite to name just two.

Wheatley Hill Farm has existed since at least 1200 when Robert de Wetelai granted some of his lands in Clayton to Adam de Hoyland. He also granted lands to Robert de Denby. Wheatley Hill Farm passed to the de Denby family and via them to the Balliol's and Burdet's until the Wars of the Roses when it became the property of the Neville family. The house was probably re-built during the late Tudor period and passed to the Hawksworth family in 1585. Peter Hawksworth was named in the muster to fight against the Spanish Armada in 1587 as a caliver (a primitive light musket) man. He died in 1590 and left the interest on the sum of 15 shillings to be shared out amongst the poor of the township, this was fraudulently converted by 1620. In 1599, his son, also named Peter, began a partnership with George Green, the millwright of Skelmanthorpe. Between them they built a water corn mill near to *'a brigg called Highbrigg'*, which was the origin of today's Highbridge Mills. In 1616 Peter Hawksworth built a new house for his son, Hilary on the North side of the dam out of the profits of the mill. The house was later re-built by another Peter Hawksworth whose initials were carved over the door along with the date of 1651. Peter Hawksworth also had a dispute with the rector of High Hoyland in 1636 when Hawksworth was accused of defrauding the rector by hiding his tithe of wool fleeces, though Hawksworth was eventually made to pay his arrears. In his will of 1614, the late rector of High Hoyland, Richard Worrall, named Nicholas Hawksworth of Wheatley Hill Farm one of his executors.

An Abraham Hawksworth of Wheatley Hill farm made his will on 18th May 1666. He described himself as a yeoman and left his worldly goods to his wife, Mary and his son and heir, Peter. Peter inherited two thirds of Wheatley Hill farm, his mother retained interest in one third, though Peter was not yet 21 so his mother was authorised to use such money as was left to see

Wheatley Hill Farm, dating back to at least 1200, it was once the home of a branch of the Hawksworth family. *W H Senior.*

to both their needs. Abraham also made provision should his wife be unknowingly pregnant and requested that his son should pay to any unborn child the some of £250 should it attain the age of 21. In his will he also mentioned his mother in law, Ellin Hawksworth, implying his wife was also his cousin.

In 1689 Wheatley Hill Farm was sold to John Rhodes of Flockton though in 1712 it was bought by William Spencer of Canon Hall, the head of a large iron manufacturing group. Spencer bought the farm in order to make use of the woodland which could provide charcoal for his furnaces, he paid £1175 for the property. In 1916 Thomas Norton of Bagden Hall bought the farm which was retained as part of the Bagden estates until their disposal during the 1950's when the farm went into private ownership.

The Hawksworth family were very widespread but the following man was a member of this illustrious clan and lived at Denby.

The Last Will of Richard Hawksworth of Denby, dated 1667

In the name of God, amen, the 13th day of April in the year of our Lord God, 1667. I Richard Hawksworth of Denby in the County of York, yeoman, being sick of body but of good and perfect remembrance (praised be God for the same) do make, ordain and declare this, my last will and testament in manner and form following:

That is to say, first and principally I bequeath and commend my soul into the hands of almighty God, my creator and most merciful father, not doubting, but that through the merits of Jesus Christ, I shall be saved; and my body I commit to the earth in hope of a joyful resurrection. And as touching and concerning my goods, cattels and chattels and temporal estates I do dispose of in manner as followeth:

That is to say, first my mind, will and true meaning is that all my debts shall be paid and my funeral charges and expenses shall be paid and borne out of my whole goods.

Also I give and bequeath unto John Hawksworth, my eldest son, 5 shillings in lieu of all the right he falleth in all my goods or personal estate. Also I give unto my daughter Abigail and my daughter, Elizabeth and to my son in law Christopher Thaborey, each of them 2s 6d in lieu and full satisfaction of any claims to my personal estate or any part thereof. Also I give unto every one of the children of my three daughters, Abigail, Elizabeth and Margaret, each of them 5 shillings a piece.

Also I give unto Joseph Hawksworth, my second son, all my husbandry gear and all the rest of my goods not formerly given, all my debts and funeral expenses being first discharged.

I give unto Richard Hawksworth. My youngest son, in consideration of all his childs part.

And also I make Joseph Hawksworth, my second son, sole executor of this my last will and testament in trust, hoping that he will faithfully discharge the same, revoking all former wills.
Witnesses: John Micklethwaite, John Crooke the Elder, (probably parson of Denby between 1657 and 1665), John Crooke the Younger.

Our final example concerns the much better known Francis Burdett who is best remembered for leaving money to found a school at Lower Denby for poor children. In his will he styles himself of Lower Denby though it is likely that he lived at Denby Hall farm which he rented from the Lord of the Manor, Sir George Savile. He was also in possession of a dwelling and land at Denby Milne called 'Pugson' which seems likely to be the same as Pogson House heading towards the bottom of Cuckstool in Denby Dale. The boundary minutes, (a written summary of the boundaries of the manor which was actually walked to ascertain its reliability and to confirm that no infringements had taken place) help to confirm this, note entry 21.

Denby Boundary Minutes 1799.

1 Common Wood Gate
2 Beck – Royds Dyke, up to
3 Pinfold Green – by Hamerton Ing
4 Long Green Top – following hollow way
5 Falledge Nook- then to the top through Hall Edge land – by a small run of water
5 Ingbirchworth Field Head (crossed out) Gunthwaite Park Wall
6 Hoyland Moor Gate – then to the right
7 (Summer Ford - crossed out) the Dam or Scout Dyke
9 A marsh called Maze Brook
9 Annat Royd House
10 Broad Stone
11 Getting Up Stone
12 Hartcliffe – crossing the bridge by Green Gate
13 (Stansfield Royd Gate - crossed out) Priest Royd Wall
14 Wood Nook
15 Allen Royd
16 Back of Cliff Style House
17 Back of Blackburn House
18 Back of (Joseph or John) Wood House
19 Moerstone (?) or Blakenhall Green – then to (house?)
20 Holling House in the Hedge

21 *Cuckstool House or Pogson House on back of ditch*
22 *Dearne Dyke – following stream*
23 *Walk Mill or Putting Mill – following stream*
24 *High Bridge Mill – then to Clayton*
25 *Marshall Mill*
26 *Park Mill*

We have come across a number of individuals mentioned in this will in previous pages. To help understand the relationships recorded a genealogical chart will be useful.

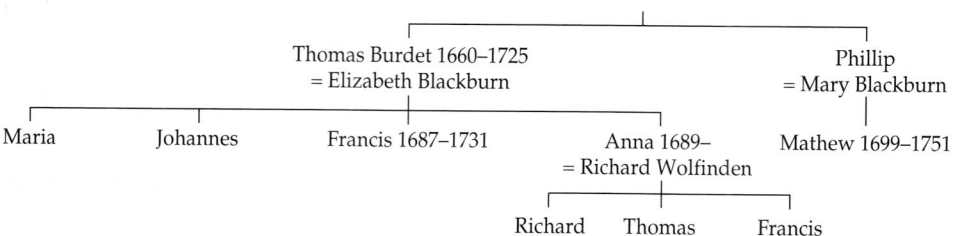

Thomas Burdet 1660–1725
= Elizabeth Blackburn

Phillip
= Mary Blackburn

Maria Johannes Francis 1687–1731 Anna 1689–
= Richard Wolfinden

Mathew 1699–1751

Richard Thomas Francis

The last will of Francis Burdett, 1687–1731, son of Thomas Burdett.

In the name of God Amen, I Francis Burdett of Lower Denby in the Parish of Penistone and County of York, Yeoman, weak of body, yet sound of mind and of good and perfect remembrance, praise be given to almighty God, am mindful to set my house in order in way and manor following.

First and principally I commend my soul into the hand of almighty God, my creator, hoping through the glorious death and passion of Christ Jesus, my Lord and saviour to obtain free pardon and forgiveness of all my sins and my body I commit to the earth to be decently buried at the discretion of my executors hereafter named and as touching the disposition of all my estate both (word?) and personal, I do give the same as followeth.

I will that all my debt of funeral charges shall be paid and discharged, then it is my will of mind and I do hereby give and bequeath unto my nephew, Richard Wolfinden, eldest son of Richard Wolfinden, late of Denby, all my lands and premises lying or being in Lower Denby now or late in my possession with all the housing and housing land and premises with all singular the appurtenances whatsoever unto the said Richard Wolfinden, his heirs and assigns forever upon this express condition, that he, the said Richard Wolfinden do learn the trade or occupation of a tanner and (word?) follow the same, but if he refuse to learn and follow the aforesaid trade of a tanner, then I do give the aforesaid land and premises with all the appurtenances unto my nephew, Thomas Wolfinden or Francis Wolfinden, to either of them that may take to learn and follow the trade of a tanner.

Also, I do give and bequeath unto the said Richard Wolfinden all the tenant right of a farm which I am in possession of under Sir George Savile lying and being at Denby Hall with all its appurtenances.

Item, I do give and bequeath unto my nephew, Thomas Wolfinden all my lands and premises lying and being at Denby Milne commonly called Pugson House (Pogstone) with all housing and housing lands and rights with all and singular appurtenances whatsoever unto the said Thomas Wolfinden, his heirs and assigns forever.

Item, I do give and bequeath unto my nephew, Francis Wolfinden all my lands and premises lying and being at Common Side in the township of Denby and now or late in the tenure or occupation of Widow Burdett with all housing and housing lands and premises with all singular the appurtenances whatsoever unto the said Francis Wolfinden his heirs and assigns forever, and also I do bequeath further unto the said Francis Wolfinden two closes or ings lying and being at backside of Thomas Robinson house and now or late in my possession and also one close called Roger Croft in Denby aforesaid with all and singular their and every of their appurtenances unto the said Francis Wolfinden, his heirs and assigns forever, also I do give further unto the said Francis Wolfinden the tenant right of a field of land (nigh?) Denby Miln known by the name of Swift Croft, of all my right (wordsx2?) same.

It is my will of mind that all my lands and premises as and above bequeathed to my, these nephews they (word?) any of them shall have, nor enjoy the above said premises until they come to their several and respective age of twenty one years. But if it should happen that any of my legatees, devisees as above, should depart this life before he or they attain to their respective age of twenty one years and have no child or children then it is my will of mind that, that part or parts so dying shall fall and descend upon their survivors, their heirs and assigns forever.

Item, I do give and bequeath unto my sister, Ann Wolfinden the sum of ten pounds yearly and every year during her natural life to arise and be payable out of the above said lands and premises equally amongst them according to their proportion but if any of my legatees above said refuse to pay and discharge their proportion of the said ten pounds, I do give my said sister, Ann Wolfinden full power to enter in and enjoy the land and premises of him, while and until what as is due with the charge shall be (word?) up and paid, and further it is my will and mind that the first yearly payment of the said ten pounds be paid unto the said Ann Wolfinden within the time of six month next of her she the said Ann Wolfinden do divide her part of that (of the said ?) with her brother Thomas Wolfinden to the intent that she may know and have her part distinct from her brother, Thomas Wolfinden and not before.

Item, I do give and bequeath unto Mary, the wife of Jonas Swift of Kexborough and legacy of £80 at the end of twelve calendar months next after my decease, conditionally, if the said Mary or any child or children be then alive.

Item, I do give and bequeath unto the poor of Denby the sum of £100, the intent of the former to be given to such poor widows and widowing poor children as may be found in need and not have of common pay.

Item, I do give and bequeath unto this present school of Denby and legacy of £100, the intent of it to teach and instruct mother poor children, in and belonging the town of Denby aforesaid and if possible both the said hundred pounds may be laid out upon lands and good, honest trustees made choice of by the inhabitants of Denby to see that the said money be put to the right use and uses, aforesaid.

Also, I do give further to my nephew, Thomas Wolfinden, the sum of £240, payable, when as he falleth to the land above.

Also, I do further give and bequeath unto my nephew, Francis Wolfinden the sum of £300 payable when as he falleth to the lands above and the interest of mean profit arising from all lands and premises above said my these legatees viz.: Richard, Thomas and Francis Wolfinden to be educated out of the same until they come to the age of twenty one years.

Item, I do give and bequeath unto my brother in law John Hadfield the sum of one shilling within twelve months after my decease, conditional he give a full discharge for the same.

Item, I do give and bequeath unto Leonard Rusby, tenant right of Slakepits, which I farm under Sir George Savile and all my right of tithe to the same.

Item, I do give and bequeath unto Rachel Ramsden, my housekeeper, a legacy of £10.

Item, I do give and bequeath unto my servant Robert Ellis, £5.

Item, I do give and bequeath unto Benjamin Green, John Kay, James Rusby, Martha Haigh, my four servants to every one of them, twenty shillings.

Francis appointed his cousin, Matthew Burdett, Elihu Dickinson and Leonard Rusby as joint executors, though were to have a problem in performing their duty.

The estates and premises devised to Richard Wolfinden were actually already in the ownership of Ann Wolfinden. The three were unwilling to act and a compromise had to be reached. Ann Wolfinden gave a bond to Mathew Burdet in which she promised to use the lands and estates for the benefit of her sons:

Anne Wolfinden, sister, next of kin and administratix with the will of Francis Burdett, late of Lower Denby in the Parish of Penistone of the Diocese of York, deceased do will and truly execute and perform the last will and testament of the said deceased for the use of the three minors, residuary legatee's in the said, Richard, Thomas and Francis Wolfinden and also as administer all his goods, rights and chattels according to law.

This was enough for the three executors to renounce their responsibilities, enabling their solicitor, Charles Clapham, to make Ann Wolfinden sole executor.

We must presume that the following inventory of Francis's goods relates to his home at Denby Hall farm. Twelve rooms plus out-housing indicates that the dwelling was of considerable size, and as we have seen from his will, he was certainly a wealthy man.

An Inventory of the goods and chattels of Francis Burdett, late, of Lower Denby in the Parish of Penistone. Appraised by us, John Hawksworth, William Smith, Thomas Smith, John Roebuck, under written, 20th August 1731.

	£	s	d
In purse and apparel	115	17	0
Range fire poker and tongs, fire shovel		16	0
3 spits, 2 iron pots and diverse iron instruments		17	0
In pewter, five stone eleven pounds and 1 dripping pan in all	2	18	0
Table and (word?) to the same and long settle	1	10	0
5 chairs, 4 little buffets and little table		10	0

Goods in New Parlour

A livery cupboard, 7 chairs, 2 buffets	1	4	0
1 bed and bedding belonging and the cushioning, little bed	2	12	0
Clock and case £3 3s 0d and little table 2s 6d	3	5	6
Feather bed (word?) 14s and other near cloth 1s6d	2	0	0
One little range 8s, one chest 6d, a little castor		8	6

Goods in the Old Parlour

One bed and bedding and hangings to the same	3	0	0
Close press £1 1s 0d, one little table 2s	1	3	0
2 chairs 5s, and desk and little chest		13	0

Goods in the New Chamber

6 chairs covered with leather and bed and bedding	3	15	0
1 oval table and 1 chest and 4 chairs	1	8	0
1 range, 1 little table, 2 buffets		7	6

Goods in Red Chamber

1 bed and bedding and hangings to the same	2	15	0
3 chests, 2 buffets, 2 chairs, another buffet	1	1	0

Goods in Chamber Over House

1 bed and bedding with some more bed and bedding	2	7	0
3 chests, 4 large arks and 2 lesser arks	2	12	0
(an ark was a kind of chest or coffer)			
Meat in one ark 32s, one dozen of cheeses 16s	2	8	0

Goods in Little Chamber

1 bed and bedding and buffet chair and desk	1	0	0

Goods in Kitchen

1 long table and buffets to the same and (longsettle?)	1	0	0
1 large cupboard 12s, and one chair 2s6d		14	6
1 range		6	6

Goods in Kitchen Chamber

1 bed and bedding to the same	1	4	0
1 long table and ark and chest, another chest	1	17	0
Certain boards 10s and certain other things	1	10	0

Goods in the Buttery

1 cupboard and churn and flask kit and kneading kit			
With certain other things in said room		16	0

Goods in the Washhouse

1 pair of (word?) frying pans, 2 brass posnets (a posnet was a Small cooking pot with feet and a handle), 3 rests, a little Cupboard and chair		18	0

Goods in the Cellar

8 barrels and a glass case, other things		18	0

Brewhouse

One brewing (pain or pan?) 30s, brewing vessels in all	2	10	0
Pan of brass 10s, malt kiln 20s, barkstone 1s	1	11	0
Certain sawn wood, an axle (tree?), buffet and stool	10	0	
2 1/2 dozen and some other old leather and warming pan	4	0	
And desk and linings in housing	8	1	0
Wheat in garner (a garner was a granary)	1	10	0

Goods in Outhousing

Seven gauges of felloes 40s, certain boards (standheck?)	3	0	0
2 wains (hay carts, 4 wheeled) and a cart (two wheeled)			
£11 10s, 1 old wain and plough and pair of Ox harrows (a spiked frame for			
leveling soil), 4 naves, felloes and others	16	0	0
Husbandry gear £4 10s in all.			
Certain gears for 3 horses	1	2	6
Cart saddle (brirk?) band 10s, 3 load saddles 6s	16	0	
Two hackney saddles and bridles 16s6d, 3 yokes, 3 heavier	1	10	0
Horses £32, Oxen £25	57	0	0
4 Cows £13 10s, 2 Swine 55s	16	5	0
5 new loads of (shilling?), being badly kept	2	0	0
7 acres of wheat in breadth of grounds	27	0	0
10 acres in two brown royds and lamb croft oates	17	0	0
Hay that's got into the barn	18	0	0
Manure in the field	4	0	0
One mortgage and bonds and bills	460	16	0
Certain cord wood (wood cut up and stacked in cords)	6	0	0
Casual book debts	146	14	7
Debts upon the (arro't?) of slate pit with slate and pavings on hill	42	1	10
In leather tanned and past tanned hides and done hides	563	17	0
Not tanned.			
1 load in tanyard	1	0	0
1 ark in the laith	12	0	
Certain bark, Wm. Smith charges himself with	6	10	0
Silver Cup	2	15	0
The due of interest in new picked bark	7	16	0
Lime brought this summer upon the ground	2	0	0
In certain huslements within and without spoon, old kits,			
Rake and spade and divers other huslements.	13	4	
Total	1582	0	3

NB: Huslements is an old Yorkshire term for odds and ends.

To complete our look at the people of the Denby District during the eighteenth century, we finally turn to a document dated 1799. It details properties at Denby which the Lord of the Manor, the Hon. Richard Lumley Savile had decided to sell off, probably because his interest in the area was minimal and he preferred to have the cash in hand. The period of enclosure was approaching and the successful husbandman now had the chance to possess their own property rather than pay rent to an absent Lord.

Sale of Property at Denby 23rd May 1799

The conditions of sale included the right of the vendor to fix an appropriate price. That 20% of the purchase money should be paid to Mr Sykes of Thornhill ten days from the date of the sale. Provided the sale was legally agreed the outstanding amount was to be paid at the house of William Kilner in Denby between 10am and 4pm on 3rd September when all rights to the properties were to be handed over to their purchasers. The same applied to free rents, suit rents and farm free rents which would also cease to be collected by Lumley Savile. In case of a purchaser refusing or neglecting to pay the balance of their acquisition all deposit money was forfeit and the lot would be re-sold to the benefit of Lumley Savile. All the conveyances were to be prepared by Mr Sykes of Mr Francis Sykes of Dewsbury at the purchaser's own expense. All mines and minerals were reserved to the Lords of the Manor for the time being but he was to have no right to sink any pits into the properties. Finally every purchaser was liable to do suit and service to the Court Leet or Court Baron of the Manor of Thornhill if required.

NB: the resulting sales in the original document are itemised after the list of lots available, I have put the details together for ease of understanding.

Some of the more interesting lots were:

Lot 1. A fulling mill at Denby Dike with the privilege of the water in the occupation of Nath. Shirt and John Horn and the privilege of the tail goit through 3 crofts in the possession of, Eliz. Robinson, Joseph Graham, John Marshall and Thomas Kaye.

Result
I John Sykes of Thornhill, aforesaid, Gentleman, on behalf of the Honourable Richard Lumley Savile do agree to sell the first lot at or for the sum or price of £60, (space for signature) and I, Nathaniel Shirt of Denby, aforesaid, Corn Miller (s.f.sig) do agree to purchase the same at or for the said sum or price of £60, subject to the written conditions.

Lot 3. A free rent of 5s 2d issuing out of a cottage and garden at Denby Dike in the occ. of John Horn, Ralph Horn, Francis Horn, William Horn, John Revel and Joshua Brook.

Result
Sold to William Horn of Denby, Worsted Weaver for £6 9s 2d

Lot 4. A close from the waste, by estimation, 2 acres, called Milner Hill, situate near Denby Dike in the occ. of William Horn. Also a free rent of 2s a year issuing out of a messuage and lands called 'Tenters', situate in Denby, afs'd.

Result
Sold to Thomas Haigh of Denby, Gentleman, for £32 10s.

Lot 5. 2 cottages and 2 crofts and 2 gardens, est. 1 acre, 2 roods, 20 perches, situate at Denby Dikeside in the occ. of Joseph Lockwood, Samuel Dawson and Mary Burdett.

Result
Sold to Thomas Kaye of Roydhouse in Almondbury, Tanner, for £40.

Lot 6. A cottage, garden and 2 crofts, by est. 0a, 2r, 12p, situate or near High Flatts in the occ. of Henry Dickinson and Samuel Jepson.

Result

Sold to Elihu Dickinson of High Flatts, Clothier, for £26 10s.

Lot 7. A barn upon the waste adjoining to Joseph and John Wilkinson's (trust est.) called 'Spring House' in Denby in the occ. of Joseph Wilkinson.

Result

Sold to John Wilkinson of Spring House in Denby, Cordwainer, for £3 3s.

Lot 9. A cottage and garden by est. 8 perches sit. on Denby Common in the occ. of Jonas Taylor and Richard Nobles.

Result

Sold to Charles Marshall of Dean Hill in Cawthorne, Tanner for £10 10s.

Lot 11. A cottage and garden by est. 16 perches sit. at Denby in the occ. of Thomas Hanwell, Joseph Green and Joseph Lockwood.

Result

Sold to David Holmes of Gunthwaite in Denby, Gardener for £12.

Lot 12. A cottage, dyehouse, garden and croft by est. 2 roods and 30 perches, in the occ. of Firth Garside.

Result

Sold to Jonathan Firth of Leak Hall, Farmer for £42.

Lot 13. A cottage and garden, by est. 6 perches sit. at Exley Gate in the occ. of John Senior and James Senior.

Result

Sold to John Senior of Exley Gate in Denby, Husbandman for £8 12s 6d.

Lot 14. A cottage and garden, by est. 6 perches, sit. at Denby Dike in the occ. of John Bilcliffe.

Result

Sold to John Barraclough of Denby, Innkeeper for £6 7s 6d.(most likely the Star Inn).

Lot 15. A cottage and garden by est. 4 perches sit. at Denby Dike in the occ. of Benjamin Morton.

Result

Sold to James Haigh of Denby, Husbandman for £4 10s.

Lot 16. 2 cottages and gardens and 4 crofts, by est. 2 acres, sit. at Denby Dike in the occ. of Jonathan Haigh and James Lockwood.

Result

Sold to Joseph Booth of Emley, Mason, for £72.

Lot 17. A cottage, barn and garden, by est. 34 perches, sit. at Birchworth in the occ. of William Rhodes and George Rollinson.

Result

Sold to Elihu Dickinson of High Flatts, aforesaid, for £12.

Lot 18. A cottage and garden, by est. 20 perches called 'Dunkirk' in the occ. of Joseph Graham, and a cottage, croft and garden by est. 1 rood, 30 perches sit. at Denby Dike in the occ. of Jonas Revel, Ab. Heliwell, Thomas Bilcliffe and Joseph Lockwood.

Result

Sold to Joseph Graham of Denby, Innkeeper for £37 10s. (a note in the margin relates: The cottage and garden at Denby Dike Side in the possession of Jonathan Revel to be conveyed to the said Jonathan).

Lot 20. A cottage and front, by est. 7 perches sit. at Exley Gate in Denby in the occ. of William Burdet, John Mosley, William Heeley and Richard Mallinson.

Result

Sold to George Hirst of Denby, Yeoman for £14 15s.

Lot 22. A cottage and croft by est. 1 acre sit. at Mooroyd Nook in Denby in the occ. of Joseph Lee and Thomas Pickford.

Result

Sold to Jonathan Firth of Leak Hall in Cumberworth, Farmer, for £30.

Lot 23. A cottage and croft by est. 1 rood sit. at Denby Dike in the occ. of Thomas Marsden.

Result

Sold to Jonathan Burgess of behalf of Hannah Burgess for £12.

Lot 25. A cottage, garden, stable and croft by est. 1 rood, 10 perches sit. at Denby Dike in the occ. of Joseph Thorp, also another cottage, croft and garden by est. 1 rood sit. at Birchworth in Denby afs'd. in the occ. of Benjamin Wrigley.

Result

Sold to Benjamin Wrigley on behalf of Ann Wrigley of Denby, Widow for £34 12s 6d.

Lot 27. A cottage, barn, mistal and 2 gardens by est. 32 perches sit. at Ingbirchworth in the occ. of William Brook and John Pool.

Result

Sold to Joseph Marsh of Gunthwaite, Farmer for £19 15s.

Lot 28. 2 cottages, 2 gardens and coal hole by est. 20 perches sit. at Ingbirchworth in the occ. of John Birkhead.

Result

Sold to John Birkhead of Ingbirchworth in Penistone, Clothier for £13 13s.

Lot 29. A cottage, mistal and garden by est. 16 perches sit. at Denby in the occ. of Joseph Senior.

Result

Sold to Samuel Thackra and Joseph Thackra of Clayton, Worsted Weavers for £10 10s.

Lot 31. A cottage, croft and garden by est. 32 perches sit. at Denby in the occ. of Joseph Micklethwaite and John Priest.

Result
Sold to John Priest of Hoylandswaine, Cordwainer on behalf of Richard Schofield of Ingbirchworth in the Penistone, Carpenter, for £14 10s.

Lot 32. A cottage and garden by est. 30 perches sit. at Denby in the occ. of Jno. Wadsworth and James Crosland.

Result
Sold to Joseph Gaunt of Denby, Clothier for £12 7s 6d. (a note in the margin relates: do not make a conveyance of this till his father's will is seen).

Lot 34. A cottage divided into 2 dwellings with a croft (heretofore occupied by Denby Town Parish) containing 1 rood, 24 perches near Denby Chapel in the possession of William Kilner and Maria Woodcock, one other cottage and croft containing 1 rood, 17 perches in the possession of Ann Micklethwaite. (lines have been drawn through much of this entry, still readable parts include, *a cottage, barn, stable, shop and 2 gardens by est, 0a, 1r, 17p, sit. at Denby in the occ. of William Kilner, Ann Micklethwaite, Jo. Beaumont, Jon Holmes and Jas. Barraclough* it is not possible to explain the crossings out but the fact that Denby Township have or had an interest could imply some sort of poor house or poor relief).

Result
Sold to William Kilner of Denby, Butcher for £68 2s 5d.

Lot 36. A cottage, barn and garden by est. 13 perches sit. at Ingbirchworth in the occ. of John Hinchliffe and William Beachill.

Result
Sold to William Priest of Cawthorne, Cordwainer for £7 12s 6d.

Lot 41. 2 cottages and garden by est. 12 perches sit. at Clayton in the occ. of James (Wareham ?), also a free rent of 18d a year issuing out of a messuage in Clayton in the possession of John and James Firth.

Result
Sold to James Firth of Clayton, Maltster, for £7 2s 6d

Lot 43. A cottage by est. 1 perch in the occ. of Eliz. Liley, also a free rent of 4 ? d issuing out of certain closes in Denby in the occ. of Daniel Dyson.

Result
Sold to Daniel Dyson of Denby, Clothier for £4 3s 4d.

Lot 44. A dwelling house, shop, dyehouse, drying house, outbuildings (word?) at about 1 acre, 3 roods of land, situate lying and being at Denby Dike Side all in the occup. of John Wood.

Result
Sold to John Wood of Denby Dykeside, Clothier, for £57.(likely to be Old Well House or Field House).

Lot 45. A tanhouse & tanyard by est. 36 perches sit. at High Flatts in the possession of Elihu Dickinson, tanner and a cottage and 3 crofts by estim. 1r, 4p, sit. at Birchworth in the occup. of John Bilcliffe and his under tenants.

Result
Sold to Elihu Dickinson of High Flatts in Denby, Tanner for £18 18s.

Lot 47. A croft situate at Denby Dyke Side by est. 1 acre and now in the possession of Joseph Lockwood.

Result

Sold to William Robinson the Elder of Denby Dyke Side, Worsted Weaver for £10.

Lot 49. A cottage, croft and garden by estim. 3 roods, more or less, called 'Cuttlehirst' situated in Clayton in the occup of – ?

Result

Sold to John Sutcliffe of Halifax, Engineer for £27.

Lot 50. 3 cottages or dwelling houses and two gardens, about 8perches, at Smithy Hill in Denby in the several occupations of Joseph Beaumont, Jonathan Holmes and James Barraclough.

Result

Sold to Elihu Dickinson on behalf of the Town of Denby for £13 10s.

Lot 51. A cottage and croft at (Muskroyd Nook?), by est, 1 rood, 30 perches in the possession of William Wilkinson.

Result

Sold to John Marshall of Lower Denby, Tanner and John Wilkinson of Denby Dyke, Cordwainer for £16 5s 6d.

Lot 52. A cottage and garden at Denby Dykeside in the possession of Widow Fretwell.

Result

Sold to Joseph Green of Thurlestone, Clothier for £3 3s.

Lot 53. A cottage, barn (word?) 2 crofts, (word? word?) by estim. 2 roods, 20 perches, also 3 closes of land by estim. 2a, 2r, 0p called 'Swift Crofts' sit. at Denby Dike in the occ. of Joseph Wood and his under tenants. Also a garden now lying open and unenclosed on the East side of the road leading to Leak Hall Green from Denby Dike Side, formerly in the possession of William Swift and belonging to the said Swift Croft (??) a mistal the (?) road leading to the common.

Result

Sold to John Marshall of Denby, Tanner for £77 15s.

In order to put a little 'human nature' back into these faceless people of the past we will take a look at an episode which took place in Lower Denby in 1822, which involved the Haigh family. The details have survived in the Court records of the Archbishop of York which took care of cases of broken marriages, divorce and adultery until 1857 when the cases were transferred to the civil court – as a result of which, they began to appear in newspapers.

The case of Elizabeth Haigh

As Elizabeth Johnson, living in London she had met Benjamin Haigh on one of his many visits to the city and decided that, on account of his wealth and goods, he was a suitable catch. They were married in the summer of 1805 at All Hallows, Barking by the Tower. She came back to Denby to live with her husband and for fifteen years they appear to have lived a normal married life. During Haigh's frequent absences on business, it appears that she had formed an attachment with a Penistone butcher, Robert Lealty, and from November 1820 until January 1822 had carried on an intimate affair with him, culminating in Robert staying the night at Haigh's house on 9th January.

The evidence of the parties concerned helps to piece together the affair. According to Elizabeth Haigh, her husband had property in Penistone worth £60 a year and shares in Clayton West Building Club and the Penistone Building Club, the latter was of long established foundation. She estimated the value of his property and stock to be £10,000. In his defence, Ben Haigh said 'that he had a house and two cottages in Penistone and Denby bringing in £39 a year. He had £120 in Beckett and Co.'s Bank in Barnsley and had money out on interest with John Coldwell, John Greenwood and John Pashley.

On the night of 9th January 1822, Ben was ill and had been sleeping in a separate room as a result. Elizabeth and Robert then went to bed together and at 2am Ben was informed that Robert was in the house. He got up and went to his wife's room, found the door locked and demanded admission. Receiving no reply he sent for a poker and began to try to break in but heard the window open and afterwards the door opened but only his wife was in the room.

Ambrose White, farmer, of Denby, aged 39, said he worked for Haigh but usually slept at home. On the 9th January, Elizabeth asked him to stay all night and sit with Ben since he was so very ill. Seeing Robert about he became suspicious, so he spoke to Lionel Hawksworth, Ben's servant about the matter. Lionel then went to see Ben's nephews, Ben and Thomas Lockwood to tell then of what he feared.

At 2am Ben Lockwood brought a note and leaning a ladder against the window climbed and knocked on the pane. When White gave Haigh the note he was told to lock the outer doors and rouse Lionel Hawksworth. Finding the bedroom door locked Ben sent White for a poker to break in the door, but hearing the window open and looking out he saw Robert in the moonlight clad only in his shirt between Ben and Thomas Lockwood. Robert was heard to say, 'It is a fair catch, I was fast asleep in bed'.

Hannah Lockwood of Flash House, Cawthorne, aged 25, a spinster and servant to the Haigh's said that at 11pm on 29th December when she was going to bed she heard snoring coming from the room where the hops were stored. Looking in she saw Robert sleeping on a bag of hops but when she told Hawksworth she received orders to go to bed and say nothing. On 9th January hearing a noise she got up and came downstairs to find Haigh, Hawksworth and White the daytel man (labourer hired by the day) with Robert Lealty.

Lionel Hawksworth of Lower Denby, aged 28, said he saw Robert in the hop room in a great coat and with thick stockings over his boots and when Elizabeth came in he left. On the 9th January he went to the Lockwoods to inform them and later went with Haigh to Elizabeth's bedroom and found her in night clothes. When Haigh saw the empty room he remarked, 'the rogues jumped out of the window'. Elizabeth replied, 'there's nobody jumped out of the window, there's been nobody in'. White on looking out said, 'they've catched him, they have him below'. Elizabeth said, 'aye, dreary me for shame of yourselves'. Taking Robert in to the kitchen he was assisted to get dressed for Elizabeth had thrown his clothes after him through the window.

The constable was then sent for to arrest Lealty. Joshua Wood, woollen manufacturer, was acting as constable for that year and came at 6am to make the arrest. As he took him away, Lealty admitted he was sleeping with Elizabeth and had to jump from the window, his clothes thrown down after him. Lealty then remarked, 'you would never have caught me if my shirt had not come up over my head as I jumped down and fastened my arms'.

Fourteen days later Elizabeth left her husband for good and went to live in Barnsley but later came to live with her father at Clayton near Denby.

The case was heard later in the year 1822 and a sentence of divorce or separation at bed and board was issued. Lealty underwent a spell of imprisonment in the House of Correction at Wakefield.

Chapter Four

A Window On Industry – the Industrial Revolution in Denby Dale & Beyond

A quick look around the district would provide anyone with the knowledge that there are few large local industries left within the area. Of these an even smaller percentage remind us of the industrial heritage upon which the modern villages are largely based. Phoenox Textiles in Clayton West (established in 1953) is one of few to come quickly to mind.

Industrial units and retail parks are a relatively modern concept yet within the area a surprisingly high number have been created. A fair amount of these are new steel and breeze block affairs, quickly assembled and conveniently located. Other edifices which house these new concerns are older, much older and are steeped in history. These are the old mill buildings which were once the heart and lungs of the area and provided employment for a multiplying populace. The individuals responsible for their foundation were pioneers, forward thinkers and driven men. Few people possessed the ability to take advantage of the times in which they lived but those that did largely created the district as we know it today. Without them it is unlikely that any of the villages within the township of Denby and just beyond it, would be as desirable, populous and affluent as they are now.

Between 1500 and 1700 all the processes involved with the manufacture of cloth were carried on by the clothier at his home except the fulling, (to scour and thicken the wool) and later scribbling (wool combing). Even in the nineteenth century the village weaver still owned his own loom, though, in many cases, he would have been supplied with raw material by the master clothier. The common or waste grounds had gradually been cleared and cultivated and dwellings with associated buildings had allowed farming and textile production to sit comfortably together on the same site since at least the sixteenth century. One such individual is mentioned in the following:

> 1587–8 – *Demise by Richard Burdett of Denby Hall, Gentleman, to William Heye of Denby, clothier, of a parcel of the demesne of his manor of Denby Hall, Yorks., for 10 years.*

Water could be found in springs almost everywhere, fuel, in the guise of peat was readily available, the land supported crops and some livestock and the weaving loom provided subsistence for the family.

Apprentices came to Denby from other villages in the area as we can see from the following two cases.

Joseph Dawson's parents originated in Shepley and moved to Cumberworth when he was born. Aged 13 he was bound apprentice to Jonathan Bamforth of Denby. After five years he moved on, to serve the remainder of his apprenticeship with Joseph Field of Skelmanthorpe who provided him with food, clothing and 18d wages a year. In April 1770 he asked to reside at Emley as a clothier.

91

John Blackburn was born at Emley but his father moved soon after to Clayton West. When John was 14 he was apprenticed to Amos Burdett of Denby, a clothier. By the time he was 28 he was applying to return to Emley to work.

Combined occupations were not exclusively reserved to farmers and weavers. William Barber, one of the Denby blacksmiths, died in 1697. An inventory of his goods listed, amongst other things, 1 pair of bellows, 1 anvil, and the other usual tools of his trade. In his smithy were 10 shillings worth of wool and yarn, he had a milk-house, 3 cows, 2 heiffer's, 1 calf, 1 horse, 2 mares, 2 pigs, and various crops of oats, barley, peas and seed wheat.

A similar case was that of John Priest, again a blacksmith of Denby, who died in 1717. Bellows, hammers, tongs, iron and all the other usual equipment was found in the smithy. Amongst his farming equipment were, 3 cows, 1 heiffer, 2 calves, 1 horse, 1 old mare, 1 pig, corn and hay. The family were also involved in the textile trade, three spinning wheels and 'shop goods, cloth and spikes etc.' were valued at £39 9s 10d. Priest had done well with his various occupations, also found was 'money and gold in several boxes £40. Bonds and a bill £144 10s 0d'.

By the early nineteenth century the power once wielded by the Lord's of the Manor had dwindled. The Enclosure Acts had regulated land ownership and far more of the middle class working men were taking the opportunity to develop their skills within their chosen fields. First amongst these were the clothiers who developed into small manufacturers. Opportunities also opened up for stonemasons, quarry owners and coal merchants. During the early part of the nineteenth century the first textile warehouses had begun to appear, work was still put out to the weavers in the upland districts but the co-ordination was controlled and managed. Scribbling and fulling mills (many of which were built on the site of old corn mills), and old dye-houses were gradually adapted, largely because they were built on or near to a source of water power, so that by the 1850's true spinning and weaving mills were finally coming in to existence. It is true that fancy weavers in the Denby area continued to ply their trade for a while longer but it was to the mill that the future belonged. The upland cottage weavers were now obliged to 'go out to work' as the mill owners sought to assemble all aspects of production on site.

Amongst early textile manufacturers in Denby Dikeside (Dale) can be found the names of John Wood & Sons (fancy woollen and worsted's), Charles Wood and Sons (fancy), William Haywood (woollen and cotton), George Peace (woollen) in 1822. By 1847 James and Edwin Wood (fancy) had established themselves and the latter John and Charles Wood appear to have merged. By 1867, John Bradford (fancy), Thomas Brierley & Sons (cotton and woollen dyers) and Worsley Brothers & Littlewood (silk, woollen, cotton and worsted dyers and dealers in silk) had arrived, Worsley Brothers were based at Spring Vale dye works in the village.

The industrial revolutionaries or pioneers also had to address the question of housing for their work force. Many of the rows of terraced cottages in the district were built or commissioned by them on land which belonged to them. Slowly these 'new men' took the place of the, by now almost defunct, Lord of the Manor. Once the local populace had worked the land for Lord Burdet who in turn was the owner of much of it but provided his tenants with crofts and cottages for rent. Although not 'all powerful' in the terms mentioned above, the mill owners did have many similar attributes to the latter. Men such as Zaccheus Hinchliffe, Jonas Kenyon, John Brownhill, George Naylor and the brothers, Joseph and George Norton were eventually to end up owning a large portion of the land in the township (and elsewhere). They provided paid work and lodgings for the villagers, at a due rent, they joined and acted for local authorities and became Justices of the Peace. This was about as close a comparison to the old courts of the Lord of the Manor as it was possible to get.

They also constructed (besides the mill buildings) some of the most important and spectacular residences in the township. Rockwood House, Inkerman Hall, Bagden Hall, Nortonthorpe Hall, Woodbine House and Hartcliffe House, amongst others, could be compared to the old Halls of the ruling gentry. It was, also, not unusual to find inter family marriage, again similarities occur between the old and the new. Lord Burdet would have been keen to see his sons and daughters marry into other powerful dynasties to increase the sphere of his and the families own wealth, power and influence and maybe even occasionally for love!

Most of these family business are now gone, some sites have been cleared and far too many names have been forgotten or consigned to the graveyards at Cumberworth, High Hoyland or elsewhere. Within the confines of this book I am unable to include as much material as I could or would like, but I would be remiss in the extreme if I did not at least pay tribute to at least some of the industrialists to which the area owes so much.

Before we examine the different families it might be useful to note some details contained in early twentieth century trade directories regarding private residents.

Name	Residence 1901	Residence 1912	Residence 1922	Residence 1936
James Brownhill	Oakfield House	Oakfield House	Oakfield House	Oakfield House
John Brownhill JP	Inkerman House			
Joseph Dewhurst	Hortulan Terrace			
James Peace Hinchliffe Kt. Bach, LLD	Not given	Inkerman House	Inkerman House	
John Hinchliffe JP	Strathdearne	Strathdearne	Strathdearne	
Thomas Albert Hinchliffe	Not given	The Royds		
Mrs Hinchliffe (wife of Zacheus)	Hartcliffe			
Arthy Kenyon	Bank House	Bank House	Ashdene	
John Kenyon	Dearneside House			
William Henry Kenyon	Bank House	Bank House	Bank House	
Frank Naylor	Woodbine			
George Wilfred Naylor	Hartcliffe House		Woodbine House	
Walter Norton JP	Rockwood House			
Thomas Norton JP	Bagden Hall	Bagden Hall	Bagden Hall	
George Harold Wilby		Birk Wood House	Norcroft Grange	Norcroft Grange
Thomas Herbert Kenyon		Royds Cottage		
Wilfred Barnes			Field House	
James Henry Dewhurst			West Cliff	
George Herbert Norton JP			Highfield House	
Arthur Turton			Hartcliffe House	
William Wood			Broad Royd	
Miss Hinchliffe (Mabel, Sir J P Hinchliffe's daughter)				Inkerman House
Duncan Alistair McGregor		Rockwood House (by 1910)		
Arthur H Wilby				Denby House
Algernon Hall				The Royds
Harold Hinchliffe				Strathdearne
Jonas Kenyon MBE				Broad Royd
William Naylor				Woodbine House
Gordon H Cran				Rockwood House

The list reads like a who's who of the Denby Dale industrialists, but who were these people and how did they get here?

THE HINCHLIFFE FAMILY

The Hinchliffe family name is derived from the Old English habitational name from West Yorkshire 'henge-clif' which meant a steep cliff. We have noted in the fourteenth and fifteenth century court rolls of Denby the name Heyngeclif, even today there are many variants of the name.

John Hinchliffe was born in 1791 at Langsett, the son of John Hinchliffe, a woollen manufacturer, and Martha Goldthorpe. Around 1810 the family moved to Barnside, Holmfirth, taking over Swan Bank Mill. After the death of his father, John moved again, this time to Scholes. He also took a wife, Harriet Brook and began a family with the birth of a daughter, Mary Ann in 1818. Noted for the 'enterprise and skill' with which he conducted his business it is also notable that he was one of the first men to introduce 'mules' into the Holmfirth district and was always an 'advocate for machinery', notwithstanding this, he was always ready to listen to the complaints of his work people.

He was involved in what became known as the 'Powlett strike'. John was one of a committee of men who drew up a scale of prices to try and regulate the unfair prices of 'piece wool' across the district. The workmen wished to abandon the procedure of paying for yarn by the 'lump' which was arbitrarily agreed according to the generosity of individual manufacturers. Their idea was to be paid according to the length of the yarn and by the weight. Initially the committee were successful but unruly elements in the workforce considered the masters were scared and the scale of payment was rejected.

Throughout the duration of the strike, which caused terrible hardship and suffering, John Hinchliffe kept his machinery running and displayed a tenacity and drive which was to stand him in good stead.

The 'Plug Riots', so named as the rioters attacked mills and drew the plugs from the boilers to stop the machinery were in full swing in 1842. Principally provoked by unemployment and wage reductions the 'pluggers' were on the march up the New Mill valley. John was warned of their approach and sent messengers to all he could rely upon in the district to meet him at Jackson Bridge Mill. John was joined by James Holmes, John Tinker, Christopher Moorhouse, Uriah Mellor (who were all involved with the mill) and a good number of employees. With the eye of a military strategist, John identified that the passage to the boiler house could be defended with a barricade and a few stout hearts.

The first attack resulted in complete panic for the rioters, evidently not locals, they realised that to attack could result in death by falling down a precipice into the river below. This panic caused the defenders to attack and calling on all in the Queen's name to keep the peace captured fourteen of the rioters. Many people were seen running towards the Sovereign Inn in their panic to get away.

Away from work, John Hinchliffe was a Liberal politician who took an active part in opposing church rates in Kirkburton parish and their abolition in Holmfirth was largely down to his influence. He was uncompromising with opponents, but fair, and although he was no great orator he rendered great service during the great free trade struggle. He also wasn't against using his skills, not to say his purse against the hated Corn Laws.

In religion, John was a Wesleyan Reformer and to his religion, as with all other areas of his life he gave one hundred per cent. He was greatly admired by all who knew him during his life and much missed when he died in 1870 and was buried at Hepworth church.

It will shortly become clear that the essential qualities in John Hinchliffe's character were inherited by the coming generations.

By the time of his death, John's family had grown up. One of his sons, John had become a farmer at Bullhouse and his fourth born son, Zaccheus, had begun to build his own empire in Denby Dale. Before we turn to him we should perhaps consider the comments of Abel Hinchliffe, son of John regarding the state of the industry and his family's place within it.

Circa 1898 written from Grimsby:
The single spinning wheel was at work in almost every house as the Penistone cloth had a good reputation for usefulness. My Grandfather had a strong ambition to produce more cloth and no sooner did he hear that an enterprising firm in Leeds had produced a machine of twenty spindles that would make better yarn than the single spinning wheel, than away he went, tried the machine and being satisfied, brought it to Langsett.

I may as well say here that my Grandfather was looked upon as a somewhat strange and outrageous character as he was a religious Republican. He also strongly held that it was impossible for the millennium to come so long as human beings had to give all their time and strength in order to procure the bare necessaries of life. There were not many asylums in those days or no doubt he might have been provided with lodgings there.

Previous to getting the spinning machine he was a popular man in the parish....but his introduction of a machine which in actual practice would do the work of thirty old machines fairly took their breath away and roused the women folk to defend themselves against the introduction of machinery that evidently meant starvation to them all. The details of his persecution are not of much public interest now, suffice it that he was glad to escape with his family and machine into an out of the way corner of the Holmfirth district where he could spin for as many weavers as he required. He even lived to introduce the first 200 spindle mules at Swanbank Mill, Underbank.

The seventh born child of John Hinchliffe and Harriet Brook was named Zaccheus, a memorable name for a memorable character, a name which lives on to this day. The name is derived from the Bible and is a variant of Zacharias, itself a form of the Hebrew Zecheriah. In the new testament he was the father of John the Baptist. Zaccheus was born in Scholes in 1835, his father being 44 years old at the time, his mother 39.

Zaccheus grew up with textile manufacturing in his blood. His father and grandfather and numerous other relations would have been ever ready to impart information and advice regarding an industry he was almost certainly expected to enter in to.

His apprenticeship was conducted with a Manchester piece merchant and would have been regarded as a lucrative opportunity by the family. Perhaps even by Zaccheus, though events did not go exactly to plan. Highly principled and endowed with the morality of his own family, Zaccheus fell foul of his employer after he accused him of dishonest practices. The story goes that Zaccheus bodily threw the merchant down the mill steps! Whatever the truth it could certainly be taken that the apprenticeship was over.

In 1850, John Hinchliffe, father of Zaccheus, acquired Hartcliffe Mill in Denby Dale. One of the major reasons for doing so was the ready supply of soft water available from the river Dearne and Munchcliffe Beck. Also, there were no plans to bring the railway through Holmfirth, but the line at Denby Dale, incorporating the new wooden viaduct was opened the very same year. On top of which a plentiful supply of energy in the form of coal for raising steam for power and heat was also available.

The 'Hartcliffe' site was of ancient derivation as can be seen from the following lease:

22 March 1617/18 – Lease for 14 years by Mathew Wentworth of West Bretton and George Burdett of Denbye Hall, Esqs., to Thomas Wainwright of Denbye, collier, of a coal mine on Hartcliffe common in Cumberworth, the lessee paying an annual rent of 20s for the first year and thereafter 23s 4d.

The Denby court rolls of 1637 note the following:

None shall drive any loadened horses or go with carts over the milne goit at Hartcliff except by the usual and accustomed way under penalty of forty shillings.

This was the maximum penalty which could be imposed by the court, and is also evidence of an early corn mill on the site.

During the latter end of the eighteenth century a fulling and scribbling mill had been built at Hartcliffe though not before 1772. It is possible that the site had been owned by the Wood family as John Wood and Sons, fancy woollen and worsted manufacturers were recorded here in early nineteenth century trade directories. Indeed, John Wood, clothier of Denby Dykeside purchased a 'dwelling house, shop, dyehouse and outbuildings' from the Hon. Richard Lumley Savile, Lord of the Manor in 1799.

By 1804 a new mill had been erected at Hartcliffe for scribbling and carding wool, the land being rented by Nathaniel Shirt (the miller at Denby Dykeside) and John Wood, manufacturer of woollen goods of Denby Dykeside for £21 per annum for a

Zaccheus Hinchliffe, circa 1880's.

Hannah Horton Peace, who married Zaccheus Hinchliffe.

period of 21 years. In 1810 the partnership broke up and Nathaniel Shirt, John Wood the elder and his son, John, agreed to carry on separately at Hartcliffe. John Wood & Sons were recorded as Fancy woollen and worsted manufacturers in 1822 prior to the latter mentioned lease expiring in 1825. A new 21 year lease was granted by the Hon. and Rev. J L Savile to John Wood and his sons, John, Joseph, and James at an annual rent of £38 again at the Hartcliffe site. Nathaniel Shirt had ceased to be a part of the equation since his death in 1813. By 1848 the Wood brothers were in serious financial trouble which inspired two members of the family to seek their fortunes in Australia and other members of the family to take to praying (staunch Wesleyan's that they were) for answers. The prayers seem to have fallen on deaf ears for by 1850 the site was owned by John Hinchliffe & Sons.

The business carried out at this time involved spinning wool into yarn and dyeing to allow fancy designs to be created by cloth manufacturers for sale to merchants and subsequently, tailors. Nine years after the foundation of the mill, Zaccheus was married at Denby church aged 23 to Hannah Horton Peace on 3rd March 1859. Their first child, a boy, named John (after Zaccheus' father) was born in the same year. Hannah was the daughter of James Peace, also a manufacturer, probably the same man noted in 1866 along with his brother Joseph working at Inkerman mill, though by 1868 the site was in the hands of Brownhill & Scatchard, therefore this was a marriage amongst equals.

They lived, at first in a house in the mill yard, which still stands today, though later on and as success developed Zaccheus was able to build 'Strathdearne' at a reputed cost of £1000 in 1893 after buying the land from the owner, Walter Norton of Rockwood House. Zaccheus was very likely to have known Walter Norton socially, aside from their manufacturing background, Walter had founded the Rockwood Harriers Hunt of which Zaccheus was a member and a noted horseman. He was also hunt secretary for many years.

Hartcliffe Mill in the early twentieth century. The Hinchliffe family home 'Strathdearne' keeps a vigil on the hillside. *C Sharp, Old Barnsley*

A very early photograph, dating to approximately 1870. In the front of the mill are Zaccheus Hinchliffe, astride his horse, presumably the one he used when hunting with the Rockwood Harriers. The young boy is his second son, James Peace Hinchliffe.

The business flourished as did his family, a second son, James Peace Hinchliffe was born in 1862, followed by Thomas, 1864, Helen, 1866 and Beatrice 1874. Though by the time Beatrice was born Zaccheus had lost his father. John Hinchliffe as we have noted died in 1870 and it was now that the business underwent a name change and became Z Hinchliffe and Sons.

Zaccheus was involved in other aspects of life away from the mill. In 1865 he became a prominent shareholder in the Denby Dale Gas Light Company. He was also the first county councillor for the Worsborough Electoral Division and was:

revered by the older generation of voters for the enlightened and progressive policy he advocated when county administration was first placed in the hands of the electorate.

He also became a Justice of the Peace and was a trustee of the Francis Burdett charity, life was nothing if not busy.

We can briefly glimpse his household due to the census of 1881, where the family is described as of 'Hartcliffe', Denby Dale:

Name	Age	Place of birth	Occupation
Zaccheus Hinchliffe	45	Scholes	Manufacturer employing 35 hands (cloth)
Hannah Horton Hinchliffe	45	Denby	Wife
John Hinchliffe	21	Denby	Manufacturer employing 35 hands
James Peace Hinchliffe	20	Denby	Manufacturer employing 35 hands
Thomas Albert Hinchliffe	16	Denby	Engineers apprentice
Helen Hinchliffe	13	Denby	Scholar
Beatrice Hinchliffe	6	Denby	Scholar
Jemima Martin	22	Penistone	Domestic servant
Mary Batty	13	Penistone	Domestic servant

A Hinchliffe family gathering dating to circa 1897/8, probably outside the recently completed 'Strathdearne'. Back row, 1st left: Thomas Albert Hinchliffe. 2nd row: 1st left, John Hinchliffe, next to him, his wife, Hannah. Far right, James Peace Hinchliffe with his wife, Narah, to his left. 3rd row: 3rd left, George Wilby, then, Beatrice Hinchliffe, 2nd right, Helen Hinchliffe, next to James Henry Dewhirst. Seated: Zaccheus and Hannah Hinchliffe.

By the 1880's all Zaccheus' sons had become involved with the company having learnt their skills from their father, by which time the textile industry in Denby Dale had greatly expanded. It was also in the 1880's that the company expanded into worsted spinning as well as woollen. In time, worsted spinning became the predominant side of the business and brought the company into dealings with hosiery knitwear manufacturers. The census returns of 1881 inform us that 35 hands were employed by the firm in that year.

Zaccheus' sons were well placed to deal with the void left by the untimely death of Zaccheus in 1896, aged only 61. He was buried at Cumberworth.

John Hinchliffe became Chairman and Managing Director after his father's death as was the eldest son's right. Born in 1859 he married aged around 30 to Hannah Mason of Leeds and had two children, Ruth and Harold (who was to succeed him), the family residing at Strathdearne. Like his father, he had interests outside the mill and was, for 37 years chairman of the Denby & Cumberworth Urban District Council. He became a Justice of the Peace and was also on the management committee for the Soldiers Auxiliary Hospital opened at the Victoria Memorial Hall in Denby Dale, a

Thomas Albert Hinchliffe, around 1910. The youngest son of Zaccheus and Hannah.

99

subject we will return to later. In his leisure hours he took a great interest in cricket and was chairman of the Denby Dale bowling club.

This interest in cricket was also firmly embedded in Thomas Albert Hinchliffe, third son of Zaccheus, born in 1864. He had followed his brothers into the family firm but was also instrumental in founding Denby Dale cricket club, indeed, he lived at the Royds, almost opposite the cricket ground until his death. He was also involved with the military hospital in the village.

The second born son achieved notoriety not just within the village but far further afield. James Peace Hinchliffe (Peace after his mother's maiden name) was born in 1862. He received his early education at Denby Dale National school but at the age of 12 entered Huddersfield college where he remained for four years and won many prizes. In 1877 at the age of 16 he began working for the family firm. Even by this early age much of his spare time was spent at the Huddersfield Mechanics' Institute where he was able to expand his knowledge of chemistry and textile technology. At the same time he was increasingly involved in the activities of the Wesleyan Mutual Improvement Society at Denby Dale, which introduced him to public speaking. In 1882, aged 20 he was made a partner in his fathers company and a few years later became Managing Director.

James played an active roll in the development of the Woollen and Worsted Research Association. Under his guidance and in collaboration with Sir Michael Sadler the first meetings were held at the University of Leeds. The result of these meetings was the establishment of the association for the whole of the country which became known as the Wool Industries Research Association which was incorporated in 1918. James was chairman of the body from 1916 to 1928 and vice chairman up until his death.

From 1898 until around 1915 James was honorary secretary to the Holmfirth Division Liberal Association and had been a delegate since 1885. He was approached on numerous occasions regarding a seat in parliament but always declined citing his heavy business commitments.

James entered county council circles as a member for his fathers old division in Worsborough in 1898. On accepting the invitation delivered by a deputation from Worsborough he told them:

> if they wanted a member who would subscribe to their various religious denominations, cricket and football clubs and so on, they must go elsewhere, as he would not 'buy' a single vote by such means. On the other hand, if they wanted a representative to look after their interests (always providing that their demands were reasonable and fair) he would use all his ability and energy on their behalf.

James was returned unopposed at each of the four succeeding elections, indeed in 1907 he became an alderman of the county council and in 1911 was appointed vice chairman. He was elected chairman in 1916 and held the office until his death.

James was also a member of the Finance, Highways and Standing Joint committees but when the West Riding County Council was charged with the administration of the Education Act in 1904 James threw all his weight behind the task of organising what was to be the largest education authority outside London. He became chairman of the Association and Attendance committee which was responsible for the expenditure of almost £1,000,000 for the provision of 150 new schools. James' belief that education was indispensable to the growth and prosperity of industry, was a large factor in his energy towards the improvement and development of technical education. His predecessors in this office included Sir John Horsfall and the Marquis of Ripon. James became vice chairman of the committee in 1911 until finally giving way in 1916 when he was elected as chairman of the County Council. On the occasion of his eighteenth re-election to this body Sir James thanked the members for, *'giving me a full time job for another twelve months'*.

James was appointed a county magistrate in 1912. He acted as chairman of the West Riding War Pensions Committee and was a champion of the grievances of demobilised soldiers, fresh from the trenches of World War One. He continued in this roll until just after the end of the Great War. He was

Swans on Hartcliffe Mill dam, circa 1900.

also chairman of the West Riding Distress committee until it was merged into the Statutory Pensions committee. Over 6000 refugees were accommodated and cared for before repatriation by a committee of which James was chairman. He also acted on a special committee at Leeds University with a view to drawing up a co-ordinated scheme of textile instruction and research for the West Riding. On top of all this, he also sat as a member on the committee for Juvenile Education in 1917 in relation to employment after the war . After a year of deliberation the committees recommendations were accepted by the then Minister for Education, Mr H A L Fisher, as a basis for the Education bill.

The steam engine which provided power for Hartcliffe Mill, removed in the mid twentieth century.

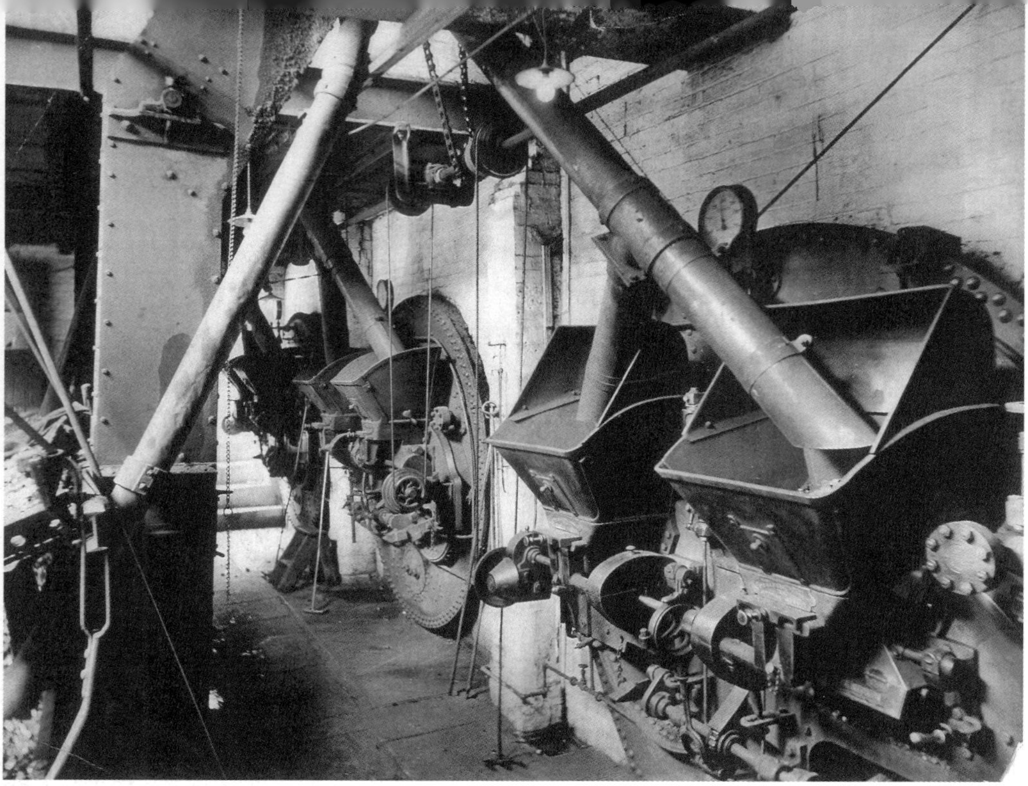

Lancashire Boilers at Hartcliffe Mill. These were used to provide steam for the engine.

How James ever found time to devote any energy to the family business will have to be wondered at, but luckily, it was in very safe hands with John and Thomas. Meanwhile Zaccheus's daughters had made marriages which produced children who were to become very important to the company. Helen married James Henry Dewhirst and Beatrice married George Wilby. The Wilbys were a well established local family and had been involved in many notable events, such as the Enclosure Act of 1802/4. George Wilby of Pogstone House in the village was a veteran of Waterloo and it would seem possible that he used his sabre to ceremonially cut the 1815 Denby Dale pie. A George Wilby was the Registrar of Births and Deaths for the Denby Dale district in 1838 though by 1867 Hugh Wilby had taken over. George lived for a time at Birk Wood House (later to become the Pie Hall) and later at Norcroft Grange. His son, Arthur Hinchliffe Wilby lived at Denby House, at the top of Miller Hill.

James's life, consisting of chairmanship of so many different committees was eventually to reap its reward. His selfless service was indicative of the new mill owning class, the drive and motivation of these eminent Victorians providing the basis for the development of society in so many different ways. In 1920 he received a Knighthood and became Sir James Peace Hinchliffe. The occasion was marked by a presentation to him of his portrait in oils by past and present members of the County Council.

Sir James Peace Hinchliffe, from a portrait dating to circa 1920.

Sir James P. Hinchliffe.

By permission of the 'Leeds Mercury.'

An early example of company transport. Dating to the early part of the twentieth century, the truck had a chain driven axle and solid tyres.

From the *Leeds Mercury*. The caption mentioned Sir James achievements and finished with 'All too few are like him – Young generation please note.'

The 'New End', after a fire in January 1934, prior to being demolished. The old chimney can be seen reflected in the dam.

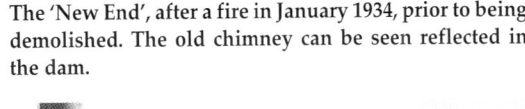

Hartcliffe Mill buildings, circa 1928. Note the shadow of the new chimney to the bottom left, which was built in 1924/5.

One of the last honours he received was an honorary degree conveyed by Leeds University which made him a Doctor of Laws. It was also in Leeds, at the town hall that Sir James figured on the platform of delegates on the occasion of the visit of King George V and his wife, Queen Mary, during the early 1930's.

A life so rich and full would seem to leave little time to any other activity but James was a Wesleyan Methodist and attended services at Denby Dale; as for leisure activities, he was a member of Woodsome Hall golf club and frequently played there in the summer.

He had married in 1886 to Narah Peace Dewhirst and had one daughter, Mabel, a further child, Reginald, died in infancy. Lady Hinchliffe pre-deceased Sir James in 1928, Sir James arranged for an altar and reredos to be erected to her memory in Denby church in 1928. A lectern was also given to Denby church on the event of his own death. Mabel became a member of several West Riding public bodies and gave invaluable help to her father in his endeavours.

Sir James died of heart failure in 1933 at his home, Inkerman Hall in Denby Dale. He was 72. The mill at Hartcliffe closed on the day of the funeral and the flag was at half mast, most of the workforce attending the ceremony. A large crowd of villagers gathered at the main entrance to Inkerman Hall to watch the cortege leave for Cumberworth. In an exceptional gesture, the family had allowed employees of Z Hinchliffe & Sons to view Sir James as he lay in his coffin at the Hall. The Rev. W H Evers conducted a private service here before departure. A number of policemen walked at the head of the cortege, being followed by around 50 representative workpeople and the six bearers. The hearse was followed by three of the firm's lorries laden with floral tributes, the principal mourners followed these in 36 cars.

The short distance to the church was lined with sympathisers, and the entrance to the churchyard was manned by six police officers to help deal with the crowds.

So many mourners arrived that a good number had to be content to stand outside the door. At the request of the family the service was a simple one and included just one hymn, '*Jesu, Lover of my Soul*'. The clergy involved were Archdeacon R C M Harvey, Rev. J J Cowan (rector of Cumberworth), Rev. G O Tibbits (vicar of Denby) and Rev. W H Evers (Wesleyan Minister at Denby Dale).

After the service the cortege was escorted to the graveside by nine policemen where Sir James was buried with his wife and infant son in a grave lined with chrysanthemums.

The high profile status of this funeral meant that it was heavily reported in the local press. It is also illuminating to read through a list of some of the mourners, though for space reasons I have had to leave out a good number.

The family mourners were:

Miss Mabel P Hinchliffe (daughter), Mr & Mrs G Wilby (brother in law and sister), Mr John Hinchliffe (brother), Mr Harold Hinchliffe (nephew), Mr H Dewhirst (nephew), Mr & Mrs A Wilby (nephew and niece), Miss M Dewhirst (niece), Mr Herbert Hinchliffe (cousin), Mr John Hinchliffe (cousin), Mrs Thomas Hinchliffe (sister in law), Mr & Mrs Thomas Field (nephew and niece), Mr & Mrs D Mallinson (nephew and niece), Mrs A Dawson (niece), and Messrs. W P and W E Peace (cousins).

The bearers were old employees of the firm:

H Mathews, H Bintcliffe, G Priest, W J Lockwood, Moorhouse Kaye and E Wood.

In addition to the latter, 37 people represented the West Riding County Council and Sir Charles McGrath (clerk) led the deputation of County Council officials, representatives of Huddersfield Town Council also attended.

Denby Dale Urban District Councillors:

S Cook (vice chairman), J Hollingworth, F Ellis, S Shepley, H N Naylor, H Grayson, G T Smith, G S Mosley (clerk), G H Senior (collector), J Firth (surveyor) and F Greenwood (sanitary inspector).

Local Authorities and Firms:

The Mayor of Dewsbury, the Mayor of Batley, the Mayor of Wakefield, Rotherham Rural Council, Clayton West Old Age Pensions Committee (W Sheard), Saddleworth UDC, Hipperholme UDC, the Mayor of Morley (representatives), Honley UDC, Upper Agbrigg Guardians committee, British Wool Federation, Cook, Sons & Co Ltd., Sir James Hill & Sons – Bradford, Lieut. Colonel Gilbert P Norton-Armitage & Norton-Huddersfield, Midland Bank-Huddersfield, Ramsden & Co-Huddersfield, Mr Algernon Hall-John Brownhill & Co-Denby Dale, Dr. S G Barker-Director of Research, British Research Association – the list is very extensive but the latter do give some idea of the esteem in which Sir James was held.

Other mourners included:

Brig. Gen. R E Sugden, representing the Earl of Harewood, Sir Jas. Baillie-Vice Chancellor, Leeds University, Mr Fred Lawton, representing Lord Barnby, Mr Thomas Norton and Mr G Herbert Norton – County Magistrates, Rev. E B Carleton-Vicar of Penistone, Sir Benjamin Dawson, Major General Sir Llewellyn W Atcherley – H M Inspector of Constabulary, Lieut. Col. F W R Brook – Chief Constable of the West Riding.

Floral tributes were numerous including offerings from the staff of Z Hinchliffe & Sons, Denby Dale cricket and bowling club, British Legion – Denby Dale branch, Montagu Hospital-Mexborough and the staff at Inkerman Hall.

Sir James was predeceased by his younger brother, Thomas, who had died in 1922 aged only 58. Of Zaccheus's sons only John remained, fortunately he and his wife had also given the family an heir. Harold Hinchliffe was born in 1890 and attended Denby Dale school. Later he had attended New College, Harrogate and Huddersfield Technical College. The first world war interrupted his studies and his working life in the family firm when Harold became a Sub-Lieutenant in the Royal Navy. He attended his Uncle, Sir James's funeral in 1933 and that of his father, John who died only two years later in 1935.

Harold was by now the only male Hinchliffe from Zaccheus' line left alive, fortunately he still had the support of Arthur Hinchliffe Wilby and Herbert Dewhirst and it was this triumvirate that saw the firm go forward. He also married Frances, the

Left to right: Herbert Dewhirst, Fred Harry Senior (receiving his retirement present), Harold Hinchliffe and Arthur Wilby, approximately 1941.

Z Hinchliffe & Sons at one time employed their own fire brigade, this picture dated from around the 1940's.

daughter of Edgar Field, a member of the Skelmanthorpe-based rug manufacturers. The couple had three children, two daughters and a son, John Norman, who was to become chairman and joint managing director of the group. Harold served on the West Riding County Council for some time and was also a Justice of the Peace. He also became the first chairman of the Denby Dale Urban District Council and served between 1938 and 1947. His leisure activities included cricket and golf and he was also renowned for being a good shot.

Left: June 1941, Frances Hinchliffe, neé Field, wife of Harold Hinchliffe, escorting Princess Margaret at Strathdearne. Articles made by the employees are displayed during a morale boosting visit by the Princess Royal during the Second World War.

Below: Aerial view of Hartcliffe Mills dating to approximately the 1960's.

Board members and managers from around 1950's. Left to right: John Hinchliffe, Charles Hoyland (Company Secretary), Walter Johnson Lockwood (Engine Tester), Edward Auckland (Director and Colour Matcher), Arnold Holmes (Teazing), George Wilby, Arthur Wilby, Herbert Dewhirst.

In 1921 the firm purchased Birdsedge Mill from the trustees of the Firth estate, the mill being situated close to the source of the river Dearne. The building was closed temporarily in 1929 during an economic slump and is now used primarily for blending wool. We will return to the history of this building in a later chapter.

The official guide to Denby Dale and District has the following to say about the company in 1959:

> Z. Hinchliffe and Sons Limited are spinners of woollen and worsted yarn. The worsted yarns are spun for the coating hosiery trade, and the qualities are from 90's to 58's and mainly in colour. The fine quality woollen yarns are spun in colours and in white for the coating and hosiery trade. Specialities include Vicuna, Cashmere, Lambs-wool and the rarer fibres.

The 'rarer fibres' referred to included Cashmere, (goats wool) a material which was limited in use until a process was developed in England towards the late nineteenth century which eased the separation of the fine undercoat from the coarse outer coat. The introduction of the wool of the breed of Merino sheep also occurred at around this time. This wool was much finer than that of the native British sheep. The Merino sheep flourish in the warmer climates of Australia, South Africa and South America but importation of the wool enabled the spinning of much finer yarns. More modern times have seen the introduction of Bactrian camel hair from central Asia and angora, from the angora rabbit.

Harold Hinchliffe died in 1955 leaving his son, John as chairman. He was ably supported by Herbert Dewhirst and further generations of the Wilby family. John joined the firm after

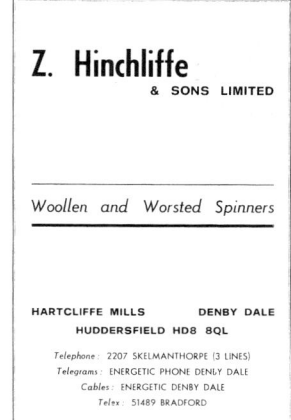

Advertisement from a 1972 'Official Guide' to Denby Dale.

107

attending school at Oundle and Bradford Technical College. He saw out his National Service in the Royal Navy (taking after his father) as a Leading Seaman. He was also a very active member of Denby Dale Parish Council and was chairman of a number of trade organisations. Taking after his great grandfather, John became the secretary of the Rockwood Harriers as well as riding with them. He also acted as a judge and steward at many hunt race meetings in the north of England.

The company also expanded, not least in terms of operational sites. As we have noted, the mill at Birdsedge was purchased in 1921, others followed at Phoenix Mills in Huddersfield, and at Ryeside Mills at Dalry in Ayrshire. The company also purchased John Woodhead (Dobroyd Mills) Ltd at Jackson Bridge near Huddersfield in 1997. Changes also continue at the Denby Dale site as new buildings replace those which are older and less suitable. It is of interest to note that a building, demolished only in recent years which stood near to the first home of Zaccheus and Hannah was once a public house. The enormous brick chimney's have gone as has the steam engine which gave power to the mill. Working practices and methods have also changed as technology has developed. During the 1970's the firm switched emphasis from worsted to woollen spinning due to a decline in the world market. In 1980/81 worsted spinning was ceased entirely.

Z Hinchliffe and Sons has stood the test of time, the company having outlived the other mills in Denby Dale, the present generations of the Hinchliffe and Wilby families continuing in the rolls created for them by their illustrious forebears.

The Hinchliffe Family

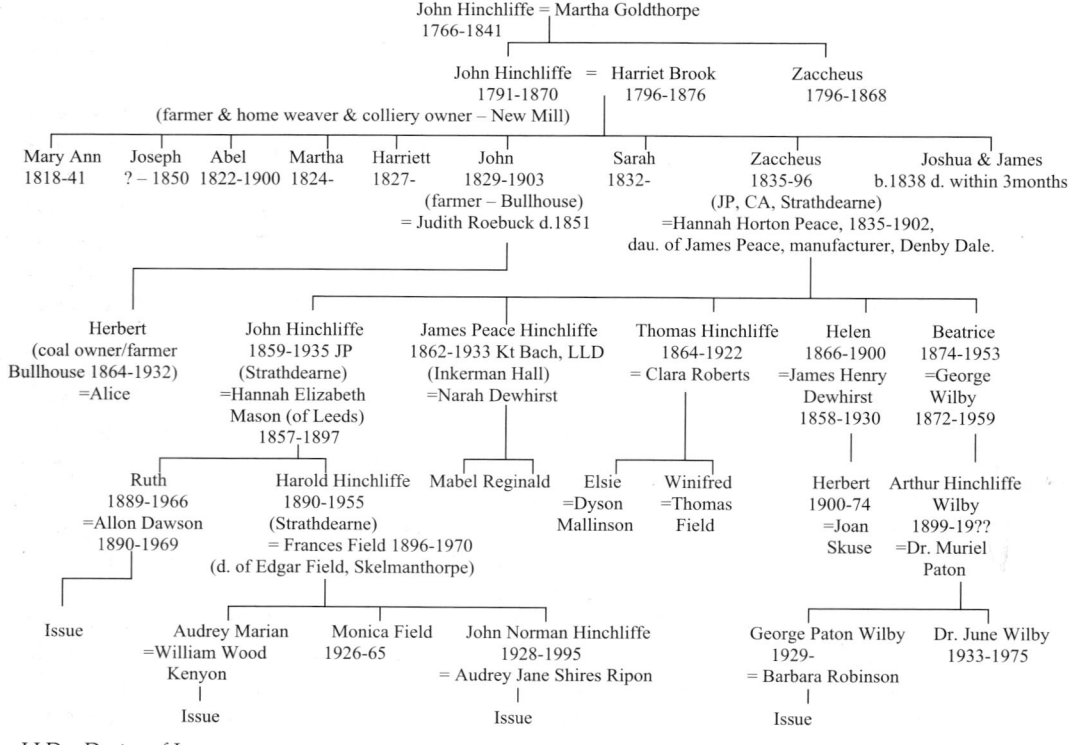

LLD = Doctor of Laws

JOHN BROWNHILL AND COMPANY

The Brownhill family derives its name from various habitations or places including one in Yorkshire. It stems from the old English 'brun' (Brown) and 'hyll', a brown hill.

Personal details regarding the Brownhill family are notably rare when considering them in the same context as the Hinchliffe family. The major reason for this would appear to be the family's sale of the business in 1961 to Qualitex Fabrics of Burnley and their subsequent removal from Denby Dale. Thankfully, members of the family do still live in and around the area, relatives born of Brownhill women who made significant marriages with other notable industrial families. The surnames of Hinchliffe, Kenyon, Wood, Naylor and Kitson all became tied in to the Brownhill family tree.

There are two schools of thought as to where the family originated. Records show a plethora of Brownhills living in the Penistone and Langsett area, perhaps they were even acquainted with the Hinchliffe family. Other sources suggest an initial migration from Bradford, whatever the truth, by 1827 they were established at Cumberworth.

Thomas Brownhill was born in 1804 and married Elizabeth Wood in 1827 at Cumberworth church. Elizabeth was very likely a member of the Wood family of Denby Dale, manufacturers whom we shall later return to. Thomas was a weaver/clothier and he and Elizabeth had at least seven children, all baptised at Cumberworth. Of all their offspring two are particularly notable, Joseph and John.

Joseph was the fourth child and third boy, born in 1834. He married a woman we know only as Fanny before 1858 and had a daughter, Elizabeth. In 1858, Joseph, along with his young family emigrated to Australia. They sailed from Liverpool on Thursday, 8 April aboard the '*Marco Polo*' and were accompanied by their Aunt Hannah along with cousins, John, Abraham, George and Tom. They landed in Melbourne on 14 July and were met by their Uncle John and Aunt Eastwood, the voyage having taken 107 days, 25 days longer than was expected.

Joseph already had relatives living in Australia, George Harrington Brownhill and his wife, Hannah Ann had arrived in Melbourne on 7th October 1841 on the '*Intrinsic*'. Unfortunately both died at an early age and their children were placed with other families. John Cochrane Brownhill was placed with a family called Lawrie (Lawry) and his sister, Rachel, was brought up by a Miss Wilson. It is likely that these are the Uncle John and Aunt Eastwood referred to latterly. Joseph kept a diary of the journey undertaken by his family; in it he mentions the wedding at Clayton West in 1858 of his cousin Abraham to Hannah. He also refers to his sister, Harriet marrying Thomas Turton.

It is interesting to note that James and Tedbar Wood of Denby Dale had emigrated to Melbourne in 1848, soon to find fortune in the 'gold rush'. It may be purely coincidence, as to date, the relevant genealogical details have not come to hand but this could imply that the Wood brothers whom we know to have met and stayed with relatives upon their arrival may have been following in well trodden footsteps. Elizabeth Wood, who had married Thomas Brownhill was almost certainly a cousin, perhaps even a sister to James and Tedbar and the gradual migration to Melbourne may have been more choreographed than has ever been thought. We will return to the story of James and Tedbar Wood later in the book.

Thomas and Elizabeth's fifth child and fourth son was a slightly different proposition. John Brownhill was born in 1836 at Cumberworth. He took after his father's trade and learnt the skills of the weaver/clothier. He was 14 years old when John and Zaccheus Hinchliffe took over the mills at Hartcliffe in Denby Dale from his probable relations, the Woods. He also witnessed the foundation of another mill a few years later by Jonas Kenyon, perhaps he was inspired by these two men. John married Jane Mary Schofield, known as Mary sometime before 1863, only five years before his partnership with a 'Mr Scatchard' began.

The 1881 census returns for Denby Dale show John living at Denby Dale, probably at Inkerman House and continue thus:

Name	Age	Place of Birth	Occupation
John Brownhill	45	Cumberworth	Worsted manufacturer employing 130 hands
Mary Brownhill	46	Clayton West	Wife
James Brownhill	18	Clayton West	Assists at worsted mill
Jane Anna Brownhill	16	Clayton West	Scholar
Jno. Thomas Brownhill	12	Bradford	Scholar
Charles Hy. Brownhill	7	Denby Dale	Scholar
Lucy Brownhill	12	Leeds (she was a niece)	Scholar
Florence Ethel Brownhill	4	Bradford (niece)	
Rebecca Hinchcliffe	23	Holmfirth	General Domestic Servant

The latter seems to suggest that before setting up the business in Denby Dale, John and his family had lived at Clayton West. Of course the births at Clayton West could also imply that Mary had been delivered of her first two children at her parents home, a usual occurrence at this time. That they had arrived in Denby Dale (to live) by 1872 is evident from the birth place of Charles Henry. There would also seem to be a Bradford connection but the nature of this is not yet clear. The two nieces in the household are the daughters of John's brother, Charles and went on to make very good marriages as can be seen from the genealogical chart. The other point to note is that Brownhills were employing 130 people only 13 years after their foundation. In the same census returns, Zaccheus Hinchliffe's labour force was 35.

Brownhill and Scatchard was established in 1868 at Inkerman Mill on the Barnsley turnpike road in Denby Dale. As to why the name 'Inkerman' was used we can only speculate. The Battle of Inkerman took place in 1854 during the Crimean War, just after Balaclava which included the famous 'Charge of the Light Brigade'. Perhaps the name was brought back to Denby Dale by a veteran of the conflict between the English and French against the Russians. The three storied building had previously been owned by the Peace family, George Peace can be found here in 1822 as a textile manufacturer and we have already noted James and Joseph, probably his sons in 1866. Had one of these sons been at the Battle of Inkerman on 5th November 1854? The Peace family were noted to be living at Inkerman Hall in 1857, one of the first mentions of the name in relation to the mill or its associated buildings. Very little is known of Mr Scatchard, including his first name! I have seen a trade directory for the Leeds area dating to the mid nineteenth century which lists a William Scatchard and in the same list (i.e.: the same village or town) a female Brownhill but this is probably pure coincidence. There is also the case of Samuel Scatchard, born in Kirkburton who by 1881 had become a 'wool piece dyer', unfortunately he was only born in 1855, though his family may have a connection. Another Samuel Scatchard was noted in Piggots trade directory of 1834 as living in Skelmanthorpe and working as a tailor so the surname was not unknown locally. Finally, a Mr. Scatchard was recorded as Managing Director of Bentleigh Silk Mills in Meltham in the nineteenth century and perhaps he is the most promising candidate. Whether the two men were linked by blood or were simply business associates is currently unknown, what is certain is that the partnership did not last very long, possibly due to disagreement or death. By the early 1880's work had begun on a new building sited lower down the valley in order to make use of the water power supplied by the River Dearne. The first building here later being known as 'number one shed' and the site was christened Springfield Mills. Inkerman mill ceased operations in the early twentieth century and was used largely as a warehouse thereafter. Only a year after the foundation of the company, John's father, Thomas died aged 65.

In 1900 John Brownhill and Company was formed; this may coincide with the departure of Mr Scatchard. John Brownhill's sons, James and Charles Henry were brought in at this time. John Brownhill and Mary Schofield had at least six children. James, the eldest was born in 1863, Charles Henry, the other major player in the family firm was born in 1872.

The family worshipped as Wesleyan's, indeed, John was given a silver plated trowel with which he laid the first stone at the new Wesleyan chapel at Thurlstone. John was also a Justice of the Peace and was a member of the Denby Dale Urban District Council until he died in 1903 and was buried at Cumberworth, his wife, Mary joined him there only one year later.

John and his family lived at Inkerman Hall which must have been acquired from the Peace family at the same time as the mill. As we have seen, after John's death, Sir James Peace Hinchliffe lived here until his death in 1933. James Brownhill had already seen to his residence by building Oakfield House a stone's throw further up the road towards Barnsley and so had no need of Inkerman Hall.

James Brownhill married Alice Naylor, the daughter of George William Naylor, who built Denby Dale viaduct. The Naylor connection was too important to hide behind the Brownhill name so they christened their son, Cecil Naylor Brownhill. Charles Henry married Annie Maud Townsend and it was his only son, John Kenneth, who was to see out the family's interests in the firm before its eventual take-over.

Surely one of the most illustrious contracts undertaken by the company occurred around 1923. A Royal wedding took place this year, that of Prince Albert, later King George VI and Lady Elizabeth Bowes-Lyon. Albert was Duke of York at this time and was not expected to take the throne but the events surrounding his brother's abdication in 1936 meant that Brownhill's now had a reason to boast – they had supplied the silk for the wedding dress of the future Queen of England.

We have already examined in the first volume of this work, numerous details regarding the company's activities but the events of 1920 saw the company change direction again.

John Brownhill & Co. became a public company in 1920 when a prospectus was issued with regard to shares. The subscription list opened on Monday 19th April 1920 and was to close on or before Thursday, 22nd April, though the prospectus makes it clear that the 1st January 1920 will be the date the business will have been taken over. The prospectus gives us some interesting details regarding the company:

James Brownhill, son of the founder, John, taken at the 'Royds', the home of fellow Director, Algernon Hall, circa late 1930's.

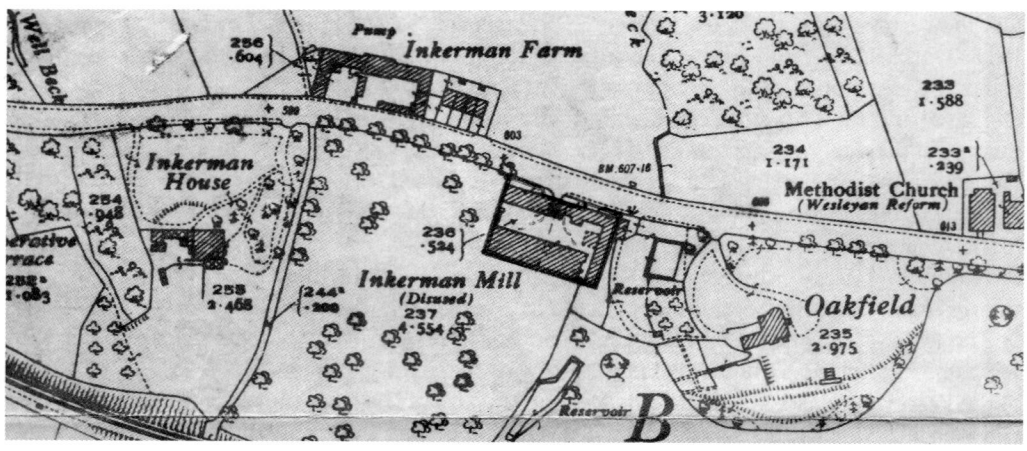

Plan, dating to 1930, of the Inkerman site in Denby Dale. It includes Oakfield House, the home of James Brownhill, Inkerman Hall and the old mill buildings.

John Brownhill & Company Ltd.
Manufacturers of cotton and silk fabrics – specialising in brocaded poplins, furnishing damasks, coutilles, linings, etc.
Springfield and Inkerman Mills, Denby Dale
(incorporated under the companies act 1908 to 1917.)

Capital £250,000
Divided into – 125,000 7$^1/_2$ cumulative participating preference shares of £1 each
And
125,000 ordinary shares of £1 each

Directors
James Brownhill (Chairman and Managing Director)
Norman Hall (Managing Director)
Charles Henry Brownhill

Bankers
The National Provincial and Union Bank of England Ltd
Solicitors
Godden Holme and Ward, 34 Old Jewry, London EC2
Morgan, Wright, Horner, Sampson & Wood, 23 Bank Street, Bradford
Brokers
Quilter & Co. 32 Old Jewry, London EC2
Potter & Co., 20 Park Row, Leeds
Auditors
Armitage & Norton, Chartered Accountants of Huddersfield, London & elsewhere.
Secretary and Registered Offices
Arthur Turton, Springfield Mill, Denby Dale near Huddersfield

The prospectus continues:

In addition to considerable home and European trade, a large export trade is done with the colonies, South America and the Far East. The orders in hand indicate that the mills will be kept running at full capacity for a long time to come and it is confidently expected the company will participate in the great prosperity of the textile trade which it is anticipated will result from the depletion of stocks throughout the world.

The freehold premises on offer comprised weaving sheds, warehouses and the usual equipment for the companies output, freehold estates in the parish of Denby totalling approximately 79 acres along with two large residential houses, eight cottages, farm buildings and water rights. The assets were listed as follows:

Land, buildings, machinery, plant etc., as valued by Messrs. Alexander Smith & Sons upon a moderate going concern basis £154,355.

Stock in trade, book debts and cash (less creditors £80,152) as per Directors valuation and certificate in the old company's balance-sheet as at 31st December 1919 £70,475.

Investments at cost (less reserve), including £20,000 war stock £20,886.

TOTAL £245,716.

Armitage and Norton also provided the following trading profits:

1916 – £13,562, 1917 – £31,745, 1918 – £34,702, 1919 – £82,411.

These figures allowed for depreciation and Directors' remuneration but not for income tax and excess profit duty.

The prospectus also reports that in early 1914 new departments of the business had been opened which had nothing to do with the war. These initiatives had, over the last few years been developed and were now profitable sections of the firms trade. All the ordinary shares of the company were kept in the hands of the Brownhill and Hall families, fully paid shares of £10 each were distributed as follows:

James Brownhill 2507 shares, Norman Hall, 1900 shares, Charles Henry Brownhill 100 shares. James and Norman also made sure of their positions by writing into the terms of the sale that they would remain in management for the next five years.

The names of some of the subscribers to the preference shares have also survived:

Victor Coope Ponsonby of Woodstock, merchant, 1 share
Oscar Wilfred Wells, Wandsworth Common, London, chartered accountant, 1 share
Herwald Ramsbotham, Hyde Park Gate, London, merchant, 1 share
Maurice S Ward, Old Jewry, London, solicitor, 1 share
TW Gowen, Coulsdon, Surrey, Clerk, 1 share
Ernest Edward Lucas, Hendon, law clerk, 1 share

The preference shares thus sold out were later all to be bought in by the company in 1936 which in effect caused the firm to become a private concern though still legally trading as a public company.

By this time, Charles Henry Brownhill was dead and his son, John Kenneth had joined the company.

The following letter dated 18th March 1930 confirmed his appointment:

To John Kenneth Brownhill Esq.,
2 Bromley Road, St Anne's on Sea, Lancs.

Dear Sir,
The arrangements made when you were over at the mill on Thursday last have now been confirmed by the Board of Directors, namely that you have been appointed as salesman at an annual salary of £250, plus all reasonable travelling expenses. We shall be obliged if you will confirm your acceptance and the appointment and if possible at the same time indicate when you will be able to join our staff.
Yours faithfully

George Senior
(Company Secretary)

The letter head lists the directors of the company, James Brownhill, Charles Henry Brownhill, Sir Frederick Eley Bart., and Algernon F F Hall.

Norman Hall (1888–1958) had by this time left the company though he had been instrumental in his younger brother, Algernon, being offered a Directorship. Norman had married Dorothy Mowat, daughter of Sir John Gunn Mowat, 1st Baronet and they lived at Birkby, Huddersfield. Algernon attended Glasgow University and Manchester Technical College and was instrumental in guiding the company through the dark years of world war two. He married Mary Law Grieg, the daughter of John and Gertrude Grieg in 1925. They lived, initially, at Carr House, Shepley and moved to the Royds (former home of Thomas Hinchliffe) around 1930/31.

James Brownhill, stood in front of Springfield Mill with some of his employees, around the late 1930's.

The mother of the brothers was Edith Hall, nee Firth, who was the daughter of Sir Thomas Freeman Firth (1825–1909) who founded Firth, Willans and Company, carpet manufacturers at Clifton Mills, Brighouse. The firm later became Firth Carpets and was eventually bought out by Readicut. The reason for the families involvement with Brownhill's may hide behind the friendship between Gertrude Sarah Grieg (Algernon's mother in law) and Alice Brownhill, formerly Naylor (married to James Brownhill) which stemmed from their days at prep school, in Ilkley.

Chairman and Managing Director, James Brownhill died in 1942, though he had no male heir to succeed him. Instead it was his daughter Marjorie Eileen who had married Lt. Col. Montague G

Norman Hall, pictured around the 1950's.

S Hopson who inherited his shares and became Chairman of the company for a time. We have already had cause to note the name of Cecil Naylor Brownhill but why did he not inherit his father's share of the company?

The *London Evening Standard* dated Friday, March 25th, 1938 tells his story very well:

Grand National Rider of 1931 Dying in Car

As tens of thousands gathered at Aintree today for the Grand National, news was received in London of the tragedy of a noted amateur jockey who rode in the 'National' of 1931. He was Major Cecil Naylor Brownhill, MC of the Irish Guards.

Major Brownhill arrived in South Africa five weeks ago. This morning he was found dying in his car on the roadside halfway between Pretoria and Johannesburg. He was in evening dress.

Algernon Hall, pictured around the 1920's.

The discovery was made by a passing motorist says Reuter. Major Brownhill was suffering from multiple injuries. The car had left the road and hit a tree. Earlier reports stated that the car was undamaged and that the police were working on the theory that Major Brownhill had been murdered.

Major Brownhill was one of the few men who have recovered from a broken neck. He was the owner of 'Drintyre' which he rode in the Grand National of 1931. He hoped to ride the horse again in the 1932 race but a few weeks before the race he had a fall at a Midland meeting.

Two years later he won the inaugural race at Hurst Park for a cup awarded in memory of Capt. R E Sassoon, another amateur jockey, who had been fatally injured in a fall at Lingfield.

In 1935 Major Brownhill broke three ribs in a fall during a training gallop and another racing accident involved a very severe internal operation.

Major Brownhill, who sailed for South Africa on January 28th was married and had one daughter. He was seconded to the South African Defence Force for liaison duty and was attached to the Military College at Roberts Heights. He served in the Royal Horse Artillery during the war, transferring to the Irish Guards after the armistice. Before he went to South Africa he was ADC to General Sir Edmund Ironside and was a General Staff Officer, Eastern Command.

NB: ADC – Aide de Camp

Major Cecil Naylor Brownhill who rode 'Drintyre' in the 1931 Grand National.

Major Brownhill married Eleanor Burman and had two daughters (not one as mentioned in the above newspaper report), but no sons. He is mentioned on his parent's gravestone at Cumberworth but does not lie there. His funeral took place in Johannesburg with full military honours in March 1938. How much he was involved in running the family business is difficult to tell but the memories of some of the veterans of Springfield mill recall a plaque which hung in Oakfield House (home of his father, James) onto which were nailed four horseshoes. Were these the shoes worn by 'Drintyre' in the 1931 Grand National?

John Kenneth Brownhill was the last member of the family to be heavily involved in the firm. Born in 1907 he saw military action during the second world war, unfortunately 4½ years of this service saw him incarcerated as a prisoner of the Japanese in Burma. Communication was difficult for him and he received no word from home. His Japanese captors did allow curt messages such as the following to be sent to his family,

Imperial Japanese Army – 17 Jan. 1944. My health is good, my best regards to Mother, Auntie Freda, Aunty Peggie, Uncle James.

The message was sent to his son, Charles and enforces just how little information young 'Jack' had received as his Uncle, James Brownhill, Chairman and Managing Director had died in 1942.

The following letter, dated 10th October 1945, was sent to him by George Senior, the company secretary for many years:

Dear Jack,
At a meeting of the Board today a resolution was passed affirming the great pleasure felt by all your co-directors at your safe return home and I was instructed to convey this to you with their congratulations and to say that they look forward to welcoming you on resuming your old place on the Board.

Their unanimous feeling is that you should now have a real holiday before once again taking up business responsibilities and as a help to that end they would like you to accept the enclosed cheque with their very good wishes. They hope to see you back 'in the team' in say, about three months.

I thought you would probably prefer this somewhat informal letter to an official typed one and take the opportunity of adding my own congratulations with, I am sure, those of all the staff. We shall all look forward to seeing you before long.

Kind regards

The company letter head is interesting in that there is now no mention of Inkerman mill, just the Springfield site suggesting that the old building had now been totally abandoned even as a warehouse, the company was also limited. Once again the directors are listed,

John Kenneth (Jack) Brownhill, circa 1940.

Weaving shed at Springfield Mill, during the 1940's.

Brownhills steam engine, 'Sarah', the pride of Bob Mellor, scrapped soon after the Second World War. Inset, Bob Mellor.

Algernon Hall along with his wife Mrs M L Hall, M R Wilkins (who was the father of the London agent Ken Wilkins), J K Brownhill and Mrs M E Hopson (the sister of Major Cecil Naylor Brownhill). John Kenneth (Jack) Brownhill was elevated to the position of Sales Director on 8 June 1948 on a basic salary of £1250 per annum.

The mill was exempted from closure during the Second World War under the 'Concentration of Industry Act' and wove silk 'man carrying', khaki material and viscose cargo parachutes and a variety of other fabrics under the utility scheme. The operations were led by Algernon Hall who was also responsible for large scale re-organisation after the end of hostilities. Scharer semi-automatic pirn winding and Butterworth and Dickinson underpick looms were brought in allowing weaver compliments to increase from two to six looms weaving 'haute couture' fabrics for London and Manchester merchants. The old Leesona pirn winders and over pick looms were scrapped as well as the old steam engine, 'Sarah' (the pride of Bob Mellor-which was sent for scrap) and line drives to the shed which were replaced by a Mirlees diesel generating set which allowed each new loom to have an individual motor drive. Trade was good up until the end of the Korean war in 1953 after which the business was increasingly impacted by over-capacity in the industry and the ever increasing amount of imports. Algernon Hall left the company in 1958 and in 1961 the shares were bought by Qualitex Fabrics Ltd. of Colne. This effectively ended the interest of the Brownhill family in the company though most of the employees were kept on as Qualitex closed down their operations in Colne and moved production to Denby Dale.

Employees working in the mills of England throughout the 50's and 60's were occasionally involved in social events such as the 'works outing' which might include huge dinners for employees, today's version of these ideas would be 'staff bonding' and take place in dreary office blocks. Brownhill's celebrated the completion of the re-equipping of the factory in 1948 or 1949 by hiring coaches to take all members of staff to Windermere for the day where they boarded one of the lake steamers for a trip.

To celebrate the re-equipping of the factory after World War Two, Brownhills decided to treat their workforce by way of a trip to Windermere and Blackpool. This included a large sit down meal at Ambleside.

One of the Windermere coaches with in front, left to right: Derek Tinsley, Freda Tinsley, Gladys Mellor, Frank Schofield, Mrs Schofield, Silvia Jackson, ?, ?, Walter Holmes, Bob Mellor.

Unfortunately, the boat had a mechanical problem which delayed matters somewhat! Afterwards a large sit down meal was eaten at a restaurant in Windermere before travelling on to Blackpool for the Illuminations and fish and chips. The mills were all encompassing, friends would

Brownhill's employees in the mill yard, left to right: Bryan Heath, Ronnie Newsome, George Radley, John Gaunt, Ronnie Fisher. Seated, Peter Lawton, circa 1950.

Employees in the mill yard: Joe Price, Bryan Heath, Peter Lawton. Seated, John Woodhead, circa 1950.

Employees in the mill yard, back row, left to right: Leslie Baker, Ann Denton, Freda Derwent, Dillys Rollinson, Christine Armitage.   Middle row: Elaine Fieldsend, Bryan Heath, Jean Hague, Derek Tinsley, Maurice Senior, circa 1950.

John Kenneth Brownhill with his wife, Patricia and their son, Charles, during the 1960's.

Thomas Brownhill = (1827) Elizabeth Wood
1804-1869   1807-1878

| James 1828- | Lister 1830- | Harriet 1832- =Thomas Turton | Joseph 1834- =Fanny ? (emigrated to Australia in 1858) | **John Brownhill** 1836-1903 **of Inkerman, D.Dale founder of Mills** =Jane Mary Schofield 1835-1904 | Jinnie (Jane) 1838- (dnm) | Charles 1840- =Anna Schofield |

| Elizabeth | **James Brownhill** 1863-1942 =**Alice Naylor** 1872-1945 | Jane Anna (Jennie) =Thomas Dewhurst | John Thomas 1868-1906 | 4 | **Charles Henry Brownhill** 1872-1931 =Annie Maud Townsend 1898-1938 | Jack =Edith | Annie | Lucy d.child | Percy **William Wood** | Florence Ethe 1877-1936 =**George Wilfre Naylor** |

| **Major Cecil Naylor Brownhill** 1898-1938 =Eleanor Burman | Marjorie Eileen 1901- =Lt.Col. Montague G.S. Hopson 1893-1974 | Freda = Dr. David Kerr | **John Kenneth Brownhill** 1907-1973 =Patricia Muriel Hopwood 1911-1985 | Peggy = Walter Webster | Isabel 1892- =**Jonas Kenyon** 1890-1978 | Constance 1894-1973 = =1)**George Kitson** =2)Jack Hollingsworth |

| Julianne Eleanor Burman 1927- =Alec Kirkbride | Anthea Louise 1931- =Peter Bennett | Guy J. 1935- =Carol Gunning | Paula M. 1937- =Iain Mitchell | Charles Robert Brownhill 1936- =Elizabeth Mary Abbey 1938- | Barbara | WilliamWood =Audrey **Hinchliffe** | Richard |

| Amanda Jayne 1963- =Denton C Guest 1958- | Lucy Victoria 1965- =William H H Charles 1964- | John Edward 1967- =Louise C Maidens 1966- |

| George D. | Freddie D. | Alice | Harry | Charlotte | Constance |

work together and eat their lunch in the staff canteen. At Christmas, the village band, whose members included many involved with the mills, such as Clifford Horsley, on his cornet, took to the streets playing carols. The mills were the major source of employment, families involved with them expected their offspring to do the same and it would be wrong to ignore the sense of community they created, disputes and problems aside.

Advertisement from the 1972 'Official Guide' to Denby Dale.

JONAS KENYON AND SONS LTD.

The surname, Kenyon, would appear to have originated in Lancashire, probably from the 'Winwick' parish area where there is a 'village of Kenyon' and a 'Kenyon manor'. The name means 'Ennions mound' i.e. a bronze age barrow once stood there. Quite when the family moved into the Cumberworth area is uncertain though a document dated the 19th June 1699 during the reign of William III proves that they had arrived by this time.

The document was an indenture made out between Edward Kenyon of Upper Cumberworth and his younger son, Joshua, a bachelor, also of Upper Cumberworth. Edward sold to his son, for £100 a messuage or tenement, 'now divided and made into two cottages', with adjoining land which were occupied by Ralf Radley and Mathew Wood, also a messuage in Upper Cumberworth which was occupied by William Peace, a close of land called 'Bathroyd Croft' in Over Cumberworth and another 5 closes called 'the two Healey closes', 'rough close', 'horse close', and 'the back three' with all rights and appurtenances. Although the properties were now held by Joshua he still had to pay rent to the Lord of the Manor for them, his mother Alice was also expressly mentioned with regard to her dowry right which was to be null and void. The document was witnessed by Richard Batty, William Kenyon and John Battye.

Edward was born around 1639 at Cumberworth and would have been around 60 years old when the document was drawn up. Although one or two generations are missing it is likely that he was an ancestor of the mill founding family. The first Jonas Kenyon appears in Cumberworth in 1739 when we find him marrying one Sarah Peace, he in turn, had a son, also named Jonas in 1740. This second Jonas appears to have remained in Cumberworth all his life, he married a woman called Lydia in 1767 although her surname may have been Goddard or Hinchcliffe. This second Jonas was involved in the following indenture, dated 1788, coincidentally perhaps? with a William Hinchcliffe:

Made on the 13th of February 1788 during the reign of George III between Jonas Kenyon of Cumberworth, yeoman and William Hinchcliffe of Kirk(burton), clothier. For a rent of 8s 8d per annum, Jonas Kenyon leased and demised to William Hinchcliffe three closes of land called 'Healy closes'. The agreement replaced an existing one which had just expired and ran from the above date for a period of 11 years. The rent was to be paid at the Feast of Pentecost and Saint Parkin in mid-winter, though in case of default of payment, Jonas Kenyon or his heirs were to have the right to re-claim the property.

> *Hinchcliffe was obliged to keep all the fences, hedges, gates and styles in good repair, 'spread on the demised premises all the hay, straw, manure, compost, dung and ashes that shall arise from … the said demised premises'. He was not allowed to cut, fell, lop or head any trees, or plough the land during the last 3 years of the lease (1797–1799). A fine of £3 per acre would be enforced if the condition was not met. The document was witnessed by George Goldthorpe and John Longley.*

Jonas and Lydia had at least two boys, John, born 1777 and Joshua, born 1788, the year the above indenture was created and also the year of the very first Denby Dale pie. It seems inconceivable that a Jonas wasn't also a part of the family but that record has not yet come to light.

John Kenyon and his wife, Sarah, were the parents of the founder of the mill in Denby Dale. Their son, Jonas, was born in 1817, the family increased with the birth of two daughters, Esther and Hannah and another son, James in 1825.

Piggots trade directory lists the following people at Dogley Mill, Fenay Bridge in 1834:

Jonas Kenyon & James Kenyon – woollen and fancy goods manufacturers.
Thomas Kenyon – scribblers and slubbers.
Archibald Kenyon – corn miller and flour dealer.(High Burton)

As the Jonas and James mentioned latterly would have been only 17 and 11 years old respectively at this time it is unlikely that the record refers to them. As Jonas is a family name it is more than likely that it is a branch of the same family, it also proves their links to the textile trade. This could be our missing Jonas. An inspection of Kirkburton churchyard reveals a number of Kenyon graves, each trying to outdo the other in prominence.

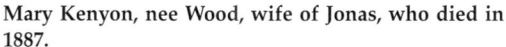

Jonas Kenyon, founder of the mill, who died in 1890.   **Mary Kenyon, nee Wood, wife of Jonas, who died in 1887.**

Jonas Kenyon founded Dearneside mills in 1854 aged 37. Whether he learned his craft at Dogley mills or elsewhere is unknown, but at the age of 37 his knowledge and skill regarding the textile industry was very firmly in place. He also had a young family, he married Mary Wood and by the time the mill opened they had six children, the eldest of which was only 12, five more were to follow in the next eight years. It is interesting to note that yet another member of a Wood family married into a textile manufacturing dynasty.

Few personal details survive regarding Jonas, though the following gives us a small insight:

Jonas Kenyon is said to have made cloth on wet days and to have farmed and played cricket on fine days.

Trade directories dating 1857 and 1866 both note that Jonas was a farmer as well as a manufacturer. He added to the mill site by buying further pieces of land from the Lancashire and Yorkshire railway company in 1861 and orders began to increase , dealings taking place with, amongst others, M. Kaufmann of Bradford and John Wood, a draper of Huddersfield in 1868.

His family grew up, the 1881 census returns listing the family at Bank House:

Name	Age	Place of Birth	Occupation
Jonas Kenyon	64	Cumberworth	Fancy Woollen Manufacturer
Mary Kenyon	59	Cumberworth	Wife
John Kenyon	34	Cumberworth	Fancy Woollen Manufacturer
Arthy Kenyon	27	Denby	Fancy Woollen Manufacturer
Mary E Kenyon	23	Denby	Daughter
Martha E Kenyon	18	Denby	Daughter
Thomas H Kenyon	9	Denby	Scholar
Bertha O W Crimshaw	4	Staningley	Grand daughter

Jonas's eldest son, John, is listed above as still living with his parents, his profession was that of a fancy woollen manufacturer, presumably with his father. Arthy Kenyon, his younger brother

An early twentieth century view of Denby Dale. The mills of Jonas Kenyon are in the centre. The old dam which supplied the corn mill with water, now buried under the Brookside housing estate, can be seen just above the mill buildings.

also became an integral member of the family firm. A testimonial survives regarding another brother, Walter, written by the then vicar of Denby, Rev. Job Johnson:

> June 23rd 1873 – *It gives me very great pleasure to be able to speak very highly of Walter Kenyon and I have known him since a child. He has some very special qualities which will, in my estimation lead to his being a good and clever man. He is very active, very industrious and takes great pains in all his engagements. He has been a pupil of mine for a long time, and I have every reason to expect great things of him. I shall be glad to know that he succeeds in the post he is now applying for.*
>
> *Faithfully yours.*
> *J Johnson*
> *Vicar of Denby*

One brother we have not yet turned to is William Henry, perhaps the most successful of Jonas and Mary's offspring. William Henry was born in 1851 and probably grew up hearing little other than fancy goods manufacturing and the family firm. By the early 1880's he had married, to Mary Ann Smith who went on to bear four children, two of which became fundamental contributors to the firm.

William Henry also made his name in another way. By around 1883 he had begun to develop a system later to become known as 'Kenyon's Undermotion'. The invention provided a *'simple and effective means of changing the order of succession of the healds by means of which a smoother and more regular action is obtained'* in the operation of a weaving loom. The device replaced the older system of springs which were placed under a loom to force down the heald shafts. The heald shafts were used to spread the healds (small rings) which lifted the ends of the yarn up from the warp. Broken shafts were common-place due to the weight being forced down by these springs which cost time and money and reduced production. At some point William Henry obviously

William Henry Kenyon, inventor of the 'undermotion', pictured around 1905.

Patent drawing of a loom incorporating the Kenyon 'undermotion'.

decided that he was fed up with the problems involved and he came up with a solution. The new device was placed under a loom and operated using a number of levers. The heald shafts were connected to these levers which in turn were sprung horizontally rather than vertically. When the heald shaft was forced down the weight was more evenly distributed and the lever was set to a certain position in order to release the shaft without undue strain being applied to the springs. The system was also versatile as it could be adapted to any number of shafts. It eased the load of the dobbie (an attachment to a loom for weaving designs) at the heaviest part of its work, i.e.: in lifting the warp out of the straight line upward, this also enabled the loom to weave uneven treads without any regularity. The weaving loom could now be put to any pattern without altering any of the under gear.

William Henry patented his invention and by 1887 had presented John Beaumont of the Yorkshire College, Leeds with two of his 'heald depressors'. Further tinkering must have gone on as amendments were made to the patent in 1889/91/92 and 1910. The 1889 patent begins thus:

1889 No. 1370
Victoria, By the Grace of God, of the United Kingdom of Great Britain and Ireland, Queen, Defender of the Faith : To all to whom these presents shall come, Greeting:

Whereas – *William Henry Kenyon of Denby Dale near Huddersfield, Yorkshire, Machine Maker*, hath represented unto us that he is in possession of an invitation *for 'An improved arrangement of levers in Kenyon's undermotion for operating the healds of looms*. That he is the true and first inventor thereof and that the same is not in use by any other person to the best of his knowledge and belief.

The machine was manufactured by William Arthur and David Crabtree, loom makers of Shipley from late December 1892. Testimonials dating back to 1888 from manufacturers in Bradford, Farsley and Halifax bear witness to the resounding success of the machine.

Whilst all this was going on the mill was steadily going about its own business. Jonas Kenyon lived to see his son's invention, but only just, he died in 1890, Mary, his wife having preceded him three years before. William Henry became Chairman and Managing Director and lived at Bank House on Bank Lane in Denby Dale in the shadow of the railway viaduct. Arthy became Managing Director, he lived at Bank House though around the time of the first world war he moved to Ashfield, also known as Ashdene and previously called Wall Royd. A son, born to William Henry in 1890 was named Jonas, keeping up the family tradition and supplying the company with its future Chairman and Managing Director.

In 1903 the firm submitted a scheme to the Lancashire and Yorkshire bank which eventually resulted in the company becoming a limited enterprise. The statement of assets and liabilities describes the basis of the purchase of Jonas Kenyon & Sons by Jonas Kenyon & Sons Ltd.

The company also continued to buy land and property in and around the village. In 1910 they purchased from Duncan Alistair McGregor and Percy Goodall Norton (the trustees of the deceased Walter Norton) and Charles Ernest Graham Norton property to the value of £195. 15s. Sometime prior to 1927 they had also acquired Lowfield House at the bottom of Miller Hill, though they sold it this year to Hilda Thorpe. They also owned some fields and a copse adjoining Manor Farm in Upper Denby which were let out to farmer, Math Webster in 1926 at £1 per annum. The document was signed by Jonas and Arthy Kenyon as Directors and Walter

The family of William Henry Kenyon, circa 1915. Back row, left to right: Walter Kenyon, Wilson Kenyon, Jonas Kenyon, James Kenyon, William Henry Kenyon. Seated: Ada Rosa, wife of Walter, Harriet Smith, next to her daughter, Mary Ann, the wife of William Henry and Clare, wife of James.

Kenyon, company secretary. Math had an option to buy the land but does not seem to have ever taken it up. A letter from Dransfield & Hodgkinson, solicitors dated 1966 took the opinion that the option to buy was now over and the agreement worthless due to Math's death. The company also owned land at Miller Hill in Denby Dale, behind the Salvation Army Hall. In 1968 it was proposed that a recreation ground for children might be built here but little came of the matter.

Interaction with the other local mill owners was inevitable, much of the property and land bought by the mill owners was acquired in order to secure water rights. In 1921, the Directors of Kenyon's reached agreement with Sir James Peace Hinchliffe, on behalf of Z. Hinchliffe & Sons regarding Bank Lane stream and water rights in general within the village.

William Henry Kenyon, as with numerous other mill owners already discussed, was involved with various local bodies, including the Wesleyan Methodist Council, and of course with local politics. The following document dates to 1904 and illustrates his popularity:

Urban District Council of Denby & Cumberworth
Election of Urban District Councillors for the above named District.

I the undersigned being the returning officer at the poll for the electors of Urban District Councillors for the said district held on the 26th day of March 1904 do hereby give notice that the number of votes recorded for each candidate at the election is as follows:

Kenyon, William Henry	159
Mathews T D	157
Cooke, Sam	154
Micklethwaite, Jno.	138

Taglis, Romeo Edwin   95
Hollingworth, Job   94

And I hereby declare the said Wm. Hy. Kenyon, T. D. Mathews, Sam Cooke and John Micklethwaite are duly elected councillors for the said district.

Dated this 26th day of March 1904

Signed : Wilfred Barnes – Returning Officer.

Returned again in 1907 (and presumably from then on), the first hint of trouble brewing came in the form of H. Grayson, T W Noble and C Senior. They issued a printed flyer 'To the Electors of the Denby Dale Ward'. In it they suggest that the water arrangements in the village had been subject to private interest and also those concerning the sewerage systems. They said that they stood for the workers and wanted to lower the rates.

William Henry, along with John Hinchliffe and Tucket Mathews issued an election poster shortly after, indignant and offended and accusing Grayson, Noble and Senior of *'inaccurate and misleading statements'*. Undeterred, William Henry continued his presence on the local board until at least 1913 and perhaps even up to his death in 1923 aged 72. He was outlived by his wife, Mary Ann by 37 years, an extraordinary achievement. She lived to be 103 years old and died in 1960, and would have known company founder, Jonas , personally and bridged the gap to the new generations.

It is interesting to note the total wages paid out by the company in 1898. An insurance policy for workmen's compensation, at a premium of £5 4s, noted that 80 employees earned a total of £3200 per annum between them. This was split into Managers/Clerks and Non-manual £200, and, Foreman/Workmen directly employed £3000.

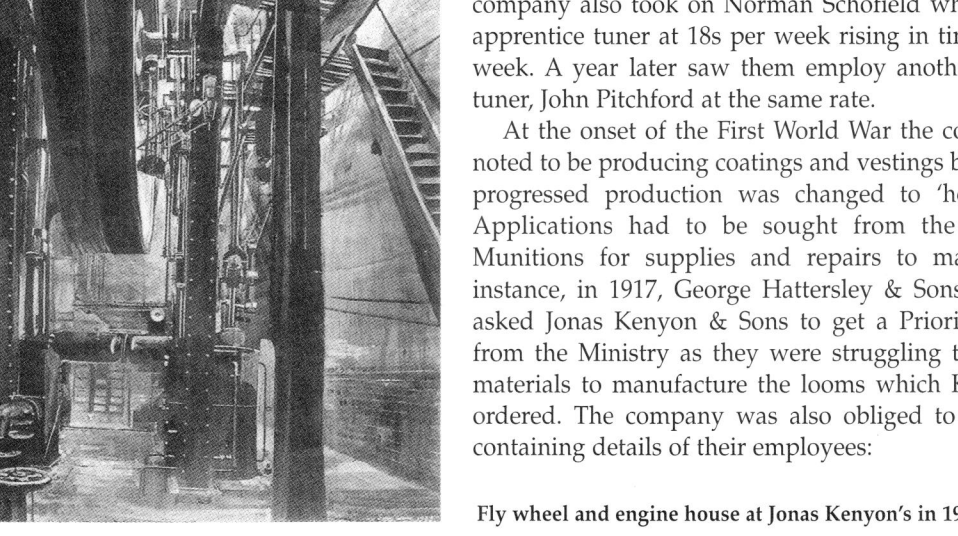

An agreement of 1906 saw the company employ Alexander Lees Small as a designer and assistant in general management at £300 per annum. The agreement was altered slightly in 1909 and endorsed to the effect that his salary was to reduce to £252 per annum in 1913. In 1914 the company also took on Norman Schofield who became an apprentice tuner at 18s per week rising in time to 21s per week. A year later saw them employ another apprentice tuner, John Pitchford at the same rate.

At the onset of the First World War the company were noted to be producing coatings and vestings but as the war progressed production was changed to 'hospital blue'. Applications had to be sought from the Ministry of Munitions for supplies and repairs to machinery. For instance, in 1917, George Hattersley & Sons of Keighley asked Jonas Kenyon & Sons to get a Priority Certificate from the Ministry as they were struggling to obtain raw materials to manufacture the looms which Kenyon's had ordered. The company was also obliged to fill in forms containing details of their employees:

Fly wheel and engine house at Jonas Kenyon's in 1972.

Return of all males over military age employed by Jonas Kenyon & Sons Ltd., Denby Dale: (all at Denby Dale unless stated).

Name	Address	Age	Occupation	Date of Birth
Thomas Blacker	High St.	66	Stoker	14 July 1851
Wright Beaumont	Briar Field.	45	Mechanic	12 Nov. 1871
George Shaw	Rock House, Upper Denby	47	Labourer	16 April 1869
Jas. Robert Waldie	Denby	50	Foreman Dyer	13 May 1867
William Heeley	Spring Bank	42	Miller Labourer	20 Nov. 1874
James Dyson	Norman Rd.	43	Dyers Labourer	3 May 1874
George Wood	Sunny Bank	59	Dyers Labourer	1 Nov. 1857
Charles Edward Firth	Sunny Bank	57	Shed Foreman	28 Feb. 1859
Arthur Schofield	Sunny Bank	45	Foreman Tuner	25 March 1872
George Henry Pell	Kitchenroyd	48	Healder & Beams	9 July 1869
Smith Kenyon	High Street	59	Twister	13 Feb. 1858
William Henry Kenyon	Bank House	65	Managing Director	2 June 1851
Arthy Kenyon	Ashfield	63	Managing Director	2 Dec. 1853
Charles K. Hanwell	Acacia Villa, Denby	61	Book-keeper	7 Nov. 1855
James Crossland	Cliffe Style	50	Pattern Weaver	31 March 1866
Frank Newsome	Norman Road	66	Pattern Weaver	2 July 1850
John Gaunt	Ratten Row, Denby	64	Pattern Weaver	20 Aug. 1852
Charles Booth	Revell Bottom	59	Labourer	9 Jan. 1858
George Wood	Lower Cumberworth	68	Hand loom weaver	Not noted
William Haigh	Dearne Terrace	54	Dyers Labourer	Not noted
R. Clarke	Denby Dale	68	Dyers Labourer	Not noted
W H West	Denby Dale	60	Labourer	Not noted
Joe Roebuck	Denby Dale	57	Not noted	Not noted

(NB: lines were drawn through the entries for George Shaw, George Wood and Charles K Hanwell – I am unaware of the reasons for this).

Defence of the Realm, Regulation 41a – Statement of all male employees of 16 years of age or over – Jonas Kenyon & Sons Ltd., Denby Dale – worsted manufacturers – 4th June 1918:

Name	Address	Marital status	Age	Date engaged by Kenyon's	Previous occupation (if engaged since Aug.1914)	Now employed as a –	Work usually employed upon
Blake J	D.Dale	Married	66	1900		Stoker	Stoker
Beaumont W	D.Dale	Single	45	1887		Mechanic	Mechanic
Heeley James	Commercial Rd. Skelmanthorpe	Married	40	1890		Foreman	Twisting Foreman
Watson Thos. W.	Commercial Rd. Skelmanthorpe	Married	36	1898		Presser	Presser
Peace Edward	Denby	Single	16	1915		Tenterer	Tenterer
Holdsworth H	D. Dale	Single	16	1915		Assistant tenterer	Assistant tenterer
Waldie J R	Denby	Married	51	1882		Foreman Dyer	Foreman Dyer
Heeley Wm.	D. Dale	Married	43	1891		Miller & Scourer	Miller & Scourer
Haigh Wm.	D.Dale	Married	54	1917	Cutter	Dyers Labourer	Dyers Labourer
Dyson James	D.Dale	Married	44	1888		Dyers Labourer	Dyers Labourer
Firth Chas.	D. Dale	Married	59	1885		Shed Foreman	Shed Foreman

Schofield Arthur	D. Dale	Married	46	1888		Foreman Tuner	Foreman Tuner	
Kenyon Jonas	D. Dale	Married	27	1907		Mill Manager	Mill Manager	
Pell G H	Kitchen-royd	Married	48	1900		Healders Beamer	Beamer	
Clarke Robert	D. Dale	Married	68	1917	Dyers Labourer	Dyers labourer	Dyers labourer	
Kenyon Smith	D. Dale	Married	60	1904		Twister	Twister	
Peace Wm.	D. Dale	Married	65	1918	Clay Grinder	Dyers Labourer	Dyers Labourer	
West W H	D. Dale	Married	61	1917	Labourer	Labourer	Labourer	
Turton Arthur	D. Dale	Married	41	1917	Weaver	Loom Tuner	Loom Tuning	
Kenyon Wm. Hy.	D. Dale	Married	67			Chairman & Director		
Gaunt John	Denby	Married	65	1894	Handloom weaver	Handloom weaver	Weaving	
Newsome Frank	D. Dale	Married	67	1893	Twister	Twister	Twister	
Crossland James	D. Dale	Single	52	1894	Shed Keeper	Shed Keeper	Shed Keeper	
Kenyon Arthy	D. Dale	Married	64			Director		
Booth Charles	D. Dale	Married	59	1914	Labourer	Labourer		
Roebuck Joe	Denby	Married	57	1917	Carter	Carter	Carter	
Hinchliffe J	D, Dale	Married	68	1917	Odd jobs	Odd jobs	Odd jobs	
Firth Ben	D. Dale	Single						
Wood George	Lower Cumberworth	Single	71	1898		Hand loom weaver	Hand loom weaver	
Heywood F	Upper Cumberworth	Single	16	1918	Bottom twister	Assistant Scourer	Scouring	
Horn H? or L	Birdsedge	Single	16	1917	Gardener	Assistant	Assistant	

During World War One the following men employed by Kenyon's saw service:

Arnold Marsden – Corporal 23197, RAF, 30 Squad, G Flight, service length – 2 years 10 months, in action in Mesopotamia. (Mechanic at the mill).

Wilfred Deacon – Gunner 239064, 885 Battery, service length - 4 years 4 months, Barracks, Kildare, Ireland. (Mill hand).

John Wm. Marsden – Gunner 188874, Royal G A, service length – 11 months, Shoreham by the Sea. (Cloth finisher).

Norman Schofield – Private 99750, 2/7 Kings Liverpool, service length – 18 months, serving hospital. (Bower Loom Tuner).

The latter is the same Norman Schofield we noted being apprenticed as a tuner in 1914.

Jonas Kenyon became a director of the company in 1918 aged 28, he married Isabel Wood, the daughter of William Wood and Lucy Brownhill thereby extending his connections with the leading families in the district. The family lived firstly, at Wall Royd but in the early 1920's moved to Broad Royd on the Barnsley road. This had been the home of Isabel's father, William Wood, who in turn moved into Wall Royd. Around 1930 William Wood moved to viaduct house, next to Broad Royd. As an aside, William Wood was the local truancy inspector! Jonas also inherited his father's desire for local government responsibilities. He first became a member of the Denby & Cumberworth Urban District Council in 1932 and remained until 1938 when reorganisation took place and the body became Denby Dale Urban District Council. Jonas remained on this committee from 1938 until 1974, a phenomenal length of service. He always stood as an Independent, his election leaflet in 1947 stated that he was opposed to party politics in Urban District Council affairs. The serving members of the council in 1959 were:

The family of Jonas Kenyon, circa 1938. Back, left to right: Jonas Kenyon and his wife, Isabel. Seated: William Wood Kenyon, Mary Ann Kenyon, (widow of inventor William Henry), Barbara Kenyon, Lucy Wood, the daughter of Charles Brownhill (brother of founder of Brownhills, John), James Richard Kenyon.

	First Elected		First Elected
Herbert Fox JP (Chairman)	1946	Norman Ibbotson	1938
Clifford Stephenson (Vice-Chairman)	1947	Joseph H Kaye	1948
Reginald Beever	1957	**Jonas Kenyon**	**1938**
George V Booth	1958	Mrs. Marjorie Lawton	1958
William Brett	1953	Cecil H Moxon	1938
H S Charlesworth	1953	William J Netherwood	1958
Arnold Fisher	1957	John Schofield	1954
Frederick Gilbert	1957	Victor Senior	1955
George A Heywood	1958	Harry Shaw	1948
James Hibbert JP	1946	Ronald D Walton	1956

The above list is taken from the village guide produced that year which makes the following note regarding Kenyon's:

the production was mainly trouserings and fancy waistcoatings but has changed over the years to the best quality worsted cloths for mens and ladies wear, both for home and export.

The Yorkshire Textile Directory of 1930 lists the firms interests as follows:

botany serges, indigo and colours, dress suiting and trouserings, white worsted serges, plain and fancy gaberdines, repps, tricotines, plain and fancy in white and colours, fancy vestings in woollen, worsted silk and mercerised cotton.

The 1959 guide contains an advertisement for the company and lists them as 'worsted manufacturers': this side of the business came to predominate all others by the 1970's.

Jonas and his brother, Walter Harold, were left very much in charge of company affairs after the death of Arthy Kenyon in 1934, though their sons were being groomed to enter the family business.

In 1964, Jonas was given the honour of making the ceremonial first cut into the Denby Dale pie of that year, following in the footsteps of his father in law, William Wood who had undertaken that responsibility on the previous occasion in 1928. He also opened the converted Birk Wood House in the village in 1972, which had been refurbished and adapted into a village hall, to become known as the Pie Hall. At the age of 84, Jonas was awarded the MBE for his services to the local council, the year in which he finally called it a day and retired from his post. Only one year before he died, Jonas Kenyon and Sons went into voluntary liquidation and closed in 1977.

The mill buildings were let out for a short time as industrial units before being sold to property developers. The old mill buildings were demolished and replaced by a housing estate, named 'Kenyon Bank' as a tribute to the family.

Jonas Kenyon, circa 1965.

The site of Dearneside mills, after demolition, it is now occupied by the 'Kenyon Bank' housing estate.

Telephone : SKELMANTHORPE 3201 (4 lines)
Telegrams :   Telex :
Kenyons Denby-Dale   51458 Chamcom Huddersfield

Cloth by Kenyon

Jonas Kenyon & Sons Ltd.

Fine Worsted Manufacturers

Established over a Century

Denby Dale, Huddersfield HD8 8TW
England

London Office :
73 Golden House, Gt. Pulteney Street, W1R 3DD
Telephone : 01-734 5569

Advertisement from the 1972 'Official Guide' to Denby Dale.

Genealogical Table of the Kenyon family
(bold type indicates involvement with the mill)

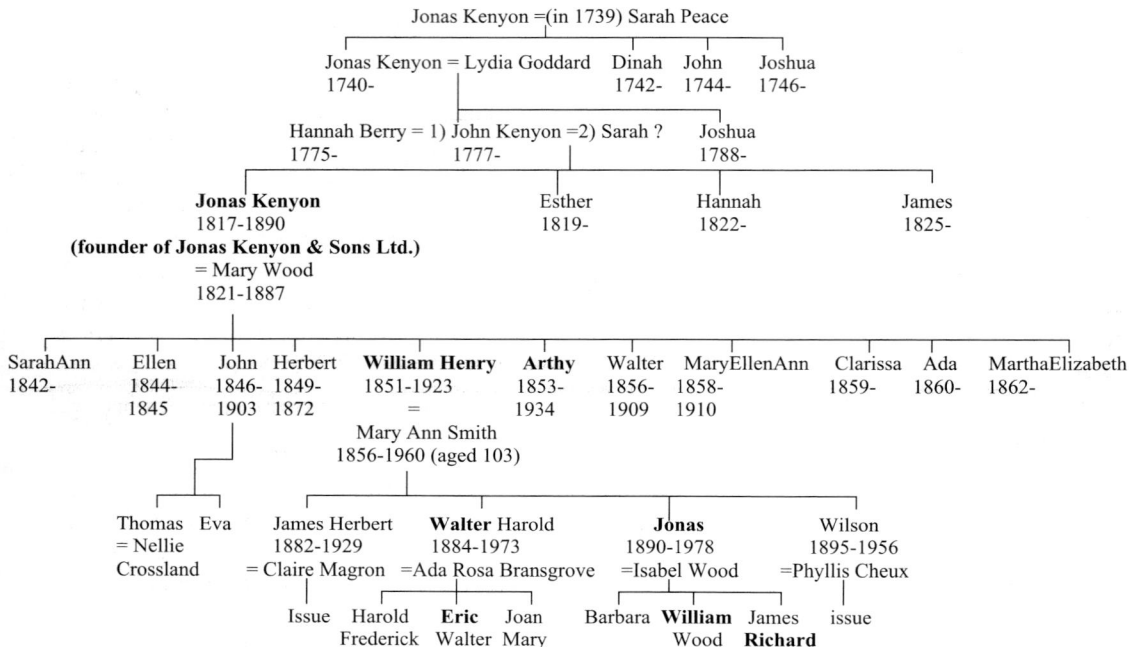

THE NORTON FAMILY

The founding father of this dynasty was Benjamin Norton who was born in 1770. He lived at High Hoyland but worked as a clothier at Cuttlehirst in what is today, Scissett. Although he undertook weaving duties himself he also supplied out weavers with the raw materials to produce finished goods which he in turn sold on. Thomas married Elizabeth Naylor and had seven children. Two of these, in particular, followed in their father's footsteps, Joseph and George.

Joseph purchased premises at Highbridge which included a corn mill and a scribbling and carding mill in 1825, he also acquired much of the adjacent land, which, after development, became the nucleus of the village of Scissett.

The mill has a history dating back to Adam de Holland's time (1246) and is mentioned in a lease of land dated 1598 by Hamnet and Robert Hide of Northbury to George Green, millwright and Peter Hawksworth. In 1657 Edward Hyde leased Highbridge corn mill to Thomas Walker. Further to this, Robert Blackburn of Papist Hall, Lower Denby and Thomas Morehouse, tanner were allowed to retrieve bark in Highbridge wood.

Joseph utilised the power of the River Dearne to drive scribbling and fulling machines though at this time continued his business on similar lines to his fathers methods. He grew dissatisfied over time at the inconvenience of having to trail raw materials and finished goods back and forth from his weavers spread in and around the upland areas of the district. His answer to the problem was to build a row of houses, known as the 'Fleet' at the bottom of Busker Lane to house some of these out workers. The buildings were designed with people in mind, each had its own well and access for goods to be moved was paramount, the looms were housed in the upper storey's where large sash windows provided ample light.

The formal agreement and permission for a turnpike road to be built in 1825 facilitated good communications and delivery routes, indeed one of the toll bars was situated at Highbridge, and Joseph wasted no time in becoming a shareholder in the enterprise. He did, however, fall foul of it as a dispute arose between him and the trust regarding his practice of tipping ashes (spent coal, probably used for steam power in the mill) at Kitchenroyd. Suddenly he was asked to pay to do something he had previously taken for granted, needless to say – he wasn't happy.

The row of houses at Busker was supposed to be the catalyst for many more but as trade and profits fluctuated the scheme was abandoned, and land was sold to other developers. It was between the 1840's and 1870's that the village of Scissett was created, largely around Norton's mills, which themselves had expanded towards Wood Street and by now only a little weaving was actually performed off the premises. It was Joseph who ran the Highbridge mill site, but he had long since been joined by his brother George who ran the mill across the road known as Cuttlehirst.

As the business developed so did the family. Joseph was first married in 1822 to Jane Lee, who bore him seven children, including Walter and Benjamin, who was the last born in 1839. His second marriage, to Emmeline Graham produced a further three offspring, including Charles Ernest Graham Norton a future Brigadier General who lived much of his life at 73 Park Street, London and who played a major roll in the affairs of the family up until his death in 1953.

Joseph was also the moving force behind the erection of a church at Scissett, his ambitions being to extend the small community which he had created and style himself as a squire and a patron of the church. In 1838 he purchased a plot of land from Colonel Beaumont of Bretton Hall who at the time was in need of ready cash. The church was duly built and consecrated in 1839 by Bishop Longley. The new church was to be regarded as a district chapel to Emley church and the patron of the living was Colonel Beaumont. The vicar of Emley, Robert Pym, was furious, claiming that the church had been illegally erected and that he would lose fees for weddings and baptisms. In 1854 the Norton family bought the

Portrait of George Norton, who died in 1865, which still hangs in the entrance lobby of the home he built, Bagden Hall.

advowson from the Beaumont's, and became patrons and appointed the incumbents as Joseph had originally wished. The patronage is today in the hands of the Bishop of Wakefield.

Meanwhile, George had married Betty Race who bore him eight children, the last of whom, Thomas, was born in 1846. George's marriage led to him having an interest in Dudfleet mills, Horbury where the family of Betty had a scribbling and fulling business, though it was eventually sold in 1905 by George's heirs. He was also noted to be a stone merchant in 1857.

William, the eldest brother of Joseph and George, had initially been a partner of Joseph's, a valuation for insurance purposes dated 1836 noted that the fixed capital for William and Joseph Norton's woollen mill was £500. Soon afterwards William decided to break away and built Spring Grove mill in Clayton West. Here he had intended to operate using a new French invention known as the Jacquard, which was capable of weaving just about anything. Unfortunately, a major slump hit the industry at this time and his business failed, the property passing to another local manufacturer, R Beanland & Co. William left the area and found employment in Almondbury but his was a rare failure in this successful family.

As we have already noted, the plug rioters were active in the district and did not neglect the activities of the Norton brothers. On 17 August 1842 a 'wild and angry mob' , as described by one witness, arrived in Skelmanthorpe from the Huddersfield area. They marched on Highbridge mill, but cavalry had been deployed in front of the warehouse and across the mill gate. The Riot Act was read and transportation threatened, this seemed to do the trick as the mob dispersed shortly after.

In 1851 Joseph Norton exhibited summer shawls, cloaks, waistcoats, table covers, alpaca gloves and winter woollen shawls at the Great Exhibition held in London's Hyde Park between

Nortonthorpe mills, Scissett, looking down towards Cuttlehirst, circa 1930's. *Old Barnsley*

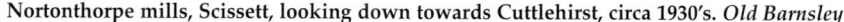

Bagden Hall, during the early twentieth century. *Old Barnsley*

May and October. The brainchild of Prince Albert, it took place in a newly constructed 'Crystal Palace'. The 13,000 exhibits celebrated Britains industrial ascendancy.

Only a year later disaster beset the brothers when a serious fire broke out at Highbridge mill in 1852, it gutted the building but true to form, rebuilding took place the resulting mill complex being christened Nortonthorpe. Around this period the firm employed approximately 110 people who worked largely in the fancy waistcoating trade.

Joseph Norton retired from the firm in 1863, though a year later he joined the newly formed Skelmanthorpe Local Board – as Chairman. In 1864 the board agreed that he could divert a footpath from Busker to Highbridge which ran through his grounds, with a new footpath running in a direct line between the latter which still survives known as 'wrapping nick'. Joseph's home, created out of the profits of his labour was Nortonthorpe Hall where he lived until his death in 1874. His brother George, died in 1865 aged only 59, though he too had built

Bagden Hall, during the early twentieth century.

Rockwood House, Denby Dale, built by Walter Norton in 1870, pictured around 1900.

his own residence, Bagden Hall, both buildings being of the same plan and specification. There is some confusion as to the year both were built. Some historians place George Norton at 64 years old when he built Bagden Hall, but this would mean that he barely lived to use it. The West Yorkshire Archive service suggest a date of the 1840's for construction of both. This would seem more likely, perhaps with later additions by Thomas and Benjamin Norton at about the same time Walter was building Rockwood House, Denby Dale in 1870.

The company was now run under the name of Norton Brothers & Co by Joseph's sons, Walter and Benjamin, and George's son, Thomas.

As we have noted, Walter built himself a home in Denby Dale in 1870 called Rockwood House, prior to this he had lived at Highfield House in Denby Dale. This was probably on land that he had recently bought from the Bosville estate at Gunthwaite as this was the year he purchased the manor of Denby from them. He married his cousin, Elizabeth Norton, daughter of his Uncle George but there were no children. Walter also became a Justice of the Peace and founded the Rockwood Harriers Hunt in 1868, keeping the hounds at his home until 1896.

Walter was a keen supporter of the church. So much so that when the rectory of Cumberworth seemed destined to be reduced to a perpetual curacy in 1881 he wrote a letter of support for the Reverend John Phillips Dickson, at that time, curate of Rashcliffe, who had been invited to take up the vacant post at Cumberworth by its people. Other letters were sent by William Kenyon and Scholefield & Co. of Nortonthorpe mills urging W B Beaumont of Bretton Hall who held the advowson, to hand over the living to the Bishop of Ripon in order to maintain the rectory. Walter and his contemporary's were successful and a new rectory was built at the turn of the nineteenth century. Walter was also disturbed by the rapid growth of the Methodist movement in Denby Dale. He donated a plot of land on Bank Lane in the village and appointed a body of trustees in

1893 to oversee and run a church, built of tin, and dedicated to the Holy Trinity, which was served by the assistant curate of Cumberworth. This iron structure was replaced by the present stone construction in 1939 and the old tin church was converted into a church hall though this was later destroyed by fire.

Walter was also an admirer of Rev. Job Johnson, the vicar of Upper Denby and can be found heading the list of donors upon Johnson's retirement in 1887:

Walter Norton Esq. £25	Harry Heath 10s	C Kilner 10s
W S Stanhope Esq. £20	Alfred Goodison 10s	Hy. H Peace 10s
Tho. Norton Esq. £10	John Micklethwaite 10s	Beanland & Co £5
J C Milner Esq. (Thurlston) £10	Joseph Gaunt 5s	Mr B Armitage (Scissett) £2
Rev. Gamaliel Milner £5	John Haigh 4s	G Stringer 10s
Mrs. Clarke (Noblethorpe) £5		
A E Bosville Esq. £5		
David Tyas 3s	Benj. Tickhill 5s	
Joshua Kaye (Dean Hill) £5	James Waldie 2s 6d	George Brook (Scissett) 10s
Mr Thomas Milnes (NetherEnd) £2	James Slater 2s 6d	Charles Townend 2s
Mr E Smithson £1	Thos. Atkinson 2s 6d	John Heath 10s
Thos. Lockwood (Cawth) £1	John Horn 2s 6d	Joseph Barraclough 5s
Henry Lockwood £1	Elijah Hudson 2s 6d	Robinson J C 3s
John Wood (NetherEnd) £2	George Broadhead 5s	George Gaunt 2s
Jonas Kenyon & Sons £2 10s	Joseph Birks (Penistone) 2s 6d	Luther Hanwell 1s
Mr Ingham Milnes £2	James Hanson (D. Dale) 5s	Job Ward 1s
Mrs Sarah Firth £3	Mrs Jane Horn 5s	Geo. Thackray 6d
A Friend 10s	E Turner 1s	Mrs Hey. Tinker (Cumb) £1
Mrs Broadhead £1	E Smith 1s	A Friend 2s 4d
Mr John Walshaw 5s	Mr Wm. Laycock Gent. 5s	Wm. Wood 10s
Mr Hy. Knowles (Ing.) 10s	Wm. Fish 2s 6d	B Mosley 5s
John Jackson 10s	Rich'd Milnes 2s 6d	A Friend (Mother ?) 10s
Mrs Sarah Roebuck 10s	Thos. Smith 2s 6d	A Friend (B??) 10s
Mr Wm. Horn 10s	Benj. Fish 5s	G H Green 5s
Thos. Holmes 10s	John Haigh 2s 6d	Mr Brownhill 10s
Jas. Stafford 5s	Alfred Gaunt 2s 6d	Arthur Dickson £1
John Burditt 2s	Robert Hirst £1	Mr Moore 10s
Frank Burdett 2s	A Friend 2s 6d	Frank Newsome 5s
Taylor Hanson 5s	Mr John Ellis 2s 6d	J Holmes 2s
Richard Beaver 5s	C Scofield 2s 6d	A Friend 5s
Wm. Town 10s	Wm. Senior 2s 6d	Mrs M A Wood (Post Office) 2s 6d
Alfred Markly Esq. £10	J H B 10s	G Wm. Morton 2s 6d
John Douse £1	J C Cockcroft 2s 6d	
Mr R Charlesworth (Cawth) 5s	Joseph Hudson (Nether Mill) 10s	
Arthur Priest 10s	C Hargreaves 10s	
Total £140 12s 6d		

Job Johnson left the vicarage in 1887 giving way to A B Orr who lasted until 1894.
Note that C Hargreaves mentioned was the schoolmaster at the time.
The booklet used to record the donations was written by John Heath in 1887.

One can only wonder as to what Walter's political leanings were, though he may well have agreed with Rev. Johnson who wrote a letter to the *Yorkshire Post* in 1830.

Rev. Job Johnson's Letter to the Yorkshire Post December 30th 1880.

Sir,

I am obliged at length to confess that my indignation has become master of my patience, which has long thriven to bear with the feebleness and imbecilic indifference of our gracious Queen's present advisers (unfortunately for this country) called the Government in the matter of the management, both at home and abroad (but especially in Ireland) of our public affairs.

Had Lord Beaconsfield been in office, the proper and only right step would long ago have been taken and murder, misrule and defiance of law in open day would not have been allowed to take place – fright and fear would not have been for weeks upon the loyal and peaceable inhabitants of the land.

Messrs. Parnell & Co. would long ago have been called to account for the treason they have been allowed so long to utter and the scandal of such a sight in view of the whole world would not have been heaped upon our beloved Sovereign and her empire to gratify the weakness and ignorance of her so called ministers.

I may be permitted, I hope, to say that I am more than astonished that the inhabitants (especially the common-sense working men) of our large towns have not ere this, risen en-masse and at once expressed their due sense of shame and righteous anger at such child play and said that these things should be so, no longer; and further, that Messrs. Bright and Chamberlain are not either the sound or true exponents of public opinion in this great country in matters so all-important to the welfare of the empire of Queen Victoria.

Dec. 28/80 J Johnson-Vicar of Denby

Walter Norton died in 1909 after which Rockwood House was taken over by Duncan Alistair MacGregor, who had been the medical officer of health for the area since 1878. Mr McGregor had married the daughter of Walter's sister, Clara Christiana and so was family. Prior to this he had lived at Riding Wood Lodge, Clayton West. MacGregor's duties and responsibilities were considerable in 1901 he was described thus:

Portrait of a youthful Thomas Norton, astride his horse, perhaps Pippin or Fanny. Bagden Hall can be seen at the bottom right of the picture.

Duncan Alistair MacGregor, MB, CM Edin., Surgeon, Medical Officer of Health and Public Vaccinator Denby District, Penistone Union and Medical Officer of Health for Clayton West, Cumberworth, Denby, Gunthwaite, Ingbirchworth and Shelley Urban District Councils.

Walter Norton owned a large amount of land which included woodlands at Upper Dearne some parts of which he developed into a kind of parkland. We will return to this in a later chapter.

Benjamin married Catherine Beckett and took over at Nortonthorpe after his father's death in 1874, as well as the company business he also held shares in the railway company, from 1874–98, most likely inherited from his father, and held land in Rhodesia. The famous Cecil Rhodes (1853–1902) had made his fortune in the diamond fields here in 1871 and by 1880 had founded the De Beers diamond company, he had moved into gold by 1887. It is interesting to note that Benjamin's step brother, Joseph (brother of Charles Ernest Graham) had dealings with Southern Rhodesia. Joseph Norton married Caroline Driffield in 1893 and the couple had a daughter, Dorothy Katherine. They lived at Pledwick House, Wakefield but ran into disaster in Rhodesia in 1896, probably out there on family business, when all three were killed. These lands would appear to have been the ones held by Benjamin in the years prior to his death in 1898. Whether the Nortons had speculated at the same time as Rhodes or had jumped on the bandwagon is uncertain. Pledwick House was sold in 1907. Nortonthorpe Hall was taken over by Benjamin's daughter, Rosalie Ann and her husband, Captain Thomas St John Belbin who were succeeded by their son, Cecil Norton Belbin. A statutory declaration in 1942 made by Percy Goodall Norton informs us that from this time it was to be used as a remand home.

Thomas Norton became a Justice of the Peace, a CBE and a Doctor of Letters. He married twice, first to Alice Ada by whom he had three children, the eldest, George Herbert went on to play a prominent roll in the company's fortunes. His younger brother was Percy Goodall Norton who became a solicitor and handled much of the families affairs in the future. When Alice Ada died, in 1897 Thomas gave Denby church a new East window dedicated to her memory. It showed Christ on the cross with the virgin Mary on the left panel and St. John on the right. Thomas's second marriage was to Jessie Jane Jardine who was awarded the MBE. He lived at Bagden Hall all his life, though he rented out Bagden Lodge, at first to George Turton until he died in 1865 and then to an old friend, John Kenworthy, a woolsorter who remained here until his death in 1887. It was also in 1887 that Thomas, in co-operation with Joseph Radcliffe of Rudding Park conveyed to Skelmanthorpe Local Board enough land to build a public cemetery, this was consecrated a year later. In 1898, Thomas bought Storthes Hall for £49,500. Previously occupied by Joseph Armitage, a member of the mill owning Milnsbridge family who had moved here a year before, the mansion and estate were sold by Charles Horsfall to Thomas, though he appears to have been acting in co-operation with the West Riding County Council to whom he immediately sold it on. The council then adapted the

The Boathouse in the grounds of Bagden Hall.

building and extended it to create a mental hospital which operated for over 80 years before it was closed down and the buildings and land were acquired by Huddersfield University. Thomas also figured prominently in local politics. The trade directory of 1901 notes the following members of the local board:

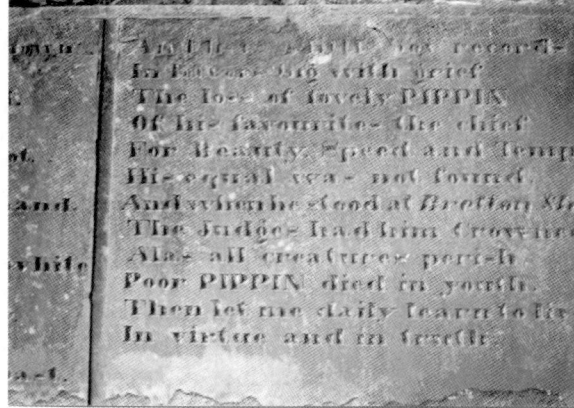

Memorials to two favoured Norton family horses, resting against the walls of the boathouse in the grounds of Bagden Hall.

These two portraits hang in the entrance hall at Bagden Hall. They are reputed to be Alice Ada and Jessie Jane Jardine, the two wives of Thomas Norton. The style of dress in the left hand photograph might suggest that this lady is in fact, Betty Race, wife of George and that the portrait was painted contemporaneously with that of George.

Chairman – Thomas Norton JP
Vice Chairman – John Hinchliffe
Retire April 1902, John Hinchliffe & William Herbert Wood
Retire April 1903, John Brownhill JP & Thomas Norton
Retire April 1904, Tom Duckett Mathews & Rev. Romeo Edwin Taglis

The acquisition of land and buildings was a big factor in Thomas's life. For instance, in 1916 he purchased Wheatley Hill farm. This was an ancient property, first noted in 1200 when it was in the possession of Robert de Wetelai. The following centuries saw the lands pass to the de Denby and Burdet families and eventually to the Nevile's during the Wars of the Roses. During the later Tudor period the house was rebuilt and passed in 1585 to the Hawksworth family. In 1689 the farm was sold to the Rhodes family of Flockton and in 1712 it was bought by William Spencer of Cannon Hall for £1175. When the Bagden estates were sold the farm was acquired by the Brook family.

In 1899 in order to deal with the problem of sanitation, Thomas reported to the UDC that the West Riding Rivers Board had complained about the quantity of raw sewage that was entering the River Dearne. Denby and Cumberworth UDC's then proposed to build a sewage works for the area. Skelmanthorpe expressed a desire to join in but Clayton West did not. It was urgent that matters were quickly dealt with, at the time there were several cases of typhoid in Lower Cumberworth. Thomas Norton said that *'Clayton West had taken the dog in the manger attitude to this for they would not have part with Denby and Cumberworth at any price'.* He also offended Skelmanthorpe by saying that Denby Dale was a prosperous village whereas Skelmanthorpe was slowly dying, for there had been no development in the place for more than 12 years.

Thomas Norton JP, DL, CBE, pictured around 1910.

Skelmanthorpe withdrew it's support for the scheme so Denby and Cumberworth went ahead on their own.

On 8th April 1933 Thomas presided over the opening ceremony of a Sunday School at Miller Hill Methodist church in Denby Dale. He did this in co-operation with James Brownhill of Oakfield, Denby Dale, who opened the school and was presented with the key of the door by the architect, Mr C Moxon of Clayton West. Both men were presented with buttonholes by junior scholars.

As with all the other local industrialists, Thomas lived a very active life up until his death in 1935. His life was commemorated by his family who donated a new East window to High Hoyland church. One obituary gives us the following details of his life. Thomas was appointed a Magistrate in 1876, he retired from the family business around 1895. He was a Deputy Lieutenant for the County and frequently sat at Quarter Sessions both at Wakefield and Leeds. In earlier days, to support his position as a Magistrate he had

Thomas Norton JP, DL, CBE, pictured during the 1930's, shortly before his death.

gone out with the Militia on more than one occasion during times of disorder. A staunch Conservative, he was first politically active in South Yorkshire, then Holmfirth division and then Penistone. He was the Chairman of the Denby Dale UDC for over 40 years. He was a Director of Martin's Bank and an Income Tax Commissioner. Thomas was a devout churchman and was a member of the Bishop's committees. Sport claimed his interest and in his younger days he was an excellent shot. He was awarded the CBE for his services during the First World War. Both Thomas, and his wife, had taken a keen interest in ambulance work and had presented a silver cup for competition known as the 'Norton Police Ambulance Cup' to be competed for annually by teams from the Staincross Division of the West Riding Constabulary. Thomas was a life long friend of fellow Magistrate, Mr E G Lancaster.

Norton Brothers & Co. became limited in 1874 and production concentrated more on fancy shawls and mantles, but disaster was just around the corner.

The American President, William McKinlay introduced a tariff on wool and silken textile imports in 1895, this along with improvements in pattern printing techniques caused an overnight and massive collapse in the fancy weaving trade. The Norton brothers were unable to absorb these changes and by 1897 they were leasing Nortonthorpe and Cuttlehirst mills to a number of firms. Scholefield and Cockcroft were one of these, manufacturers of rugs and fancy woollen goods. Other rentals included the lease of Cuttlehirst mills to Lewis Crowther in 1899 by Walter and Thomas Norton and Charles Frederick Dyson. In 1906 a part of the Cuttlehirst site was leased to Edward & Henry Blackburn by George Herbert Norton and Charles Scholefield. In 1895 R Beanland & Co. leased a room and power at Nortonthorpe mills. This slump affected the village as with the major employer in trouble further development became impossible and unnecessary and employees had to find work elsewhere.

Nothing if not enterprising, the brothers joined up with Scholefield and Cockcroft, largely due to the

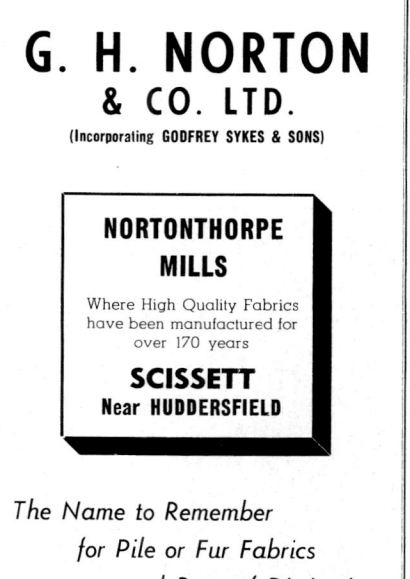

Advertisement from the 1972 'Official Guide' to Denby Dale.

efforts of George Herbert Norton, Thomas's son in 1899. The company now being known as Norton, Scholefield and Cockcroft was based at Nortonthorpe mills and ran from around 1901 to 1913 when, upon the death of Charles Scholefield, George Herbert took over the business in its entirety. Now known as G H Norton & Co. manufacturing consisted of 'shawls, mantle cloths, trimmings, table covers, mats, travelling rugs, toy cloths, plush and plushette, imitation furs and astrakhans',the firm becoming limited in 1939. George Herbert lived in Denby Dale at Highfield House where he died in 1950. After his death the mill was run by Alick Oxley, who was Managing Director.

Financial difficulties within the textile industry were common place in the late 1970's and 1980's, as we have seen Brownhill's and Kenyon's in Denby Dale closed their doors at this time. G H Norton went into receivership in 1984. The firm did run for a short while after as Norton (Weaving) Ltd. and is listed in the Yorkshire and Lancashire textile directory of 1986 as manufacturers of 'woven pile and fur fabrics for linings, furnishings, footwear, toys, rugs, under blankets, paint rollers etc. The respite was only a brief one and by 1989 Nortonthorpe mills had become an industrial park, as with the Brownhill's and Kenyon's sites in Denby Dale.

Within Nortonthorpe mills today can be found an integral and cherished relic of the industrial past of the building: a rare Pollit and Wigzell (based in Sowerby Bridge) patent three piston rod tandem compound steam engine. The engine had initially replaced a steam powered beam engine known as 'Ben' in 1886. It was originally christened the 'Empress' after Queen Victoria who was Empress of India. An overhaul in 1906 also saw a name change when George Herbert and his wife Ethel May had a daughter, Violet Alys, a granddaughter for Thomas Norton of Bagden Hall. The steam engine, now called 'Violet' was compounded in 1929 to 350 hp and was fitted with a Corliss valve high pressure cylinder in 1931. Violet gave good service until 1962 when she was retired after the installation of full electricity. In 1976 she made a comeback during a period of extreme power cuts.

Thankfully, during the period 1993–95 she was restored and is occasionally run as something of a tourist attraction.

Nortonthorpe Hall and Bagden Hall stand as a reminder of the family's success, built in true mill owner style, both buildings overlook their owners main concern in life, the mill. Although the family is now gone from the district the memory of them survives. Nortonthorpe has become a school catering for children with special needs. After a period of extensive restoration by Jack Braithwaite between 1989 and 1992 Bagden became a high quality country hotel, with a nine hole golf course and is regularly host to wedding receptions and other functions.

Nearly all the family were buried in High Hoyland churchyard in special plots. Amidst the iron railings lie for all eternity, the founder of the dynasty,

'Violet', the Norton factory steam engine, which has been restored and is 'steamed' from time to time at Nortonthorpe mills as a tourist attraction.

The Norton Family

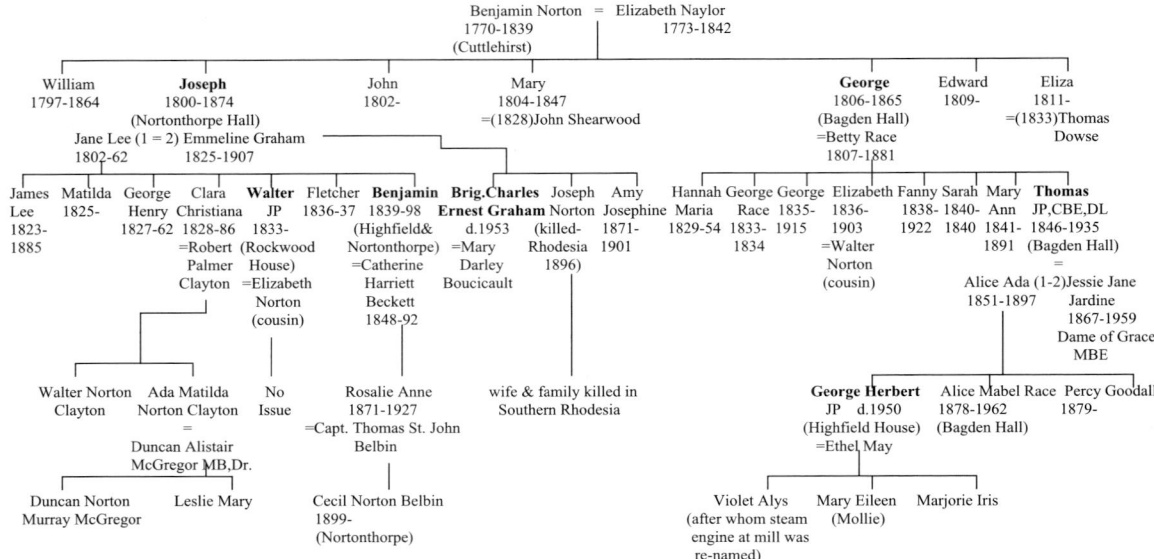

Benjamin Norton, with his two sons, Joseph and George, along with their offspring, Walter, Benjamin and Thomas, along with their numerous wives and children.

Why have we considered the Norton family in the context of this book, which is primarily concerned with the Denby district? Two reasons to consider; one, we have already seen how the manor of Denby included the site of the mills and Bagden from various court rolls, manorial surveys and suchlike and so the information is here on merit. The other reason involves the amount of land and buildings acquired by the firm in and around Denby Dale during the nineteenth and early twentieth centuries and the families involvement with municipal bodies and projects during that time.

The family's estates and property around the area began to accrue from the mid nineteenth century. For example, George Norton (Senior) leased land at Upper Denby to George Turton in 1848. He also made an agreement with a Joseph Newton to lease him land at Gilthwaites, Cumberworth in 1863, this was almost certainly included in a sale of land at Gilthwaites in 1939 to the Denby Dale UDC to allow them to build the housing estate. George was also involved with land conveyancing at Hartcliffe, Cumberworth, as well as at Skelmanthorpe, Clayton West and Horbury in 1859. His brother, Joseph was also involved, he made an agreement in 1863 with John Spencer Stanhope of Cannon Hall regarding rights at Highbridge Wood, Scissett. Joseph's son, Benjamin had acquired Lower Busker Farm and its neighbour, Busker Farm by 1870, though the latter was hit by fire in 1922 (after his death) the family undertook improvements in 1926. Benjamin also held the deeds to the Travellers Inn, Denby Dale which was finally sold in 1927. Later documents include the sale of land at Lower Cumberworth by George Herbert Norton to the Cumberworth Brick and Tile Company in 1941, and the sale of the Reading Room at Kitchenroyd in 1951.

Ultimately, the deaths of the leading members of the family paved the way for much of their estates to be sold off. Walter died in 1909, Benjamin in 1898, Thomas in 1935 and Charles Ernest

Graham in 1953. The period between 1938 and 1955 saw George Herbert Norton selling buildings at Cuttlehirst mill to Maurice Buckley of Hirst Buckley & Co., manufacturing stationers of Scissett. During 1934/5 the executors of Walter at Denby Dale began to sell off the Rockwood estate, including Toby Wood Farm, and land at Upper Denby for which a map exists showing coal and clay deposits identified there. More of this estate was sold in 1953, this was after the death of the last manufacturing Norton, George Herbert. The Bagden estate went under the hammer during the period 1957–59, the trustees of Thomas Norton included furniture, pictures and other goods within the sale. The families reign was over, it had lasted just over a hundred years.

We will now examine just a small amount of the enormous archive material held in Huddersfield to illustrate the latter:

DENBY DALE GAS LIGHT COMPANY LTD

The memorandum of association for the company was dated 13th April 1865. It describes its objectives as manufacturing and producing inflammable air or gas, from coal tar and oil and lighting therewith the streets, highways, factories, shops, dwelling houses and other buildings in Denby Dale and for a radius of two miles in every direction from the boundary of the village.

The capital of the company was £2000 divided into 2000 shares of £1 each and the major shareholders were:

Name	Address	Occupation	No. of shares
Walter Norton	Highfield House, Clayton West	Manufacturer	**100**
Thomas Lee	Netherend, Denby	Farmer	10
John Wood	Newhouse, Denby Dale	Corn Miller	25
Joseph Whitaker	Denby Dale	Land Valuer	10
Thomas Brierley	Denby Dale	Dyer	50
Zaccheus Hinchliffe	Denby Dale	Manufacturer	**100**
Henry H Peace	Denby Dale	Manufacturer	20
John Brierley	Denby Dale	Dyer	10
Josh. Firth	Highflatts	Land Agent	100
	All in the County of York	**Total shares taken**	**425**

The document was witnessed by Charles Holmes, Corn Miller of Denby Dale.

As we can see, Walter Norton is one of only three men to hold a hundred shares, it is also interesting to see that one of his co-subscribers was a man we have met previously, Zaccheus Hinchliffe, two men, as usual, at the forefront of change and innovation. A future account holder with the company was William Henry Kenyon. In 1867 the secretary was John Brierley, he was succeeded by Thomas Ellis (1889, (Walter Lister was the manager), Francis Hobson (1901), William Wood sec. and James E Curtis (1912), Curtis become secretary in 1922, and William A Heap (Manager & Secretary) and G H Senior (Collector) in 1936.

A series of tenancy agreements has survived relating to farms in Denby from the late 1920's and early 1930's. These not only show just how much land the Norton family had acquired but also include the names of the fields involved and their acreage. The farms involved all seem to have been owned by Brigadier Charles Ernest Graham Norton of 73 Park St, London. He was in fact acting on behalf of the estate of Walter Norton of Rockwood House, his half brother who as we have noted died in 1909. Brigadier Charles was by now the oldest male heir to his father,

Joseph, who had built Nortonthorpe Hall. Acting for him in Yorkshire were the solicitors Walker, Hall and Norton, Norton being Percy Goodall Norton, the son of the Brigadiers cousin, Thomas.

Schedule of land and premises relating to Toby Wood farm, Denby Dale, tenanted by James Lodge.

No. on Ordnance Survey Plan	First Part Name of Close	Area in Acres
566	Farm house, farm buildings and yards	.831
567	Kitchen Croft	1.291
568	Cote Close and building	4.582
571 (part of)	Shrogg	.425
575	Stubbing Bank	3.347
574	Little Close	1.276
573	Long Close	2.500
572	Low Rangebrough	2.805
570	Hills	2.662
608	Upper Ward Close	3.750
609	Far Rangebrough	4.669
610	Near Rangebrough	5.085
612	Fruit Carr	2.468
616	Near Apple Tree Royd, Far Apple Tree Royd, Ley Close and Low Ing	15.120
618	Round Flatt	4.785
562	Upper Norwood	3.826
563	Low Norwood	3.704
565	Lower Pingle	2.081
563	Upper Pingle	2.972
560	Pingle	3.960
559	Round Field	5.318
556	Long Ing	8.095
Total		85.552

Second part:
All that land known as Schofield's pasture situate in Denby, aforesaid, 6.495 acres.

Third part:
Long Shackles and New Park – 14.910 acres.
Total area 106.957 acres.

James Lodge and his son Joseph can be found at Toby Wood during the late nineteenth century. Both men were heavily involved with shire horses and it was their animals which were used to draw the 1887 and 1928 pies through Denby Dale. The trade directory of 1901 notes that James and Sydney Lodge (brother of Joseph) were farming here, though a Thomas Denmar also farmed a part of the site at this time. Tom Lodge, son of Joseph, was the last member of the family to work the farm, something he did for 60 years before taking well earned retirement. He continued the families associations with shire horses and is a popular judge at shows around the country.

27th March 1920
Schedule of land and premises relating to **Moist Holme Farm, Upper Denby**, tenanted to William Bastaby but the document was prepared to enable Joe Mosley to take over at a rent of £45.

No. on Ordnance Survey Plan	Name of Close	Area in acres
738	Farm house, farm building etc.	.331
735	Croft	.856
737	Moist Holme	2.910
692	Upper Shackles	4.143
694	Great Close (part of)	5.070
696	Great Close (part of)	10.493
695	Great Close (part of)	3.738
748	Allotment	5.450
734	Common	3.799
743	Common Field	2.851
743a	Common Field	2.723
739		4.579
Total area in acres		**46.943**

28th March 1928
Schedule of land and premises relating to **Denroyd Farm, Upper Denby**, previously tenanted to Mr. J M Priest, now to be let to Fred Nicholson of Low Fold Farm, Upper Denby for £85 per annum.

No. on Ordnance Survey plan.	Name of Close	Area in acres
114	Farm house, farm buildings and stack yard.	.764
113	Croft	1.802
111	Far Croft	1.842
108	Upper Buck Croft	3.619
147	Stainlands	5.662
115	Field	1.296
116	Grass Yard	1.937
96	Brick Croft	5.009
706	Long Lemon Acre	2.583
707	Broomfield	3.115
704		1.637
705		1.679
701		3.237
700	Stonepit Close	2.582
697	Great Close	3.647
586	Near Wall Royds (about)	6.485
582	Far Wall Royds	10.407
578		3.174
Total area in acres		60.447

28th March 1928

Schedule of land and premises relating **to Low Fold Farm, Upper Denby**, to be let to Fred Barden of Park Head Farm, Cumberworth for a rent of £62 per annum.

No. on Ordnance Survey Plan	Name of Close	Area in acres
117	Farmhouse, farm buildings, yard and garden (not including cottage and garden now in the occupation of Hugh Beever)	About-.668
119	Line Yard	.778
141	Ing and Calf Croft	2.804
144	Great Croft	4.842
145	Field	1.759
146	Field End	.759
121	South Croft	About-.1.630
125	Ditto	1.775
124	Croft and Barn	.646
123	Croft	2.365
122	South Croft	2.041
112	Long Close	1.771
107	Lower Buck Croft	3.491
579	Lower Ward Close	3.300
580	Square Close	2.406
581	Shoeboard	4.720
587	Marl Ing	2.030
606	Steep Close	6.751
Total area in acres		**44.536**

6th June 1931

Schedule of land and premises relating to **Moor Royd farm, Upper Denby**, in the possession of Julia Haigh, though at her request the tenancy was to be transferred to her son, George Thomas Haigh, at a rent of £19 10s per annum. The Haigh family were Quakers, and had been tenants of this property for many years, John Haigh and his wife Hannah, can be found here in 1762.

No. on Ordnance Survey Plan	Name of Close	Area in acres
684	Long Lands	2.985
685	South Croft	2.851
686	Square Close	1.967
688	Cross Lands	3.138
687	Penny Royd	5.137
613	Ing	1.294
689	Part of Little Moor Royd	(area on plan includes other lands)
690	Part of ditto	Ditto
758	Allotment	1.244

During April 1949 letters were sent out by the Rockwood Estate requesting payment of rents for the following properties:

Mr R D Mosley – Moistholme Farm, Denby £10

Mr Stanley Kaye – Moor Royd, Upper Denby £9 15s

Mr Joseph Lodge – Toby Wood Farm, Denby Dale £66

Mr Fred Barden – Lowfold Farm, Upper Denby £32 7s 8d

Mr Walter Hudson , Upper Denby £2 2s

Mr Henry Broadhead, Upper Denby £3 5s

Mr Fenton Senior – Munchcliffe Lodge, Denby Dale £4 10s

Mr R A Pickford – Denroyd Farm, Upper Denby £37 8s 6d

Mr Harry Turton, Upper Denby £6

(a tenancy agreement was also made out in 1938 for Dry Hill Farm, Lower Denby).

Another interesting set of documents regards the lease of fishing rights at Square Wood reservoir, near Toby Wood Farm, Denby Dale.

The matter began when Robert Wright of Crofton House, Upper Cumberworth wrote to Percy Goodall Norton on 1st April 1943. Mr Wright was a disabled veteran of the first world war. Now aged 61, he had served for 20 years as an Executive Councillor at Storthes Hall. He admitted in the correspondence that he had put 20 trout into the reservoir thinking he was not trespassing. He goes on to say that he did not want the fishing rights for himself, just permission to fish there and said that he took great relaxation from fishing in the fresh air.

The Denby Dale Urban District Council had been leased the rights to the water supply at Square Wood on 12th November 1891 by the Norton's. In 1892 they constructed the reservoir which had a capacity of 2,000,000 gallons to supply the lower levels of the township. Tanks were also supplied at Rusby Wood, Birdsedge (100,000 gallons) and another small reservoir at Moist Holme, Upper Denby (30,000 gallons) to supply the higher levels and parts of Cumberworth. Included in the lease of 1891 were fishing rights which entitled each member of the council to receive, on application, six tickets per annum permitting them to fish at Square Wood with up to five friends. There were usually six or seven members on the board so around 120 persons a year were given permission to fish.

The question of fishing rights seems to have been raised before Mr Wright sent his letter. On 8th October 1942 the Clerk of the council, J Haigh, wrote to C E G Norton's solicitors informing them that the board refused to give up their rights to fish and preferring the banks to remain unused. In a further letter, Percy Goodall Norton noted that 'up to the present time board members had never asked for tickets' i.e. 21st April 1943.

Matters moved on apace, Percy Goodall Norton was also approached by Ralph Noel Berry who lived at Low House, High Flatts, perhaps in collusion with Mr Wright? He was granted permission to fish with rod and line only, by the Norton executors for £3 per annum, the agreement to be for seven years. He was also authorised to stock the reservoir with trout and only persons invested with his permission were to fish there. Mr Berry also requested that he might run a small hatchery from his home to keep up the stock levels.

Of course, this was the reservoir which had supplied the contaminated water causing the outbreak of typhoid in Denby Dale in 1932. A letter dated 22nd May 1943 from C E G Norton to Percy Goodall Norton said, *'I think the reservoir is quite safe from contamination, but no doubt Mr. Berry will have made his own enquiries'.*

The decision seems to have annoyed the local council somewhat! A rather 'snotty' letter was sent by them on 24th July 1945, somewhat after the event. In it they noted that Mr Berry had stocked the reservoir with trout and that he claimed to be the owner of the fishing rights. It goes on to refer to their own letter of 7th October 1942 when they refused to relinquish their rights. The problem was nipped in the bud by Percy Goodall Norton, when he stated that the rights were held by the lessor in 1891 not by the lessee – therefore the board did not have a say.

Even the woodland owned by the family was significant. The trustees of Walter Norton's, Rockwood Estate sold in 1934/5:

the following timber, now standing and growing in woods near to Rockwood House:
47 Oak trees, 54 Beech trees, 27 Sycamore trees, 2 Ash trees and 1 Elm tree.
695 Oak Poles, 98 Birch poles, 96 Ash and Elm poles, and 14 Larch poles.
All to be sold with bark and top wood.

Alfred Hill of Cawthorne was in charge of the sale, the timber was to be 'shown' to prospective buyers by a Mr John Sadler of Newhouse, Denby Dale.

We could go on, but the latter serves to illustrate a little of the extent of land ownership enjoyed by the Norton's. There were many reasons for acquiring it to this extent, not least for coal, clay and water rights. As we have seen the Norton's were not the only people to invest in land. At some point during the nineteenth century Jonas Kenyon had come into possession of a part of Town Field at Lower Denby, probably because of the coal deposits there. Town Field ran from, roughly, the East of Haley Well in Upper Denby down to the Barnsley and Shepley turnpike road. It was originally owned by Josias Wadsworth in 1748, when it was in the occupation of Jonathan Gaunt, though by 1805 Daniel Dyson was the tenant, indeed, Dyson owned land which abutted it. The enclosure map of 1802 notes that it was owned by Sir Charles Kent and Mrs. Varelst, who also acquired 'Little' Town field from George Tyas in 1816.

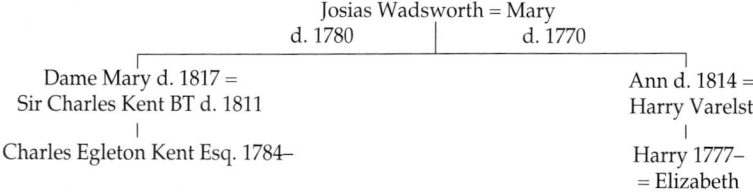

Sir Charles Kent of Farnham St. Geneveve in Suffolk (later Sir Charles Kent Bt.) married Mary Wadsworth (later Dame Mary) in 1770 at Wadsworth in Doncaster: they were joined here by Mary's sister, Ann, who married Harry Varelst of St James Square, Middlesex, at the same time. When old Josias Wadsworth died his lands in Penistone, Hoylandswaine, Silkstone, Denby and elsewhere were inherited by the latter whose names are very prominent on the map accompanying the enclosure award for Denby.

Later nineteenth century maps note that Denby colliery was sited at Town Field between the turnpike road and the railway bridge along with a shaft behind the town school and a pit behind Stocks Hall. The footpath used by Denby miners to reach the site still exists, known as Coal Pit Lane. If you take a walk down here from Upper Denby look for Haley Well, once you can see it be aware that the fields to your right as far down as the Barnsley Road were once 'Town Field'.

Jonas Kenyon was not alone in his desire to mine and supply his business with cheap coal for steam power. Nortonthorpe Colliery was well established by 1912 and Zaccheus Hinchliffe & Sons also mined in Denby Dale, unfortunately, by 1875 many wells in the village had been contaminated

Arial view of the site, formerly Kitson's, in Denby Dale, taken in 1973 when it was run by the Hepworth Group. To the right of it is Prospect Terrace. *(Simmons Aerofilms).*

due to this operation. During the early 1900's coal was also mined by Joseph Flack at Upper Bagden, John Horn at 'Top O' Hill', Cumberworth, William Longley at Lower Cumberworth, Joe Kitson & Sons at Bank Royd, Denby Dale, Naylor Brothers at Pinfold, Denby Dale, Stringer and Jagger at Clayton West and numerous others.

Besides coal mining the area was also extensively worked for stone and clay. Joe Kitson and Sons was founded in 1878 manufacturing clay pipes and other earthenware goods. Raw material was brought from newly opened clay pits behind Denby Dale school. A disastrous fire engulfed many of the buildings on 23rd August 1915. The company eventually became a part of the Hepworth group. In 1901 a small brick works at Cumberworth was taken over by the Wood family and re-named the Cumberworth Brick and Tile Company. This was also, later, taken over by the Hepworth group. We now turn to the villages most famous exponents to utilise the properties of clay.

Kitson's works, after a disastrous fire in 1915, the site has now been re-developed as Denby Dale Industrial Park. *Old Barnsley*

THE NAYLOR FAMILY

The Naylor family were involved with the brick manufacturing trade since at least the 1730's in Scholes. Daniel Naylor (1710–79) had handed the brickmaking business to his son, Samuel, and he in turn to his son, Joseph who was also a clothier. George Naylor (1814–79), son of Joseph, was the first real pioneer of the family. Instead of going along with the quarrying, farming and brick-making side of the business he branched out and founded a railway contracting business. This was the heyday of the railway and by 1852 there were over 7000 miles of track in Britain. George Stephenson's *Rocket* had been designed in 1830 and steam power had become King of the transport industry. The industrial revolution was very much upon the country, but the manufacturing industry needed more speed than was available using the limited turnpike roads or canals which were largely superseded by the railways by 1840.

George Naylor had two sons, George William Naylor (1847–88) and Thompson Naylor (born 1855) who became very involved in the family firm, by now known as Naylor Brothers Contractors of Scholes. The business was eventually, awarded a contract in 1877 by the Lancashire and Yorkshire Railway Company to replace the creaking wooden viaduct in Denby Dale with a stone built construction. George had by now retired and the business was run by his two sons, their tender was £27,650 and they quoted an estimated time of $2^1/_2$ years to completion. The line had been surveyed by Joseph Locke (1805–60) a man with the right credentials to do so. He was an associate of Isembard Kingdom Brunel and George Stephenson. Born near Sheffield, he left school aged 13 and went to work for George Stephenson and would have been an intimate of his during the development of the 'Rocket'. He learned the art of surveying as well as railway engineering and construction, and went on to create many lines, including some in France. Various difficulties ensued including ground subsidence, but the twenty one great arches were finally raised by 1879. The line was opened on Whit Sunday , 16th May 1880 when the occasion must have held a sense of pride for George William and Thompson and also of loss, as their father, George, had died the previous year. Unfortunately the contract lost money, the great railway boom was beginning to subside, not helped by the mass construction of non profitable lines during the 1860's and 70's which caused untold problems for operator's in the late nineteenth and twentieth centuries. Despite this, Naylor Brothers had enhanced their reputation, and had delivered a difficult job on time, further contracts followed over a wide area.

Whether they fell in love with Denby Dale or perhaps they just wanted to be near their masterpiece, one thing is certain, in 1881 the family moved from Scholes into the village where George William built a large home, known as 'Woodbine' which, naturally, overlooked the viaduct. By this time manufacturing, as we have seen, in Denby Dale was expanding rapidly. Hinchliffe's, Kenyon's, Brownhill's and the Norton family had begun to develop into major concerns in the area. The achievements of the Naylor's certainly elevated the family into this manufacturing elite.

We can find the family, newly arrived in Denby Dale, in the 1881 census returns:

Name	Age	Occupation	Place of birth
George William Naylor	33	Contractor (Railway)	Cleckheaton
Hannah Naylor	31	Wife	Cleckheaton
George Wilfred Naylor	10	Scholar	Brighouse
Alice Naylor	8	Scholar	Cleckheaton
John Francis Naylor	6	Scholar	Cleckheaton
Mary Elizabeth Gawthorpe	13	General Domestic Servant	Denby Dale

(NB: a further child, Emma Isabel was born soon after the census was taken).

Left: George William Naylor, builder of Denby Dale viaduct, who died in 1888.

Construction of the viaduct arches continues, finally completed in 1879.

As we can from the above table, George Wilfred Naylor was 10 years old at the time of the move. He started work in the family business aged 16 but only two years later, in 1888 his father died at the very early age of 41, this left George Wilfred aged 18 with a widowed mother, Hannah, herself only 38, and two young sisters to care for. His nickname 'push Naylor' developed in the classroom, now became a useful asset as he took on his responsibilities with gusto. His Uncle, Thompson Naylor now took on the roll of Senior Partner and the two of them successfully completed a contract to build a viaduct near Buxton, which had been on going at the time of George William's death.

By 1890 George Wilfred had split from his Uncle to found a sanitary pipe business, aged only 20 he had skills in civil engineering, quarrying and surveying amongst others, though his work took him away from his family on many occasions. Eventually Thompson Naylor left England for Canada, along with his two sons, they arrived in 1912 (thankfully not aboard the Titanic – which sank the same year) and was soon involved with extensive new projects on Vancouver harbour.

The site of Naylor operations in Denby Dale was an ancient piece of farm land known as Bromley's, once farmed by the Horn family. The coming of the railway had split the land in two but also had the advantage of providing a ready transport system on the firm's doorstep. Large clay deposits were also to be had which were suitable for making glazed pipes and of course all mineral and water rights were purchased with the land.

In 1898 George Wilfred married Florence Ethel Brownhill and moved to Hartcliffe House immediately next to the Bromley site. This left his mother and sisters with 'Woodbine' to themselves. Florence Ethel was the daughter of Charles Brownhill and the niece of John, who founded his company at Inkerman mill in 1868. In 1881 she was living at Inkerman House with her Uncle John, indeed, George Wilfred's sister, Alice went on to marry James Brownhill, son and heir of John so family ties between the two clans must have been good.

George William Naylor's children, circa 1881. Left to right: John Francis, Alice, Emma Isabel and George Wilfred.

Thompson Naylor, circa 1892, seated on the steps, presumably with his children.

George and Florence's first child, Edith was born in 1900 and she was followed by two boys, William and (Charles) Eric. After George's mother, Hannah's death in 1915 he moved his family back into Woodbine House. His two sons went on to attend Penistone Grammar School before joining the family business.

A period of expansion followed, in 1926 Naybro Stone Ltd. was formed and was based at a factory at Longton, Stoke on Trent with a quarry at Newcastle Under Lyme, this business catered for the pre-cast concrete industry. William Naylor was largely responsible for this and went to live at Newcastle Under Lyme. A calcium brickwork's was also bought at Lower Upnor near Chatham with a wharf on the river Medway. Later Naylor Brothers (Stoke) was formed to combine the group with pipe sales in Denby Dale.

In 1929 George Wilfred leased land at Wall Royd in Denby Dale on which to build a garage. His dealings were with the solicitors, Hall, Walker and

Naylor shunting engines around 1900.

William Naylor, son of George Wilfred, circa 1927.

George Wilfred Naylor, founder of the sanitary pipe business, who died in 1932.

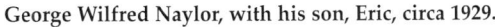

George Wilfred Naylor, with his son, Eric, circa 1929.

Eric Naylor, son of George Wilfred, circa 1927.

John Francis Naylor, brother of George Wilfred, 1927.

Early Naylor's transport, at Upper Denby, On the left is George Hodgson, right, Ernest Heath, circa 1930.

Norton, i.e.: the trustees of the Norton estate. George clearly had no time for niceties of type written letters as his cheque was despatched along with a hastily scrawled note on company letterheaded paper. The letter head notes the partners: George, Frank Naylor (John Francis, his brother), William and Eric Naylor his sons and proudly ascertains *'Contractors to the Admiralty, War Office and Crown Agents.'*

Frank Naylor had by now become involved on the sales side of the operation and was responsible for forming Naylor Brothers – Sheffield as the main selling agent. He was also given the honour of making the first ceremonial cut into the 1896 Denby Dale pie.

Tragedy struck the family again in 1930 when Eric died as a result of severe burns sustained in a fire at the above mentioned garage. Only two years later and George Wilfred himself passed away aged 62, he was buried at Cumberworth.

Frank Naylor, about to perform the first ceremonial cut into the 1896 Denby Dale Pie.

'Grace', the Naylor's steam engine, which was a double acting compound type. It provided power and electricity for the factory until superseded by full electrification in the 1940's. Power for the engine was provided by Lancashire type steam boilers, this also provided heat for drying clay products.

William Naylor now found himself bereft of most of his immediate family though Frank lived until 1943. He left Newcastle Under Lyme and moved back into the family home at Denby Dale where he saw all aspects of the company grow before 1938 when they were incorporated as separate limited company's.

The Second World War saw William join the 5th Duke of Wellington's Regiment of the Royal Engineers as a 'sapper', though he was soon on indefinite leave as a result of his ability to keep factories, producing concrete products for the war effort, going.

During World War Two a number of temporary changes were made. The wharf at Chatham was taken over by the Admiralty and it became requisite for women to be employed in pipe manufacture for the first time. All the kilns had to be blacked out to prevent them being seen by enemy aircraft overnight. When the USA entered the war the Americans took over the goods yard at Denby Dale station and used it as a transit depot for gas bombs. These were not always handled with the necessary care required and in the event of danger a large bell was rung to warn the employees at Naylor's of the possibility of a gas leak so allowing them time to don gas masks.

In 1945 a disastrous fire occurred which destroyed around three quarters of the works site. Many of the machines were salvaged but financial crisis ensued due to lack of adequate insurance. In typical 'bullish' fashion the firm re-built the site in cast concrete, made, of course, by themselves, though they may have had little other choice due to shortage of materials caused by the war. Later in the year the family experienced even more heartbreak when William Naylor was killed in a car

Kiln workers, in full battle dress during the Second World War.

accident. His two sons, George and Allan, aged only 16 and ten years old were still at school and it is a testament to the then Directors and Board members that the company continued to run effectively up until the Naylor boys could assume control.

George joined the company in 1947 and assumed the title of Managing Director in 1950 at the age of 21. In 1948 the company bought Actons Stoneware Ltd. at Cawthorne and began working clay here. The site was re-developed during 1961 and included Europe's first salt glazing continuous tunnel kiln. This kept manual handling of the pipes down to a bare minimum and only one other company in the world had achieved this high level of mechanisation. Denby Dale continued to produce special pipe fittings and larger diameter pipes and was also home to the sales and accounts offices.

The company continued to make favourable progress throughout the second half of the twentieth century. Embracing new technology and even opening their own laboratory in 1951.

By 1990, the firms centenary year, the group included the following companies:

Naylor Brothers Clayware, Naylor Bros. – Denby Dale Ltd., Naylor Bros. (Structural Products) Ltd.

A busy day in Naylor's jointing shed, circa 1940's.

The changing face of company transport. This photograph dates to the very late 1940's or early 1950's.

A mid-twentieth century aerial view of the Naylors site in Denby Dale. Note the now demolished family home, 'Woodbine House', towards the bottom centre of the picture. It is easy to see the proximity of the railway and its effectiveness in facilitating the transportation of goods, the station is to the left of the photograph.

The re-built Naylors works after the fire of 1945.

Associated companies were, Readymix – Huddersfield Ltd., Naylor Myers Ltd., Johnson's Wellfield Quarries Ltd., Blastmaster Int. Ltd., Mobile Concrete Pumps Ltd. and Honley Skip Hire Ltd.

The Denby Dale site was finally closed down on Sunday, 3rd October 1993 and production transferred to Cawthorne. The loss of 72 jobs was compensated by the creation of 55 new ones at the Cawthorne site.

Naylor Myers is the only remnant of this historic company still to be seen amidst a site which has been almost totally cleared of its buildings to make way for the Bromley housing estate.

The last day. Naylors closed down the Denby Dale site on Sunday 3rd October 1993. The workforce pictured were those who were being transferred to Cawthorne.

The Naylor Family

Joseph Naylor (only son) 1780–1843

George Naylor (third son) 1814–1879

George William Naylor
(2nd son) 1845–1888
Hannah 1850–1915

Thompson Naylor

George Wilfred ('push') Naylor
1870–1932 = Florence Ethel Brownhilll
1877–1936

John Francis (Frank)
1874–1943

= Alice
James Brownhill

Emma Isabel

Edith 1900–   William 1901–45   Charles Eric (Eric)
1904–30 =
Esca May

George Holdsworth   William Allan Naylor

Within this chapter we have examined five of the most important and influential families born out of the Industrial Revolution. It would be impossible to include every family detail and the progression of the industries that they were involved with. It is also uncertain as to just how much they interacted with each other. From a quick glance at the genealogical tables we can see that over the years they were eventually, almost all related to each other. What of their co-operation in public service? The foundation of a military auxiliary hospital in 1916 brought at least some of them together. Indeed the lists of the various committee members read rather like a who's who of the local area, with certain exceptions.

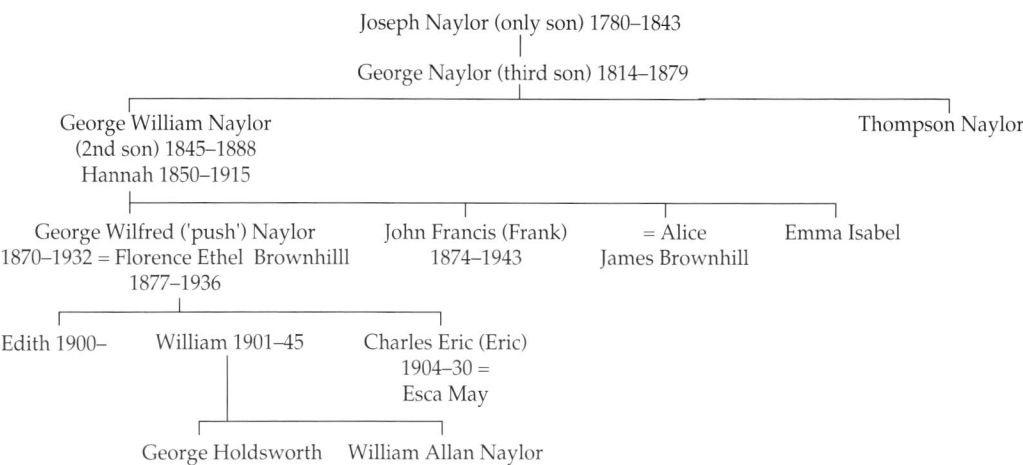

The old Naylors site has now been re-developed into the Bromley housing estate.

DENBY DALE AND DISTRICT JOINT MILITARY AUXILIARY HOSPITAL

On 2nd October 1916, John Hinchliffe JP, then acting as Chairman of the Denby and Cumberworth Urban District Council received a letter from Lieutenant Colonel Marshall, the officer in charge of the war hospital at Huddersfield. He asked if it was possible for Denby Dale to provide accommodation to convalescing patients as pressure on the beds he had available was too great.

The requirement was for a house, preferably with its own grounds to allow outdoor recreation and it would require the people of the village to staff and equip the hospital and provide medical attendance. A competent matron would also be required.

A meeting in the council room on 3 October decided to go forward with the idea. William Henry Kenyon, George William Moxon (a veterinary surgeon and assistant overseer and collector of poor rates), and Arthur Turton were to speak to the Trustees of the Wesleyan church in Denby Dale with regard to converting the Memorial Hall. Carr House at Cumberworth was also touted as a possible venue.

An executive committee was also formed: S. Cook, J. Barrow, William Henry Kenyon, Thomas Albert Hinchliffe, W Longley, George William Moxon, Dr. Duncan Alistair McGregor, Dr. Banham. Rev. Romeo Edwin Taglis, Rev. A Currie(Vicar at Cumberworth), W H Wardle, W B Redhead, Mr Harold Hinchliffe (deputising for his father, John, who was ill).

A further meeting attended by Alderman James Peace Hinchliffe JP and James Henry Dewhurst saw Mr Furman Hunt McGrath (of Birdsedge mill) appointed as Chairman.

Alderman Hinchliffe had approached the West Riding County Council and suggested the scheme regarding the Memorial Hall which was currently being used as an infants school. The council were amenable to the idea and arranged for the children to be moved out of the building leaving it available for a hospital.

A sub-committee consisting of Alderman J P Hinchliffe, Dr. Banham, Rev. J F L Orton, James Henry Dewhirst and T Shield approached the Wesleyan trustees for the first time on 16 October.

The committee met on 23 October in the council room at Denby Dale and were now bolstered by representatives from Skelmanthorpe and Clayton West. Joining the above named were: John

The Victoria Memorial Hall, Denby Dale, circa 1940. *Old Barnsley*

Thomas Field, George Herbert Norton, F Exley, C E Field, H Beanland, A M Beardsell, Arthy Kenyon, W Longley, E Blackburn, Charles Kilner Hanwell, Wilfred Kaye, Jas. Waites, B Senior and H Cockshaw. John Thomas Field JP was elected Chairman of the Hospital Committee. He was the brother of Edwin Field of Skelmanthorpe and lived at 'Longroyd' on Pilling Lane in the village, now a nursing home. His family had been involved with the textile industry since at least 1770 in Skelmanthorpe. Successive generations had broken away from the family business and founded their own firms, Edwin built Tentercroft mill in Skelmanthorpe and manufactured pile fabrics. The meeting continued with Alderman Hinchliffe supplying all the details of the proposed scheme which, by now had become an operation to provide 50 beds. F H McGrath was elected Vice Chairman, E L Ferrall, the Manager of the London City and Midland Bank, Penistone, and Thomas Albert Hinchliffe were elected joint treasurers. T Shield and H Cockshaw were elected joint secretaries.

The agreement with the Wesleyan trustees, after various suggestions and amendments was passed to J W Piercy, solicitor, in Huddersfield for ratification.

With the building now available, secretary T Shield was able to advertise for a matron at £60 per annum, and a trained nurse at £40 per annum, he placed the advertisements in the *Nursing Mirror, Nursing Times* and *Yorkshire Post*. He also advertised for two cooks at £30 per annum in the *Yorkshire Post* and *Huddersfield Examiner*.

A ladies committee was also established to deal with all the domestic appliances, equipment and beds deemed necessary for setting up the hospital. The ladies committee met for the first time on Wednesday 1st November 1916, again in the council room. Present were: Mrs T Norton, Mrs T A Hinchliffe, Mrs J P Hinchliffe, Mrs Banham, Mrs Redhead, Mrs G W Naylor, Mrs Bell, Mrs Beanland, Miss Armitage, Mrs C E Field, Mrs W Bell, Mrs E Field, Mrs P R Jackson, Mrs F Child, Mrs Jas. Waites and Miss Yardley. Mrs Thomas Norton was elected President, Mrs J P Hinchliffe, Vice President and Mrs T A Hinchliffe, secretary. Mrs J T Field and Miss Norton came on board soon afterwards. Sub committees were set up which included Mrs MacGregor and Mrs

The Hospital Committee: Back row: T A Hinchliffe, H Cockshaw (Joint Secretary), Dr C W R Banham, G H Norton (JP), E L Ferrall (Treasurer), A M Beardsell, W Longley, J Barrow, T Shield (Joint Secretary). Front row: W H Kenyon, Dr D A MacGregor, F H McGrath (Vice Chairman), J T Field (JP, Chairman), J Hinchliffe (JP), Jas. Waites (JP), J Bedford.

T A Hinchliffe for Denby Dale, Mrs T Norton and Miss Norton for Scissett and Mrs G W Naylor, Mrs Banham and Mrs J P Hinchliffe who were elected as the staffing committee for Denby Dale.

The presence of Thomas Norton and others was appropriate if for no other reason than that they were involved in the opening ceremony of the Hall on 11th July 1903. Other's involved in the ceremony were Mrs Brownhill, Mrs J. P. Hinchliffe, Mrs T.A. Hinchliffe, Miss Naylor, Miss S.S. Moxon, Mr G.W. Moxon, Mrs Tedbar Wood, Mrs Norton of Bagden Hall, Mr John Hinchliffe and Mr Charles E. Field.

The agreement for the use of the Memorial Hall was signed on 13th November 1916 by J T Field, C E Field, J Hinchliffe, W Longley, Jas. Waites, R J H Beanland for the Hospital committee and by A Turton, G W Moxon and W A Heap for the Wesleyan trustees.

Applications had by now come in for the post of matron which had been reduced to three for interview on the 17th November. The position was given to Miss M A Meadows of Leasowe, Cheshire.

An appeal for funds was now made in the various districts involved, as the cost of running the enterprise was estimated at £1200 for the first year and £400 for the next year. Although £830 had already been subscribed, the shortfall had to be met.

The committee had by now informed Lieutenant Colonel Marshall of their progress who wrote back to Chairman, J T Field informing him of his acceptance on behalf of the War Department of their generous offer. It was to be a 'Class B' auxiliary hospital and each patient was to be granted an allowance of 2 shillings per day. The hospital was to be under the County Director of the British Red Cross Society and St. John's Ambulance Brigade.

From the 17th November the Memorial Hall was a hive of activity. Baths and a stove room were fitted by contractors who, once finished, were followed by an army of volunteers who went in to clean the place up. The ladies committee busied themselves acquiring linen, blankets, crockery and cutlery. Committee member, Furman Hunt McGrath of Sunside, Cumberworth, who owned Birdsedge mills supplied material, ready cut to be turned into blankets. The ladies committee and pupils at Denby Dale council school undertook this task, stitching all the material by hand. Thomas Hinchliffe loaned a gramophone and Jas. Waites offered to ask Mrs J Kaye about borrowing her piano.

The Matron, Miss M A Meadows RRC.

The opening day was fixed at 9th December as a result of which, the matron, Miss Meadows was asked to be in residence by December 5th. She was joined there by the sister, Miss B Mainprize. The pair were in charge of a number of teams of V.A.D.'s (Voluntary Aid Detachment of Nurses) recruited from the local villages and known, for example, as Denby Dale Contingent or Skelmanthorpe Contingent. It was resolved that the hospital would be open to visitors on Saturdays between 2 and 4pm. Visitors from long distance would be admitted on presentation of their rail ticket. Mrs Child took up the position of Entertainment Secretary assisted by Jas. Waites and James Henry Dewhirst.

The opening ceremony was attended by, amongst others: Colonel C E Duncombe CBE, Lieutenant Colonel W L W Marshall RAMC, Major Rowell, Mr F H McGrath (vice chairman of the committee), Mr John Hinchliffe (chairman of

James Henry Dewhirst, Member of the Hospital Committee.

the DDUDC), Dr. D A MacGregor, Dr. Banham, Mr Thomas Norton CBE JP, Mr Thomas Albert Hinchliffe (treasurer), Mr & Mrs William Henry Kenyon, Mr James Henry Dewhirst and most of the other members of the committee. After a brief prayer and the National Anthem, Chairman, J T Field stated that £1030 had already been promised towards the £1200 required for the running of the hospital.

Lieutenant Colonel Marshall thanked the committee for their efforts before Colonel C E W Duncombe declared the hospital open. Thanks were given to them both on the proposal of Thomas Norton, after which guests were able to tour the building.

The first soldiers arrived on 12th December, in time to celebrate Christmas. Gifts were handed out, each man awoke to find 5 shillings on his locker. Pipes, wallets and fountain pens as well as tobacco and cigars were provided by both male and female committees. Turkeys and plum puddings were served at dinner, the tables being presided over by Chairman, John Thomas Field, John Hinchliffe, Dr. MacGregor, Dr. Banham and William Henry Kenyon, these men having forgone a part of their own Christmas Day with their families.

Two of the earlier patients admitted to the hospital were Lance Corporal H Mitchell, Duke of Wellington's Regiment, a native of Almondbury and Private Percy Fitt. Both were awarded the Military Medal at the hospital by Lieutenant Colonel Marshall on 10 March 1917.

To break the monotony and to assist with morale and recuperation the patients were encouraged to take part in a concert on Friday 1st June 1917. Songs and sketches ensued along with Miss Beanland of Huddersfield, who played violin solos and Miss Dewhirst who delivered a clever recitation in dialect. Lance Corporal Hirst of Skelmanthorpe, recently a patient but now discharged returned and sang to great applause. Privates Farmer and Morris provided comedy and the evening concluded with a sketch entitled 'Dr Diaculum' which saw Privates Dryden, Wright, Smith and Taylor perform a mock amputation, on Dryden's leg!

Committee member, Thomas Hinchliffe of the Royds in Denby Dale had taken the chair on a night which had raised £20 8s 6d for hospital funds.

Another ceremony was performed on the first anniversary of the opening of the hospital when Lieutenant Colonel Marshall decorated Bombardier Hallsworth, RFA, with the Military Medal and Belgian 'Decoration Militaire'; this led to a 'gala' afternoon. Bombardier Hallsworth had walked into a swamp amidst heavy shell fire to save a wounded man, he succeeded and got the injured soldier to a hospital, this won him the Military Medal. On the same day he continuously tried to repair telephone wires destroyed by enemy barrages. He succeeded, for a short time only, but did get information through to the observing officer. During the battle at Messines his battery was heavily bombarded but when a message came through from headquarters he ran through shell fire to where the officers were taking cover, this brought him the Belgian decoration.

Christmas 1917 arrived, more gifts were distributed and cygnets, turkeys, plum puddings, chocolates and oranges were served up at tables presided over by J T Field, Dr. Banham, Dr. MacGregor and Thomas Norton. This was followed by a Boxing Day fancy dress dance for the patients and staff. Around one hundred people attended and saw the 'Pearl King and Queen win first prize. Bombardier Hallsworth was second as 'a coster' and Corporal Bagnall, a 'clown' was third. Even Father Christmas came along!.

On 7th March 1918 the resignation of Sister, Beatrice Mainprize was accepted as she had gained a similar position in Walthamstow. Mrs A Kenyon took over her duties on a temporary basis until May when the services of Miss Nora Bugbird were engaged

In the meantime Dr. MacGregor's wife, Ada Matilda Norton Clayton had attended a meeting in Leeds called as a matter of urgency due to the escalation of hostilities in France. Extra beds were being called for, but it was decided that Denby Dale, Clayton West, Cumberworth and Skelmanthorpe were doing all they could.

The committee were keen to increase the size of the recreation room, though due to difficulties in financing and acquiring materials they had decided to approach Clayton West Golf Club with a view to borrowing the club house. The golf club agreed to a loan for the duration of the war at the hospital committee's expense. The job of moving the building to Denby Dale was undertaken by J Holmes & Sons.

The 11th November 1918 saw flags and bunting displayed in every conceivable place of the hospital. A whist drive was organised by the Matron amongst the VAD nurses and soldiers, as the feelings of relief overtook the world at large. A communication received from Colonel Duncombe and Lieutenant Colonel Marshall suggested that the hospital should close on 28th February 1919.

Patients still in residence were again treated at Christmas in 1918. John Thomas Field, Thomas Norton, Thomas Hinchliffe, Dr. MacGregor and Dr. Banham presided at the dinner tables. Boxing day again saw a fancy dress dance, this was given in the Council school, the arrangements for which were in the hands of Mrs MacGregor and Thomas Hinchliffe. Around 180 people attended.

Saturday the 28th saw a whist drive and dance in Denby Dale school. In the centre of the room was a large Christmas tree laden with presents. These were taken off later in the evening by headmaster, Sam Shepley, and handed to Mrs Jonas Kenyon to present to the soldiers and staff. Corporal Davidson thanked the committee on behalf of the soldiers and then dancing and games took over, Sam Shepley acting as MC.

Things began to wind down in the new year. Nora Bugbird, the hospital sister tendered her resignation on 17th January and Miss Meadows was recommended for the Royal Red Cross. A victory ball was also planned under the guidance of Thomas Hinchliffe and the ladies committee. The question of the disposal of all the equipment was also dealt with. It was decided to hold a public auction to raise funds for the restoration of the Memorial Hall, any profits remaining thereafter were to be split between Huddersfield Infirmary and the Blind Soldiers Fund, St. Dunstans.

Colonel Duncombe returned to Denby Dale one last time to preside over the events of the closing ceremony, he was aided in this by John Thomas Field, JP, J P Hinchliffe (Chairman of the West Riding County Council), John Hinchliffe JP, William Henry Kenyon, Doctors MacGregor and Banham,

Doctors, MacGregor (seated) and Banham in the makeshift hospital.

The Denby Dale contingent of the VAD Nurses.

F H McGrath and Rev. C Pollard MA. J T Field read a letter from Lieutenant Colonel Marshall, who, due to illness, was unable to be present, thanking the committee and people of the village for all their efforts. The V.A.D.'s were thanked and awarded brooches for their service. Colonel Duncombe made special mention of Mrs. Norton (Jessie Jane Jardine wife of Thomas) of Bagden Hall and congratulated her on her being made an M.B.E. by the King. He remarked that the work of Mrs Norton was well known to him since he had taken up the office of Director of the V.A.D. Hospitals in 1916. Matron Meadows was also singled out for praise as were the efforts of the committee.

Alderman James Peace Hinchliffe then gave a speech referring to the enormous loss of life and the men and women who had come forward to serve their country. He also mentioned the signing of the League of Nations agreement, which had taken place the day before to try and prevent any future conflict on the scale just seen. Little did they know. He also informed the gathering that an agreement had been made with the County Council (remember that he was the Chairman) for all the hospitals equipment, its Matron and some of its staff to be transferred to Alverley Hall Institution near Doncaster (a home for disabled soldiers and sailors), it was also hoped that some of the V.A.D.'s might go as well.

He finished by thanking Colonel Duncombe and was seconded by Thomas Norton. Dr. MacGregor then reported that although the hospital had had some very serious cases there had been no deaths. Thomas Norton and William Henry Kenyon thanked Chairman J T Field for his efforts and Rev. Taglis from Upper Denby proposed that a vote of sympathy be sent to Lieutenant Colonel Marshall. Proceedings were brought to a close by Rev. C Pollard MA, Wesleyan Minister at Denby Dale before refreshments were provided by the ladies committee.

From the opening of the hospital, 12th December 1916 to the closing on 28th February 1919:

Average cost of each inpatient per day	£0 2s 10.519d
Average cost of each inpatient	£5 7s 6.984d
Total number of beds available	40
Total number of patients resident daily (total daily counts)	30218
Unoccupied beds	2102
Average number of patients resident daily throughout the period	37.396
Number of patients admitted	924
Average number of days each patient was resident	32.703
Number of patients discharged	924
Discharged for duty	146 (15.8%)
Discharged for light duty	600 (64.93%)

Discharged for further treatment	75 (8.11%)
Discharged for Medical Board examination	28 (3.03%)
Transferred to other hospitals	21 (2.272%)
Removed under escort	13 (1.406%)
Recommended for discharge	4 (.454%)
For munition work	1 (.108%)
For employment	36 (3.89%)

The victory ball was held at Denby Dale school on 22nd February 1919 to celebrate the end of the war and the achievements of the hospital. On 25th February Mrs MacGregor presented a silver tea service to Matron, Miss Meadows from the Denby Dale V.A.D.'s. She had already received an attaché case and a silver fruit dish from the Clayton West and Skelmanthorpe V.A.D.'s. On top of this the King awarded her the Royal Red Cross in *'recognition of valuable nursing services under British Red Cross Society and the Order of St. John of Jerusalem'*.

J T Field, John Hinchliffe and T Shield met a deputation from the West Riding County Council, including James Peace Hinchliffe, on 7th March. A price of £450 was agreed for the hospitals equipment and all the staff were to be retained by the County Council, and thus the life of the hospital and its associated committees came to an end.

Many of the family names that we have considered in these pages still survive in the Denby district and beyond. Their legacy surrounds the present inhabitants of the area in their mill buildings and family homes and of course the monumental viaduct. As with the old Burdet Lords of the Manor, their influence over the district has diminished and so a new wave of smaller industrial concerns has taken over.

Woven into their story are the names of other local industrialists, the Fields of Skelmanthorpe, Joe Kitson & Sons, Dawson's of Skelmanthorpe, Beanlands of Clayton West and numerous others. The area was alive with manufacturing from the period around 1850 and for those who took their opportunities the rewards were plentiful, though not easily gained.

As the number of people employed in the mills increased, terraced accommodation was built to house them. This in turn attracted smaller business to the area, cobblers, butchers, grocers, hardware, animal foodstuffs, Doctors, tailors, beer retailers and so on. Cricket, bowls, tennis, and a Working Men's Club arrived to add to the traditional craftsmen of the township. This process is still ongoing as Denby Dale grows and flourishes.

Chapter Five

Denby Dale in the late Nineteenth and early Twentieth Centuries

Heading from Scissett, one must pass through Kitchenroyd to get to Denby Dale, here pictured in the early twentieth century. *Old Barnsley*

8 Kitchenroyd

I. Wray, P.O. Scissett

Wakefield Road, Denby Dale, around the 1940's. To the left can be seen the site of the present day garage, the petrol pumps at this time, at the front of the premises, abutting the pavement. A Lewis Ellis can be found in the 1936 trade directories as running a motor garage. *Old Barnsley*

H Brownhill's general store, which has now become the World of Wine corner shop, opposite the village school. H Brownhill may have been the same man (Herman) who developed a confectionery business with a man named Shaw from at least 1901. A Herman Brownhill can be found in the Cumberworth parish registers between 1897 and 1899 where he was noted to be an Innkeeper, in Cumberworth. There is no known connection with the mill owning family of the same name. Note the lack of pavement outside the buildings which have in recent times become Italian and Indian food outlets and a Dental surgery, which closed in 2003. The premises of Hirst's carriage company can be seen occupying the site of the present day Doctors surgery, (the low building with the sloping roof). *Old Barnsley*

Trade Directory 1822 – Denby Dale

Mr George Wilby
John Schofield – Blacksmith
Gabriel Tyas – Boot & Shoe Maker
Joshua Morley – Butcher
John Lockwood – Joiner & Cabinet Maker
David Green – Shopkeeper & Carrier
John Hobson – Shopkeeper
Thomas Kilner – Wheelwright
John Sanderson – Academy

Thomas Totton (Turton?) – Boot Maker
Edward Horn – Butcher & Beer Retailer
Joshua Moxon – Corn Miller
George Biltcliffe – Shopkeeper
William Heywood – Shopkeeper
Benjamin Lockwood – Shopkeeper
Isaac Charlesworth – Plumber
John Mitchell – Dyer

Wakefield Road, Denby Dale, early twentieth century. The Upper Corn Mill buildings can just be glimpsed on the extreme right. Some years later, a BP petrol filling station was erected on this side of the road, just a little way up from the corn mill. *Old Barnsley*

General view, Denby Dale.

Taken from Miller Hill, this view of the village was taken prior to the demolition and burial of the Lower corn mill, (centre, left), the site was covered by waste from Kenyons who were enlarging their premises in 1917/18. *Old Barnsley*

An early view of Denby Dale. The Lower corn mill has gone and allotments cover the site. A skyline of chimney's overlook the White Hart as the road bends up towards Cumberworth. Note that the Salvation Army building has not yet been erected. This dates the picture to between 1917/18 and 1927. The local corps of the Salvation Army were established on 11 September 1884 in a wooden hall near the centre of the village (possibly the wooden structures seen here, on the same site). The first officer was Captain Mary McIver. The foundation stone for the new hall was laid in 1926, the corps meeting here until it was disbanded in Denby Dale in 1970.

Denby Dale. 404.

Trade Directory 1838 – Denby Dale

George Wilby – Registrar of Births etc.
John Berry – Beerhouse
Joshua Morley – Butcher
John Peace – Manufacturer
John Wood & Sons – Manufacturers
George Bincliff – Shopkeeper
John Hobson – Shopkeeper

John Mitchell – Dyer
Jonathan Schofield – Blacksmith
Edward Horn – Butcher
Thorpe & Hirsts – Manufacturers
Joseph Gaunt – Farmer
David Green – Shopkeeper

Wakefield Road, Denby Dale, circa 1890. Behind the unknown gentleman's head is the building which now houses Marsden's hardware. Originally, below here, was the blacksmith's and farrier's shop, run for many years by Douglas Heath.

Wakefield Road, Denby Dale, circa 1920's. We even have a lady posing for the camera on the left just after J H Greens. The lady looking in to the shop window on the right may have been considering buying sweets as this was, at one time, Bedford's sweet shop. *Old Barnsley*

A merchant on Wakefield Road, Denby Dale, during the early twentieth century. Wesley Terrace can be seen in the background. The man in the photograph may have been called Billy Bray, as faint pencil writing on the picture can still, just, be discerned.

Trade Directory 1847– Denby Dale

Elijah Whitaker – Valuer & Farmer

James & Edwin Wood – Fancy Manufacturers

Thomas Kilner – Wheelwright

Edward Horn – Butcher

J. R. & C. Wood – Fancy Manufacturers

John Lockwood - Wheelwright

Norman Road, around the 1930's, complete with early motor car. Note the men standing outside the Working Men's Club taking a keen interest in the picture. One of Kenyons mill sheds can be seen below the distant trees. *Old Barnsley*

NORMAN ROAD. DENBY DALE.

The bottom of Norman Road, enduring late snow on 24th April 1908. Kitsons mill chimney's can be seen in the background.

APRIL 24th 1908.

Norman Cottage, Denby Dale, early twentieth century, which once stood near to the present day tennis courts.

1951. The Croft. Denby Dale.

The Croft, Denby Dale, early twentieth century. The Croft was situated after the chemists on Wakefield Road and before the beginning of Prospect Terrace. The picture shows a building, now demolished, which was probably once part of a smallholding to the back of the gardens on Prospect Terrace.

Trade Directory 1866 – Denby Dale

John Schofield – Blacksmith
Jonas Kenyon – Farmer
John Robinson – Farmer
Noah Green – Shopkeeper
Sarah Haywood - Shopkeeper
John Hobson – Shopkeeper

Henry Ellis – Farmer
James Peace – Farmer
George Wilby – Farmer
Giles Haigh - Shopkeeper
Charles Hobson – Shopkeeper

Rockwood Lodge, at the bottom of the drive leading to Walter Norton's old home, Rockwood House, in 1928.

Looking back through Denby Dale from the Prospect Hotel in 1928. J H Green's can be seen on the left and the chemists shop on the right.

A 1928 view looking from the top of Norman Road up towards the viaduct. The Prospect Hotel is in the centre. Note the differing modes of transport!

Cottages to the West side of the viaduct in Denby Dale, early twentieth century. *Old Barnsley*

Trade Directory 1867 – Denby Dale

John Bradford – Fancy Manufacturer
Noah Green – Shopkeeper
Enoch Revell – Lime Merchant
Hugh Wilby – Registrar (Births & Deaths)

Henry Ellis – Coal Owner & Farmer
John Lockwood – Joiner
Thomas Schofield – Coal Owner
Mrs Mary Peace – Fancy Manufacturer

Catchbar, Denby Dale, 1928.

Denby Dale railway station during the early twentieth century. Station Masters have included: Joseph Clegg (1866/67), John Robinson (1871, he was also a bone setter!), and Ezra Arthur Brogden (1912). *Old Barnsley*

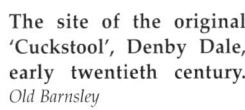

The site of the original 'Cuckstool', Denby Dale, early twentieth century. *Old Barnsley*

175

'Church Fields', Denby Dale. Looking on to Bank House, one time home of the Kenyon family, taken around the 1920's, prior to the building of the stone church.
Old Barnsley

A long forgotten sight. A steam train crosses Denby Dale viaduct.

Carr Bridge or the 'Rotten Bridge' in 1907. The remnants of this bridge can still be seen, below the present day structure, which allows access from the Upper Dearne Woodlands to the footpath heading towards Toby Wood Farm.

Trade Directory 1871 – Denby Dale

John Brearley – Dyer

James Peace – Fancy Woollen
  Manufacturer, Holywell Mill

Worsley & Littlewood – Dyers

The 1928 'Pie' procession makes its way past Hartcliffe mills on the Barnsley Road (K-line).

Trade Directory 1889 – Denby Dale

Mrs Lattice Green Child – Coal Owner

Mary Ann Revell – Lime Merchant

Arthur Ebenezer Wilby – Auctioneer/Surveyor

Moses Worsley – Grocer

Denby Dale Working Men's Club (William Wood, sec.)

William Tetley – Farmer, Gilthwaites

Fred Wood – News Agent

'Top Road', Denby Dale, early twentieth century. Now commonly known as K-line. The mills of Z Hinchliffe can be seen along with their family home, Strathdearne.

Top Road,   Denby Dale.

The moment is near. The 1928 Pie in the final stages of cooking at the corn mill at the bottom of Miller Hill. Miller Hill can be seen continuing upwards to the top right of the picture.

This picture shows the old gas storage vessel, looking from the bridge over the River Dearne at the bottom of Miller Hill, towards the cricket field, in the 1970's. The gas holder, used to store town gas, until required by customers in the area, was formed from a series of short, large diameter tubes which could rise or fall depending on the quality of gas stored. When the area switched to North Sea Gas, the holder was used to smooth the peaks and troughs of demand. The holder was removed during the 1980's. *W H Senior*

Map, dated 1906, which shows the location of the gas vessel in Denby Dale.

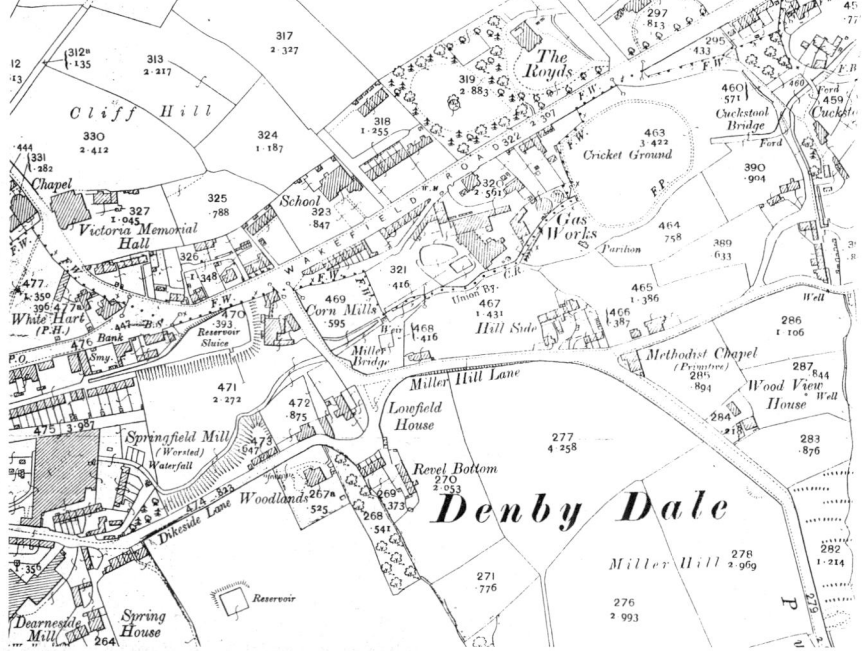

Denby Dale Band, 1889. Probably in front of the Prospect Hotel. The sign above the door reads, 'Beer, Porter and Tobacco'. INSET: Details of Denby Dale Band's achievements over the years.

Denby Dale Band in 1938. Members include: Hector Buckley (back no.5), Raymond Cunningham (front no.7), Wilson Moorhouse (front no.8).

Denby Dale Band 1956, possibly taken at Woodlands, the Doctors house in the village. Back row: A Whitwam, Harry Lockwood, Tommy Kaye, Roy Wainwright, Syd Blackburn, Johnny Garrett. Middle row: Clifford Horsley, Beaumont Wood, Keith Whitehead, Jack Fisher, Harry Lockwood, Desmond Roebuck, Wilson Moorhouse, Richard Horn, Edwin Cunningham, Malcolm Lockwood. Front row: Raymond Cunningham, Lawrence Wainwright, Dennis Haigh, Reggie Beever, Noel Thorpe, Eddie Wilkinson, Malcolm Broadhead, Stanley Schofield, Clarence Boyles. Seated on the floor: Andrew Lockwood, John Kenyon, Barrie Whitwam.

Denby Dale Band, around 1950, possibly at Oakfield House, former residence of James Brownhill. Members include, Harry Morley (back no.5), Wilson Moorhouse (back no.7), Raymond Cunningham (middle no.6), Wilfred Lockwood (front no.4), Clifford Horsley (front no.6).

One of Denby Dale Band's keenest rivals, Upper Denby Band, circa 1951. Back: Kathleen Webb, Mrs Jack Fisher, ?, ? Woodcock, ? Woodcock, Jack Fisher, ?, Robert Chilton, ?, ?, ?. Middle: Norman Horn, Fred Nicholson, Annie Haigh, Alfred Fisher, Norman Mitchell, ?, ?, ?, Nellie Horn, Ivy Moorhouse, Mrs Woodcock. Front: Rafe Barber, Mr Pickford, Delariver Burdett Haigh, Stewart Noble, Mr Woodcock, Douglas Mitchell, Wilson Moorhouse, Norman White, Richard Horn, Jim Harley. Cross legged: ?, ?.

Trade Directory 1901 – Denby Dale

Henry Barden – Shoemaker
Arthur Beever – Tailor & Music Teacher
Emma & Jane Braithwaite – Grocers
George Brown – Surgeon, Woodlands
Alfred Castle – Tailor
William Chilton – Miller (Steam & Water)
Denby Dale Water Works –
   Charles Hinchliffe, Manager
Loxley Wilson Ellis – Grocer & Printing Agent
William Fitton – Yeast Dealer
James Hanson – Grocer
Walter Heath – Joiner
Joe Hirst – Shopkeeper
Walter Holmes – Furniture Dealer
Samuel Kay – Blacksmith

Wilfred Barnes – Clerk & Collector to UDC
Biltcliffe Dental Co. Ltd
Thomas Brierley & Sons – Dyers
Brownhill & Shaw – Confectioners
Mrs Nancy Child – Painter
Mrs Eliza Ann Crossland – Shopkeeper
George Dyson – Shoemaker
Miss Maud Ellis – Milliner
Joseph Henry Green – Grocer & Corn Merchant
Joe Hardy – Tailor
J & J Heywood – Drapers
John Holmes - Joiner
John Horn – Farmer & Dyer
Miss Isabella MacDonald – Dress Maker
George William Moxon – Veterinary Surgeon

Arthur Edward Mathews – Butcher
Arthur Peace – Clothier
Scissett Co-Operative Society
  (Charles Patterson, Manager)
Sheffield Union Banking Co.
  (Frederick Crawshaw, Manager)
Charles Townsend – Druggist
Moses Worsley – Grocer

Miss Lillias Robinson – Dress Maker
Harry Senior – Music Dealer
Fred Stephenson – Hairdresser
Miss Frances Wood – Post Office

Upper Denby school, probably late nineteenth century.

Trade Directory 1912 – Denby Dale

Florence Bansgrove – Infant School Mistress
Cecil Walter Ramsay Banham – Surgeon, Woodlands
John Thomas Atkins – Coaldealer
George Blacker – Hairdresser
Albert Castle – Tailor
Denby Dale Club – Charlie Senior, sec.
Denby Dale U.D. Water Works –
  Fred Greenwood – manager
Henry Grayson – Shopkeeper
Harry Hanson – Shopkeeper
William Arthur Heap – Butcher
William Jubb – Plumber
Tom Duckett Mathews – Butcher
George William Moxon – Veterinary Surgeon
Thomas Robertshaw – Dentist (Friday's)
Willie Thorpe – Greengrocer
Robert Walsham Wright – Drug Store

Sam Shepley – School Master
Walter Armitage – Shopkeeper
Arthur Beever – Tailor & Music Teacher
James Arthur Braithwaite – Saddler
Misses B & E Coldwell – Drapers
Denby Dale & District Sanitary Laundry –
  George Robert Senior, proprietor
Albert Dawson Froggatt – Boot Maker
Noah Green – Shopkeeper
Haigh & Lockwood – Joiners
Miss Lizzie Horn – Farmer
Ernest Littlewood – Shopkeeper
Thomas Milnes – Butcher
Fred Peace – Shopkeeper
Shaw & Brownhill – Confectioners
Arthur Wooley – Miller (water)

Denby Dale cricket team in 1905. Thomas Hinchliffe, son of Zaccheus, was instrumental in founding the village cricket team around the late nineteenth century. Over a hundred years later it is still going strong. A National Lottery grant of £320,000 coupled with the clubs own fund raising total of over £50,000 meant that improvements planned for the ground in 1995 could finally be carried out in 1998. Support was also given from the Foundation for Sport and the Arts, Huddersfield Common Good Trust, Kirklees Council, Lords Cricket Headquarters, Denby Dale Carnival, the Pie Trust and others. Sponsorship also came from the present day directors of Z Hinchliffe & Son who, fittingly, lent the company name to the new building. The pavilion was completed in 1999 and incorporated modern changing facilities and two community rooms for village groups. The official opening of these new facilities took place on 22 August 1999. George Wilby of Z Hinchliffe & Sons cut the ceremonial ribbon and Audrey Kenyon (sister of the late John Hinchliffe), released 200 balloons to start a very special match. To celebrate in style Denby Dale men's first eleven took on the England women's cricket team. Watched by a crowd of about 1000 people, the England ladies batted first, making 135 for 7 wickets but they were beaten by the Dale men, who only just scraped the win. The cricket field was put to another use on 2 July 2000, to celebrate the new Millennium. People drawn from nine schools and eleven churches from Denby Dale, Clayton West, Cumberworth, Skelmanthorpe and Scissett put on an outdoor musical performance called Hopes and Dreams, which was based on the Lords Prayer. Hundreds watched the performance, the choir and orchestra being conducted by Jane Hobson, other attractions included a pig roast and local bands.

Expectant supporters of Denby Dale cricket team in the early twentieth century.

Denby Dale cricket ground, during the 1970's, before re-development. Cuckstool Road can be seen on the skyline.

Trade Directory 1922 – Denby Dale

Robert Richmond Archibald – Medical Officer of Health, Woodlands
Andrew Barden – Shoe Maker
Dr. John T Blaxdell – Surgery
Central Garage (J W Turton) – Motor Engineers
Denby Dale Club – Edwin Hanson, sec.
Ashley Fretwell – Fried Fish Dealer
Oliver Haigh – Joiner
Elizabeth H Horn – farmer
Charles Kilner – Butcher
London Joint City & Midland Bank (E L Ferrall, Manager)
Ida Robinson – Shopkeeper
Denby Dale & District Sanitary Laundry – F. Wong, proprietor

Ernest Armitage – Shopkeeper
Arthur Beever – Tailor
James Arthur Braithwaite – Saddler
John J J Cope – Drug Store
Dronfield & Brownhill – Blacksmiths
J H Green – Grocer
Joe Heywood – Draper, Birkwood
Jubb & Taylor – Plumbers
Mrs Hedley Kitson – Coal Dealer
Miss Ellen Smith Revell – Manure Merchant
Sam Armitage – Pastry Cook

The 1887 Denby Dale Pie is drawn to its burial site at Toby Wood. Sidney Lodge leads the procession.

Celebrations on Sunny Bank around the early twentieth century. The road separates Sunny Bank from the Slade, where the present day youth club and children's play area now stand.

Salvation Army gathering 1909 in front of J H Green's grocers and corn merchants.

More scenes from the Salvation Army gathering of 1909, upon the occasion of General Booth's visit. Booth founded the movement in 1865.

A school feast in Denby Dale from around 1905.

Trade Directory 1936 – Denby Dale

Fred Bates – Inkerman Farm
Francis Andrew – Chemist
John Thomas Ashton – Baker
Harry Bedford – Shopkeeper
Arnold Dearnley – Boot Repairer, Miller Hill
Wilfred Garner – Hairdresser
W A Heap & Son – Butchers
George Lee – Butcher
Midland Bank Ltd
Arthur Priest – Fried Fish Dealer
John William Rowley – Ladies and Gents.
   Tailor & Outfitter
Frederick W Stanger – Wireless Engineer
Martha Townsend – Newsagent & Post Office
Percy Wilkinson – Boot Repairer
Eliza Thackray – Dress Maker & Costumier

James Buckley – Farmer, Dry Hill
George Herbert Arnison – Physician, Woodlands
Winifred Barraclough – Confectioner
Central Garage (Hirst Bros.) – Motor Haulage
   Contractors
Lewis Ellis – Motor Garage
J H Green – Corn Millers
Cyril Jones – Physician & Surgeon, Millbrook
Arthur Lockwood – Joiner
Granville Mosley – Clerk to UDC
Charles Ross – Newsagent
Smithson & Littlewood – Builders
Tom Stringer & Sons – Tailors
United Yeast Co. – Royds Cottages
J Hirst & Sons – Grocers
Denby Dale Club (Frank Allot, sec.)

The unveiling of the War Memorial in Denby Dale on 21st July 1923.

The 1928 Denby Dale Pie procession, heading up High Street. The chemists shop can clearly be seen as can the London Joint City & Midland Bank on the corner of Norman Road.

Dr Arnison hands over his patients in Denby Dale to Dr Mitchell in 1946. Back row: Rene Morley, Barbara Roebuck, Mrs Dawson, Mrs G Lockwood, Mrs Lockwood, Mrs Mate. Seated: Mrs Mitchell, Dr Mitchell, Nurse Hartigan, Dr Arnison, Mrs Williams, Mrs Hopkinson. We have already noted the names of the early district Doctors in MacGregor, Banham, Brown and Archibald. We can also mention, Dr Bleasdale and this photograph shows their successors. The practice, in Dr Arnison's time was centred on the buildings which now host the newsagents in the village. The Doctors residence was at 'Woodlands' on 'Hillside', or Dearneside Road. Doctor Mitchell continued in practice until around 1972/3 when he was succeeded by Dr's, Buxton, Scott and Wood. These were in turn joined by Dr Samanta and formed the basis of the group practice which now operates from Skelmanthorpe, with a surgery at Denby Dale.

Dr Mitchell took part in the choosing of the Denby Dale Coronation Queen in 1951, at the village School. The decision was made in favour of Maureen Sowerby. Back row, left to right: Catherine Coldwell, Dr Dennis Mitchell, Mrs Joan Mitchell, Hazel Hollingworth. Front row: Margaret Lockwood, Sheila Lloyd, Stewart Kilner, Maureen Sowerby, Judy Benson, Rita Wood, John Horsley, Carol Newby.

The Coronation Queen is crowned and sits upon her throne. Jonas and Isabel Kenyon stand behind the Queen. Mrs Algernon Hall stands on the right behind the girl holding a cushion, (Catherine Coldwell).

Feast day celebrations in approximately 1956. Denby Dale band accompany the school children, here pictured at the Gilthwaites housing estate.

Denby Dale village centre during the 1970's. Joe Mosley's fish and chip shop, Carol Anne clothing, the old Co-op and Barradell's village stores can all be seen. Note the lack of traffic and parked cars! *W H Senior*

Greenfeeds premises during the 1970's. The Green family can be found in Denby Dale at least as far back as 1822, when David Green was recorded as a shopkeeper and carrier. By 1866, Noah Green had taken over, he was succeeded by Joseph Henry Green who in 1901 was described as a grocer and corn merchant. Another Noah Green was recorded in 1912 as a shopkeeper, but J H (Joseph Henry) was recorded as a grocer in 1922 and corn miller in 1936. *W H Senior*

This spectacular bus crash at the bottom of Miller Hill occurred around 1974. The brakes of the bus failed and it crashed through the wall of the bridge, the cabin ending up in the stream below.

Present day Denby Dale from the air. The Naylor's and Kenyon's sites are now covered by new housing estates. The premises of Kitson's underlay Denby Dale Industrial Estate. *Courtesy of the Huddersfield Daily Examiner*

Aerial view of Denby Dale, 1997, featuring Gilthwaites, Cuckstool and the cricket pitch.

Chapter Six

The Story of the New Inn – and a look at other Inns in the District

✧

In volume 1 of this work I briefly examined the history of the New Inn at Upper Denby. Now, with the co-operation of the current owner of the property I am able to give a far better picture and include details never before published.

We know that the public house was operating by 1838 but prior to this the building seems to have been a dwelling only.

An indenture was made on 23rd April 1808 between George Turton, Surgeon and Apothecary of Denby and Abraham Mullin of Halifax, Druggist, Benjamin Rose of Sheffield, Druggist and Joseph Wreaks of Sheffield, Merchant along with several creditors of George Turton.

George was in debt to Mullin and Rose and to Robert Wreaks who had died and was represented by his administrator and son, Joseph. George was evidently in serious financial trouble and had been arrested by Joseph Wreaks for non-payment of £28 4s prior to the indenture being created. Turton had no choice, his *'goods, chattels, household stuff, furniture, stock in trade, book debts, sums of money, land, including a parcel at Denby and effects whatsoever'* were legally made over to Mullin and Rose. They were given the right to dispose of them however they saw fit in order to recover their debts. The *'necessary wearing apparel of George and his wife and*

The Turton Family

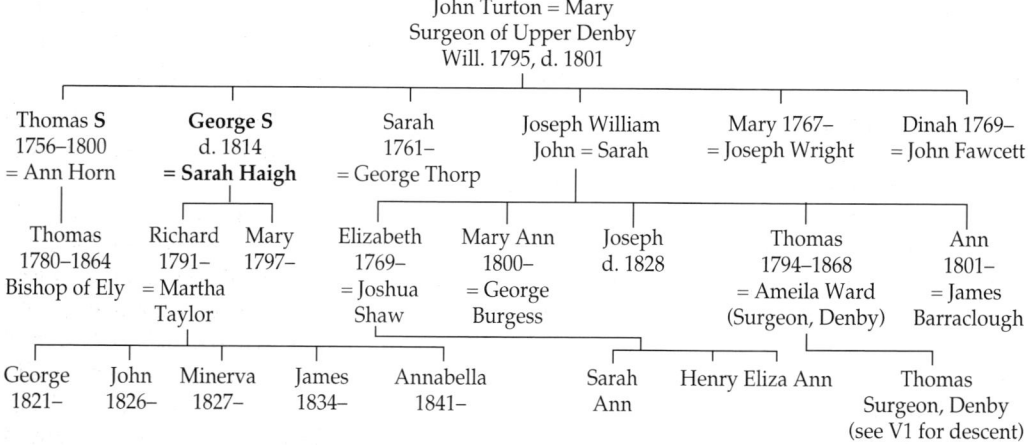

John Turton = Mary
Surgeon of Upper Denby
Will. 1795, d. 1801

| Thomas **S** 1756–1800 = Ann Horn | George **S** d. 1814 = **Sarah Haigh** | Sarah 1761– = George Thorp | Joseph William John = Sarah | Mary 1767– = Joseph Wright | Dinah 1769– = John Fawcett |

Thomas 1780–1864 Bishop of Ely

Richard 1791– = Martha Taylor

Mary 1797–

Elizabeth 1769– = Joshua Shaw

Mary Ann 1800– = George Burgess

Joseph d. 1828

Thomas 1794–1868 = Ameila Ward (Surgeon, Denby)

Ann 1801– = James Barraclough

George 1821– John 1826– Minerva 1827– James 1834– Annabella 1841–

Sarah Ann

Henry Eliza Ann

Thomas Surgeon, Denby (see V1 for descent)

NB: Elizabeth Turton and Joshua Shaw ran the Wagon & Horses Inn at Lower Denby.
S - Surgeon

family' were the only things exempted from the deal. Wreaks was also to be paid out of the proceeds collected by Mullin and Rose.

George is reputed to have lived at a property now known as 'The Old Tavern' formerly the New Inn public house. He was a member of the successful family of 'Denby doctors' of which Thomas Turton of Pinfold and his son, also called Thomas were the most successful.

One has to wonder if there was bad blood between George and the family as surely he could have called upon them to aid him in his time of need, though pride remains a very likely contender for his loss.

A further document would appear to suggest that George had retained an interest in the property. An indenture was made by Benjamin Rose and Richard Turton (a weaver) of Denby to James Seddon, also of Denby, a dyer, on 27th June 1825. Seddon paid 5 shillings to Rose and Turton in order to buy the property described thus:

> *all that piece or parcel of land situate and parcel of the green, number 49 in the place annexed to the award of the commissioners for the Inclosure of the Common of Denby aforesaid containing by survey, 6 perches bounded by a road on or towards the east and south by an allotment awarded to William Kilner, on or towards the west by an ancient inclosure of Joseph Gaunt.*

The rent of a pepper corn (a nominal value) was to be made during the first year by Seddon after which he became sole owner of the property. The document also mentions Sarah Turton, who was the widow of George Turton mentioned previously. The indenture was witnessed by Richard Turton, James Barraclough and Jonathan Firth.

Made a day later than the above document, this document relates to the release of land at Denby by Benjamin Rose and others to James Seddon. This document again refers to the 1808 indenture whereby Abraham Mullin and Benjamin Rose took possession of George Turton's property. By this time Abraham Mullin had died though the date is blank. George Turton had also passed away in 1814, leaving his wife Sarah (described as his relict) and his eldest son, Richard as his heirs. Somehow, Sarah Turton had retained some interest in the land referred to in the document:

> *… the said George Turton and the said Sarah Turton (who is entitled to dower in such piece or parcel of land and hereditaments) for the greater satisfaction of the said James Seddon and for releasing and extinguishing the dower right or title of the dower in such piece or parcel of land … have agreed to join in the conveyance thereof in manner hereinafter mentioned for the further sum of £2.*

James Seddon made his payments for his house and lands, £5 to Benjamin Rose and £2 to Richard and Sarah Turton this very day as acknowledged at the end of the document. He was now in full possession and his rights were affirmed.

George Turton acquired the above mentioned land from Joseph Gaunt sometime prior to 1802 as it is noted on the plan which accompanies the enclosure award. Never once in the latter documents is a messuage or home referred to though the documents are all tied to the building which became the New Inn. Number '49' on the plan is definitely the site of the later public house. It is possible that George and his family lived elsewhere in the village and the land had been a speculative acquisition by George in more affluent times. When Rose and Mullin confiscated all his goods to pay off his debts he must have held an interest in the latter mentioned land. His son Richard, probably on behalf of his mother after his fathers death in 1814, is involved in the sale to Seddon, acting with Benjamin Rose. If a house existed here in 1808, Turton may have mortgaged it to his creditors and continued to live here, perhaps even paying a rent. From Rose acquiring an interest in the property in 1808 to 1825, the date of sale, a period of seventeen years had elapsed. This would suggest that Sarah Turton had decided to leave, perhaps to live with her son.

James Seddon seems to have done very nicely in acquiring the land as mentioned above. By indenture, dated 20th December 1825, between himself and Joshua Brook of High Flatts, yeoman, he agreed to mortgage parcel of land, (noted to be number 49 on the Enclosure Award map and detailed exactly as described above), upon which Seddon had built a cottage for £100. This is the first mention of a dwelling existing upon the site. If George Turton had lived here, the edifice must have been pulled down in order to build a new one.

Seddon's wife, Susannah, was included in the document in an amazingly long list of do's and do not's, this was in reference to her dower portion which was to be null and void. This perhaps a result of Seddon's experiences when he bought the property and land and had to pay £2 to Richard and Sarah Turton. Seddon seems to have used the land and dwelling as collateral for a loan from Joshua Brooke, at an interest rate of £5 per annum per £100 which was to be paid on 20th June. When the loan was repaid, Seddon and his wife, Susannah were to be re-admitted to the ownership of the property and Susannah was to be made eligible for her dower portion.

By Easter, 1832, things had gone badly wrong for James Seddon. A detailed invoice has survived from this time sent from William Stephenson, solicitor, to Joshua Brooke for work undertaken to retrieve the money owed by Seddon, totalling at £39 17s 10d. Seddon had defaulted upon the interest payments and now, seven years after the original agreement was drawn up, Brooke had had enough. Some of Stephenson's charges make for interesting reading:

> *Writing letter to Messrs Tindall & Varey Solicitors, Manchester with writ and instructions to procure warrant thereon and get defendant arrested 3s 6d.*

> 8th May – *Journey to High Flatts and attending you thereon & horse 7s 6d.*

> 8th May – *Defendant having gone to gaol instructions for declaration 6s 8d.*

> 15th September – *Journey to Cross Pipes and attending meeting of creditors, out all the afternoon and horse 7s 6d.*

> 18th October – *Attending sale at Denby on our road from Penistone 10s 6d*

By 13th July 1832, James Seddon was noted to be living at Grosvenor Street, Chorlton Row near Manchester. It seems likely that he had fled from Denby once times had become financially difficult which may have prompted Brooke to have taken action against him in the first place. On the same date an indenture was created between Samuel Sturgis of Lincoln's Inn Fields, the Government appointed *'Provisional Assignee of the Estate and Effects of Insolvent Debtors in England'* and William Stephenson of Holmfirth on behalf of Joshua Brooke. James Seddon's occupation had changed from a dyer to a 'mechanical chimney sweep' and he was now referred to as an insolvent debtor, as a result of which he was languishing as a prisoner in Lancaster castle. The indenture legally signed over the land and building to William Stephenson 'for the use, benefit and advantage of the creditors of James Seddon' who, it was noted, was to be entitled to a share in the dividend of the said estate if it should make so much. That Seddon tried to cover his tracks whilst in Manchester becomes obvious when we see how many times he moved home, details we get from a notice posted by William Stephenson in the London Gazette regarding a meeting of creditors at the Cross Pipes, Birdsedge:

The London Gazette, Friday, August 24th, 1832

*Notice is hereby given, that a meeting of the creditors of **James Seddon**, formerly of Denby, in the Parish of Penistone, in the County of York, Woollen Dyer, then of Bailey Street, Manchester, in the County of Lancaster, Assistant to a Woollen Manufacturer, then Ashton Street, Manchester, aforesaid, Labourer, and late of Grosvenor Street, Chorlton Row, near Manchester aforesaid, Mechanical Chimney Sweeper, an insolvent debtor, who was lately discharged from Lancaster Castle will be holden on the 15th day of September next, at the hour of Three o'clock in the afternoon precisely, at the house of Mr. Joseph Nightingale, the Cross Pipes Inn, in Cumberworth, in the said county of York, in order to assent or dissent from the Assignee conveying over to the mortgagee the real estate of the said Insolvent, for the principal and interest now due thereon to such Mortgagee; and in case of dissent, to approve and direct at what place such real estate shall be sold by auction.*

The meeting was duly held and it was decided that the property would be auctioned on Thursday the 18th of October *'at the house of Mr Joseph Brooke, the Star Inn, Denby….between 5 & 7 o'clock in the evening'*.

One presumes that Joseph was a near relative of Joshua. At the auction, Joshua Brooke out-bid any opposition with a total of £126 10s. A document was drawn up dated 10th November 1832 releasing the property from William Stephenson to Joshua Brooke, it goes on to say that Brooke was owed £100 along with a further £24 10s for interest. The remaining £2, Brooke paid to Stephenson, though it is unlikely that James Seddon saw a penny of this.

A John Brook, probably a relative of Joshua Brooke, can be found running the New Inn in 1838, the earliest mention of the building being used as a public house. By 1857, John Hanwell had taken over as the landlord, he was succeeded by his wife Mary. The Hanwells were employed by Seth Senior and Sons, brewers who took over the tenancy of the building sometime around 1838. The building was surplus to Joshua Brooke's requirements and it was only natural that he let it out for rent. The census returns of 1841 note Joshua Brook, aged 76, an agricultural labourer and Joshua Brook, 55, farmer of High Flatts. Our Joshua Brook must be the High Flatts farmer, he would have been around 39 years old at the time he lent James Seddon the £100. By 1841, the John Brook running the pub seems to have left, one presumes that John Hanwell had recently taken over.

By 1884 the ownership of the New Inn had fallen into the hands of the Green family. Still running as a public house, rented by Reuben Senior (son of the brewer Seth) at a yearly rate of £19, Mary Hanwell was the landlady. Tamar Green, the wife of Amos Green who was a retired publican died on 12th December 1884 at Netherfield Villas, Thurlstone aged 59. Tamar was the owner of the New Inn rather than her husband, one can only presume that it was bequested to her by one of her immediate family. It is unknown as to whether Amos Green was ever its landlord.

On 1st March 1886 the property passed to Elizabeth Moulton, of Green Villa, Penistone, a 'lineal issue' of Tamar Green, therefore we may presume that Elizabeth was the, by now married, daughter of Tamar. An Inland Revenue document drawn up to calculate succession duty declared that Elizabeth was born on 9th December 1852 and that the net annual value of the New Inn was £18 (annual rental £19 less £1 for repairs). Elizabeth was charged duty of 1% which came to £2 15s 3d after the annuity for a life aged 32 on £18 was valued at £291 8s 4d in order to inherit.

Less than two years later, Seth Senior & Sons contacted Elizabeth, the death of Seth's son, Reuben had left a void and on checking their records they had realised that their lease on the New Inn would soon expire, a letter dated 1st March 1888 requests her permission to continue. Elizabeth replied in the affirmative and at the same terms as before.

An indenture was made between Elizabeth Moulton of 1, Dunollie Road, Kentish Town, London (the wife of George Moulton) and Louisa MacKenzie of 74 Burlington Road, Bayswater, London on 29th May 1894. The document describes Louisa MacKenzie lending Elizabeth Moulton £100 (we seem to have seen this situation before with regard to this building!). Elizabeth conveyed to Louisa:

> all that messuage, public house, dwelling house and premises known as the New Inn Tavern with the stable and outbuildings thereunto belonging situate and being at Denby, in the parish of High Hoyland in the County of York and which said premises are now in the occupation of one **Mary Hanwell** to hold the same together with the appurtenances unto and to the use of the said Louisa MacKenzie in fee simple for securing payment on the twenty ninth day of November, one thousand eight hundred and ninety four of the principal sum of one hundred pounds as the mortgage money with interest thereon at the rate of six pounds per centum per annum.

Elizabeth did not long survive her inheritance as she died on 21st June 1901 leaving all her property to a Thomas Shaughnessey, and indeed her debt to Louisa MacKenzie!

> Be it known that Elizabeth Moulton (wife **of George Moulton**) of the Elephant and Castle Hotel, Westgate, Wakefield in the County of York, formerly of 1, Dunollie Road, Kentish Town in the County of Middlesex who at the time of her death had a fixed place of abode at the Elephant and Castle Hotel aforesaid within the district of the West Riding of the County of York died on the twenty first day of June 1901 at the Elephant and Castle Hotel aforesaid.
>
> And be it further known that at the date hereunder written the last will and testament (a copy whereof is hereunto annexed) of the said deceased was proved and registered in the District Probate Registry of His Majesty's High Court of Justice at Wakefield and that administration of all the estate which by law devolves to and vests in the personal representative of the said deceased was granted by the aforesaid Court to **Mr Thomas Shaughnessey**, the sole executor named in the said will.
>
> And it is hereby certified that an affidavit for Inland Revenue has been delivered wherein it is shown that the gross value of the said estate within the United Kingdom (exclusive of what the deceased may have been possessed of or entitled to as a Trustee and not beneficially) amounts to £312.16.0 and that the said affidavit bears a stamp of £2.10.0.
>
> Dated the fourth day of October 1901.

Thomas Shaughnessey obviously encountered problems in receiving the rent due to him from Seth Senior & Sons for the New Inn. He instructed his solicitors to apply for £9 10s being rent due to him on 13th January 1902 and mentioned that Mrs Moulton had died and her will had been proved. Problem solved! A cheque duly arrived and was acknowledged on the 18th. It wasn't all one way traffic of course, on 17th May 1902 the same solicitors wrote to Shaughnessey at the Upholsterers Club, 117 Gower Street, London informing him that the £100 due to Louisa MacKenzie was now due. Evidently Shaughnessey did not have the necessary funds, therefore he took out a mortgage on the New Inn of £150 at 4% interest with James Senior of Seth Senior and Sons, sitting tenants of the New Inn. Out of this Louisa MacKenzie was to be paid off along with some of his other debts.

The New Inn was again used as collateral against the loan to guarantee re-payment. By 12th July 1904 Thomas Shaughnessey had decided that his bequest from Elizabeth Moulton was more trouble than it was worth and he instructed his solicitors, Claremont and Haynes to contact Seth Senior & Sons to ask whether they were prepared to make him an offer on the premises. In reply, probably from James Senior, they pointed out that it was unusual for them to put a price on someone else's property and were not prepared to make this an exception but, if Mr Shaughnessey would like to put a fair price on the premises they would consider the option. They also pointed out that:

> *no doubt he (Shaughnessey) is aware that it (the New Inn) is in a poor village with two more licensed houses close by and on the hill where there is no prospect of improvement.*

Shaughnessey responded by quoting a figure of £500 but James Senior came back with an offer of only £450 suggesting that if it was not acceptable perhaps an auction might better test the market value. The matter dragged throughout July, Shaughnessey refused to accept the £450 on offer and eventually Senior's relented and agreed the £500, on 27th July they sent a cheque for £50 as deposit. Shaughnessey probably fought for £500 as he knew that the mortgage, borrowed from Senior's of £150 would now have to be paid back in full.

On 31st December when the conveyance was drawn up, it noted that the interest accrued upon Shaughnessey's debt to Senior had been paid up to date and that only the £150 was due. Thomas Shaughnessey received a payment of £350 from James Senior and with it his interest in the Inn was finished.

Seth Senior and Sons continued to hold the property until they were bought out by Hammonds United Breweries of Lockwood who in turn were taken over by Bass Charringtons, the New Inn eventually ceased trading in 1963, when it was converted into a private residence.

Still in public life, after the New Inn was converted into a private home, Mrs W Wheable began a Youth Club for Denby children, here pictured in January 1977. Back, left to right: Graham Pickford, William Marsden, Julian Barden, David Richardson, Andrew Holmes, Ian Slater, David Goodwin, Winifred Wheable. Middle, left to right: John Richardson, Alison Badbury, Rachel Goodwin, Beverley Stead, Suzie Hepworth, Dawn Booth, Phillipa Goodwin, Ruth Haigh, Suzie Goodwin, Gillian Barber. Front, left to right: Alison Lee, Judith Leeming, Sheila Booth, Fiona Lee.

The following is by no means a complete listing of every public house and tenant in the area but it does illustrate how many Inns had been established around the district, excluding Beer Houses and is a basis for further study.

PUBLIC HOUSES IN DENBY AND ITS DISTRICT

Joiners Arms – Denby Dale

1822	Joseph Lockwood
1834	John Lockwood
1838	Ann Lockwood

White Hart-Denby Dale

1842/1847/1857/1866/1867	Ann Lockwood
1871/1889	John Lockwood
1901	Thomas Firth
1912/1922	John Jewitt
1936	William Darren

From the latter two panels we can hazard a guess that the Joiners Arms may have undergone a name change between 1838 and 1842, just as it did in the mid 1990's when it became known, albeit briefly, as Mr Boons. The landlady is the same and she remains here until at least 1867, the pub being run by the family for at least 77 years. The first John Lockwood appears to have been a joiner in these days when a public house was run as a secondary occupation.

Prospect Hotel – Denby Dale

1889/1901	Charles William Kilner
1912	William Dyson
1922	William Dyson
1936	Harry Addy

The Wellington – Upper Denby

1834	Joshua Shaw

The White Swan – High Flatts

1838	Jonathan Jubb

The Rose & Crown – Ingbirchworth

1822	John Mellor
1834	George Barraclough
1837	Jonathan Brown
1838	George Barraclough
1861/1871/1877/1889/1901/1904	Thomas Holmes
1912	Charles Langley
1922	John Scholey
1936	Charles Henry Wilkinson

The Prospect Hotel, Denby Dale, Peckett Row is to the right, probably during the 1950's. *Old Barnsley*

An early twentieth century view of Pump Row, High Flatts. One of these cottages was once the White Swan public house.

The Travellers Inn – Denby Dale		Cross Pipes Inn – Cross Pipes, Birdsedge	
1838	John Holden	1832/1834/1838	Joseph Nightingale
1857	Michael Braithwaite	1842	Charles Murgatroyd
1877	Joseph Dalton	1847	George Murgatroyd
1889	Jane Dalton	1857/1871/1877	Charles Murgatroyd
1901	Timothy Mitchell	1901	Reuben Smith
1912	Charles Harmwell	1912	Mrs Martha Smith

A very early photograph of the Rose and Crown at Ingbirchworth. Thomas Holmes' name can clearly be seen on the pub sign. Holmes was the landlord here from 1861 until 1901. Note that the building pictured, faced the opposite way to today's public house. *Old Barnsley*

The Cross Pipes Inn, Birdsedge, which closed in the 1920's.

The Travellers Inn & Druids Tavern, later just the Travellers Inn – Ingbirchworth

1871	Thomas Roebuck
1877	Ann Roebuck
1889/1901	John Dickinson

The Crown – Birdsedge

1877	John Tinker
1901	Joseph Sedgwick
1912	Arthur Lodge
1922	Ernest Thorpe
1936	Herbert Horn

The Star – Upper Cumberworth

1838/1842	George Rusby
1847	George Rushworth
1857/1877	George Smith
1901/1912	William Brook
1922/1936	Roland Brownhill

Red Lion – Upper Cumberworth

1838/1842	George Jakeman
1847	John Jakeman

The Star – Lower Cumberworth

1838/1842	Ninah Kilner

The Crown Inn, Birdsedge, which closed during the 1960's.

Cumberworth School and Cross Road

Staring at us from the end of the road is the Star, at Upper Cumberworth, the school is on the right, circa early twentieth century *Old Barnsley*

Foresters Inn – Lower Cumberworth

1847	Richard Kilner
1857	Thomas Kay
1901	James Peace
1912	Charlie Lockwood
1922/1936	John Henry Lockwood

Dunkirk Inn-Lower Denby

1866	Elizabeth Burgess
1867	Allen Booth
1871	Sarah Johnson
1877	Emma Johnson
1889	Walker Haigh
1922/1936	James Gill

Wagon & Horses – Lower Denby

1799	Joseph Graham
1822	William Hague
1838	Joshua Shaw
1841	Elizabeth Shaw nee Turton
1861	Mrs Senior
1867/1871/1881	John Johnson

Globe – Skelmanthorpe (probably)

1838	Joseph Gawthorpe
1857	Edward Gawthorpe
1866	Charles Littlewood

Horseshoes (Three) – Skelmanthorpe

1838	Joseph Gawthorpe
1857/1866	Samuel Peel

Grove – Skelmanthorpe

1838	John Senior
1857	James Jubb
1866	Jonathan Greenwood

Commercial Inn – Skelmanthorpe

1857/1866	Joseph Eastwood

Royal Oak – Skelmanthorpe

1838	Joseph Hay
1857	N Fisher

Windmill – Skelmanthorpe

1857/1866	John Berry

Commercial Inn - ?Lower Cumberworth?

1857	Hezekiah Tinker
1877	John Shaw
1901	Herman Brownhill
1912/1922	Mrs Mary Ellen Woodhouse

Crown – Scissett

1857	John Schofield
1866	Thomas Ely
1912	Sam Farrington
1936	Thomas Rusby

Queens Head – Scissett

1857/1866	Richard Roberts
1912	Tom Wilfred Crossland
1936	Thomas Mathews

The Duke William – Clayton West

1822/1838/1857	Thomas Gelder

This Inn stood at the Guide Post leading to Church Lane but had become a farm by 1939.

One Inn not featured in this list is the White Bear, also in Clayton. Nothing survives of this edifice today.

Commercial Inn – Clayton West

1838	Samuel Liles
1857	Thomas Farrington
1901	Mrs Julia A Douglas
1912	Fred Hobson
1922	John T Gibson
1936	Risdon Armitage Woodcock

New Inn – Clayton West

1822	Eli Clegg
1838	John Brettoner
1857	James Rawnsley
1901	Joseph Barber
1922	Harry Sanderson

Shoulder of Mutton – Clayton West

1857	George Tinker
1901	Milton Shaw
1912	Joseph Batty
1922	Edgar Rhodes
1936	Ada Rhodes

Woodman – Clayton West

1838/1853/1857	Thomas Hall
1901	John Bedford
1912	David Allott
1922	James Smith
1926	George Puddephat
1936	John Oates

The George Inn – Upper Denby

1857/1861/1866	Enoch Taylor
1881	Nancy Taylor
1882/1889	George Taylor

1901/1904	Alfred Taylor
1909	Joseph Airton
1917	Benjamin Slater
1926	Edward Daniel
1927	Genny Buckley
1930–1958	Frank & Mabel Widdowson
1959–1970	Jim & Dot Barber
1971–1992	Roy Barraclough
1992	Martin & Carol Brook
1993–1999	Steven & Jill Slater
1999–2000	Ken Hunt
2000–2002	Joan Eastwood & Clare Davis(solely in 2002)
2002–present	Graham & Tracy Mallinson

The New Inn – Upper Denby

1838	John Brook
1857/1861/1866/1867	John Hanwell
1881/1889	Mary Hanwell
1901	Hannah Pearce
1904	Harry Thorpe
1912/1917	Sam Wing
1927/1930	Percy Cartwright
1950 app.	Walt Martin
1952 app.	Eric & Joyce Bailey
1954	Doug & June Fisher
1958–63	? Fisher

The Star – Upper Denby

1799	John Barraclough
1822	Amos Barraclough
1830	Thomas Burdet
1832	Joseph Brook
1838/1857/1861	John Firth
1866/1867/1881/1889	Aaron Hanwell
1901	Wilson Green
1904	Joshua Swainson

The Globe/Cherry Tree – High Hoyland

1838	Ely Clegg
1889/1901	Thomas Holden (also a farmer)
1912/1922	Robert T Gill

The Cherry Tree or Globe, at High Hoyland, early twentieth century. *Old Barnsley*

The Globe Inn existed in 1281 when the Archdeacon visited the parish and Archbishop Corbridge probably passed it on his way from Kirkburton to Doncaster in 1305. It was built of timber and plaster and for centuries was known as the Cherry Tree derived from the orchard which existed behind the present day Inn. In the 17th century the timber structure was replaced with stone. In the 19th century the name was changed to the Shoulder of Mutton and later to the Globe but the reasons for this are unknown.

The Rag & Louse, later the Fountain Inn

1871	George Huscroft
1889	Mrs Caroline Sykes
1912	Edward Woodhead
1922	George Rowe
1936	Archie Moorhouse

The trade directories list the latter as 'Beer Retailers' and do not mention a specific name for the Inn. This is unusual which leads me to suspect that the name 'Rag & Louse' was used as a sarcastic term of endearment by the locals, perhaps in its early days. Older residents may remember that an old stage coach in a bad state of disrepair stood in the car park until comparatively recent times.

Chapter Seven

Of the Wood family and their endowment of Denby Dale school; and typhoid in the village

The story of the Wood family and particularly two half brothers, has been published before. '*A Memoir of Mr James Wood – Including Notices of other Members of his Family*' was written by Thomas Williams and published in 1883; Williams was certainly a friend and possibly a relative. His narrative, though over wordy and hardly explosive is worth a read for anyone who should wish to know more. I have based the following highly selective narrative upon this work as it is about time a little more of their story was told to a more modern readership. Details concerning the village school which they helped to found have also previously been published in a centenary booklet produced in 1974 based largely on the thesis of Margaret Kendall. Again I have been highly selective in the material I have used but again it is time that some of this information was commercially available again. The original booklet is excellent and I would recommend it for further study.

John Wood (1755–1831) was a passionate Wesleyan Methodist and was responsible for introducing this branch of religion into Denby Dale. He had split from the organisation at Shelley when they went over to the new connection in 1797 and had begun holding meetings in his textile warehouse, indeed, employees at the family firm of John Wood and Sons were frequently employed to prepare the buildings for their Sunday purpose. Old Well House, and Field House on Wakefield Road seem to have been the site of this early activity, though we noted in a previous chapter that the family ran a fulling and scribbling mill at the Hartcliffe site in Denby Dale.

In 1799 a purpose built chapel was erected and a dwelling for the preacher, due to the efforts of John Wood and his brother Joseph, thus the future of Methodism in Denby Dale became secure.

John was possibly the son of Joshua Wood who died at Cumberworth in 1786. A John Wood, along with two others valued his fathers effects, farm stock and working equipment. Among the household goods were items such as a milking kit, a piggin and wood boul, a warming pan, iron bakestone, bread creel, mattock bill, sett pot, dresser, delf cases, pot hooks and pewter dishes. Joshua was a farmer as well as a manufacturer. On the farm he had a cow and heifer, two horses, a cart, hen chickens and a cockerel valued at £21 9s 11d. His hay in the barn, the corn in the field, harrows, plough and manure were worth £15 16s. Since he was a manufacturer of cloth this was also valued. Finished cloth was valued at £30. He had two packs of size and two sheets with 3 cwts of Redwood for dying, all worth 18 guineas. His working tools were considerable and included a cloth press, six pairs of sheers, 2 shear boards, teazles (or tazzles), a spinning jenny, a pair of looms, a pair of cards, a dyevat and tenter, all worth £26.

Amongst his debtors were merchants in Yarmouth, Downham Market and Gretna Green. The list also included local men such as Jonas Kenyon of Cumberworth, John Ellis of Denby Dale and John Hinchliff of Clayton West.

John was married three times, though he had children only with his first wife, Hannah. These were, John, James, Joshua, Joseph, William and a daughter. As his family grew older and produced offspring of their own it was expected that all these Grandchildren would call on their Grandfather on their way to morning service. John became known as a skilful healer, using simple remedies and cures, he became known as the Denby Dale practitioner.

The Wood family business, textile manufacturing, which we have examined in a previous chapter, hit financial trouble prior to 1848, it seems likely that the death of John Wood in 1831 had heralded the beginning of the decline. One of the major reasons cited by the family was their failure to protect by patent, a method for producing or finishing Orleans fabrics which had been developed by them. This was fabric made of a cotton warp and worsted weft. Employees had delivered the details of the process to competitors denying the Wood brothers their chance to become very wealthy. Changes in the manufacturing industry compounded the problems which became so serious that senior members of the Wood family took to praying at the chapel in order to change the outlook.

James and Tedbar Wood, grandsons of John Wood, realising their prospects within the family firm were poor, decided to try their luck on the other side of the world, and perhaps hoped to try and reverse their families fortunes. Their emigration was endorsed and supported by the senior members of the family.

James, born in 1811, was the youngest son of James Wood and his first wife, Hannah Hinchcliffe. Hannah died in 1815 aged only 28 and James re-married., to Hannah Tinker and began another family which included Tedbar, who was again the youngest of the brood, born in 1825.

James's childhood involved the usual pursuits available in this pre-technological age. Marbles, tops and leapfrog to name a few and he also 'devoted himself heartily to the games of cricket and football'. He also had a reputation as a good swimmer. He was placed for a time at a private boarding school at Rawmarsh before 'accommodating himself to the will of his father' and coming to work in the family business. Involved in the production of fancy vestings, dress goods and other such fabrics, James had a particular affinity with the dyehouse. Though he was also known as his fathers 'head gardener' as he was blessed with green fingers.

The emotions of James and Tedbar are unrecorded, it may well have been their idea to try and make their fortune abroad, they must have relied on their faith to give them the courage and strength to embark on such an adventure. James's last sermons in the Sunday school must have been entertaining before the two brothers left Penistone station in 1848 heading for London docks bound for Victoria, Australia. James was 36 and Tedbar 23 years old. The half brothers were not the first people from Denby Dale to try their luck in Australia. Members of the Brownhill and Schofield families had also emigrated and it is possible that all were related to each other though more research will have to be undertaken to prove this.

James and Tedbar boarded the '*Sultana*' on Monday 3rd April and began the long journey to the other side of the world. Tedbar sent a letter home regarding the voyage, which recorded that both brothers soon became sea sick, this lasted for between 8 or 10 days, the roughest seas being on the passage through the Bay of Biscay.

James made a personal journal of the trip, from Plymouth they went to the Bay of Biscay, along the coast of Portugal passing Madeira and Palma and one of the Cape Verde Islands then onward to South America passing Trinidad. Around this time James was injured during heavy seas which caused the ship to heave violently and unexpectedly. He was flung down an open hatchway and was soaked to boot, the ship then heaved again and threw his head against the wall cutting him. Conditions worsened and became so bad that the two men manning the ships wheel had to be lashed to it to avoid them being washed away and to keep the ship on course. To add to the brother's misery, Tedbar also injured himself when he fell from a ladder and scolded his arm with the hot tea he was carrying. The weather and consequently the sea must have abated by the 12th of June when James's journal notes that, *'we honoured Cumberworth feast well : fresh bread with ham and salt beef to breakfast, parkin to lunch, fresh roast pork, preserved potatoes and bread pudding for dinner'*; they were at this time just off the Cape of Good Hope.

The brothers had a very poor journey, another vessel, the *'Mahomed Pasha'* had left London ten days after them and arrived in Melbourne fourteen days before them. They finally disembarked on Sandridge Pier, Melbourne on 21st July 1848 and went to stay with a cousin, Mr T Bray, who lived at Geelong, for about a month. Thomas Bray had married Mary Tinker – probably the sister of Hannah Tinker, mother of Tedbar.

James and Tedbar began their bush life at Cowie and Steads station, on the banks of the Moorabool River, 12 miles beyond the town of Steiglitz. Interestingly, in 1883, the station was known as Emly Park, this was about three days from their base at Geelong. They worked as gardeners and shepherds for a wage of £20 a year plus rations. James was largely based around the station but Tedbar was mostly in the bush, where he could earn a little more, and communication between them was difficult but the ox drawn bush cart would take messages as well as supplies. Within three months, James had sent money home to distribute amongst his fathers creditors, anxious in his desire to lift the disgrace of his family. James, and probably Tedbar later progressed to being wool sorters but James's career soon altered, sometime between 1849 and 1851 he became a partner in a timber merchants business in Geelong along with the proprietor, Mr Dean, the business being re-named 'Dean and Wood'. The partnership had initially been offered to Edwin Wood, brother of Tedbar who had followed his kin from England in 1849, arriving in Melbourne on the 'Madagascar' on the 5th August. He declined the opportunity in favour of his half brother.

Then life really changed! Gold was discovered in Victoria in mid 1851. Gold hunters began to overrun the country but James initially resisted the temptations. Not so his half brother Edwin who formed a number of other Methodists, including his cousin, Joseph Bray, into a working group. They headed for the gold fields of Ballarat and pitched their tent at the base of Black Hill. Only a few days after their arrival Edwin was required to return to Geelong to attend to urgent business, he was replaced by James at the dig. They were initially unsuccessful, though after they moved on, to Mount Alexander their fortunes improved, a further move, to Forest Creek (now Castlemaine) saw further success.

The rewards were rich enough for the party to be armed on transporting their gold away, James refused a gun, preferring to lose his gold then take another mans life. The group were followed for a time but their pursuer eventually gave up hope and went in search of easier pickings.

After this episode James went back to 'Dean and Woods' timber yard. Mr Dean was soon to retire due to ill health and return to Glasgow. James didn't miss his opportunity, he, and Tedbar and another brother of Tedbar's, Benjamin, again the son of Hannah Tinker, who had also subsequently followed them to Australia, formed a partnership. After the launch of 'Wood Brothers – Timber Merchants' sums of money began to flow home. Payments had already been made by the brothers to creditors of the family business back in Denby Dale and their fortunes in the gold fields and in their partnership at the timber merchants eased family fortunes significantly. A letter from James to his brother, John dated 1854 saw £100 being sent home for 'fathers creditors' and more followed. Money was also donated to Denby Dale chapel to keep it out of debt. The decision to seek success in Australia had been a fantastic success story. The brothers' Uncle, Joseph Wood wrote in 1856 that, *'the chapel is just able to pay its way……without your kind donation we should have been in debt'*.

In 1854 the brothers purchased land in North Geelong which fronted Little Ryrie Street for £810. They then constructed a six roomed, weather board house, which was only a five minute walk from the wharf and had a good view of the bay and shipping. They also moved the business from Market Square to Little Ryrie Street where they built sheds and an office.

In 1857, after nine years, James decided to return home, partly for family reasons and partly for business on behalf of Wood Brothers. One would also imagine that he must have missed his old home and friends and family and felt the need to re-acquaint himself with them all. He was accompanied by his spinster sister, Sarah, who had kept house for the brothers for a number of years, she was to remain in Denby Dale.

They sailed aboard the '*Anglesey*' and, *'a very cordial welcome awaited his return'*.

James made a number of visits on his return, largely to firms which had long been associated with the family. He paid out considerable sums of money to these in order to clear more of his fathers creditors, though his father had died in 1850. He also travelled to the home of Mr G Nicholson of Badsworth, York, where he met his cousin Mary Wood who was also visiting.

Their friendship grew and they became close, Mary agreeing to marry him after a relatively short space of time. The ceremony took place on 8th October 1857 in Grosvenor Chapel, Manchester, James was 45 years old. The couple spent two months longer in England before, after saying all their goodbyes, and presumably having furthered the interests of Wood and Sons they left for Australia aboard the clipper '*Norfolk*'. The trip was a poor one for Mary as she was sea sick for most of the journey and James also noted, in a letter home, to his mother and sisters that three people had died during the journey and had been buried at sea. They were accompanied by Mary's brother, Charles's three children, Ann Amelia, John and Thomas Turton Wood and two of James's brother, John's children, James and Benjamin Green Wood who all settled in different areas of Victoria. They arrived in Geelong on 9th February 1858 after a voyage of 68 days.

The business at Geelong was flourishing, the brothers had by now built quality accommodation for themselves, and they were even making forays into the textile industry. Unfortunately, not all was good news, in March 1868 the home and timber yard narrowly evaded destruction by fire. A blaze broke out at a sawmill 10 yards away and the embers from this were blown onto the Wood brothers property, their buildings consisted largely of timber and broke out in flame. Fortunately they were equipped with a large underground water tank and a good pump and they were able to successfully tackle the flames. A similar timber yard, three times as far away was also set on fire.

Being responsible Methodists the brothers supported and founded a number of charities they also undertook to aid the poor whenever possible. James became an influential Methodist preacher, he served on the Geelong Hospital Committee, the Geelong Infirmary and Benevolent Asylum (1867 & 1868), the Geelong Protestant Orphan Asylum from 1864 until 1881. He was a member of the Homeopathic Free Dispensary until his death. He was also a founder of the Geelong Female Refuge from 1872–79. This was not at the expense of sending money home, for example, £100 was sent in 1854 with the promise of more to come.

Benjamin retired and returned home in 1858, Tedbar returned to England in 1860. James's health began to gradually decline from 1879, he was by now, 67 years old, he passed on the timber business to his nephews, James and Thomas Turton Wood sometime after 1872. It was also in 1872 that James and a number of others purchased land which was a part of the Wesleyan Methodist church thereby continuing the families support for the movement. In fact, James had been involved with the Wesleyan movement in Yarra Street since 1847. James and his brothers had taken enormous risks and endured numerous hardships. Their story is a tremendous testament to their faith, their devotion to charity and strength of mind and spirit, without them Wood Brothers would have ceased to exist in their own time and the Methodist movement in Denby Dale would have been significantly poorer. On his arrival in Victoria James was, at 6 feet tall, *'square shouldered, well limbed and well kept'* but the years of hard toil and long hours took their toll. James health started to decline in 1879, he passed away in 1881 in Geelong aged 70, married to Mary for 23 years, she outlived him by 10 years, passing away in 1891, aged 77.

James's will was dated 28th September 1880 where he describes himself as a 'timber merchant, now out of business'. He left nearly all his worldly goods to his wife though he made a special case for his sister, Mary, who had kept house for him before her return to England, when he left her an annuity of £50 per annum. James had also made provision for a large number of bequests to made upon the death of his wife, after all his real and personal estate were disposed of. The chapel at Denby Dale was to receive £200, the same amount was also to be paid out to numerous brothers, sisters, nieces and nephews. Various charities benefited to the tune of £100 each, James had become a very rich man during his lifetime as the latter bequests illustrate, though he was more than benevolent with it.

James Wood, pictured before his death in 1881.

Edwin Wood remained in Australia until his death in 1900, as we have seen, Benjamin Wood returned to England in 1858. In a letter to his brother, James dated 23rd May 1881 we find him living at Park Mill House, Clayton West, the census of the same year noted him as a retired general agent, widower. He was still involved with activities at Geelong. On 16th January 1883, described as of Denby Dale, Benjamin purchased land in South Geelong. He later sold it on to William Miller Wood, son of Edwin who was a farmer. Tedbar, on the other hand, had, as we have seen, returned to England in 1860, where he too found a wife, Louisa who bore him a son, James Beaumont Wood in 1864, the family living at the ancestral residence, Field House. In the 1881 census Tedbar is described as a retired timber merchant, his son as a land surveyor. Like his brother, Benjamin, Tedbar remained involved with activities at Geelong. On 3rd November 1896, Tedbar sold a parcel of land at Cowie's Creek to Stephen Barclay of North Geelong for £20. Tedbar's Australian exploits had left him in a financially

James Beaumont Wood, son of Tedbar, circa 1884.

sound situation, but, true to family form, he didn't keep it all for himself. The family were not only largely responsible for Methodism in Denby Dale, but also for its village school.

Tedbar not only donated a large sum of money towards the creation of a school he also put some aside for the erection of a village hall, unfortunately the bank involved with this transaction went into liquidation and the money was lost. The village eventually got its hall situated next to the Methodist chapel and christened the Victoria Memorial Hall.

Tedbar Wood, with his wife, Louisa and their son, James Beaumont Wood, aged around 2 years old, dating the picture to around 1866.

Geneealogical Table of the Wood family

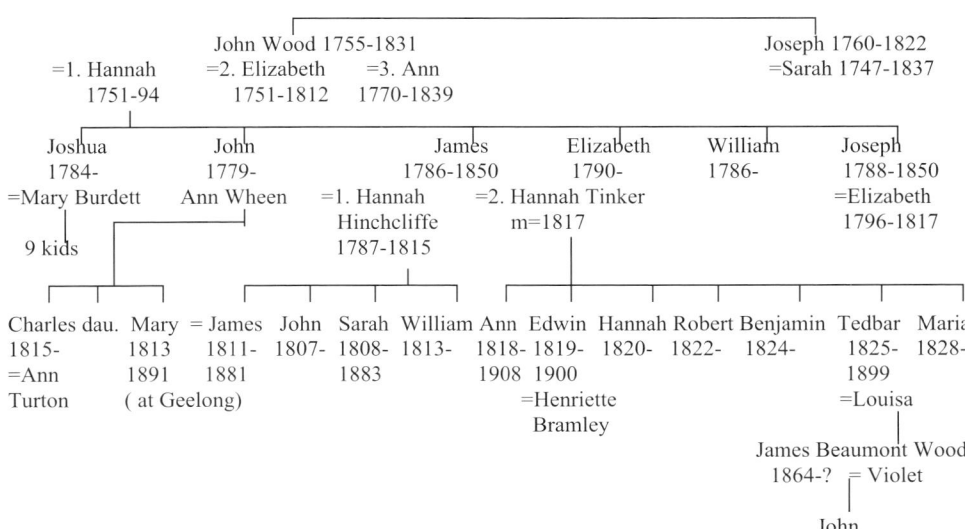

Denby Dale school, early twentieth century. *Old Barnsley*

DENBY DALE SCHOOL

Tedbar Wood was elected Chairman of the new school which was opened on 6th July 1874. Founded by public subscription, any contributor who donated £1 or more could become a manager. William Newsome was the first master, he was assisted by his wife who looked after the infants, his daughter, Fanny, a pupil teacher and his son, Willie, a candidate pupil teacher/monitor.

By the middle of the first September, 257 scholars had been admitted, though it was normal for only 60 to 100 to actually attend as the older children split their time between education and working for half the week. Other village events also reduced attendance levels such as potato picking, harvesting and feasts. Alongside the usual subjects of reading, writing and arithmetic the syllabus included geography, scripture, needlework (girls) and singing.

The expenditure of the establishment in these early years involved the master receiving £150 per annum and pupil teachers £15 per annum. Some of this money was recouped from scholars who were charged between 3d and 9d per week depending on age and circumstances. A large piece of coal was considered an excellent substitute for school pence!

In January 1875, Newsome was asked to hand in his resignation. He had been outspoken in his views regarding the shortcomings of the school. Heating problems, flooding, water supply, along with the fact that the school buildings were hired out for village dances, concerts and meetings which occasionally resulted in damage were all cited by him.

On top of which both his children, Fanny and Willie had failed their pupil teacher examinations and the board of managers refused to pay his wife a salary.

Wilfred Barnes took over on 19th April 1875 and his initial enthusiasm helped to buoy attendance's. After only two or three years interest had again begun to wain and children were eventually to be threatened with the sack from their jobs in the mills if they were continually absent from school.

Mr Barnes also inherited his predecessor's problems with the buildings and conditions of the school. An entry made in the log book on 9th October 1876 noted that the girls yard was flooded

Denby Dale school children in 1898. A young Jonas Kenyon sits seventh from the left, cross legged. It is possible that the scholar sitting cross legged, fifth from the left, is a young Harold Hinchliffe.

and that the girls had to walk on stepping stones to avoid being ankle deep in water. Leaking drains often emptied into the school and two of the girls toilets, facing the school were without doors! Disease was common, diphtheria occurred in 1876 and a measles outbreak in 1887 caused the school to close for five weeks. Mr Barnes recorded that during an outbreak of influenza, 'every ailment is it!' and that attendance suffered greatly.

Funding became a whole lot easier on the advent of the 1891 Assisted Education Act. Fees for scholars dropped to between 2d and free (for infants), naturally these rose throughout the following years as salaries and equipment were subject to inflation.

School life at this time included, amongst other things, military drill in the school yard and poetry recital. This included learning works of up to 80 lines for standard 3 and 150 lines for standards 4 to 7, it would be interesting to see how many of today's children could do the same! A fifteen minute break was allowed in the morning, but if inclement conditions prevailed this was cancelled and lessons continued as usual.

Just before the turn of the century dissatisfaction was being expressed by the government regarding the schools' accommodation. A report dating to 1904 noted problems including overcrowding, despite two newly built classrooms, poor cloakroom accommodation, poor ventilation and washing facilities, and difficulties regarding playground segregation and quality.

At various times the Victoria Memorial Hall had been pressed into service as overspill accommodation for the infants but it had never been a very good solution. Although plans for change had been drawn up in 1900, it had not been possible to implement them due to an overdraft of £380, this caused the Board of Education to withhold the annual grant, thereby exacerbating the problem.

At a management meeting it was decided to ask the Board of Education to take full control of the school and on 25th July 1905 the Local Education Authority took charge. Improvements were made which re-dressed much of the latter and by 1911 the buildings looked much as they do today.

In the midst of all this change there had also been another change of Headmaster, Wilfred Barnes having retired in 1903. It was Sam Shepley who had overseen the school's interests as it passed into local authority control.

Increasingly, attention was being paid to health matters, not just in school but also within the village. A medical officer first visited the school in 1904 and inspections began in 1908, the same year in which toothbrushes were first provided. Biltcliff Dental Company can be found in the village in 1901. These measures didn't stop an outbreak of measles which closed the school for a short while in 1912.

Problems over non attendance due to work related commitments were just about stamped out due to a bye-law of 1912. Mr Shepley considered this would 'almost entirely stop the half time system', and keep children at school until they were 14 years old. It is interesting to note that a protest strike occurred on 25th November 1912 by five boys who objected to this new rule, though Mr Shepley dealt with them on their return! The last of the half timers left school in 1912 and the new law made its impact.

By 1922 the curriculum included gardening, largely fruit and vegetables, and handicrafts (boys) and cookery and laundry-work (girls), swimming lessons and even occasional trips out

Denby Dale Council school, October 1954. Back row, left to right: ?, John Lindley, Paul Tann, Joyce Smith, Keith Lockwood, June Sowerby, Keith Kirkbright, James Hollingworth, Olga Cole, Billy Stewart, Arthur Watkins, Elizabeth Booth, Anthony Mountain. Middle, left to right: Linda Brown, Leslie Kenyon, Stella Huddleston, Iris Beaver, Lynn Marsden, Donna Lockwood, Anne Lodge, Pauline Tarbuck, Carol Newby, Jean Craven, Elizabeth Venables, Janet Rawson. Seated: Jean Rawson, Denise Frankland, Maxine Hodgson, Hilary Stott, Kay Lockwood, Janice Heath, Denise Loukes, Christine Rhodes, Jill Copley, Sandra Dearnley.

Denby Dale schoolchildren around 1955. Back row, left to right: teacher unknown, ?, ?, ?, S Pell, S Woodhead, I Thackra, ?, ?, P Hyde, A Wood, V Schofield, D Bostwick, ?. Middle, left to right: J Cook, K Wadsworth, G Morris, A Fisher, J Choppin, R Smith, E Greaves, S Ryan, C Birks, R Birks, ?, B Sharpe. Front, left to right: K Hirst, S Simpson, K Booth, J Hobson, M Wilkinson, M Wood, C Euston, S Ball, S Schofield, V Firth.

to Ripon, Bridlington or even Giggleswick, where in 1927 pupils were able to observe a total eclipse of the sun. Deliveries of school milk and a dental clinic were also provided.

Health was still a major concern though school closure was very infrequent, an outbreak of influenza in 1918 had been serious enough to cause this but a worse disease than ever before occurred on 18th September 1932, the school log notes that, *'school closed for the remainder of the week on account of a terrible outbreak of typhoid fever'*. We will return to this subject a little later in the chapter.

In 1934 Sam Shepley retired and Mr F Taylor took over. His reign was much like the last and school life continued in its regular way until 1st September 1939 when all the children were sent home. The government had declared war and a state of emergency was in operation which meant that all schools were to close immediately until further notice. Denby Dale re-opened on 11th of September. Evacuees began to arrive from London in 1941 and by 1944, 71 were attending the school regularly. In the midst of this terrible time the school began to serve dinners, this service began on 4th December 1941 and cost 5d each. It was also during the war years that Skelmanthorpe Secondary Modern school was completed, late in 1940, known today as Scissett Middle School. On 6th January 1941 all children over 11 years old were transferred here along with two teachers. Denby Dale now became a junior mixed and infant school.

Fortunately the school never suffered any damage and all the precautions regarding bomb shelters for the children and emergency procedures never had to be implemented. Peace was declared on 7th May 1945 and after the summer holidays only 9 evacuees returned to continue their lessons.

The school now ran on similar lines to today's establishment, throughout the 1950's, as in other schools, choosing a May Queen was very popular though this tradition has died out today. Changes in the local industries working policies regarding holidays dictated some change in the calendar year for the school as closures had to be in tandem with the mills. One of the largest changes was the building of large new housing estates, such as the one at Gilthwaites in the 1960's. Pressure on attendance levels increased substantially and temporary classrooms were erected to try to alleviate this.

Mr Taylor left the school in 1966 and was replaced by Eric White as Headmaster. His initial and worst problem was overcrowding. The school had been built nearly one hundred years ago and was now struggling to cope with its antiquated layout. Lessons were even held in the porches and kitchens! More temporary rooms were acquired but enormous feats of planning and accommodation were necessary to keep the school running. Mr White left the school in 1973 having seen its population double in just seven years. He was replaced by Tom Smith who was to take the school forward and combat the overcrowding problems by over-seeing the schools interests at a site for a new building. Tenders were advertised in 1973, but it took another three years to achieve the goal of 'splendid school premises'. Pupils moved to the new site at the top of the Gilthwaites estate at Easter in 1976, your author being one of them!

The old school house became the doctors surgery until 1994 when purpose built premises were constructed just across the road. The old school buildings became a nursery school and in 1978 the buildings in the school yard were utilised by Kirklees Library.

The new school was split into three distinct areas, these for the three age groups which would attend before transfer to Scissett. Doors to classrooms were rejected for curtains and classrooms surrounded a shared area for each year where lectures could be taken and dinners served. A central hall played host to morning assembly, PE lessons and Christmas plays amongst other things. There were also separate playgrounds for each year which were patrolled by dinner ladies during break times.

Tom Smith had as his teaching staff, for the youngest children, Mrs Bennett (who played the piano) and Mrs Bloggs (Butterfield), the intermediate children were looked after by Mrs Dean, Mrs Butterfield and Mrs Russell (who also played the piano but was more noted for her metre long wooden ruler!). Mr Wright, Mrs Chilton and Mr Bassindale saw to the final year pupils.

And so the vision, dedication and charity of the Wood family eventually resulted in a modern and popular school for today's society. Health problems are now insignificant compared to the past and education as a whole has now become the central pillar upon which our children base their lives. How much different might this story have been if Tedbar Wood had not put his hand in his pocket all those years ago?

Ava Horn, 1937.

Foundation of Local Schools	
Denby Dale – Wakefield Rd.	*1874–1976 (then a nursery)*
Denby Dale – Gilthwaites 1st	*1976–present*
Upper Denby	*1864–present*
Lower Denby	*1769–1876*
Birdsedge	*1911–present (prior to this there had been a Quaker establishment)*
Shelley High School	*1974–present*
Skelmanthorpe Secondary Modern – Scissett Middle School	*1940–present*

The Recollections of a Typhoid Victim in Denby Dale

Ava Horn was born on 16th of December 1919 at Wood Nook Cottage, Denby Dale. She was the youngest of nine sisters, the first of whom, Ida, was born in 1903 followed by Lena (1907), Ethel (1909), Mabel, Blanche (1914), Gladys (1916), Grace (1917) and Minnie (1918).

Wakefield Road, Denby Dale showing Prospect Terrace and the pub of the same name. The shops to the left, at one time, included a chemists, run by Francis Andrew, Hopkins bakers and Seniors watch sellers. Circa 1930's.

The parents of this large female family were Harry and Annie Horn, née Lockwood who had married around 1902. Harry, born in 1882 was by Ava's birth 37 years old, a man of imposing stature and nature who invoked a relatively strict upbringing upon his children. Money was scarce and frivolity frowned upon, nothing went to waste, though his regime was tempered by the fact that he worked shifts as a miner at Spring Wood Colliery between Bretton and Clayton West. This gave Annie nominal control and her attitude was far less austere. This should not detract from Harry's character or personality, he was a hard man but fair dealing with difficult circumstances on a pitiful budget, he was a man of his time. Few people today, if any could even contemplate this task and for that he, like others, should be applauded.

Ava well remembers Harry coming home from the pit, cut and bleeding and regularly wet through, evidence of the working conditions at the pit and the size of the shafts he was mining. Strangely enough, though she smiles to remember it, she does not remember him ever taking a bath! He would wash his hands and face and Annie would scrub his back but nothing else. Either he used the tin bath in front of the fire after all the girls had gone to bed, not unreasonable or, the pit had washing facilities.

A typical day for him would be to call at the Prospect Inn (now the Dalesman) and have a couple of pints with a friend, Redfearn Laundon he would then set off to the pit around lunch time. Later in life he changed his allegiance to Denby Dale Working Men's Club.

Harry Horn with his granddaughter, June, around 1946.

Salvation Army gathering in 1909. The Prospect Hotel is on the left. A little above it are the cottages at Wood Nook.

His method of transport to the pit was a push bike, better than walking and relatively cheap though not altogether safe.

Sometime around 1942 he came off his bike at Kitchenroyd and broke his leg, aged around 60, only a few years before retirement.

Happily he recovered and soon after a bus route became operational thereby solving any more problems in this direction. Ava remembers the incident well from the worry it caused the whole family, she was also pregnant with her first daughter, June at this time.

Prospect Terrace, to the right of the picture. The square building at the end of the terrace on the left is the Prospect Hotel. The terraced building with the fancy front porch, nearest to us on the right was once a drapers run by the Misses B & E Coldwell. It later became a hairdressers, run by Wilfred Garner. *Old Barnsley*

Of course shift work was rotated and Harry was well used to working through the night, this meant that he largely slept throughout the day and woe betide any of his girls making too much noise and waking him up!

Wood Nook was rented from a Mr Gill of Skelmanthorpe at around 3/6 a week. The property lay next to a small stream which gave the sisters excellent opportunity for adventure, catching frog-spawn and sticklebacks and playing in the water, it also lay next to 'Bricky Wood' (probably Brick Wood due to the activities of nearby Kitson's clayware manufacturers). The wood provided a free playground and offered the young girls one of their few opportunity's to escape their slightly austere existence, and helped to make up for the distinct lack of toys. The highlight of which was receiving a penny on a Friday and going to the shop to spend it on a bag of broken biscuits and out of date sweets. Indeed, it was not until many years later that the girls were given their first doll, a Christmas present from elder sister, Lena, though she nearly made a hash of it! The doll had been stored in Harry and Annie's wardrobe and Lena, who had been out with her husband to be, George Harrison, had forgotten to get it out before her parents went to bed. As she dare not tiptoe through after arriving home late, it was a somewhat belated surprise on Christmas morning.

Whilst on the subject of Christmas Ava's regular present list contained a new penny, an apple and an orange and a spice pig – to which, when she told me- she went 'yuck'. Keep in mind that this was the only occasion in the year when she was presented with fresh fruit.

It was also in the Bricky Wood that the family lost its only pet. Molly was a Yorkshire Terrier and whilst playing in the wood had suddenly been attacked by a Red Setter belonging to nearby Kitson's. The Setter killed Molly and it was Harry that went to bury her body in the wood.

Wood Nook was originally two cottages, Harry, Annie and their family living in the left hand cottage as one looks from the modern day road. Albert and Jane(y) Sharp occupied the right hand side, a couple who were heavily involved in the Salvation Army, perhaps due to the visits of General Booth to the village during the first decade of the twentieth century. Indeed, Ava's sisters, Ida and Ethel both went on to become prominent members of the Denby Dale branch of this august organisation.

The aforementioned Mr Gill also owned two other cottages, now demolished, which stood close by Wood Nook, the site now being occupied by a red brick dwelling. Also close by was an old Chinese Laundry, once run by a Mr. F. Wong, which today seems an odd business to have been operating in Denby Dale, activities had ceased by Ava's time but her mother told her about it. The buildings after this were occupied by the Green family who made animal feeds and this little section of Denby Dale was completed by the Prospect Hotel, the landlord of which was William Dyson who later gave way to Harry Addy.

Living arrangements inside the family cottage were somewhat cramped. All the sisters slept in the attic, two to a bed, (the fourth born sister, Mabel had died only eight months after her birth), this meant that when Ava was 3 years old her eldest sister, Ida was 19, Lena 15 and so on, the different levels of maturity must have provoked some interesting conversations and privacy must have been an impossibility. There seems to be a reason as to why there was a four year break between the births of Ida and Lena. Harry and Annie had decided that it would be useful if Annie went out to work. To be able to do this they would have to refrain from having any more children for a while. It also meant that Ida had to be looked after. Ava cannot remember who undertook this responsibility but did mention that her mother told her that Ida may not have been treated in as correct a manner as one would expect – we will leave this matter.

Harry Horn and Albert Sharp tending poultry at Wood Nook around 1930.

At least the attic boasted four small, narrow windows and was not constantly darkened. One of the things all the girls would have loved was a piano, realising how impossible this would always be they created their own, silent version! One of the window sills lifted up, similar to a piano lid, here they played to their hearts content, and never had to worry about waking their father! Surprisingly, the girls did eventually get a real piano, bought for £20 at an auction on Barnsley Road though Ava cannot remember where the money might have come from.

Below the attic slept Harry and Annie, though one part of this room was partitioned off. This other half contained a wardrobe and a dressing table. The room downstairs was as usual a kitchen, living room and bathroom boasting a fine stone flagged floor. A small keeping cellar led off from here and was entered by just one step. This was more Annie's domain and was used to store foodstuffs created by her. Nettle Beer was one of her speciality's, nettles were gathered and mixed with yeast and sugar and then left to ferment in the cellar, before being drunk by all in these days without cans and bottles of pop, or indeed, safe drinking water!

Annie also baked regularly, averaging around two stones of bread a week in the shape of loaves or tea cakes. A rare treat were current tea cakes topped with icing! A more regular treat was Pudding Tin Cake on a Sunday, this was the most important culinary day of the week. A dinner with meat would always be provided for the girls. Harry kept hens and ducks at the cottage and had no qualms about ringing their necks. He also had permission to shoot on lands belonging to his Uncle Jim, between Naylor's Clayware and Cumberworth, and also at his Auntie Lizzie's property at Stubbing, up Hollin Edge, off Common Lane. As an aside, in these politically and socially more circumspect times it is interesting to note that Harry kept his 12 bore in the wardrobe! He also borrowed ferrets to go catching rabbits and kept them in a bag under the kitchen sink, the girls would be well warned not to open the cabinet doors on these occasions.

Harry's knowledge of flora and fauna was also excellent, he was able to supplement his families diet by gathering wild berries, nuts and mushrooms, particularly a type of mushroom that Ava remembers had a blue stalk. To add to this he kept a vegetable garden and proved his green fingers whenever food was required. One thing Harry would never have anything to do with was chips!, *'not a proper dinner'*, was his usual response, though week day meals did consist of soup, stew and meat and potato pie. Surprisingly breakfast for the family was also good, bacon and eggs just about every morning. For a poor family the latter seems to be a good diet but Harry's Uncle Jim owned a farm and there was always work for good slaughter men. Harry could get a very good price on a side of bacon after a few hours working for Jim. Indeed, Uncle Jim did what he could for the family and occasionally even supplied them with a goose.

Harry's father had died very young and his mother had re-married to her husband's brother, Jim. He was the youngest of three children, Polly and William being his siblings. His mother had four other children but when money was being handed out after family deaths Harry was never to be a recipient. Perhaps Uncle Jim, his father's younger brother had taken it upon himself to see to Harry's families interest to the best of his ability as and when money allowed.

Annie had the usual, laborious tasks of bringing up a large family. In time Ida and Lena became old enough to help with the younger daughters but Annie preferred to do the bulk of the work herself, including painting the rooms. The girls attic bedroom was painted in pink but the paint, known as distemper used to come off if you touched it or brushed it with your clothes. Washing was long, arduous and drawn out. Sheets for instance would be put into water and rubbed with soap, such as carbolic. They would then be rubbed on a washboard before being put through a mangle and then hung out to dry or put on clothes rails in front of the fire.

This difficult, yet happy family life was severely disrupted on 17th of September 1932. Lena and Ava had for some time been ill, laid up with flu. The symptoms were headache, sweating and loss of appetite amongst others. Annie had brought in Dr Arnison who had diagnosed the illness and to attempt to contain the virus the two sisters were put into the same bed, Lena was 25 years old, Ava, just 13. Ava became so bad that she took to sleeping in her parents bed between her mother and father. On the night of 17th the first case of Typhoid in the village was identified. A blood test taken from Lena confirmed the worst and it was two very frightened and upset girls that were wrapped in red blankets and led out of the house at tea time to the awaiting ambulance amidst rumours of others, also in trouble.

A land drain at Square Wood reservoir had been contaminated with sewage which had infected the drinking water. Just by turning on a tap for a drink of water, Lena and Ava had put their lives at risk.

One can only wonder at the fear which must have been felt by the family, let alone by all the other villagers. Ava's sister, Grace seamed to be the worst, perhaps she knew she had taken a drink from the tap, whatever the reason upon which her fear was based it proved to be correct and she ended up suffering the worst rigours of the disease. She began talking and singing in her sleep and lost all her hair. Whilst in ear shot of Ava and Lena, who had been taken to Mill Hill Hospital near Dalton, Dr Bleasdale of Denby Dale was heard to comment, *'there's a girl from Denby Dale seriously ill at Meltham – a Grace Horn'*, what a way to find out about your sister. Grace was taken ill a little after Ava and Lena and getting news from home was not all that easy. Visiting was facilitated by the taxi company of Fred and Edwin Hirst of Denby Dale, who, by order of the Denby Dale Urban District Council, were paid to take relatives to see inmates. Perhaps this was an attempt by the Council to make amends as Ava remembers Arthur Laundon, whose father was a member of the Council telling her that warnings regarding the sewage running into Square Wood had gone unheeded. She also remembers Lena telling her that their mother and Blanche had come to see them, but as inmates were confined and isolated, Annie and Blanche were restricted to standing outside the hospital and waving! Ava had found it impossible to stand and look or wave as her legs had become so weak. It would seem that their father, Harry never came to visit.

The two sisters were destined to stay here for seven weeks, Ava slept for most of the time, sweating and shunning all food. Patients survived on a diet of milk and water and she attributes a sudden spurt of growth in her height to this. Indeed, when she left hospital she had risen to almost her full adult size, though she was also of an age to grow.

Denby Dale Council school, 1928, just 4 years before the typhoid disaster. Pictured are the combined classes of Miss Snape and Miss Berry. Back row, left to right: May Hirst, Gladys Cooper, Bessie Lockwood, Edith Fisher, Eddie Booth, Leslie Stricker, Ellis Roe, ? Crossland. Second row: Bessie Holmes, Vera Roberts, Barbara Kenyon, Louise Auckland, Alice Cooper, Connie Mosley, Irene Morley, Audrey Hallas, Kenneth Hirst, Ken B Smith, Arnold Mellor, Ronnie Newsome. Third row: Barbara Firth, Joan Curtis, Ethel Laker, Freda Hudson, ? Bell, Alice Stanger, Cyril Lockwood, Percy Shaw, Dennis Fisher, Thomas Fretwell, Douglas Noble, ? Thorpe. Fourth row: Ava Horn, Violet Simpson, Horace Auckland, Kenneth Smith, James Lodge, Charles Hinchliffe, Bessie Holt, Hilda Mudd.

Enema's were widely used to treat the problem, an unpleasant procedure, but as bowel movements were adjudged to be the key to the process of healing they were undertaken.

A three year old patient from Denby Dale, used to say to her nurse whilst being treated in this fashion, *'ya mucki fing'*, typifying patients attitudes to this particularly undignified treatment.

There were other problems in hospital, one girl from Denby Dale even ended up with lice!

Above all this, the underlying current of thought with all the patients was their chance of survival. People who were known to them occupied many of the surrounding beds. Ava watched as the body of a lady she knew was pushed past, Lena just turned to her and said, 'don't look'.

Watching these harrowing scenes, knowing that one also had the disease must have been the most frightening experience in most of these peoples lives, let alone that of 13 year old Ava.

As patients' bowel movements became more regular and normal the liquid diet was modified slightly to junkit and jelly, semi liquid food which prepared them to begin eating more normally once again, this was after about six weeks. Patients were soon told that they should expect something special for their first solid meal in these last few days of their stay. Ava waited with baited breath to see what sort of tantalising morsels were to be brought before her and failed to disguise her disappointment when a freshly made plate of scrambled egg appeared!

Lena was pronounced fit a week before the Doctor and Matron told Ava that she was ready to go home. Hirsts taxi's were employed to bring the patients home though relatives could not travel to the hospital as there would not be enough room in the car to take them and the returning inmates.

Wakefield Road, Denby Dale, looking down towards Prospect Terrace on the right, in 1906.

Blanche and Ava link their mother, Annie's arms whilst in Land Army kit, during the Second World War.

Harry Horn, holding granddaughter, Carol, circa 1949.

Ava travelled home with, amongst others, Dorothy Littlewood and was dropped off at the Prospect in Denby Dale, just a short walk home to Wood Nook. Unfortunately her emaciated legs were so weak that even this distance was a struggle and on reaching home she went straight to bed.

Ava and Lena and subsequently Grace all beat typhoid but paid a further six months service to the disease recuperating. The council arranged for some ex-patients to be taken to Blackpool for two weeks with the usual autocratic attitude that 'the sea air will do their recovery the world of good'.

Ava and Lena caught the train at Denby Dale station and went to stay at a boarding house run by Fred Firth, an acquaintance of their fathers, the council paid for their train tickets and their two weeks but nothing else and so the two sisters could do little but walk around as they had no money to spend.

Grace was sent to a convalescent home, the location of which has now been forgotten.

Around eight months after contracting the disease Ava returned to school, she did not know that the schools had been closed for some time while the disease was rampant and that attendance's had been down, only 30 out of 166 children attended when they did re-open. She was obviously a long way behind with her studies and could not participate fully in lessons. The Headmaster, Mr Sam Shepley (a man held in high regard by many) virtually abandoned her as she was due to leave the following year anyway. This left Ava in a poor position and she did what any self respecting, quick thinking child would do, she copied the work of her cousin, Irene Morley only she was very crafty in her methods. Making sure she got one or two questions wrong on purpose she fooled the master in to thinking that she had done the work herself, on being told to do the incorrect questions again she duly supplied him with the correct answers! Always assuming that Irene herself had got them right.

Genealogical table of the Horn family

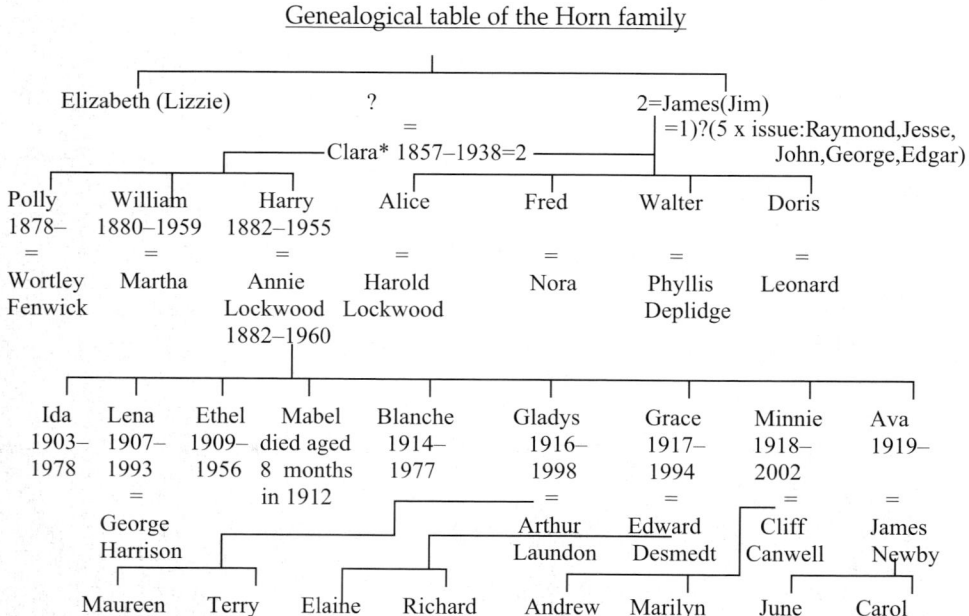

* After Clara's husbands death she married his brother.

Ava left school aged 14 in 1933 and spent around a year at home before beginning work at Jonas Kenyon and Sons textile manufacturers in Denby Dale when she was 15. Only seven years later, in 1940 she was called up for the Land Army, she was accompanied by her sister, Blanche who although too old to be called up volunteered to go anyway. The pair went first to Ashford in Kent, threshing, and then on to Sleaford in Lincolnshire picking potatoes. After this Ava ended up on Newby's farm in Emley where she met her future husband, James (Jim), by whom she had 2 children, June and Carol. Unfortunately the marriage fell apart soon after.

She moved back to her family in Denby Dale, who had moved home prior to Ava's wartime service and taken a step up by renting number 1 Prospect Terrace in approximately 1936, a much bigger house for them all.

After Ava had presented her father with two Grandchildren he seemed to mellow and spent a lot of time fussing them, playing with them and giving his love and affection. He had been extremely unlucky not to have had a son within a family of nine and must have rued his luck when his daughter presented him with two more girls. This denied him the chance to teach a Grandson how to hunt and garden and to talk about football with perhaps over a pint, though it must be said that these two girls gave him much comfort in the latter years of his life. Harry died in 1955.

Ava took over the running of the family after her mother suffered a debilitating stroke eighteen months before she died in 1960.

Blanche, Minnie, Gladys, Grace and Ava Horn, 1935.

Left to right: ?, Joyce Beever, Mrs Roberts, Doris Lockwood, Leonard Smith, Nora Garrett, Elizabeth (Lizzie) Horn, John Phillips, Ethel Horn, ?, Gladys Horn, Mrs Stephenson, (the made up people are unidentified), Janey Sharpe (in spotted dress), Annie Lockwood, Harry Horn, taken during celebrations for the Coronation at Wood Nook, in 1935.

Chapter Eight

Ingbirchworth

e have already come across many mentions of Ingbirchworth within the pages of this book. This chapter will take a look at just a few other interesting people and features of the village's past.

Domesday Book 1066: Ingbirchworth was included with Thurlstone.

Alric and Halfdan had 9 carucates of land taxable; 5 ploughs possible there. Now Ilbert has (them). Waste. Value before 1066 £4. Woodland pasture $1^1/_2$ leagues long and as wide.

The first thing to note is a comparison of Ingbirchworth and Thurlstone with its neighbour, Denby at this time. In Denby, Upper and Lower, there was only a third of the land mentioned above under cultivation. At Denby only $1^1/_2$ ploughs were possible as against 5, there was $^1/_2$ a league more woodland than Denby and the value of £4 is astronomical when compared to the 10s of Denby. The one word which renders Ingbirchworth and Thurlstone of less value than Denby after the conquest is 'waste' which refers to William the Conqueror's 'Harrying of the North' when he and his army destroyed every living thing and its habitation in order to quell rebellion in the North of England. It is difficult to say just how much of the latter entry refers to Ingbirchworth, although the acreage given in the *Victoria County History* may reflect similar areas, Ingbirchworth 1105 acres, Thurlstone 8116 acres.

There were a number of individuals who claimed to be Lords of a part of the manor of Ingbirchworth, though it must be said that the Burdets seem to have held a prominent position in this role until their sales of the manor between 1600 and 1643. The association with Denby is ancient as we find that Robert de Denby gave the monks of Roche Abbey free passage through his lands at Birchworth towards the grange of Eniker, or elsewhere. This probably relates to the late twelfth or early thirteenth century. Another early document, probably twelfth century, tells us that a Grant was made by William son of John de Penistona to Ellias de Binchewrd of 20 acres of land etc., in Penistona (not to be transferred to religious or Jews) at an annual rent of 3s in silver.

During the reign of Richard II, (1397/98) William Dronsfield of West Bretton was noted to be holding land in Ingbirchworth, he also held land in Cumberworth.

On 27th August 1577 a commission sat in Pontefract to determine the names of the persons who held lands in chief of the Duchy. This became known as 'Barnards Survey'. The list included, Henry Burdet of Denby, Francis Burdet of Birthwaite and Robert the son of Robert Rockley who held Ingbirchworth.

Aside from the court rolls and other manorial documents already examined our next important record is the poll tax of 1379. Everyone aged 16 or above had to pay 4d, though a graduated scale was applied to the more affluent.

POLL TAX 1379
Roger Dickson 6d
Adam de Micklethwaite and his wife Alicia 4d

William de Thurgoland and his wife Isabella 4d
William de Walton and his wife Agnes 4d
Margaret Smalther 4d
Magota Micklethwaite 4d
Magota de Walton 4d
William Notte and his wife Alicia 4d
John, servant of Roger Dickson 4d
Total: 3s 2d.

The above list sees the early association of the name of Micklethwaite with the village. The name derives from the old Norse 'mekil', large or big, and 'thwaite', meadow. Professor David Hey suggests that the clearing in question was sited between Cawthorne and Silkstone, now known as Banks Hall. The following documents will enable us to view a little of the village's leading family and their contemporaries, though it would be wrong to confuse the families influence and power with their landlords, the Burdets, even though a number of them made excellent careers for themselves as we shall see.

> *1433 – In the feast of the invention of the Holy Cross (3rd May). Charter dated at Yngbircheworth, confirming a grant from Thomas son and heir of Robert Walton of Yngbircheworth to Thomas son of Richard Roberts his heirs and assigns for ever; of one yearly rent of 2s issuing annually, at the terms of Pentecost and Saint Martin in the Winter by equal portions, out of all and singular his lands and tenements, with all their appurtenances in the town and within the boundaries of Yngbircheworth.*
>
> *Power of entry and distress were authorised in default of payment and the document was witnessed by Master Robert Polayne, Vicar of the church of Penyston, John Barnby, William Turton, John Ranowe, and Richard Smyth of Barneslay.*

> *1486/7 – January 4th in the second year of Henry VII, from Nicholas Burdet esquire son and heir of Aymer Burdet esquire and Elizabeth his wife, to William Turton; to cater for them and in their names into seven oxgangs and meadows, with all messuages tofts and crofts adjoining with all their appurtenances in the town and territories of Yngbyrcheworth and to take possession; and after taking possession to deliver to Thomas Burton of Wakefield his heirs and assigns, according to the form and erect of a certain charter indented then already made by the said Nicholas and Elizabeth.*

The grant was confirmed the day after with Thomas and his heirs to pay 32s to Nicholas and Elizabeth and their heirs for ever at the feasts of Pentecost and Saint Martin in Winter by equal portions and also making and doing two days extra service at harvest each year for ever. It was witnessed by John Moxon, Robert Riche and William Turton.

I have left the following document in its original form to allow us to see the spelling of English before it was standardised:

> *1538 – July 21st in the 30th year of Henry VIII. Acquittance, as follows: ' be it known to all men where this present wryttyng shall come, to so reyd and here. I Agnes Charlesworth of Yngburchworth in ye pariech of Penyston in ye Countie of York haue resayved ye day of makyng hereof a sertayn soame of money of Richard Mykkyllthwayt my kynsman in full contenttacion and pamentt of all manner of dewttes, dettes or demandes and ye wiche pamentt the said Richard, his heirres and executorres shall be dyschargd and this my present wrytyng shall be a sufficientt*

acquictance and dyscharge for euer. In wytnes whereof I the same Agnes Charlesworth in my virgynite hayth setto my seall.

NB: *An acquittance was a discharge from an obligation or debt.*

1539 – *May 5th in the 31st year of Henry VIII. Whereby John Mosley of the parish of Cawthorne in the County of York, yeoman acknowledged that he had received of Richard Micklethwaite £13 6s 8d of lawful money of England, the day of the making thereof, in part of payment of certain lands and tenements for 21 years term letting unto the same Richard and his assigns.*

Witnesses: John Ward, Richard Vesse, Henry Crawshay, Charles Burdett and Charles Slack.

1540 – *December 12th in the 32nd year of Henry VIII. From John Mosley of Ingbirchworth in the parish of Penistone and Jennet his wife, cousin of Thomas Turton to Richard Micklethwaite of the same place, yeoman, of half of one close called the … Felde, with appurtenances in, the Feldes of Ingbirchworth aforesaid, for the term of 12 years, then next for to come, yielding and paying for the same … it was agreed between the parties that the lessee should not be called upon to pay tithe; and the consideration for granting the lease was £9 10s 8d.*

1542 – *December 1st in the 34th year of Henry VIII. Acquittance by John Mosley of Ingbirchworth and Jenet his wife by which they acknowledged that they had received from Richard Micklethwaite of the same £10 and he and his heirs and executors were acquitted and discharged forever, the said acquittance being made at Penistone. Witnesses: Ralph Wordsworth, William Addy and Edmund France.*

1546 – *31st March in 37th year of Henry VIII. Bond of John Mosley of Ingbirchworth, yeoman, to secure to Richard Micklethwaite the sum of £40 to perform covenants contained in a certain indenture of even date made between the said John Mosley and Jennet, his wife of the one part and the said Richard Micklethwaite of the other part.*

1546 – *October 5th in the 38th year of Henry VIII. Bond of Robert Brodehede (probably Broadhead), of Ingbirchworth, husbandman, in the sum of £40 to secure to Richard Micklethwaite of Ingbirchworth, clothier, the performance of the award of Thomas West, yeoman, William Riche, yeoman, Richard Woodcock, clothier and Robert Holme, clothier, its arbitrators, indeferently elect and chosen betwix the said Robert Brodehede of the one party and the said Richard Micklethwaite of the other.*

1553 – *26th June in the 7th year of Edward VI. Charter confirming a grant from John Mosley of Cumberworth and Joan his wife to Richard Moor of two closes called Bromfeld and Narlynge lying in Ingbirchworth between lands of Jered Rockley on the south and lands of the said John Mosley on the north and abutting on lands of the said Richard at both ends, to have and to hold the said two closes with their appurtenances to the said Richard his heirs and assigns forever. Witnesses: Thomas Walton and Ralph Walton.*

1555 – *Easter, April in the 1st and 2nd years of Phillip and Mary. Final concord, made at Westminster between William Turton, plaintiff and John Mosley and Johanna his wife, deforciants, concerning one messuage, one … fifty acres of land, eight acres of meadow, six acres of pasture, four atfts of wood and bramble, … acres of … and heath with the appurtenances in Ingbirchworth.*

1555 – *November 15th in the 1st and 2nd year of Phillip and Mary. Charter confirming a grant from John Mosley of Cumberworth in the County of York, yeoman, and Joan his wife, kinsman and* next heir of Thomas Turton, deceased, to William Turton of Denby in the said county, yeoman, of that their messuage with its appurtenances in Ingbirchworth and one meadow lying near to the said messuage, as it lay there between the King's way on the south and one stream there called Birchworthwater on the north and abutted on land of Richard More on the west, one other meadow there called Hespyn Yngs lying between the land of Thomas Walton on the south and north and abutted upon the King's way on the east, one other enclosure of pasture called Le Highfeld, as it lay there between the lands of Richard More on the south and the common of Ingbirchworth on the north, and abutted on land of Thomas Walton on the east; and all that enclosure of land meadow and pasture called Arkyncrofte as it lay there on the west of a certain water called Scout water and on the north by a certain stream called the Meresbroke, with all rights, advantages, commons and casements whatsoever to the said messuage and to all and singular other the premises, belonging or appertaining; to hold the same to the said William Turton, his heirs and assigns to the use of the same William his heirs and assigns forever, of the Chief Lord of the fee, for services. Appointment of Christopher Wilson and Robert Jelott as attorneys to deliver seisin. Witnesses to the giving of possession, Robert Holme, Thomas … , Richard Micklethwaite and Hugh Gylett.

1566 – 30th June in the 8th year of Elizabeth. Bond of Thomas More of Braywell in the county of York in the sum of 80 marks, to secure to Richard Micklethwaite of Ingbirchworth, clothier, the performance of covenants. Witnesses: William Wordsworth, yeoman, John Scott, yeoman, Robert Saunderson, yeoman, Henry Burton, Thomas Shepherd and John Smyth.

1566 – 1st July in the 8th year of Elizabeth. Grant from Thomas More of Braywell yeoman to Richard Micklethwaite of Ingbirchworth, clothier, of a certain annuity or annual rent of 2s payable at the feast of St. Martin in the winter, issuing out of a certain messuage and certain lands, meadows and pastures with their appurtenances in Ingbirchworth aforesaid at one time in the occupation of Ralph Walton, to hold the same rent unto the said Richard Micklethwaite his heirs and assigns to the use of the said Richard forever. Power to distrain if the rent was in arrears for twenty days. Witnesses: William Wordsworth, yeoman, John Scott, yeoman, Robert Saunderson, yeoman, Henry Burton, Thomas Shepherd and John Smyth.

1576 – 19th June in the 18th year of Elizabeth. Marriage settlement, whereby Richard Micklethwaite of Ingbirchworth, yeoman, in consideration of a certain marriage, then shortly to be solemnized between Richard Micklethwaite, son and heir apparent of him the said Richard, of the one part and Mawde Hawksworth, one of the daughters of Richard Hawksworth of Brodok (Broad Oak), yeoman on the other part, gave, granted, and by that his then present writing, to the said Richard Micklethwaite and Mawde Hawksworth, all those his enclosures, lands, meadows, and pastures called or known by the name or names of Arken Croft or Arken Crofts with their appurtenances in Ingbirchworth and then in the tenure or occupation of the said Richard Micklethwaite or his assigns, to have and to hold…. with their appurtenances, to the aforesaid Richard Micklethwaite and Mawde Hawksworth for the term of their natural lives, or the longer liver of them then to the heirs between them lawfully begotten, and in default of such issue to the right heirs of the said Richard for ever paying thenceforth annually to the church wardens of Penistone for the time being 10s. Witnesses: (Jn. Hn.) West, John Micklethwaite, Anthony Micklethwaite, William Walton, Thomas Catlen and Thomas Slack.

1576 – 1st July in the 18th year of Elizabeth. Grant from Richard Micklethwaite of Ingbirchworth, yeoman, for divers causes and considerations him thereto moving to Mawde Hawksworth of a certain annuity of yearly rent of 20s issuing and arising out of and in all his messuages, lands and tenements in Ingbirchworth aforesaid at the feast of St. Martin the Bishop in the month of November and Pentecost by equal portions, to have and to hold the said annuity or yearly rent of 20s to the said Mawde Hawksworth, immediately after the death of the said Richard Micklethwaite during her life. Power of distress in default of payment. Witnesses: (Jn. Hn.) West, John Micklethwaite, Anthony Micklethwaite, William Walton, Thomas Catelyn and Thomas Slack.

1576 – 7th July in the 18th year of Elizabeth. Charter confirming a grant from Peter Hawksworth of Wheatley Hill (Clayton West), yeoman, and Thomas Slack of Worsbourdale to Richard Micklethwaite Senior of Ingbirchworth, yeoman, of all and singular their messuages, lands, tenements, meadows, feeding, pastures, woods, underwoods, commons with their appurtenances in Ingbirchworth at one time in the tenure or occupation of Richard Micklethwaite, Senior, during the term of the natural life of the said Richard, except certain parcels of land, meadow and pasture called Arken Crofts, to have and to hold the same….during the term of his natural life, without impeachment of waste. Witnesses: Ralph Micklethwaite, John Micklethwaite, John Henry West, William Walton, Richard Crosley, Thomas Catelyn.

1580–1 – 12th February in the 23rd year of Elizabeth. Richard Micklethwaite, senior, of Ingbirchworth, husbandman, in £30 to secure to Richard Micklethwaite of the same place, husbandman, the indemnity of the said Richard Micklethwaite, junior, his heirs, executors and administrators, against all claims against Anthony Micklethwaite of Ingbirchworth, clothier, for and concerning one obligation, wherein the said Richard Micklethwaite junior together with the said Richard Micklethwaite senior stood bound jointly and verally to the said Anthony Micklethwaite in the sum of £20, being covenanted, granted and agreed in one pair of indentures made between the said parties …the demise and grant of two closes called Anat Roides or Oxcloses. Witnesses: Richard Micklethwaite, John Walton and John …

1590 – 14th May in the 32nd year of Elizabeth. Inquisition held at Barnsley before Edward Frothingham esquire, escheator, ? Wilkinson, gent., Robert Cusfurth, John Rishworthe, Humphrey Christopher, John Walton, Nicholas Wood, William Hobson, James Liversedge and Francis Skerowe junior who said on oath that Richard Micklethwaite, the day before his death, was seised in his demesne as of fee, of and in one messuage or tenement in Ingbirchworth with the appurtenances belonging, lying and being within the town and territories of Ingbirchworth and Thurlstone. To wit; 14 acres of meadow, 100 acres of arable land, 40 acres of pasture and a certain close called Arken Crofts, containing by estimation … acres; 100 acres of moor and common with the appurtenances in Ingbirchworth aforesaid, and of 16 acres of meadow and pasture in Thurlstone and of one messuage or tenement in Cawthorne; to wit 6 acres of meadow, 4 acres of arable land, 6 acres of pasture and common of pasture … and from thence being seised by his charter and writen indenture, the 5th day of June in the 18th year of Elizabeth, which gave, granted, enfoeffed and confirmed to Peter Hawksworth of Wheatley Hill and Thomas Slack of Worsbourghdale and their heirs forever. … after the death of him the said Richard, senior, to the use and benefit of the said Richard, junior and the heirs of his body of him the said Richard, junior and Matilda his wife, lawfully begotten. … and lastly the said jurors said on oath that the said messuage or tenement and all the said premises in Ingbirchworth aforesaid were held of the chief lord of the fee there, in free and common socage by fealty and valued per annum in all outgoings beyong repairs, 20s and that all the said premises, with their appurtenances in Thurlstone aforesaid were held of Edward Savile, esquire as of his manor of

Thurlstone, in free and common socage, by fealty at a rent of 2d …and all the said premises in Cawthorne were held of Maria, then wife of Thomas Mounteney and then formerly wife of Thomas Walton of Walton, deceased as of the manor of Cawthorne.

And that the said Richard Micklethwaite died xo day of August then last past, 1589 and the said Richard Micklethwaite was his son and next heir and was aged at the time of the death of the said Richard, his father, 30 years, and that the said Richard Micklethwaite senior, on the day on which he died, neither had nor held any other or more land.

NB: Socage was a free tenure without the obligation of military service. It could be inherited without restriction although the heir paid a fee to enter the land. Free socage involved fixed and determinate services to the Lord. It was abolished in 1660.

At the beginning of the English Civil War troops were raised, equipped and provisioned by the landowners. They were required to contribute financially though many deeply resented it, indeed, those that were against the King had all the more reason to refuse support. The following document may shed light on the split loyalties of the Micklethwaite family at this time.

1639 – *'Forasmuch as complainte is made to me by Anthony Micklethwaite of Ingbirchworth that Richard Micklethwaite and John Nicholls of the same, being equally charged with him and John Micklethwaite there at the charge of a corslet for his Majesties service do notwithstanding refuse to contribute and paye such moneys towards the charge thereof as and one by them for the same.*

These are therefore in his Maties names to charge and command you that forthwith you cause them the said Richard Micklethwaite and John Nicholls to come before me or some other deputy Lieutenant of the Riding to make answer to the premise and to be dealt with according to the law.

Hereof fail not at your peril given at Rockley under my hande the 24th day of June Ano Dom 1639.

Robert Rockley

The Micklethwaite family were also involved in poor relief,

and there is the hands of John Micklethwaite of Ingbirchworth (of Upper House), and Christopher Micklethwaite of Mathorn £3 given by John Bilclyffe of Water Hall Mill left to the poor of the parish of Penistone. And they are to pay to the poor of the said parish yearly on St. Thomas day (21st December), 5s. 1640.

Further members of the Micklethwaite family can be found in *Hunter's South Yorkshire volume 2* when he made note of important memorials within Penistone church:

Elias Micklethwaite of Denby Hall, died 1735 and Sarah his wife, the daughter of John Bedford of Flockton, died 1703. Richard Micklethwaite of Ingbirchworth, died 1730 aged 80, Josias Micklethwaite of Ingbirchworth, died 1756 aged 45 and Olivia, daughter of Mr Micklethwaite of Ingbirchworth, died 1723.

Possibly the most successful member of the family was Elias Micklethwaite, son of John Micklethwaite and Mary Stainsby. Born in 1556 at Ingbirchworth, his keen nose for a business deal took him to York where he worked as a merchant. His star rose and he went on to become the Lord Mayor of York twice and was also a burgess in parliament. He married Dorothy Jacques and had 10 children, though Dorothy died less than a year after giving birth to the tenth child, named Elias. Undeterred, Elias went on to re-marry to a woman we know only as Magdalina,

Geneaological Table of the Micklethwaite family of Ingbirchworth

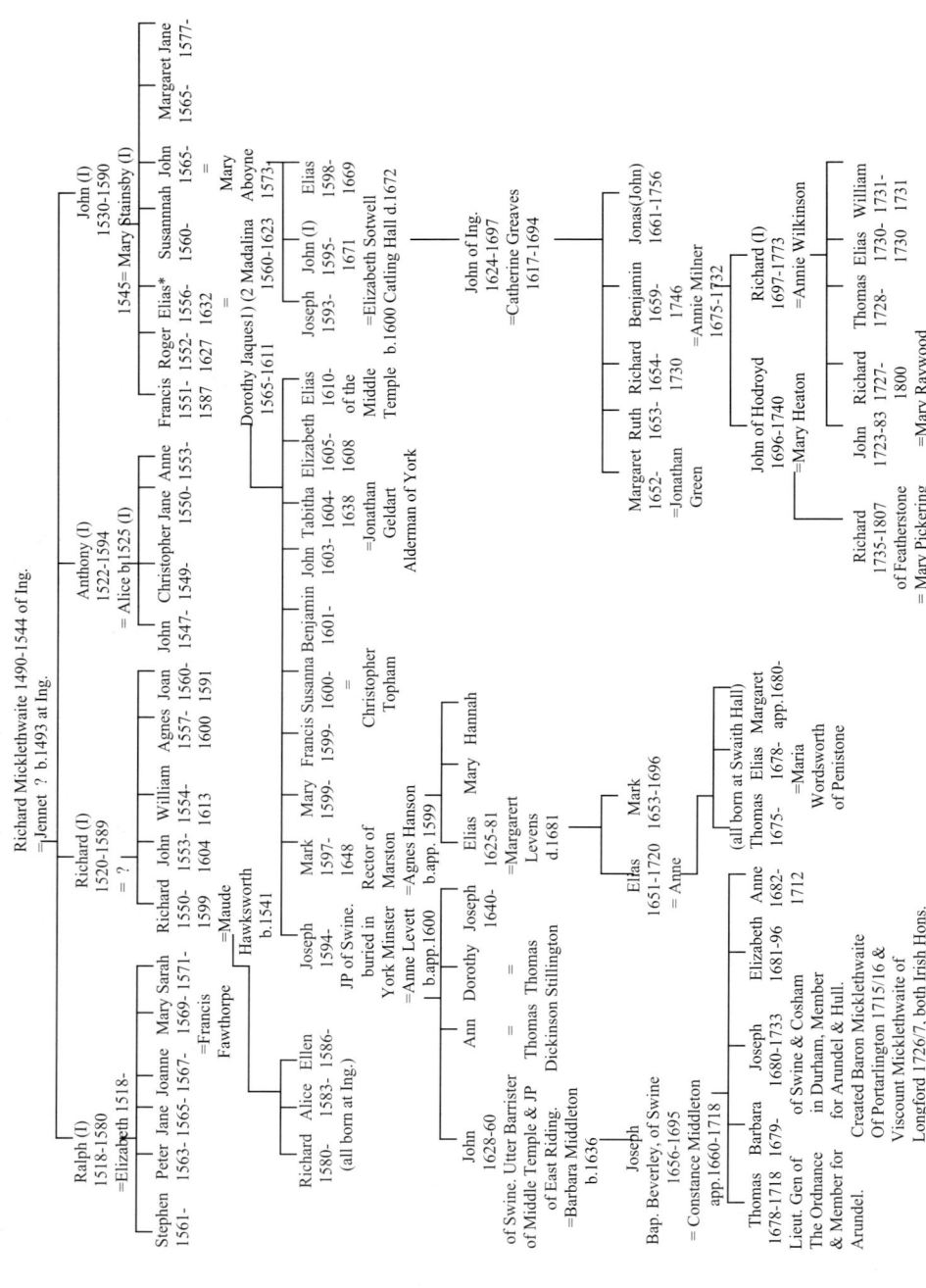

I = Lived at Ingbirchworth
* = Twice Lord Mayor of York

though there were to be no more children. Elias died in 1632 aged 76, leaving some of his children to emulate him, such as his eldest son, Joseph who became a Justice of the Peace and was buried in York Minster.

As we have seen, a large number of the family remained at Ingbirchworth some of whom were included in the Hearth Tax Returns of 1672:

Mr John Micklethwaite	5	John Micklethwaite (son of Richard)	4
John Micklethwaite (son of Anthony)	4	John Blakey	4
William Barber & forge	3	Mrs Eliza Shirt	4
George Shaw Snr.	1	George Shaw Jnr.	2
George Firth	2	John Ellis	2
John Roebuck	1	John Haigh	2

Robert Moore – Collector, John Haigh – Constable. (12 houses with a total of 34 hearths)

In the decades after the restoration of King Charles II the standing army was dispensed with and a countrywide militia formed, the local regiment was commanded by Sir Michael Wentworth and included, in 1680, John Micklethwaite who was a pike-man. This John was the grandson of an earlier John Micklethwaite who was the brother of Elias, Mayor of York. His father who was also named John, died in 1697. He was a farmer and his equipment was valued at £9 1s 4d at his death. He was also in possession of, 5 cows, 4 oxen (£35), 6 steers, 2 heifers, 3 stirks (bullocks or heifers under 2 years old), 3 calves (£29), 1 horse, 2 pack saddles (£4), 99 sheep (£27 10s), seed and ploughing (£6 10s).

Within the court rolls of Denby, previously examined there were also entries that related to Ingbirchworth which give us some of the names of the occupants during the eighteenth century:

1733 – The jurors say and present that Jonathan Shaw who held by the same services and yearly rent of 1s 6d one messuage and lands in Birchworth and one sixth part of another messuage late Hinchliffe's, is dead and that Hannah and Rebecca are his daughters and heirs and under age.

And also they say and present that Richard Micklethwaite who held of the Lord by the same services and yearly rent of £1 12. 0. one messuage and lands in Birchworth is dead and that Jonas Micklethwaite is his nephew and next heir.

And also they say and present that Benjamin Barber who held of the Lord by the same services and the yearly rent of …… one messuage and lands in Birchworth, is dead, and that by marriage settlement the same is now held by his wife.

1740 – The jurors say and present that John Roebuck who held under the same tenure and yearly rent of 1s6d one messuage in Ingbirchworth, is dead and that by his last will he devised the same to Jonathan Roebuck, his son.

1751 – Hannah and Rebecca Shaw, daughters and co-heirs of Jonathan Shaw who late held of the Lord of this manor by fealty, suite of court and the yearly rent of one shilling and sixpence a messuage and lands in Birchworth and one sixth part of another messuage formerly Hinchliffe's have conveyed the same to Mr William Fenton.

Where did all these people live? Green Farm, Willow farm and Annat Royd (a clearing named after a woman) all date to at least the seventeenth century, and Grange End Farm, which has a date stone of 1624 and was built by John Micklethwaite.

Grange Farm, Ingbirchworth, 1982. *W H Senior*

By the 1640's at least a part of the farm buildings had become known as the Angel Inn, a busy coaching house catering for commercial travellers using the trade route between Halifax and Sheffield. The route followed the old road from Penistone to Shepley though this has now been diverted due to the building of the reservoir, the remnant of the old route finishing at the Fountain Inn on Wellthorne Lane. The house has large cellars where kegs of ale were stored and included buildings associated with the keeping and maintenance of coach horses. It is rumoured that a large field opposite the Inn was the burial ground of tired horses which were slaughtered and interred there. That the building was the biggest in the immediate area is supported by the fact that it was sold in 1840 for the princely sum of £3000. Records seem to imply that a building stood on this site from much earlier times and it is the only conceivable candidate for the ancestral home of the earliest Micklethwaites. The earliest we know of was Adam (1379 Poll Tax) who was succeeded, around three generations later by Richard who was born in 1490 and died in 1544, therefore it is likely that the John Micklethwaite who built much of the present property was in fact only re-building on an ancient site.

The Angel Inn was regularly visited by Adam Eyre, the famous diarist who was also related to the Micklethwaite family, by using the following probable, family tree, we can now see how:

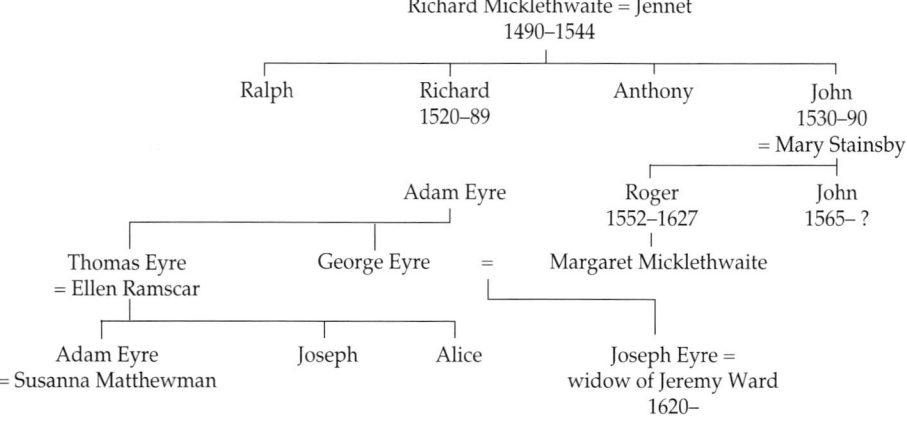

The trade directories of the nineteenth and early twentieth centuries reveal the extent of agriculture as the basis for the local economy. Not for Ingbirchworth the large fancy weaving trade or other textile oriented occupations. These are not complete lists, and the publicans have been listed earlier:

1838

John Hanwell – Blacksmith and Victualler
Samuel Taylor – Shopkeeper
Joseph Charlesworth – Farmer
Jonathan Greaves – Farmer
Joseph Hendre – Farmer
John Hobson – Farmer
Francis Horn – Farmer (owner)
Benjamin Jackson – Farmer
James Jenkinson – Farmer (owner)
Joshua Marsden – Farmer
Joseph Milner – Farmer (owner) & Miller
James Strafford – Farmer
James Taylor – Farmer
Charles Webster – Farmer

John Holmes – Wheelwright & Carpenter
Joshua Calvert – Farmer
Thomas Crookes – Farmer
Benjamin Hallett – Farmer
Jha. Hinchcliff – Farmer
Burton Horn – Farmer (owner)
Joseph Horn – Farmer (owner)
John Jackson – Farmer
Charles Knowles – Farmer
Benjamin Marsh – Farmer
Samuel Rusby – Farmer
Charles Taylor – Farmer
William Ward – Farmer
William Wrigley – Farmer (Annat Royd)

1871 – Letters via Penistone by foot post.

Joseph Hobson – Grocer
Mr John Jackson
John Wood – Shopkeeper
Joshua Biltcliff – Farmer
Thomas Crookes – Farmer
John Haigh Jnr. – Farmer
Joseph Horn – Farmer
William & John Horn – Farmers
George Jackson – Farmer
William Jackson – Farmer
John Knowles – Farmer

John Holmes & Sons – Wheelwrights
Thomas Jackson – Shoemaker
George Beaver – Farmer
James Strafford – Farmer
Charles Taylor – Farmer
James Taylor – Farmer
Luke Taylor – Farmer
Charles Webster – Farmer
John Wood – Farmer
Henry Knowles – Farmer
George Huscroft – Beerhouse (prob. Rag & Louse)

1889 – PO – Denby, John Micklethwaite receiver.
Gunthwaite and Ingbirchworth Local Board meets at the Rose and Crown Ingbirchworth on the last Monday in the month at 7pm.
Clerk – Alfred Hawes – Penistone
Treasurer – Frederick Crawshaw – Penistone
Medical Officer of Health – Duncan Alistair McGregor
Surveyor & Inspector – Thomas Lee – Oxspring
Collector – Henry Knowles – Ingbirchworth
Benjamin Haigh
Richard Beaver – Farmer/Mason
Samuel Burdett – Cow Keeper
Henry & Jonathan Crookes – Farmers
Thomas Crossley – Farmer
Taylor Hanson – Farmer
George Jackson –Farmer
Henry Knowles – Farmer/Ass. Overseer/
    Collector to Local Board
Ira Mitchell – Farmer (Annat Royd)

William Holmes – Wheelwright/Joiner
Henry Horn – Farmer
Francis William Horn – Farmer
William Horn – Farmer
William & George Horn – Farmers
Benjamin Jackson – Farmer
John Jackson – Farmer
Charles Lockwood – Farmer
Thomas Poole – Farmer
James Strafford – Farmer

Mrs Sarah Roebuck – Shopkeeper
Mrs Caroline Sykes – Beer Retailer
   (probably Rag & Louse)

Robert Taylor – Farmer

1912

Barnsley Poor Childrens Camp (James Sinclair,
   Dodworth Rd. Barnsley Hon. Sec.)
Tom Hanson – Farmer
Walter Hanson – Shopkeeper
John Henry Horn – Shopkeeper
John Jackson – Farmer
Job Knowles – Farmer/Assistant Overseer &
   Collector for Gunthwaite & Ingbirchworth UDC
Frank Lyles – Farmer, Greengates
Edwin Roebuck – Shopkeeper
Charlesworth Swallow – Farmer

Frank Burdett – Farmer & Surveyor to Gunthwaite &
   Ingbirchworth UDC
Taylor Hanson – Farmer
Hanson Holmes & William John – Wheelwrights
George Jackson Jun. – Farmer
Miss Sarah Jackson – Farmer
Charles Lockwood – Farmer
Wilfred Poole – Farmer
Mrs Mary Stafford – Farmer
Edward Woodhead – Beer Retailer
   (prob. Rag & Louse)

1922

James Mills
James Bramhall – Farmer, Spicer House
Taylor Hanson – Farmer
John Henry Horn – Shopkeeper
John Jackson – Farmer
Charles Cyrus Laycock – Farmer & Collector of
   King's taxes, Ivor Bank
Oliver Metcalfe – Farmer
George Rowe – Beer Retailer (prob. Rag & Louse)
Fred Stafford – Farmer
Wilson Webster – Farmer, Greengates

Benjamin Beever – Stone Mason
Frank Burdett – (as latter)
William Holmes & Sons – Wheelwrights
John Jackson Jun. – Farmer
Job Knowles (as latter)
Joseph Lockwood – Farmer
John Rhodes – Farmer
Edwin Stafford – Farmer
Charlesworth Swallow – Farmer

**Silver Jubilee parade, for King George V, led by Denby band,
heading towards Ingbirchworth, down Fallage Lane in 1935.**

1936

Benjamin Beever – Stone Mason
Sam Burdett – Farmer & Surveyor & Sanitary
   Inspector G & I UDC
Mrs A A Hanson – Farmer
Mrs Isabella Horn - Shopkeeper
Albert Kaye – Farmer, Grange Farm
Henry Knowles – Farmer
Charles Cyrus Laycock – Farmer, Ivor Bank
Archie Moorhouse – Beer Retailer (prob. Rag & Louse)
John Smith – Farmer, Annat Royd

George Beever – Motor Engineer
Gunthwaite & Ingbirchworth Memorial Institute
   (Roebuck Turner sec.)
John William Holmes – Wheelwright
Fred Jackson – Farmer
George Knowles – Farmer
Job Knowles (as latter)
Joe Lockwood – Farmer
Luke Mosley – Farmer, Spicer House
Edwin Stafford – Farmer

INGBIRCHWORTH RESERVOIR

Authorised by the Barnsley Local Board Act of 1862, it is 59 feet deep and contains 293 million gallons of water. Completed in 1868 it has a surface area of 23 hectares and the dam height is 20 metres or 65.6 feet.

As can be seen from the plan, Summer Ford bridge is now sunk under the water. This crossing had been used from more ancient times and was mentioned in the sale of the manor of Denby by George Burdett in 1636/7 as 'the Somerford'. Perhaps the crossing was only possible during the Summer months, when rain fall was lower, as the name suggests. In periods of extreme drought it sometimes becomes visible as the photographs show, though one wall has suffered more than the other. After its initial submerging the bridge first reappeared in 1884 and has continued to do so in 1893, 1900, 1921, 1947, 1948, 1973, and 1976 when your author walked upon it only to sink into a large patch of mud and cause his father much consternation! It has also been extant at least once in the mid 1990's. One must presume that the old corn mill had by 1868 ceased to function as the mill race would have been totally flooded by this time. It provides drinking water for the Barnsley area. The reservoir is today a haven for wildlife, particularly wildfowl and is also home to Plumpton Fly Fishing Club, founded in 2002.

Its near neighbour, Scout Dyke, was built between 1923 and 1928, covering 38 acres and is 40 feet deep. Scout Dyke is of ancient derivation and is even referred to in the deposition of the Denby 'witches' in 1672. This reservoir provides 'compensation water', ie: water power was used for powering corn mills, waterwheels and later for steam power. Scout Dyke was built solely to keep these going after the other sources were tapped.

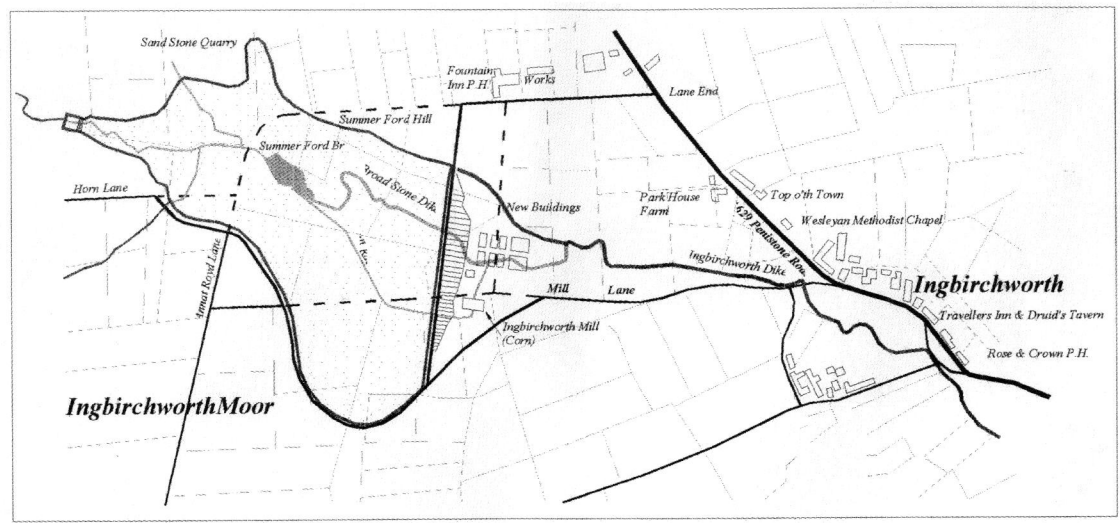

Summer Ford bridge, probably in 1921.

The camp at Scout Dyke once consisting solely of Nissen huts was begun in 1935 by Barnsley Borough Council who purchased the huts built to originally house the workmen who built the dam. During 1939–45 an American transit camp was built on the other side of the road and Barnsley Council took this over when the GI's left. This camp was replaced with the present purpose built building in 1966. The centre was now able to be used all year round unlike the Nissen huts which were only usable in Summer.

Ingbirchworth was always a part of the parish of Penistone. The only other religion to be established in the village was the Methodist church, formerly the Wesleyan chapel dated to 1829. In 1893 trustees of the chapel decided that because of over crowding an extension should be built. The old part then became the Sunday school, the new chapel being built on funds raised by public subscription. It is noteworthy that the complete extensions, plus furniture, fixtures and fittings, including hymn books were completed for the sum of £1000. County Councillor John Dyson JP of Thurgoland laid the first stone and other stones carried the name of the donor. The chapel changed from Wesleyan to Methodist in 1938.

Gathering to commemorate the cutting of the first sod of Scout Dyke reservoir, 22 May 1924.

Ingbirchworth Methodist church, centenary celebrations in May 1994. *W H Senior*

Aerial view of Ingbirchworth taken in 1997, the Ings Way housing estate is to the centre of right.

Chapter Nine
Birdsedge & High Flatts

The earliest recorded mentions of the village today known as Birdsedge refer to it as 'Burs Edge' or 'the Burs Edge'. This would refer to the obvious lump or ridge of land as one looks back from the village towards High Flatts and Denby. It was included in George Burdet's sale of his manor in 1637 as 'the Bursedge' which also mentioned 'the Castle Hills', an obvious reference to the earthwork on Windmill lane, named after the windmill which stood here in the nineteenth and early twentieth centuries. The famous diarist, Captain Adam Eyre also made mention of the place in his journal, which began in 1647, '...to Birchworth Moor, to Burdesedge, thence to Denby'.

'Burdesedge' was a place Captain Eyre passed through fairly regularly. Note the subtle change in spelling! Known previously as the 'Burs edge', Eyre seems to have been the first writer to coin the term Birdsedge. This is not to say that he was responsible for the name as a note in the Denby court roll of 1733 informs us:

> and also the jurors say and present that Ephraim Burdit who held of the Lord of this Manor by fealty, suite of court and the yearly rent of ... ... one messuage and lands at Burs Edge, did convey the same to John Clarkson of Silkston, Clerk.

Birdsedge farm (now converted into living accommodation and known as Birdsedge farm Mews) has a date-stone of 1638 and it is not unlikely that this was the 'messuage and lands' which Ephraim Burdett rented from the Lord of the Manor in 1733. This area was also marked on 19th century maps as 'Old Birdsedge'.

An early twentieth century view of Birdsedge. Note how extensive the mill buildings once were. Birdsedge Farm stands in the foreground, this is most likely the place which was farmed by Ephraim Burdett during the 1730's. One of the old farm buildings bore a date-stone of 1638.

As we know, spelling at this time was a hit and miss affair, but as Eyre included the 'd' in 'birds' in a written journal it is possible that this was how the place was referred to, by and large, in his time. It could also be that it was around the mid seventeenth century when the name Birds Edge began to evolve.

The area was undoubtedly known by its topographical situation as with many other places from more ancient times in the locale. There was no village here to speak of but there were a small number of tenant farmers, the easiest way for them to describe where they lived was to say at the edge of the burr or 'the burs edge'. It is also possible that the 'edge' part of the name was originally written 'sedge' which implies coarse grass, or uncultivated common land. That our earliest mention of the place dates to only the early part of the seventeenth century does not mean that it had not been known by this name for many centuries before – only that the whereabouts of earlier records which refer to it are at present unknown.

The final possibility is that the area was originally known as 'Burdet's Edge', ie.:the edge of the Burdet Lords's lands. Did a gradual corruption, perhaps known to Adam Eyre, take the 'Burd' element from Burdet and become Burdsedge?

High Flatts literally means, level ground, high up. An apt description, our earliest mention of it comes in the year 1453 by means of a lease dated 13th December in which Lord of the Manor, Aymer Burdet rented to John Parkynson a bovate of land in Over Denby called 'Mortenlande' and an assart called 'Heghflatt' for 5s per annum. An assart, was cleared woodland which had been enclosed and adapted for arable purposes. As with Birdsedge, the name probably goes back much further.

We will begin this chapter by taking a look at the leading families to have dwelt here.

THE DICKINSON, FIRTH AND WOOD FAMILIES

Associated with the villages/hamlets of Birdsedge and High Flatts are three families in particular, all of whom were very prominent supporters of the Quaker movement. Although both villages broadly came under the over-lordship of the Burdet and then, Savile families, (parts of Birdsedge were in the Cumberworth township) the families of Firth, Wood and Dickinson grew into a sort of upper middle class yeomanry. We have already met with a number of the individuals who follow in the pages of this work, be it in the Court Rolls or manorial sales, the information which follows is supplementary to this.

The Dickinson family

The Dickinson families association with High Flatts goes right back to the 'Quaker dawn'. John Dickinson raised his family at High Flatts before giving way to his son, Edward who is noted to have licensed his home as a dissenting place of worship in 1689. The family is also noteworthy for the Christian name Elihu which reached its zenith with two individuals who lived during the eighteenth and early nineteenth centuries.

To distinguish between the two we will use their professions to identify them – a practice which has been used a number of times before.

Elihu Dickinson – the Clothier

Elihu was a Quaker of considerable status, wealth and property. Responsible for founding Birdsedge mill around 1799, (a subject we will return to later), he can regularly be found in a number of documents reproduced in this book acquiring property, he was also instrumental in efforts to provide relief for the poor. He is known to have dressed entirely in 'drab', according to J N Dransfield, this should be taken to mean the typical and simple Quaker apparel of the day. He married Martha Beaumont in 1781, the daughter of Abraham Beaumont of Deershaw. She was *'very much indulged by her father'* and according to Joseph Wood (the leader of the High Flatts meeting at this time who we will turn to later), she *'possessed very little education'*, though *'demeaned herself in other respects to gain the esteem of friends'*.

Elihu became a very well respected member of monthly meetings and was also an elder of the High Flatts meetings, besides being possessed of a large amount of property. Perhaps it was this rather than his character or religion that attracted his wife in the first place. Martha Dickinson seems to have suffered from the beginnings of a mental breakdown prior to 1799 and had become awkward, embarrassing and disruptive at meetings. The result of which saw Elihu write to Joseph Wood in November 1799 informing him that as a result of his wife's behaviour he would no longer be attending meetings. The letter goes on to state,

> *I have no opportunity of writing a letter when she is at home nor nothing else in my own house. But if I have anything to write that I have an objection of her seeing I take pen, ink and paper unknown into the Meeting house for to do it.*

Elihu was desperately trying not to send his wife to a retreat in York founded by the Quaker's for treating mental disease. Probably the most sympathetic group of people of the age, the stigma attached to sending a member of his family was still too great for Elihu.

Though supported admirably by his fellow Quaker's, Martha's illness became worse. Records show that she fought with an S Haigh and hit him with a 'rod', sadly Elihu was ultimately given little choice and Martha was sent to York. Unfortunately, though she improved after treatment she did not stay for long enough and returned home only to fall straight back into her old ways. The Quaker fraternity at High Flatts seem to have little idea as to what to do with her next. They talked, pleaded and cajoled her into behaving and tackled problems by leading her out of meetings or asking her not to attend at all.

How this affected Elihu and Martha's two children is difficult to say. Their son, Edward committed suicide in 1817 aged just 31. His sister, Mary, who married John Firth was noted to have had a difficult home life because of her mothers problems. Whether by grief, exhaustion or pure old age, Elihu died shortly after his son in 1817 but was survived by his wife for a further thirteen years.

Joseph Wood wrote the following after Elihu's death,

> *he had been in declining state of health for upwards of half a year before his change, but at last was unexpectedly removed......in respect to his character amongst men he was a quiet and peaceable neighbour, a man of uprightness, integrity and strict punctuality in all his dealings. A considerate landlord not oppressing his servants but endeavouring to do unto others as he would wish to be done by.*

Elihu Dickinson the Tanner

The son of Elihu Dickinson and Mary Aldham, was notable for his style of dress, appropriately all in leather as befitting his profession. He was described by historian, J N Dransfield *as 'a dapper little man, conspicuous in hair powder, light gaiters and white stockings'*.

He married twice, first to Sarah Sutcliffe and after her death to Elizabeth Rothwell, who local tradition asserts was responsible for first coining the name 'Denby Dale' for the village then known as Denby Dykeside. Sarah Sutcliffe appears to have been a woman of considerable means, Joseph Wood made the following comment in a letter of 1772:

I was pleased to hear that Elihu Dickinson the Tanner was so well married ... he tells me his wife's fortune is ten thousand pounds.

During his lifetime he built Mill Bank House at High Flatts as a home for his family and made his mark in numerous areas of industry. Besides his tanning business he was also a farmer, colliery owner, corn miller, timber and stone merchant and land valuer. By 1792 he had acquired an interest in coal pits at Fulshaw and by 1799 was digging coal at Denby Dale. Dransfield notes that Elihu purchased large amounts of bark for his tanneries, some of which he bought off Howden and Grainfoot farms in the Woodlands, this appears to have been carried by women, from there to Langsett, where there were no houses on a very poor road of some 8 miles.

J N Dransfield goes on to state that Elihu attended Huddersfield market, 10 miles away by 8 o'clock am in both summer and winter, which displays a drive and tenacity of tremendous strength. As an aside, Dransfield mentions the following which shows that people were used to travelling on foot over lengthy distances,

Joshua Dyson of Denby, near Penistone, a quaint but not at all a temperate old Quaker, used to say they become 'weaker and wiser'. The old man was accustomed to attend all the markets around and always walked. I have seen him many a time at Penistone very late at night on his way back from Sheffield.

Despite his hectic work load, Elihu led a very long and active life, a case reported by Dransfield from a newspaper report at York Assizes states the following,

One of the witnesses for the plaintiff was Mr Elihu Dickinson, a most respectable and venerable-looking old gentleman of the Society of Friends, who is in his profession a land valuer had been employed to inspect the farm occupied by the plaintiff and to estimate the allowances to which he was entitled by the custom of his country. Mr Scarlet: Will you allow me, Mr Dickinson, to ask how old you are? Witness: I am now in my 80th year. (The appearance of Mr Dickinson betokens a hale and happy man of about 60). Mr Justice Bayley: Ah! Mr Scarlet, this land valuing is a far better occupation than the law. (A laugh).

Elihu became an elder at High Flatts and regularly dealt with discipline and finance matters. Thankfully, before the rest of us wilt under his shadow even he was not beyond a rebuke. His contemporary, Joseph Wood admonished him in 1798 for drinking too much alcohol!

Thread Mill Farm, Birdsedge. The building to the right of the barn was provisioned with the typical weavers windows on the second and third storey's, (the third storey has now gone). One presumes the spinning/weaving activities which took place here, gave rise to the name of the farm.

Elihu died in 1829, his estates were sold after the death of his grandson, Herbert Camm Dickinson in 1875, these included Thread Mill Farm at Birdsedge, Dearn House Farm, High Flatts and Mill Bank House.

In 1886 Mill Bank House became a home for the 'restoration of inebriate women of the working and middle classes'. Rules appertaining to the running of the establishment included, 'no immoral women can be received'. Some element of success was achieved, as in 1895 a number of former patients returned to encourage those now undergoing treatment, but there were failures, indeed, one patient had to be removed to a lunatic asylum and two others were expelled for insubordination. Patients did not come exclusively from Yorkshire and women from as far away as London and Cheltenham were admitted. As befitted a Quaker run establishment of this sort the home was created and run upon religious ideals.

Genealogical Table of the Dickinson's of High Flatts

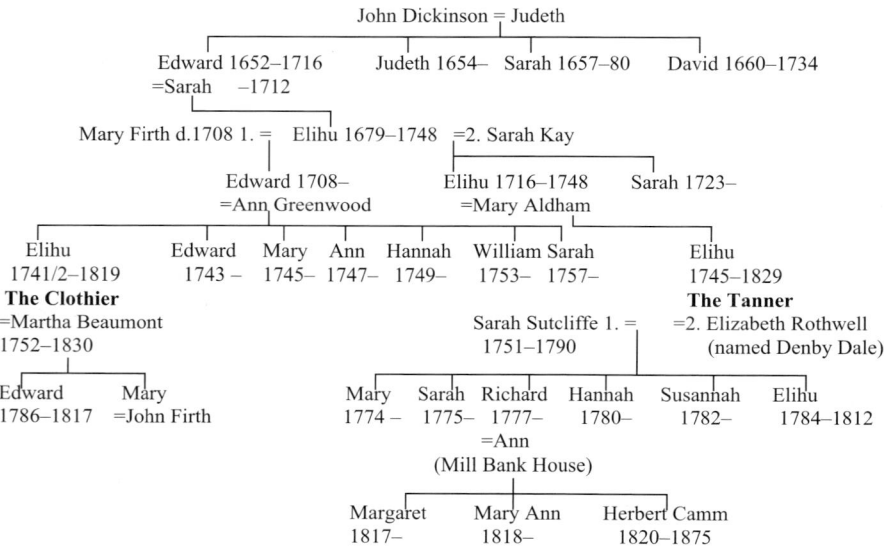

The Firth family

Towards the end of the seventeenth century, one of a number of Firth families was noted to be living at Lane Head, Shepley, just a stones throw from Birdsedge. The traditions of this family reports that they were descended from James Firth who had lived at Leak Hall, between Denby Dale and Lower Cumberworth. Leak Hall is of very ancient derivation, and was once an estate of large dimensions. As Denby Dyke Side had yet to evolve, Leak Hall was probably the chief centre of habitation between Denby and Cumberworth. William Jessop granted his lands here to his brother, John in 1376, and Richard Wentworth's rental of 1469/70 suggests that this family were his tenants. John Jesope granted the tenement called 'Leyke' to tenants in 1490.

In 1544 John Jessop of Shepley, yeoman, transferred one quarter of his messuage called 'Leikhall' to his niece, Joan Jessop of Cumberworth, daughter of his brother, Edward. In 1550 a survey was made of John Jessop's property in connection with the proposed marriage between Alice, daughter of William Turton of Upper Denby and Henry, son of John Jessop, who was the heir to a very large and desirable estate. Alice's father, William, was a benefactor of Penistone Grammar school, upon his death in 1559 he left lands in Bagden and Denby to provide 40/- a year for the poor. He also left certain lands near Wakefield Road, Clayton, to provide rye flour for the poor of the village. When the new road was built this was changed to a monetary payment, by 1885 the charity was transferred to Consolidated Charities and the interest received was distributed twice every year to the poor of Clayton. The survey was carried out by Richard Wentworth of Bretton, Edmund Oxley of Clayton and Thomas and Edward Firth, clothiers on 28 November 1550. The boundaries were described as being 'two acres of land joining a close held by Wentworth on the south and bounded on the east, north and west by boundary stones joining Birke Royd, Smith Royd, Nabb Acre and Denby Common.

An agreement for the marriage to take place was reached on 12th February 1552 by John Jessop, Henry Jessop and Charles Turton of Upper Denby with Henry Burdet (Lord of the Manor of Denby), William Turton of Upper Denby and Thomas Horne of Cumberworth. The families agreed that Henry Jessop should marry Alice Turton and provide for her in case her husband should die before her, all the woods, meadows and pasture lands in Cumberworth Half which had formerly belonged to Thomas Firth, clothier. All this property was to be enjoyed by Henry and Alice for their lives before passing to their heirs.

By December 1552 the marriage had hit trouble and a quarrel had broken out between the families which was taken to arbitration. The arbitrators were Godfrey Bosville, Ralph Jenkinson of Upper Denby and John Micklethwaite of Ingbirchworth. Evidence was produced to show that Henry Jessop had lent William Turton £20 (about £700 in modern terms) which had not been redeemed and Turton had not handed over the sum of £6 3s 4d which he promised to pay Henry for marrying his daughter. Evidently Alice had complained to her father about her husband for the deed states '… *for not well ordering and dandellying of the said Alice …by the said Henry and all other quarrels between them*'. The arbitrators made an award that Turton should enjoy the £20 for a further period and then deliver to Henry Jessop, '*one cow at noyte*' (a cow in milk after calving) in satisfaction for his wife's dowry. If any further quarrel arose between Henry and Alice which they were unable to settle peaceably they were to bring the matter to arbitration.

A deed of about 1550 describes Leak Hall as lying in the township of Shepley which suggests that Cumberworth Half may have been a hamlet of Shepley in the 16th century. It is currently unknown as to whether the feofee's of 1490 were the Firth family.

James Firth had a son, John, baptised in 1597, he in turn had two sons, Thomas (of Leak Hall) and John, who became a Quaker. This John Firth has been confused with his namesake who purchased Shepley Hall though family legends regarding a John Firth's activities during the civil war, the gunning down of the vicar of Kirkburton's wife, which I related in V1 seem to be untrue. As the Lane Head John was not born until 1645 he cannot have taken any part in the civil war. Interestingly, the other John Firth never became a Quaker and could not have been convinced by George Fox at Nottingham as Fox was not a prisoner here until 1648 and the events to which the legend alludes occur in 1643. Perhaps there is no smoke without fire, but we need better evidence than currently exists to believe this family 'fairy tale' any more!

The semi-legendary John Firth of Lane Head had registered his house as a dissenting place of worship (Quaker) in 1689, he had previously been persecuted for his beliefs in 1683. His son, Joseph, re-licensed it in 1694/5 under his own name, this is most likely due to the death of his father. Joseph married Martha Haigh and had three children. All of these married into another celebrated High Flatts Quaker dynasty, the Dickinsons, the eldest son, another Joseph Firth married Hannah Dickinson. Joseph and Hannah had three children, including another Joseph and it was down to the latter two Joseph's that the families fortunes were built. Joseph II and Joseph III were also far more active as Quakers than Joseph I and saw to affairs at Lane Head and acted as representatives at other meeting houses further afield. As farmers, Joseph II and III acquired large amounts of land in and around Shepley at the time of the Enclosure Act of 1820. Joseph III ploughed his fields with two yoke of oxen respectively named Mathew, Mark, Luke and John.

Joseph III married Martha Greenwood and had a son in 1752 named John who in turn married Ann Burrow and had four children including Joseph IV and John. By this time Lane Head had ceased to be a meeting house and the family naturally turned its attentions to High Flatts. Ann Burrow was noted in the Leeds Mercury in 1780 as *'the handsome young lady with £1000 fortune'* though it was never forthcoming! Ann became a prominent member of the High Flatts Quaker fraternity but she died of jaundice aged only 39.

The couples son, John became a clothier at Fulstone in partnership with his brother in law, Samuel Woodhead. He married Mary, the daughter of Elihu Dickinson the clothier at High Flatts where they made their home at Low House though they never had any children. John is remembered for establishing a First Day School at his home for children of both sexes of poor parents in the area which ran for many years. A lifelong Quaker, he refused to pay church rates and appeared before magistrates in 1841 three times in five weeks for this. Three years before he died he began suffering from a disease which affected the brain, the attacks grew worse and his lucid moments less frequent, he died in 1847 and was buried in the Quaker cemetery at High Flatts.

It was through John Firth's brother, Joseph that the family line continued at Lane Head. His daughter, Mary was the last of this long line of Quakers, when she died in 1898 Lane Head passed to her nieces who used the house as a summer home until 1920 when it was sold to William Hallitt of Huddersfield.

Genealogical Table of Firth family, Quakers of Lane Head

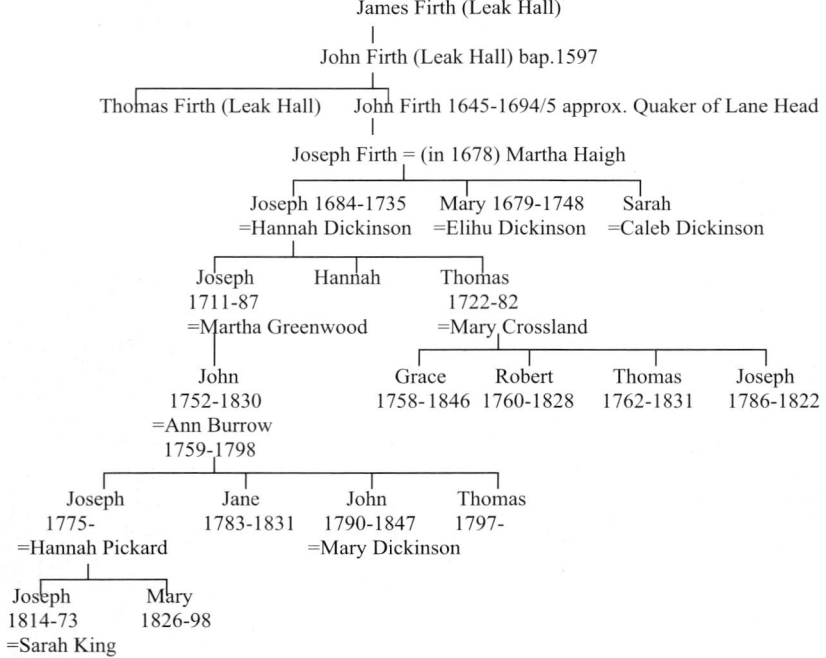

The Wood family

The Wood family were long associated with Newhouse, between High Flatts and Birdsedge. Abraham Wood married Rebecca Green at High Flatts meeting house and went to live at Newhouse with Joshua Green, presumably Rebecca's father or brother. Joshua died here in 1710 and Abraham took over the tenancy of the farm, he was granted a 21 year lease on the property by William Bosville at £14 0s 6d per annum. Abraham ran the farm alongside his other interest as a clothier, in 1709 he took on an apprentice, Bartholomew Hoyle of Cumberworth, and in 1713 he signed an agreement with his own youngest son, Samuel for the same. At his death in 1747, Newhouse passed to Samuel who so impressed his landlord, William Bosville that he was offered an indefinite lease upon the property of £24 per annum. Samuel was persecuted for his Quaker beliefs, was branded a heretic and was sent to York Castle for non-payment of tithes for three months. His energy in industry allowed him to become, at the very least, moderately wealthy. He married Susannah Walker and had seven children, the eldest of whom, Joseph, became a noted character in his own time.

Joseph was born at the 50 acre farm of Newhouse in 1750 and was educated at the boarding school at High Flatts before following his father into farming and textiles. He travelled widely from 1767 to meetings all over northern England and at the age of 29 in 1779 he became a minister. His travelling had introduced him to many eminent personages within the Quaker fraternity of the day and he became one of the most powerful preachers of his era. He never married, having given himself up to his vocation, he also abandoned his profession as a clothier.

Much of what is known about Joseph comes from his journal which he began at the age of 17, this lists the places he visited, various letters and encounters with numerous friends. The journal covers the massive span of 55 years from 1767 until 1821.

Newhouse became a popular place for Quakers to stay, pilgrims expressing a desire to meet with and learn from a master teacher. As we have seen, Joseph was eminent enough to admonish

An early twentieth century view of New House, Birdsedge, tenanted by the Wood family from at least the eighteenth century. The picture shows the later Victorian house and the older edifice which was demolished in the 1970's. *Old Barnsley*

Elihu Dickinson, an elder of High Flatts for over indulging in drink. At leisure, Joseph enjoyed a pinch of snuff and on his way to meetings he would call at an Inn along the way and partake of a little rum and water or a quart of mulled ale.

On 25th March 1821 Joseph appeared in his ministry at High Flatts for the last time, he died at 5 o'clock the following morning aged 71.

After his death, Newhouse passed to his nephew, Robert Wood. Robert was the son of Joseph's brother, Samuel who had married Mary Firth and settled at Netherend farm near Denby. Samuel became a clothier but his activities in hunting and shooting led him to neglect his finances and eventually he left for Ireland whilst his friends sorted out his debts, he was also noted to be a heavy drinker. On Samuel's return from Ireland, his father in law settled him and his family on a farm at Haddenley, probably to try and avoid further embarrassment.

Samuel's eldest son, Robert was born at Netherend though after his marriage to Mary Andrews he moved to Shelley. As we have noted, in 1821 he moved into Newhouse, after his death in 1840, his father, Samuel, moved in with his widow and her children until his death in 1842.

Robert Wood's seventh born, John Wood inherited Newhouse, noted to be a farmer and manure merchant he also dealt in a variety of fertilisers including *'Peruvian Guano'*.

Like his forbears, John was a committed Quaker, he refused to pay a rate of 1 penny in the pound to Denby Chapelry in 1853, was a lifelong teetotaller, and, along with Joseph Firth, he founded Birdsedge Day School. Around 1855 he was granted a 99 year lease on Newhouse by the Bosville estate, though he was required to spend £500 on improving the property. The present Victorian house is the result of this, the old dwelling finally being pulled down in the late 1970's being ruinous.

John Wood married twice, his first wife bore him three children, his second, two more. The youngest of these, William Herbert (Will) died from typhoid in 1902 which saw his wife and family leave Newhouse and sever the family links with the property.

During 1986 whilst repairing a section of dry stone wall at Newhouse the owner discovered a lead plaque concealed in the wall it bore the following inscription:

O thou treacherous rogue John Wood of Newhouse Denby Dale I make this that thou rest not night nor day but be like the waters of the troubled sea tossed to and fro without a resting place and that thou cannot sleep night nor day nor that thou cannot die until thou confess the wrong that thou hast done me TG & JG and my fathers house by aiding and assisting a forged will and robbing him and all his sons out of land and money signed in the mighty name of God – Amen.

The back of the plaque bears a pattern of numbers which have been identified with the Moon and Saturn and strongly indicates a belief in magic or the occult. No proof of a forged will has been discovered and the matter remains a mystery.

Souvenir mug, commemorating, Joseph Firth and John Wood, the founders of Birdsedge day school, during the late nineteenth century.

Genealogical Table of the Wood family of Newhouse

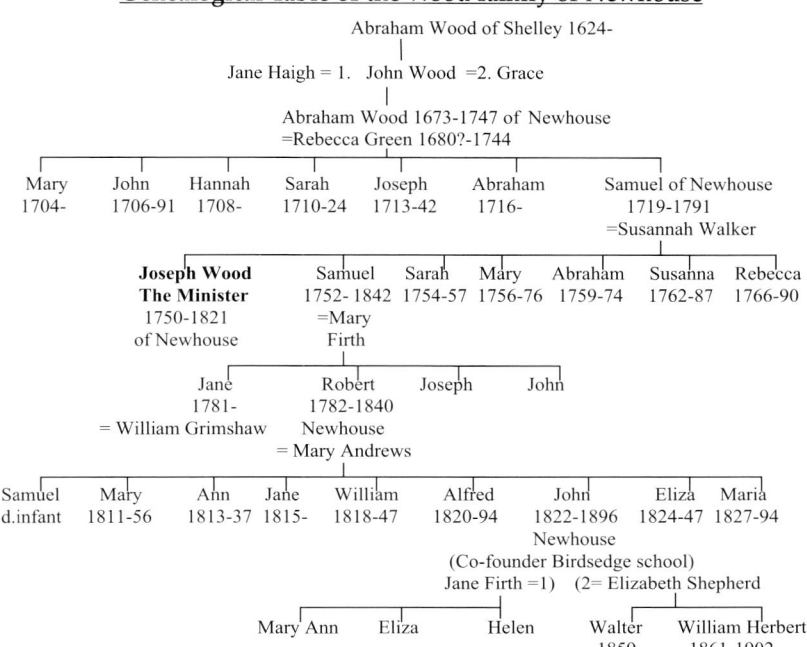

Abraham Wood of Shelley 1624-

Jane Haigh = 1. John Wood =2. Grace

Abraham Wood 1673-1747 of Newhouse
=Rebecca Green 1680?-1744

| Mary 1704- | John 1706-91 | Hannah 1708- | Sarah 1710-24 | Joseph 1713-42 | Abraham 1716- | Samuel of Newhouse 1719-1791 =Susannah Walker |

Joseph Wood The Minister 1750-1821 of Newhouse / Samuel 1752-1842 =Mary Firth / Sarah 1754-57 / Mary 1756-76 / Abraham 1759-74 / Susanna 1762-87 / Rebecca 1766-90

Jane 1781- = William Grimshaw / Robert 1782-1840 Newhouse = Mary Andrews / Joseph / John

| Samuel d.infant | Mary 1811-56 | Ann 1813-37 | Jane 1815- | William 1818-47 | Alfred 1820-94 | John 1822-1896 Newhouse (Co-founder Birdsedge school) Jane Firth =1) (2= Elizabeth Shepherd | Eliza 1824-47 | Maria 1827-94 |

Mary Ann / Eliza / Helen / Walter 1859- / William Herbert 1861-1902 d. of typhoid Newhouse sold

We have noted that a boarding school had been set up by the Quakers of High Flatts, in operation from the mid 18th century, this being due largely to the drive and tenacity of the leading families examined previously. A pupil between 1764 and 1767 was James Jenkins, originally from Bristol he had arrived, via London, after a lengthy and problematic journey at High Flatts. The school was at that time run by Joseph Shaw and alongside school work Jenkins attended meetings where he noted that *'Friends of these parts, when preaching, tremble greatly'*. He comments:

> *Nearly all the inhabitants of the village of High Flatts and its immediate vicinity were Friends, the occupation of some of them was farming, but by far the greater number were engaged in the manufacture of woollen cloth......the dialect of the country is barbarous, and some of the words so little English that none but a Yorkshire-man can understand.*

Most of the 50 boys were probably boarded at Low House Farm (the home of Edward Dickinson) though Jenkins and five others boarded with Joseph Shaw, a man noted to be a little on the stingy side. The boys were driven to supplement their diet, which had included so much salt liquor that they had drunk large amounts of water which led them to wet their beds overnight for which they had been fined their penny a week pocket money. Jenkin's goes on to relate that, *'we now and then borrowed a few potatoes from the fields of Edward Dickinson without his knowledge or consent'*. Jenkins lot did improve and he eventually became Joseph Shaw's deputy when he was called to meetings.

The Quakers also founded adult schools which were originally begun to teach poor people to read and write. The High Flatts adult school began in 1908 in the Meeting House, it was also deemed necessary that people should spend a 'holiday' together. To this end the Rest House later known as the Guest House above the Meeting house at High Flatts was re-used, formerly the First Day school. The building was sold in 1925 and two old army huts were erected at Strines nearby now called the 'Guest House' though this suffered economic difficulties and it was sold to Barnsley Corporation in 1930's who used it to accommodate evacuees.

Another First Day School was begun around 1865, again largely run and supported by the Firth, Dickinson and Wood families, its two leading lights were Joseph Firth and John Wood. Sometime between 1877 and 1899 the High Flatts First Day School, which was now housed at Three Wells above the Meeting House, closed due to falling numbers, this coincided with the foundation of National schools and a number of new Acts of Parliament which made education more readily available for all. Attempts to re-start the enterprise were made in 1899 but these were unsuccessful.

Not to be beaten, the foundations of the present day Birdsedge school were laid by the Quakers who ran a school in what is today's village hall until this was replaced in 1911 by a purpose built structure, now a primary school.

BIRDSEDGE MILL

Maps do not record the presence of any sort of mill here until around 1800. Many of the mills built in the nineteenth century replaced pre-existing structures, usually fulling or scribbling mills but this does not appear to have been the case at Birdsedge. The enclosure map for the area dated 1802 shows a water powered corn mill and a dam and was constructed by a man we have already met, Elihu Dickinson, the clothier (1741/2 - 1819). Elihu, as we have noted earlier in the book, bought up a significant amount of land when Lord Savile sold much of his Denby estate in 1799. Twelve fields to the side and at the back of the mill were owned by Elihu. His cousin, Elihu, the tanner, owned much of the land on which the school is now built along with Four Row and Ten Row and the present Wesleyan Methodist chapel, this he had bought from the Miss Walkers of Papist Hall, Lower Denby. The water course for the mill dam was largely on the tanner's land which leads to speculation that the two men were not only related but also supportive friends.

The enclosure map also shows the turnpike road, reputedly built by Blind Jack of Knaresborough at a cost of £340. The map's date of 1802 confounds other reports that the road

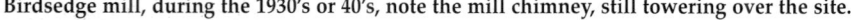

Birdsedge mill, during the 1930's or 40's, note the mill chimney, still towering over the site.

was not built until 1825, though it may have been re-surfaced at this time. The road's construction may have coincided with the building of the mill as Elihu the clothier was nothing if not an entrepreneur and would have realised the enormous difference a good quality trade route would make to his business all year round.

It seems likely that the earliest activity at the mill would have revolved around fulling and scribbling. Elihu's death in 1819 may have led to a William Dickinson taking over the operation, but the mill itself passed to the Firth estate through the marriage of Elihu's daughter, Mary who married John Firth in 1817. That it was running in 1843 is certain as records show that a James Batley of Birdsedge was convicted this year for an offence under the factory act.

It is probable that Batley worked for Hirst, Thorpe and Company, scribbling and fulling millers of 'Birdshedge Mill' who had established themselves sometime between 1819 and 1843 and rented the mill from the Firth estate. This company was dissolved in 1845, though two partners, William and Charles Hirst carried on. In 1852, two partnerships were recorded as fancy woollen manufacturers, William, Charles and Henry Hirst, and, Edward Hirst and Company. The Hirst brothers were recorded in 1857 as woollen manufacturers but in 1862 as fancy woollen manufacturers. By 1866, William and Charles Hirst had been joined by Edwin Hirst and they continued until at least 1873, the mill was occupied by fancy goods manufacturers in 1889 and was by now consuming 1100 tons of coal each year. By 1912 Furman Hunt McGrath had taken over the business which was recorded as worsted manufacturing, he remained here until at least 1921, he lived at Sunside House, the former home of Thomas Armitage, also a woollen manufacturer who can be found here in 1857. McGrath became an integral member of the committee formed to run the Military Auxiliary Hospital during the first world war in Denby Dale, indeed, he was responsible for manufacturing the blankets for the beds.

The mill was finally sold by the trustees of the Firth estate in 1921 to Z. Hinchliffe & Sons of Denby Dale, it closed during a slump in trade in 1929 but has survived to the present day and is primarily used for blending wool. The buildings were listed in 1981.

The entry to Birdsedge mill and Willie Ellis' shop, circa 1920.

Weavers at Birdsedge mill during the 1920's.

Mary Smith, on the right, at work in Birdsedge mill during the 1920's.

A tragedy occurred in 1940 when Jack Senior of 6 Park Head, a boy in his early teens was skating on the mill pond which was iced over but beginning to thaw. As the ice gave way Jack slipped into the water and though he hung on to the edge for around 40 minutes as rescue attempts were made he eventually slipped under and drowned as nobody had been able to get to him.

TWENTIETH CENTURY BIRDSEDGE

Many of the houses built in Birdsedge were erected to house the working population of the mill. Terraced housing such as Four Row and Ten Row sprang up from around the 1850's onwards. The trustees of the Firth estate seem to have held on to the rentals of at least some of these properties and then, after the estate had been purchased by Z Hinchliffe and Sons the rentals continued. On 20th August 1925 Hinchliffe's sold number 1, Ten Row to James Kaye which probably signalled the companies policy towards the housing involved with their purchase of the mill.

Terraced cottages across from Birdsedge mill, originally built to house its employees. The old Quaker school, now the village hall, can be seen on the left of the photograph, at the end of Ten Row.

Although largely a one street village by 1945–50 there were approximately 680 people living between Sunside and the end of High Flatts. As the modern practise of knocking cottages through to create larger living accommodation continues the names of the rows of cottages have, in some cases become somewhat irrelevant, but farm conversions and some new building have seen the growth of the village into the modern age.

Around 1950 the following people lived at Ten Row, opposite the mill:

No. 1. Tom and Emma Dearnley with their daughter Caroline. Tom was an excellent dry stone waller.

No. 2. Mr and Mrs Haywood

No. 3. Mr Arthur Tyas – the property being a cobblers shop, which was known by some as 'Obe's'. Arthur Tyas was a first world war veteran who also sold pop and crisps from the shop which gave local children somewhere to go at night as the only other place of recourse was the Crown pub, the landlady of which, Mrs Horn, would not have let them in anyway. The Crosspipes Inn had a reputation as a 'bit of a rowdy house', so this was not an option either. Arthur Tyas actually lived at New Brighton, he worked at the shop between 8am and 10pm six days a week. His family included four daughters, Mavis, Mabel, Marlene and Wendy.

The cobblers shop was known to some children as 'Obediah's' as they believed that to be Arthur's name, shortened to Obe's as is a child's want.

No. 4. Mr and Mrs Briggs, their son Trevor and a daughter.

No. 5. Mr and Mrs Bower.

No. 6. Mr and Mrs Lindley, their son Bernard and daughter Nancy.

No. 7. Wilfred and Mary Jane Mosley.

No. 8. Mrs Tinker and her daughter Florrie.

The former school at the end of Ten Row, disused from 1911 on the erection of a larger school just up the lane was purchased by public subscription and became the village hall. It is administered by a committee of volunteers under the guidance of elected trustees. In 1940 it was the home of the YMCA for Gentlemen, the Ladies club met in the little room next door. Gertrude Mosley was the secretary of the Ladies club which eventually became the Women's Institute and remained so until she reached her 80's.

The new school erected in 1911 was large enough to accommodate 200 pupils though the average attendance in 1912 was 104, under the mastership of William Holt. The school had replaced the National establishment which in 1901 had provision for 100 scholars though again the average attendance was much less at only 70, Henry Marsh was the master at this time. The new school was the scene of excitement during the Second World War. This was at the time that Mr Butcher was the Headmaster, ably supported by Miss Broadbent and Mrs Riding. During the war years bombs used to be stored and stacked at the side of the road, these included gas bombs which arrived at local stations. The road surfaces had been improved from the ash and dirt of earlier times to help facilitate the transportation of equipment and weaponry. As a result of this American soldiers used them to race their bomb laden lorries through the village. On one

Birdsedge schoolchildren, pictured in 1907/8.

Birdsedge school, opened in 1911, in the early years of its life.

occasion a lorry turned up school lane and his brakes caught fire. The soldier jumped out of the cab and abandoned the vehicle. The bombs he was carrying did not have fins or detonators and so were usually harmless - unless an explosion set them off – a blazing truck would certainly have been enough to trigger them. Another American soldier was at the road junction and he ran into school to alert the staff and effect an evacuation. He then ran back outside and let down the tail gate of the truck, got up into the cabin and reversed quickly before pulling up sharply. The bombs rolled out of the back of the lorry and disaster was averted.

As far as religious matters were concerned, the people of High Flatts were a part of Denby parish but Birdsedge was split by the young river Dearne, which rises in the fields immediately above Park Head at the Northern end of the village. This portion belongs to Cumberworth parish, the southern end belonging to Denby parish. Other than the established church religion, aside from the well supported Quaker movement, took time to infiltrate the area. Eventually a Wesleyan Reform chapel was built in 1868 on Birdsedge lane, before this, believers had met in each others homes. The only monument of note is the following:

Esther Rusby, the beloved daughter of Charles and Emma Rusby, who departed this life January 17th 1870, aged 14 years.

The Rusby family have a long history in the Denby district, indeed, to the North West of the chapel is Rusby Wood plantation, amidst which water tanks were constructed in 1892 containing 100,000 gallons to supply Birdsedge.

The increased housing in the village naturally brought with it the need for

An early twentieth century view of Birdsedge Wesleyan Reform church, which was built in 1868.

services, though it must be said that agriculture was still the predominant occupation in the area.

The trade directories of the nineteenth and early twentieth centuries make interesting reading, though it should be noted that I have abridged the Birdsedge entries as half of the village lies in Denby parish and the other half in Cumberworth. I have also omitted the public houses as these have been examined in another chapter.

1838 – all at High Flatts
Pvt. John Ellis-Stone Mason
John Firth – Gentleman
Luke Holmes - Beerhouse
John Senior – Shopkeeper

John Ellis-Colliery Owner
Jonathan Jubb – Blacksmith (also landlord of the White Swan Inn)
Richard Wood – Farmer

1847 – at Birdsedge
William Ellis – Stone mason
William Pickford – Shopkeeper

Joseph Mellor – Farmer

1857 – at Birdsedge
William Ellis – Stone Mason
Fanny Pickford – Shopkeeper (Crosspipes)
George Rusby – Farmer

Joseph Mellor – Farmer
Abraham Beaumont – Farmer
William Woodhead – Shopkeeper

1857 – at High Flatts
Francis Burdett – Joiner/Builder/Grocer
Joseph Jubb – Blacksmith/Farmer (probably the son of Jonathan who ran the White Swan)
Sarah Burdett – Farmer

George Norton – Stone Merchant
William Beaumont – Farmer
John Ellis – Farmer

1866 – at Birdsedge
John Beaumont – Farmer
George Rusby – Farmer
George Boothroyd – Tailor

Edward Hirst – Farmer
William Woodhead – Shopkeeper

1866– at High Flatts
George Beaumont – Farmer
Francis Burdett – Farmer/Wheelwright/Shopkeeper
George Smith – Farmer
George Norton – Stone Mason

Samuel Brown – Farmer
Samuel Rusby – Farmer
Ben Ellis – Stone Mason
Charles Rusby – Stone Mason

1871 at Birdsedge
Edward Hirst – Springfield
George Rusby – Farmer
William Woodhead – Shopkeeper

John Beaumont – Farmer
Edward Horne – Shopkeeper

1871 at High Flatts
Herbert Camm Dickinson

Joseph Briggs – Farmer

1889 at Birdsedge
John Bickerdyke – Farmer

Wilson Herbert Horn – Farmer

1889 at High Flatts

Mrs Burdett
Allott Brothers – Builders
Mrs Ann Blacker – Shopkeeper
Burton Rusby – Farmer

Mrs Firth
Ingham Milnes
John Kaye – Farmer
Jn. Wood – Farmer and Manure Merchant

1901 – at Birdsedge

Pvt. John Dowse
Herbert Wilson Horn – Grocer
Sarah Charlesworth – Shopkeeper (Crosspipes)

William Child – Fancy Goods Manufacturer
William Henry Thickett – Farmer

1901 – at High Flatts

John Kaye – Farmer

James Norton – Farmer

1912 – at High Flatts

Pvt. Henry Senior – Low House
William Bartaby – Farmer
John Thomas Kaye – Farmer

Edward Allott – Builder
Samuel Cook – Shopkeeper

1912 – at Birdsedge

Willie Ellis – Post Office/Grocer
Henry Moorhouse – Farmer
George Charlesworth & Son – Shopkeepers
   (Crosspipes)

Sam Jepson – Farmer
Geoffrey Moreland – Farmer
George Norton Peace – Farmer - Sunside

1922 – at High Flatts

Pvt. Miss Brook – Low House
Edward Allott – Builder

Pvt. William Robson – Middle House
Samuel Cook & Son – Shopkeepers

1922 – Birdsedge

Willie Ellis – Post Office/Grocer
Alfred & Arthur Moorhouse – Farmers

Walter Davidson – New House – Farmer
Young Men's Christian Assoc. (J B Heywood – secretary)

1936 – at High Flatts

Pvt. Clement Roebuck – Broomhill
William Robson – Middle House
Percy Cook – Farmer

Pvt. Charles Liversidge – Low House
Edwin Allott – Builder
Norman Naylor – Upper House –Butcher

1936 – at Birdsedge

Tom Ellis – Farmer
Willie Ellis – Post Office/Grocer
Thomas Smith – Farmer
Pvt. R Brown – Sunside

Lewis Dearnley – Painter
Clarence Haigh – Poultry Farmer – Springfield
Beardsell Charlesworth – Shopkeeper (Crosspipes)

The above list excludes some of the individuals we have already met. Sarah Charlesworth, of Park Head, mentioned in 1901, took steps to provide for her children, Beardsell and Emily by setting them up in business, in January 1901, with a shop at a cost of £1000. The above records note that Beardsell had taken over by 1936. This shop survived the twentieth century, becoming a Post Office and general store before it began to suffer at the hands of the Supermarkets and the nearby Petrol Filling Station which became a Londis outlet. The last remaining shop in Birdsedge shut its doors in 2001. It had largely taken over from the establishment run by Willie Ellis close

to the mill. A regular site at this shop was the owners Bulldog which sat in the shop window, one day a cat ambled past and the dog took it upon itself to jump at the window, which shattered, in order to see off the offending feline. Willie Ellis had been in business since at least 1912 and when it finally came to his retirement in the 1950's the future of the shop

Willie Ellis' shop, and next door, the home of Charlie Kendall. The two swapped houses in the 1950's when Charlie took over the business.

was, for a time, secured. Charlie Kendall lived in the adjoining cottage and agreed to take over the enterprise, so, naturally, the two of them swapped houses! Charlie's shop remained a Post Office and Grocers at ground level, but he began selling furniture from the basement and at the back. Charlie later moved his furniture business to Shrewsbury Road, Penistone, though later a man called Sparking bought the shop site and converted it into premises for a haulage company.

UPPER DEARNE WOODLANDS

These woods, split in half by the young River Dearne lead away from Birdsedge towards Denby Dale with Cumberworth to the North. They are of ancient origin, past owners include the Wentworth's of Bretton Hall, the Bosville's of Gunthwaite and more recently, Walter Norton of Rockwood House, Denby Dale who finally brought the woods into single ownership. Latterly, Hepworth Building Products Ltd. took over the woods in 1970. They are managed by a local

Rockwood Lake, created by Walter Norton during the late nineteenth century.

volunteer group known as the Upper Dearne Conservation Group who meet at the village hall in Birdsedge.

Walter Norton spent time and money on landscaping the woods and river, the project took place between 1880 and 1895 in a number of stages. This landscaping also included a pond, originally fed from Park Dike by means of an underground channel. Later, the course of Park Dike was altered to flow into the pond and an inlet was created from the Dearne. Once completed the pond was 100 metres long by 20 metres wide and several feet deep. It contained an island near the upper end and a curving stone spillway at its exit. Walter Norton evidently enjoyed his woods as he grew older and used the money acquired from his families textile business to create a private haven for himself before he died in 1909. By the 1970's much of the pond had silted up and only a shallow area of open water remained. Winter storms and vandalism damaged the top of the spillway and the remaining water drained out. Remedial work undertaken between 1998 and 1999 saw 8000 barrow loads of silt removed by local volunteers which helped to restore the pond to around half the area of the original, though at a depth of just 18 inches.

The woods are home to a large variety of wildlife, information signs note that Tawny Owls, Pied Flycatchers, Treecreepers, Goldcrest and Nuthatch are all breeding successfully. Some of the most interesting dwellers in the woods are also its smallest!

Red Wood Ants have populated much of the woodland floor, believed to be the only colony in Yorkshire and one of only a very few in England they are extremely rare this far North. In excess of 70 nests were found in 2002, and these are monitored during summer to see how many are actually occupied, with a view to assessing whether management of the woodlands needs to be changed in any way.

Finally, we must mention the pride with which the occupants of Birdsedge treat their village. The erection of a sun dial in 1953 in the small roadside garden at the front of the new school commemorates the Coronation of Queen Elizabeth II. But matters closer to home celebrate the community as a whole. A carnival was held from the mid 1940's but gradually interest died off. Its modern day replacement is a village festival which takes place on the school playing fields. Usually blessed with excellent weather, the festival takes place on a Saturday in July, a local history exhibition is held in the village hall and entertainment is provided in a number of marquees. Folk music forms a large percentage of the day and a concert is held in the main tent in the evening, largely down to the efforts of Birdsedge based folk group, Artisan. The day includes food and drink, children's shows, brass bands, agility dog display's, vintage vehicles and is always very well attended.

Appendices

✧

APPENDIX 1 – Extracts taken from Penistone Almanac.

NB: *The Almanacs were a record of the past year, therefore the first date, in bold, is the date of the Almanac, the second date is of the actual occurrence.*

1910 – May 1909. Death of Mrs Mary Ann Revell, of Denby Dale aged 89. For over 30 years she attended Penistone Market in the capacity of lime merchant, she having taken up the business on the death of her husband, Mr Enoch Revell.

1910 – May 1909. Two sisters, Gertrude and Lena Headley of Upper Denby, whilst driving on the Penistone Road by Ingbirchworth, saw two men kicking and beating another, whilst on the ground and pluckily went to the rescue. They succeeded in capturing one of the assailants, after a struggle with three of his companions, put him into the trap and gave him into custody at Denby. The young ladies were afterwards presented with gold watches by the Watch Committee, in recognition of their plucky conduct.

1912 – June 1911. Opening of new Council school at Birdsedge. Cost including site, £2,657 18s 2d.

1912 – September 1911. Death of John Micklethwaite, sub-postmaster at Denby, and a prominent Conservative, at the age of 85.

1914 – Recent Local Wills. Mr W Laycock, of Gunthwaite Hall, left £1,436.

1919 – September 1918. Mr George Jackson, farmer, Ingbirchworth, received official news that his son, Private Albert Jackson, 2nd Notts. and Derby. Rgt. was killed in action in France on 14 July aged 21.

1919 – Recent Local Wills. Mr John Thomas Brownhill of Denby Dale whose death occurred on 16 September left estate valued at £3,105 2s 9d. Mr James Brownhill of Oakfield, Denby Dale, is his executor.

1920 – November 1918. Mr and Mrs J Jackson of Willow Farm, Ingbirchworth, received news that their son, Rfn. T Jackson, London Regt., died in hospital in France from gas poisoning; formerly employed at Messrs. Hinchliffe & Sons mill in Denby Dale.

1922 – May 1921. Mr T A Hinchliffe of the Royds, Denby Dale, presented to the village a field known as 'Swift Croft', 3$^{1}/_{2}$ acres, for purposes of cricket ground and bowling green, which was formally opened by Mr T A Hinchliffe (cricket) and Mr John Hinchliffe, JP, (bowls).

1923 – Recent Local Wills. Mr Thomas Albert Hinchliffe, Denby Dale, woollen and worsted spinner, left £62,049.

1924 – Local Wills. Mr Wilfred Barnes of Field House, Denby Dale, died, 28 December 1922 left £4,767. He was for many years clerk to the Denby & Cumberworth UDC and had, not long ago, retired from the position of schoolmaster at Denby Dale.

1925 – Recent Local Wills. Dr Duncan Alistair MacGregor (67) of Exmouth, formerly of Clayton West, left £2,682 (net personalty £2,604).

1930 – Recent Local Wills. Dame Narah Peace Hinchliffe of Inkerman Hall, Denby Dale, wife of Sir James Peace Hinchliffe and daughter of the late Joseph Dewhirst, left estate of the gross value of £2,454 with net personalty of £2,341. Mr Joe Hirst, Norman Road, Denby Dale, grocer, left £2,089 17s 6d, with net personalty £2,056 2s 8d.

1931 – Recent Local Wills. Mr James Henry Dewhirst of Westcliffe, Denby Dale, formerly Chairman and Managing Director of Messrs. Bairstow, Sons & Co. Ltd. wholesale clothiers, Huddersfield who died 6 August 1930, aged 71, left gross estate to the value of £36,931 8s 7d, with net personalty £33,498 16s 7d.

1933 - Recent Local Wills. Mr Charles Henry Brownhill, 59 years, 2 Bromley Rd, St Annes-on-Sea, cotton manufacturer, a director of John Brownhill & Co. Ltd., left £17,106, net personalty £15,198.

1933 – Re. – typhoid fever at Denby Dale. The first case was that of a young woman living at Quaker Bottom, notified on 17 September after her return from Scarborough.

1934 – December 1932. Denby Silver Prize Band gave a concert in Penistone Town Hall in aid of the sufferers of typhoid fever in Denby Dale. A balance sheet was issued by the Denby & Cumberworth UDC showing receipts to 4 Jan. 1933, for the relief fund to be £1,147 8s 6d.

1934 – September 1933. Death of Sir James Peace Hinchliffe, CA, LLD of Inkerman Hall, Denby Dale.

1934 – Recent Local Wills. Mr George Wilfred Naylor of, 155 Reads Avenue, Blackpool, formerly of Denby Dale, sanitary pipe manufacturer, who died 1 July 1932, aged 61 years, left £6,462 19s 2d, with net personalty £6,435 14s 2d.

1935 – January 1934. Serious damage, estimated at several thousand pounds done by fire to a storage house at Hartcliffe Mills, Denby Dale, belonging to Messrs. Z Hinchliffe & Sons, worsted spinners. The four storey warehouse was completely gutted.

1935 – June 1934. Death of Mr William Wood, (75), of Viaduct House, Denby Dale. From 1908 to 1929 he was Divisional Education Clerk for the district in and around Penistone.

1935 – Recent Local Wills. Sir James Peace Hinchliffe of Inkerman Hall, Denby Dale, left £76,284, net personalty £73,551. Mr Arthy Kenyon of Ashfield, Denby Dale, Chairman of Jonas Kenyon & Sons, left £5,624, net personalty £5,100. Mr William Wood of Viaduct House, Denby Dale left £1,141, net personalty £286.

1936 – December 1934. Jubilee celebrations of the Denby Dale Corps of the Salvation Army.

1936 – January 1935. Inquest on Charles Hirst Dearnley (53), of Cumberworth, whose body was found in Square Wood reservoir. A verdict of 'drowned himself while temporarily of unsound mind' was returned.

1936 – February 1935. Adjourned inquest at Denby Dale on Clifford Burton, of Royd Moor, Thurlstone, who was killed by the falling of a chimney at Naylor Bros. Sanitary pipe works in Denby Dale, during high wind.

1936 – May 1935. Denby Dale Brass Band won the 100 guineas gold cup in the open qualifying competition at Belle Vue, Manchester. Ninety two bands competed. Mr Albert Cook, bandmaster has played in brass bands for 40 years. He received a gold medal from the 'Brass Band News' in honour of the band's success.

1936 – Recent Local Wills. Mr Thomas Norton of Bagden Hall, left £202,749 (net personalty £169,419).

1937 – November 1935. The stocks at Upper Cumberworth were removed from the road opposite the schools and placed in the churchyard.

1937 – March 1936. Thomas H Ellis, 24, of Wakefield Road, Cumberworth, shot himself at his mothers house in Denby Dale. A verdict was recorded that the deceased shot himself while in the fit of a depression.

1937 – March 1936. Celebration supper at Denby Dale Working Men's Club on the members winning the Dearne Valley Billiards Cup and becoming champions of the Domino league.

1937 – June 1936. Trailer laden with cattle overturned on Chapel Hill, Denby Dale. The cattle were unhurt.

1937 – Recent Local Wills. Mr John Hinchliffe of Strathdearne, Denby Dale, yarn spinner, formerly Chairman of Z Hinchliffe & Sons Ltd., left £75,298 (net personalty £75,136).

1938 – June 1937. Death of Joseph Wood, 70 years, of Co-operative Terrace, Denby Dale. He was a member of Denby Dale band for 32 years and three sons are playing members.

Denby Dale Carnival, Saturday 7 August, 1937. Jointly organised by the Brass Band and the Bowling and Cricket Clubs, the event was an outstanding success. The Carnival Queen (Miss Marion Scott), was crowned by Mrs Harold Hinchliffe, wife of the Chairman of the Urban District Council. The Queen's attendants were, Doreen Dyson, Marjorie Brown, Hilda Mudd, Barbara Roberts, Nancy Hartley, Barbara Senior and Jean Hirst. The Queen was dressed in silks woven in the village.

1938 – June 1937. Percy Chandler (20) of Holmfield, Clayton West, fatally injured while working at Messrs. Naylor's, Denby Dale.

1938 – June 1937. Denby Dale Band awarded 1st and 2nd prizes at the Flockton Brass Band Contest.

1938 – August 1937. Denby Dale Band awarded two cups and 2 first prizes at Haworth Brass Band contest. Hade Edge were 2nd in both cases to Denby Dale. Eight bands took part.

1938 – August 1937. Denby Dale Carnival.

1938 – October 1937. Employees of Z Hinchliffe & Sons Ltd., Denby Dale given an outing to Blackpool.

1938 – Coronation Celebrations at Denby Dale, 12 May 1937. The day reached its climax in the lighting of the bonfire in Norman Park. It was lighted by Mr James Brownhill, who was escorted from his home at Oakfield to the site by torchlight procession. The brass band was in the park and when the fire was lighted they played the National Anthem and led community singing.

1939 – December 1937. Presentation to Miss Bransgrove, mistress of Denby Dale infants school on retiring after 40 years. Mr Harold Hinchliffe of Denby Dale, offered to give £2000 towards a dance hall and swimming bath if Denby Dale would raise £1000.

1939 – January 1938. Presentations to Mr William Turton, on retiring after being employed at Messrs. J Brownhill & Co. Ltd., of Denby Dale, for nearly 60 years.

1939 – Recent Local Wills. Major Cecil Naylor Brownhill, Irish Guards, of Dolphin Square, London, a noted amateur steeplechase rider, son of James Brownhill, left £36,952 with net personalty £35,364. Mr H A Kitson, Westleigh, Denby Dale, pipe manufacturer left £33,493 8s 9d (net personalty £30,667 0s 9d). Mr J T Field of Long Royds, Skelmanthorpe, formerly of Edwin Field & Sons Ltd. Former Chairman and for nearly 40 years member of Skelmanthorpe Urban Council, left £197,556 (net personalty £190,954) on which £47,367 estate duty has been paid.

1940 – November 1938. Denby Dale Brass Band awarded first prize £10, and the Parkinson Cup, at Wakefield Band Contest. Conductor was Mr N Thorpe.

1940 – November 1938. Harry Dalton (21) of 4, Birdsedge Hill, Birdsedge, killed at Denby Lane End when walking home from church by a car driven by Mr F W Rowe, of St John's, Penistone. A verdict of death by misadventure was returned.

1940 – December 1938. Retirement of Harry Holmes (57 years service), Mr Charlie Senior (53 years service), Mr John Dransfield (51 years service) from the employ of Messrs. John Brownhill & Co Ltd., Denby Dale. Presentations were made at the mill.

1940 – December 1940. Rockwood Hunt meeting at Rockwood House, home of Mr and Mrs H Gordon Cran, cancelled owing to snow and inclement weather.

1940 – Recent Local Wills. The Rev. G O Tibbits, of Upper Denby vicarage, for 12 years Vicar of Denby, who died on 4 January 1939 aged 57, left gross estate of £1,492 10s 5d, net personalty £943 18s 3d.

1942 – June 1941. The Princess Royal paid a visit to the Red Cross Depot at Bagden Hall, Scissett and saw an exhibition at Strathdearne, Denby Dale, of articles made by the workers. John Desmond Schofield (24) of Sunny Bank, Denby Dale, a telegraphist in the Navy, died of wounds received through enemy action.

1942 – July 1941. Death of Councillor W A Heap (74), head of Heap & Sons butchers, Denby Dale.

1944 – November 1942. Among the messages broadcast from Cairo was one for Mrs Rose Tyas of Denby Dale, from her husband, driver James Tyas, RASC, in the Middle East.

1944 – November 1942. Corporal Walter D Heath, R Tank Corps of High St., Denby Dale, reported a prisoner of war in Italian Hands. He had been missing since 20 June 1942. He served in France, Dunkirk and the Middle East and was wounded near Tobruk. He has a brother and a sister in the forces.

1944 – May 1943. Arnold Victor Ellis (56), a tailor of High Street, Denby Dale and a six year old London evacuee, were killed when the car in which they were travelling, skidded and fell down a 30ft. drop into Sally Wood, New Mill.

1944 – May 1943. Presentation at Messrs. Z Hinchliffe & Sons, Hartcliffe Mills, Denby Dale, to Mr Arthur Gill, who had completed 50 years service with the firm.

1944 – October 1943. Flight Sergeant Donald Mudd (28), RAF., of Miller Hill, Denby Dale, killed in action. He was an air gunner and rigger with Coastal Command, and had 1,400 hours operational flying, including over Russian Convoys, the Mediterranean and Norwegian Fjords, and shadowed the 'Bismarck' – German battleship.

1944 – Recent Local Wills. Mr John Francis (or Frank) Naylor, Riverdale Rd., Sheffield, formerly of Denby Dale, sanitary pipe maker, left £19,908 gross, net personalty £19,795.

1945 – March 1944. Guardsman Harold Burdett (28) of Inkerman Cottages, Denby Dale, reported missing since 9th Feb. now believed to be in enemy hands.

1945 – April 1944. Cpl. W Desmond Heath, Royal Tank Corp, of Denby Dale, spoke on BBC Radio. He was in the leading tank to capture Halfia Pass. He has served in France (Dunkirk), the Middle East, was wounded at Tobruk and was for a time, a prisoner of the Italians.

1945 – July 1944. £1,351 was raised in Denby Dale UD, for Holmfirth flood relief fund.

1946 – February 1945. Flt. Sgt. Ralph Townsend, son of Coun. and Mrs Townsend, of Denby Dale, presumed killed on air operations.

1946 – February 1945. Petty Officer George Bower, of Highfield Farm, Denby Dale, met his cousin, Sub-Lt. John Leach of Clitheroe, out in Ceylon.

1946 – February 1945. Percy Brown of Denby Dale, borer, killed by a fall of roof while at his work at Messrs. Stringer & Sons, Springwood Colliery, Clayton West.

1946 – May 1945. P/O. John Horlsey, RN., of the White Hart Hotel, Denby Dale, awarded the DSM. Guardsman, Harold Burdett, of Inkerman Cottages, Denby Dale, arrived home after 15 months a prisoner of war. Two Denby Dale brothers, Jack and Fred K Fisher, of Leak Hall Crescent, after being prisoners of war since St. Valery, June 1940, arrived home. Trooper John W Thorpe, of Low Field House, Denby Dale, taken prisoner of war at Tobruk, 1942, returned home. Pioneer Norman Laundon (28) of Syke House, Denby Dale, taken prisoner at Boulogne in May 1940, arrived home.

1946 – October 1945. Birdsedge Knitting Party for the Forces ceased operations. They had completed 3,858 articles.

1947 – June 1946. Retirement of Mr Wilfred Haigh, after almost 60 years service as a tuner at Messrs. J Brownhill & Co., Denby Dale.

1947 – June 1946. Gunner William Hirst (23) of Prospect Terrace, Denby Dale, drove a tank in the London Victory Parade.

1947 – July 1946. Miss Audrey Hallas of Denby Dale, won first prize in Contralto Class at the 'Mrs Sunderland' Musical Festival at Huddersfield.

1949 – February 1948. Mr Fred Bates of Inkerman Farm, Denby Dale, took part in a broadcast in 'Farmers half hour'. March 1948 - Local farmers Mr Geo. Hirst and Mr Fred Bates of Denby Dale, broadcast in a visit by the BBC to Barnby Hall Farm, Cawthorne.

1949 – April 1948. The body of George Henry Hirst (67), woollen feeder of Prospect Terrace, Denby Dale, was recovered from an aqueduct near Hartcliffe Mills, Denby Dale.

1949 – August 1948. The body of Gordon Senior (16) of Denby Dale was recovered from Square Wood reservoir, Denby Dale. A verdict of death by misadventure was recorded. He was a good swimmer.

1949 – August 1948. Presentation to Miss Lily Windle, of Upper Denby, by workpeople of the woollen dept. of Z Hinchliffe & Sons, Denby Dale, where she had been employed for 46 years, on her retirement.

1949 – August 1948. Sir Don Bradman, world famous Australian cricketer, visited and was shown around the mills of Jonas Kenyon & Sons, at Denby Dale. He had lunch with Mr Jonas Kenyon and signed autographs for enthusiasts.

1949 – August 1948. Mr William Haigh, aged 85, of Denby Dale, was hit by the ball during a cricket match at Denby Dale. He was wearing glasses at the time and the glass splinters so damaged the right eye that it was subsequently removed.

1949 – Recent Local Wills. Mr Edwin Allott, of Rockley House, High Flatts, builder and contractor, who died 19 June 1948 left, £7,823 7s 4d. gross, net personalty £7,786 12s 4d.

1950 – December 1948. Mr Fred Bower of Denby Dale, roundsman for Messrs. H Norton & Sons, Scissett, for 34 years, retired.

1950 – January 1949. Death of Mr Fred Crosland (81) of Denby Dale. He had been emplyed by Z Hinchliffe & Sons, for whom he was head dyer for nearly 70 years, working for three generations of the Hinchliffe family.

1950 – April 1949. Presentation of a pipe and silver salver to Mr G H Norton of Bagden Hall, by the Barnsley West Riding Magistrates Court, to mark his 50 years as a magistrate.

1950 – August 1949. Miss Audrey Hinchliffe, of Strathdearne, Denby Dale, was awarded first prize in the British Show Jumping Assoc. Championship at the Royal Lancs. Show at Blackpool.

1950 – Recent Local Wills. Miss Mabel Hinchliffe of Inkerman Hall, Denby Dale, daughter of the late Sir James, left £25,670 7s 3d gross (net value £25,356 12s). Mr Fred Cook of Norbreck, Wakefield Road, Denby Dale left £15,204 10s 10d gross (net £15,093 15s 8d).

1951 – November 1949. Golden Wedding of Mr and Mrs Willie Ellis, of Birdsedge, formerly of Birdsedge Post Office, for 35 years.

1951 – December 1949. Members of Denby Dale UDC, objected to the proposal to commence open cast coal operations in Deffer Wood, near Clayton West.

1951 – May 1950. The family of Mr Harold Nightingale were left homeless when their home at Park Head, Birdsedge, was entirely destroyed by fire.

1951 – May 1950. Denby Silver Band won the fourth section of the Brass Band contest at Belle Vue, Manchester, gaining 192 points out of a possible 200.

1951 – July 1950. The fund for the Nightingale family, whose house was destroyed by fire at Birdsedge, was closed at £359.

1951 – September 1950. Maurice Leyland, the former Yorkshire and England cricketer, presented the Holden Cup to Denby Dale cricket team, with replicas for the players. Present was Mr T Thackra, who has been playing with the club for 29 years.

1951 – October 1950. Nortonthorpe cricket club, Scissett, won the Central League Campionship.

1951 – Recent Local Wills. Mr George H Norton of Bagden Hall, Scissett, and of Tan-y-Bryn Road, Colwyn Bay, Chairman of G H Norton & Co. pile fabric manufacturers, Nortonthorpe Mills, left £199,173 14s 2d., £196,144 5s 5d. net duty paid £81,569.

1951 – District Property Sales. October 1950. Over 300 acres of freehold farms in Skelmanthorpe, Denby, Denby Dale and High Flatts areas, sold under the direction of the executors of the late Mr G H Norton of Bagden Hall, Scissett, fetched high prices. The 13 lots made £14,220, only one lot was withdrawn. Mr Arthur Brook bought Leak Hall Farm, Denby Dale for £1,125. Dry Hill Farm, Denby and six cottages realised £3,050, Leak Hall Farm and cottage, Denby Dale £1,900, Wither Wood, Denby Dale, £525, Common Side Farm, Common Lane, Denby Dale, £800. Accommodation land included, Gilthwaites Lane, Denby Dale, £800, and adjoining Zion Chapel, Denby Dale, £450.

1952 – February 1951. Denby Dale UDC decided to erect the 1952 allocation of houses by licence (25) at the Gilthwaites Lane site.

1952 – March 1951. Denby Dale Brass Band celebrated its centenary honouring three members for long service, Mr Harry Lockwood (63 years), Mr Herbert Firth (43 years) and Mr Fred Hudson (42 years). Among those present were 6 brothers called Wood having between them 140 years playing service and three Cunningham brothers having 88 years service, one having two sons now playing.

1952 – April 1951. Mr Arthur Horsfall, stationmaster at Denby Dale was appointed stationmaster and goods agent at Meltham. Mr E Piggott, clerk at Denby Dale was appointed stationmaster at Hipperholme.

1952 – June 1951. Mr Walter Hudson, Low Fold, Denby, retired after 60 years with J Kitson & Sons Ltd., pipe manufacturers of Denby Dale. Mr W Wainwright who had 61 years service made the presentation.

1952 – July 1951. The body of Mr T R Haigh (50) of Upper Putting Hill, Denby Dale was found in a reservoir near his home. A verdict of death from misadventure was recorded.

1952 – September 1951. Alexksander Gryszel (40) a Pole living at Denby Dale, re-visited Arnhem, Holland, seven years after being parachuted there.

1955 – District Property Sales. February 1954. The model freehold licensed T.T. dairy farm, Fall Edge Farm, Upper Denby, with vacant possession, and approx. 57 acres of land was sold by A E Wilby & Son, auctioneers to Mr Geo. Holmes, for £6,250.

1955 – May 1954. 'Oakfield', Denby Dale, a freehold residence, including two flats, with vacant possession, was withdrawn when offered for sale by A E Wilby & Sons, auctioneers.

1957 – November 1955. 100 tons of hay was destroyed in a fire which gutted a barn at Denby Hall Farm, tenanted by Mr Eric Peace.

1957 – April 1956. Miss Mabel Norton (78) of Bagden Hall, secretary treasurer of Wakefield Diocesan Mothers Union, has been organising MU outings for 56 years.

1957 – April 1956. Denby Dale Brass Band were placed 2nd at the North Eastern area Brass Band Contest at Bradford.

1958 – October 1956. Mrs Mary Ann Kenyon of Ashfield, Denby Dale, attained her 100th birthday. Congratulations included a telegram from Her Majesty the Queen. Mrs Kenyon is the widow of the late Mr William Henry Kenyon, Managing Director of Messrs. Jonas Kenyon & Sons, who died in 1923.

1958 – November 1956. Friend Garratt (57) of Kitchenroyd, Denby Dale, received fatal injuries when he was struck by a motorcycle ridden by Michael Kilner of Denby Dale, who received head injuries in Wakefield Rd., Denby Dale.

1958 – November 1956. Denby Dale Brass Band reached the finals of the National Brass Band Championship in London. They were un-placed. With the band travelled Mr Harry Lockwood, who joined the band in 1888, now 82.

NB: *Personalty – personal estate, all the property which, when a person dies, goes to the executor or administrator, as distinguished from the realty which goes to the heir at law.*

APPENDIX 2 – High Hoyland
Poll Tax 1379
John Robinson and his wife Alicia 4d
Richard Machun 4d
John Brys (Brice) and his wife Dionisia 4d
William Grall and his wife Johanna 4d
John Oxspring and his wife Johanna 4d
John Shepherd and his wife Katerina 4d
Peter Belamy and his wife Anabilla 4d
John Bythebroke, (tailor) and his wife Elena 6d
Walter Myrell and his wife Margery 4d
William Bithebroke and his wife Elena 4d
Total: 3s 6d

Lords of the Manor
Originally a part of the great holdings of Adam fitz Swain, his lack of a male heir resulted in his two daughters inheriting from him. This is why there were two rectors at High Hoyland until 1687.

We have noted the de Hoyland and Burdet families as Lords but when Richard Burdet split High Hoyland and Denby due to his displeasure at his eldest son, Aymer, Thomas, his second son, after serious legal arguments, inherited High Hoyland and made his residence at Birthwaite. His line continued until the last Frances Burdett of Birthwaite, who was described as 'profligate' was forced, by financial necessity to sell the manor, along with lands at Dykeside and Kexborough to Sir Mathew Wentworth of Bretton Hall soon after 1675. The village remained part of the Bretton estate until 1958. Later trade directories note that, Wentworth Blackett Beaumont of Bretton Hall, in 1901 and Viscount Allendale of Bretton Park was the Lord of the Manor in 1912.

It is also noted that during the reign of Richard II (1397/8) William Dronsfield of West Bretton held land here, until at least 1407.

The Church
We noted in V1 that the site of the church was ancient. A Saxon cross dated to approximately 800AD has been found there, and other material of this early period has been discovered and is now built into the north wall of the nave. It is possible that the cross was a marker for an early Christian preaching station as the religion grew in popularity. Aerial photographs have revealed marks on the ground that indicate that there was an Iron Age settlement at High Hoyland more than 2000 years old. The primitive road track from the church across the top of Hoyland Bank to Winterhill farm is an Iron Age road leading towards Denby and Penistone. Hilltops were favoured sites for early pagan

centres and the early Christian missionaries were encouraged to re-use these sites when setting up their own preaching stations. The earliest church seems to have been founded by around 1150 by Adam fitz Swain though nothing survives of this edifice, save the material now built into the nave wall. This church was bigger than the present edifice and it's first priest was called Robert which we know from a disputed presentation between the descendants of Adam fitz Swain, his son in law William de Neville against Adam de Hoyland heard in 1200, he was followed by John and then Simon who witnessed two deeds in the 1240's. The Norman font of High Hoyland now resides in Skelmanthorpe church after being removed during re-building work in 1804. It features an odd pair of heads which take the place of flowers on the tree scrolls of two panels. This form of decoration first appeared at Lastingham in 1073 which dates the font to the generation after the conquest.

On 17th August 1247 Archbishop Walter de Gray appointed Rosfredus de Farnetino, an Italian Canon lawyer from a village near Florence to be his proctor at the Papal court. Farentino was not to contract loans nor debts to be paid by the diocese. The Archbishop had to provide him with a salary and so awarded him the benefice of High Hoyland which was empty by lapse with the consent of Pope Innocent IV, on 17th June 1250 though it is unknown as to whether Farentino ever came to the village. In 1275 Farentino was given leave of absence in order to attend to his affairs in Rome and was ordered to provide a suitable replacement. By 1282 Farentino was dead and Archbishop Wickwane appointed Ralph de Burelle to the first mediety at High Hoyland, he resigned in 1302 but died before his resignation took place. In 1303 Archbishop Corbridge instituted Thomas de Langton who was only in minor orders being a subdeacon to the rectory. Because of this the Dean of Doncaster was ordered to sequester profits from the benefice for the payment of a man in priests orders. The second

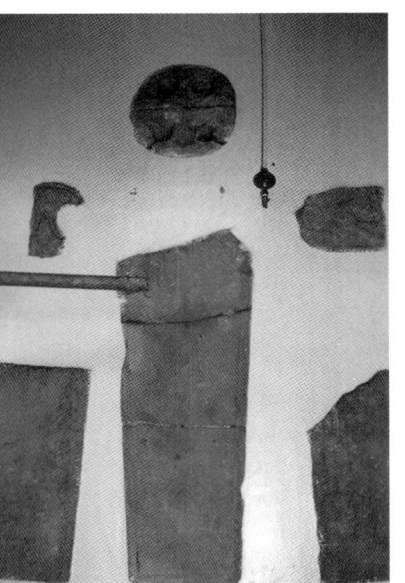

The remnants of an early Christian cross and other material, built into the north wall of the nave at High Hoyland church after re-building took place between 1904 and 1908.

mediety was occupied by Richard de Swinton who resigned in 1267 after being instituted by Archbishop Godfrey de Ludham, formerly rector of Penistone. Swinton had been the secretary of Archbishop Gray and had been granted this mediety on the death of his patron.

The church was always a poor one, no wealthy family having given it patronage and after the Black Death the tithes were not enough to support one rector let alone two. The church has undergone a number of changes though the most substantial part remaining is the tower which has a date stone of 1679. Joseph Hunter commented upon the height of the church and the fact that a beacon had stood here in the south west corner of the churchyard in the seventeenth century. He went on:

High Hoyland church during the early twentieth century. *Old Barnsley*

to this circumstance must, I suppose be attributed that the justices of the peace, at a Sessions held in the fifth year of King James I (1607/8) laid an assessment on the inhabitants of Hoyland for the erection of a steeple to their church. They had at that time only a little shed of boards. This was resisted on the part of the inhabitants, and the church of Hoyland had no steeple till the year 1679. This is the date on the present tower; but I have seen a receipt dated 25th May 1673 from John Moore, the builder of it, to Sir Matthew Wentworth, for £10, the last of five payments of £10 each towards the work.

John Moore was the mason and Thomas Hawksworth the carpenter who worked on the construction. In 1804 much of the old church was demolished and re-built, the nave of which was replaced between 1904 and 1908, this was when the Saxon material was incorporated into the nave wall and a large number of the ancient monuments inside the church were removed and destroyed. It is difficult to tell just how much demolition took place although from old photographs it would seem the early twentieth century re-building did indeed see only the tower survive. I am informed that a small number of the architectural features of the earlier edifices still survive, including a number of medieval arches, indeed, some parts of the church are now blocked up and there is even a tale of a missing crypt! It is described in Kelly's trade directory of 1912 thus:

The old church of All Saints is a plain building of stone, consisting of chancel, nave and a western tower, containing 6 bells, it is now used only as a mortuary chapel, having been disused for divine service since 1875 when a new church was erected at Clayton West: in the churchyard is a stone recording the death of Ann Copley, in 1707 at the age of 105 years

Although High Hoyland never grew into a large village its church covered the ecclesiastical affairs of a wide area which included Clayton West, Scissett, Bretton and parts of Cumberworth and Skelmanthorpe and as we have seen was an important centre for the manorial administration of its Lords, the Burdets.

The building was eventually taken over by Bretton College and opened its doors very rarely, though a service was held in 1981, the very last, but in 2003 they sold it to Mrs Alison Johnson, a private individual whose associations with the church came about due to a family tragedy. She has turned the building into an art gallery and has begun work on cleaning up the churchyard. It would seem that High Hoyland church, which was becoming something of an eyesore, is now in capable and loving hands and it is to be hoped its future is as successful as its past.

Rectors of High Hoyland Church

1st Mediety	2nd Mediety
1251 – Rosfredus de Ferentino	? – 1267 Richard de Swinton
1280 – Alexander de Vaus	1267 – Robert de Saint Laurence
1282– 1302 Ralph de Burelle	
1303 – Thomas de Langton	1280 – Alexander de Vaus
1304 – William de Burton	1303 – Walter de Halton
1309 – William de Hyde	William de Savile
1349 – John de Crosland	1349 – John de Brampton
John de Walton	1366 – Thomas de Mathersley
1379 – John Bettison	1367 – Robert Club vel de Midelton
1427 – Henry Faldon	1371 – William de Midelton
1465 – John Porter	1372 – John de Hopton
1497 – John Dughtiman	1378 – Robert de Pykering
1511 – Edward Bayne	William Ashberry
1545 – Thomas Barlow	1400 – David Qwitchurch
1576 – Arthur Kaye	1417 – John Southwell
1592 – Robert Kaye	1421 – John Ainsworth

1603 – William Wilkinson
1623 – Anthony Binns (or Benns)
1642–1662 – Robert Inman
1662 – Henry Bubwith
1687–1725 John Brooke

1434 – John Dighton
1460 – Thomas Staynton
1511 – John Suthilde (or Sotehill)
1549 – Richard Shanne
     George Tailyour
1591 – Richard Worrall
1614 – John Galley (or Gale)
1615 – William Appleyard
    … Carvile
    William Heron
1687–1725 John Brooke

The two medieties were united in John Brooke from 1687, though the medieties were to be split again as we find in 1743 that Thomas Dawson held the second mediety, he was the master of Congleton Grammar school in Cheshire so visits were very infrequent. John Burton held the first mediety. He was succeeded by, amongst others, Robert Hodgson, died 1807, John Alcock, died 1810, and by 1825 Charles Bird. He died in 1867 and was succeeded by Fitzgerald Wintour. One name not in the above list is John Caltorne who occurs in deeds of 1398 and 1404. It is unknown as to which mediety he belonged.

The latter list is made up from the notes of Joseph Hunter who, largely, listed the incumbents by the date they were presented to the living, it is likely that there are gaps in the list and a number of individuals have probably been forgotten.

David Quitchurch, rector around 1400 was convicted of robbing the offertory box and taking the oblations.

Thomas Battelot was rector in 1549 though does not appear in the above list as I am unaware as to which mediety he belonged. In 1549 he found himself in serious trouble when he performed the marriage of Robert West, who was 7 years old and Elizabeth Beaumont who was 9. The respective families involved were endeavouring to look after their own futures and found a receptive priest in Battelot. When the case came to light Battelot was ordered to perform a humiliating public penance. The marriage was declared null and void, thankfully, Robert West had refused to share his wife's bed, believing her to be his sister.

Frequent disputes occurred between rectors of the two medieties after 1570. The Wentworth's of Bretton owned the rights to one living (Amabel's portion) and naturally appointed a rector who held their own religious beliefs, which were Anglican. The Savile family of Thornhill held the other living (Maud's portion) but they were puritans, with Calvinistic leanings, two rectors supporting different doctrines within the same church!

In 1624 Anthony Benns was rector of one of the medieties of the church, he was also tutor and chaplain to Lady Anne Savile at Thornhill.. He found himself in trouble when he secretly married Thomas Edmunds, footman to Lady Anne Savile to Anne Cookson, daughter of Henry Cookson who was not yet 21. The marriage took place in the great chamber of Lady Savile's home at Thornhill. Henry Cookson was outraged and cut his daughter off from his estate and threatened punishment and revenge upon Anthony Benns. Lady Savile was also furious when she heard of the marriage. She deprived him of his salary and from teaching her children, which caused Benn's to have to survive on the very poor living derived from the church. Henry Cookson and his daughter eventually made their peace and she was restored to the family fold.

In 1662 Robert Inman was ejected from his living, he was a puritan and non-conformist, probably originally presented by the Saviles.

Henry Bubwith and William Heron held the two medieties in 1669 when the pair can be found fighting over the funeral of a child of William Deighton who lived at Park Mill, Clayton West. William Heron had taken to drinking heavily and often fought and quarrelled with people, including his wife and mother in law whom he beat and bruised causing them to take refuge with neighbours. Once, when she refused to allow him in her home he threw stones through her windows! He called Bubwith a fool, 'thou art sick, thou wearest a cap' during the funeral service and continued his assault at the graveside.

Roger Hodson was the last of the full time resident incumbents, he married the heiress of the Greaves family, he held the incumbency from 1785 until 1807.

His successor was Christopher Bird who held the position until 1866, though he spent most of his time in Northumberland, due to his friendship with Mrs Beaumont of Bretton Hall who had awarded him two livings there. This meant that High Hoyland was served by poorly paid curates. Bird paid only one visit each year to the village when he came to collect his tithes from farmers. The continued negligence of the eighteenth century allowed the Wesleyan's to fill the vacancy for religious leadership and the decline of High Hoyland church had begun. It was too far removed from the people it served who lived in the villages which had grown as a result of the Industrial Revolution. Fitzgerald Thomas Wyntour succeeded Christopher Bird and he decided that the building had become redundant and that activity should be moved down into the valley at Clayton West. After opposition was voiced, Wyntour got his wish and after 1875 High Hoyland became a mortuary chapel only, though it was used for occasional Summer services after the restoration of 1908.

APPENDIX 3 –
Cumberworth Poll Tax 1379
Staincross wapentake
Robert Farthing and Constance his wife 4d
Johanna del Byrkes 4d
John de Royds and Cecilia his wife 4d
John Farthing 4d
Robert Hobson and Alicia his wife 4d
Giliaum Spyser 4d
John de Riley and his wife Cecilia 4d
Adam del Legh, (diker) and his wife Johanna 6d
    (a diker was a ditch or trench digger).
John de Wortley, (mawer) and Magota his wife 6d
John Elcock, (tailor), and Emmot his wife 6d
John son of John Elcock 4d
William Forster and Elizabeth his wife 4d
John Milner and his wife Margaret 4d
John de Saurebe and his wife Margaret 4d
John, son of John de Saurebe 4d
Total: 5s 6d

Aggbrig wapentake
Robert de Riley and his wife Agnes 4d
William Jessop and his wife Agnes 4d
John Thomson and his wife Alicia 4d
William de Lipheued and his wife Alicia 4d

Thomas Milner and his wife Isabella 4d
Walter del Brome 4d
John Alcock 4d
Galfridus Nadeson 4d
John Thomson 4d
Agnes Hunt 4d
John Jessop and his wife Alicia 4d
Johanna, daughter of John Jessop 4d
John de Riley and his wife Agnes 4d
Agnes de Rilay 4d
Adam de Hinchcliffe 4d
Elizabeth, daughter of Adam de Hinchcliffe 4d

Clayton West Poll Tax 1379
Richard de Mosley, (smith) and his wife Isabella 6d
John Grobbar and his wife Annot 4d
Robert Byngge and Emmot his wife 4d
Thomas Dawson, (smith), and Margaret his wife 6d
Richard Grelle and Matilda his wife 4d
Alice Riche 4d
Nicholas Riche 4d
William Shepherd and his wife Margaret 4d
Thomas de Wylam and Cecilia his wife 4d
Thomas Tagon and Annot his wife 4d
Total: 3s 8d

APPENDIX 4 – Penistone Church – the Clergy

In 1229 there were two medieties in Penistone. One was held by Simon de Rupibus and the other by Geoffrey de Ludham. In 1232, Archbishop of York, Walter Gray consolidated the two in the person of Geoffrey de Ludham, de Ludham, as we have noted earlier, became Archbishop of York himself in 1258 and was buried in the Minster when he died in 1264. Prior to Thomas Bryan the position was that of Rector, Bryan was the first Vicar. The incumbents, with some omissions were as follows:

1281 – Henry de Barton	1574 – John Sotwell
1313 – Richard de Walton	1597 – 1602 – George Goodwin
1313 – William de Nevile	1602 – Francis Oley
1331 – Richard de Rotherham	1619 – 1633 – Jonas Rook
1349 – William de Stainton (1373 & 1378)	1633 – Mathew Booth
1413 – Thomas Bryan	1635 – 1642 - Peter Toothill
1418 – 1458 Robert Pulleyn	1642 – Timothy Broadley
1458 – William Wordsworth	1649 – John Didsbury
1495 – Robert Bishop	.... – 1689 Henry Swyft
1498 – Robert Amyas	1690 – 1717 - Edmund Hough
.... – 1542 – Robert Watts	1717/18 – Edward Jackson
1545 – John Herbert	1722 – Thomas Cockshutt
1550 – 1560 - Robert Skires	1761 – Samuel Phipps
1560 – 1570 -William Crosland	– Good Eyre
1570 – 1574 – Thomas Bosvile	1809 – Martin Naylor (till at least 1825)

We have already come across Robert Pulleyn and his links to the Burdet Lord's of Denby. He died as Vicar of Penistone in 1458. In his last will he directed his executors to provide 7lbs of wax, to burn about his body at the time of his funeral, to every person present he left 12d, to every parish clerk 4d, to every other clerk 2d, to the four orders of friars he left 13s 4d. The next Vicar, William Wordsworth seems to have been a friend of Pulleyn as he is left a bequest in Pulleyn's will.

APPENDIX 5 – Visitations to Denby Chapel/Church

In 1627 the second chapel was built at Denby, to be used only for Mattins and Evensong. In 1637 the minister at Denby was cited before the Archdeacon's court for administering the sacraments in Denby chapel, which had not yet been consecrated.

Archbishop Drummond's Visitation 1764

Denby: There are 120 families and 11 Quakers taught by Henry Dickinson at the Quaker Meeting place. There is a school with a salary of £4 paid to Theophilus Swann the master. There is no vicarage house but Divine Service is performed twice each Sunday at 11am and 3pm. There are 250 communicants who walk to Penistone, for the communion is not celebrated here.

In 1829 the furnishings of the chapel were returned as being a pulpit, a reading desk with a cushion of green shag, two prayer books, two surplices, a pewter basin for Baptisms, the Royal Arms, the Creed and Lord's Prayer on boards and a bell given by Lady Beaumont. The minister received one shilling for a funeral during the week but only sixpence for one on Sunday. The parish clerk received a salary of 20/- a year, 6/- for ringing the bell and 8d for digging a grave.

Bishop Longley's Visitations 1837–1853

Denby: There was no house for the curate who lived near the chapel in a private house. When I visited the chapel in Autumn 1837 I found it in so miserable a condition that I strongly recommended an attempt be made to raise money for its rebuilding. Here the population was 2000 with church seating for 200. There were two services each Sunday but there were never any celebrations of Holy Communion. For this the parishioners had to walk to Penistone. The Methodists and Ranters had built a chapel each in the parish.

1870

Denby was a parish of 1700 people – it included a large part of Denby Dale. The new church could hold 300 but the average congregation was 40 and there were no communicants. The pews in church were rented out and the services were depressingly dull. Dissent was rising and at a meeting to elect new trustees for the management of the church school all those elected were in favour of secularising education.

APPENDIX 6 – Denby & District Volume 1 – Addenda:

p. 66. Arabella Burdett married 26 February 1620/1 at Wragby to Richard Bullock of Pontefract. Susan Burdett married 18 May 1592 at Barnsley to Alexander Ryshforth.

p. 67. Hune Burdett was Agent to Lionel Cranfield (1575–1645), Knighted 1613. Created Earl of Middlesex in 1622 at Cranfield's estates at Frobisher Hall, Altofts in the parish of Normanton.

p. 82. Herrer Rich (possibly a mis-transcription for Aymer) married 13 May 1587 at Almondbury to Alice Burdett between 10 & 11 o'clock in the morning. Alice may be the Alice, daughter of Henry Burdett on the pedigree on p. 66.

p. 92. Dorothy may have been the Dorothy Burdett buried at Emley, 17 September 1654. If so she would have been in her early 80's.

p. 92. Matthew Burdett & Dorothy Colthurst did indeed marry in 1600 as is recorded in Paver's Marriage Licenses.

p. 93. Grace, daughter of Matthew Burdett married in 1634 at Kippax to William Fleming, Yeoman.

p. 94. Mary, daughter of Tobias Burdett married, ..?.. Smithson and Sarah, her sister also married. Both were dead before 1727 and both left children.

Their sister, Ann, married (as his second wife), Francis Barrowby of Thirsk, Gentleman (1674–1726). She was buried, at her own request at St. Michael le Belfry, York.

Denby & District Volume 1 – Corrigenda:

p. 92. Matthew was probably not the fifth son of Nicholas but one of the eldest. By 1612 he is described as 'son and heir' of Nicholas which implies that any elder brothers had already died without issue.

Bond in £24 by Matthew Burdett of Denby, Gent, son and heir of Nicholas Burdett, late of Swawell, Gent, deceased. Dated 27 July 1612.

Darton Parish Registers are missing 1561–77 but the following children of Nicholas were baptised after that:

Samuel -3 September 1578, Reginald – 11 December 1578, Arthur (later of Cawthorne) – 28 .....1581, Valentine (later of Silkstone) – 10 September 1583.

Not all of these are mentioned in Nicholas' will but records exist of all having reached adulthood. Fitting the other children in before 1578 implies that Matthew was born not later than around 1570. Nicholas Burdett of Silkstone (d.1666) was the grandson of Nicholas of Swawell, not his eldest son. He was the son of Valentine, b. 1583, (see above).

The spelling of Delariviere seems to have been invented by Joseph Hunter. The historical records normally give 'Delariver' or 'Delaryver', although 'Dallriver' is also used.

Despite the date of 1527 given for Edmund Colthurst's birth in Burkes Landed Gentry, it now seems he was not born until at least 1544 as there are records of Wardship in the State Papers which indicate he was still a minor (i.e. under 21) in 1564.

Thomas Delariver Esq. of Brandsby died about 1558 (not 1577). Hence Dorothy was not even born when her grandfather died.

Thomas Delariver's four illegitimate daughters were Jane, Thomasine, Eleanor and Elizabeth (not Martha). Incidentally, Jane had a different mother from the other three, who were full sisters.

Nicholas Burdett of Swawell in his will of 1598 mentions his master, John Savile (not Sir John Neville). This ties in with the fact that his son, Matthew, married, two years later, Dorothy Colthurst of Howley Hall, Batley. This was the seat of Sir John Savile (later Baron Savile of Pontefract). It would seem that Dorothy was a ward or guest of the Savile's and there appears to be little doubt that Sir John played a part in bringing this important marriage about. It is unlikely that Sir John would have secured a marriage for any younger son of his old retainer which suggests that Matthew was the heir by this time.

p.94. Matthew Burdett (1692–1725) son of Samuel, did not marry Ann Arsland as shown in the pedigree. Ann Arsland is a misreading by one of the sources of Ann Crossland who married Matthew Burdett (1699–1751) the drysalter. (See pedigree on p.96).

Matthew (1692–1725) married as her second husband, Mary, the widow of William Couldwell. She was several years his senior. She is the Mary Burdett of Commonside, Penistone, who left a will in 1734. By her first husband, Mary was the mother of William Couldwell (d.1783) who's interesting epitaph in Denby churchyard appears on p.122. This explains why his tombstone also records Amos Burdett (1724–1798) who was his half brother.

Mary, may be the Mary Newton who married a William Couldwell at Cawthorne in 1706.

p.245. James Oates lived (1823–1852) the dates in the pedigree are those of his father, John. Amos Burdett died 1798 not 1799. Ann Arsland should be Mary Couldwell, widow. Grace, daughter of Matthew Burdet & Dorothy Colthurst married William Fleming.

p.247. Matthew Burdett died in 1632 not 1597. His Uncle John's wife was Cecilia (see p.91).

Bibliography

✿

Addy, John, Selected notes from Parish magazines
Addy, John (Editor), *A History of the Denby Dale Parish*, DDUDC 1995
Arnold, Peter, *Methodism in a West Yorkshire Village*, Denby Dale Methodist Church 2001
Barratt, Nick, *Tracing the History of Your House*, PRO Publications 2001
Bower. D & Knight. J, *Plain Country Friends*, Wooldale Friends Meeting Society 1987
DDUDC, Denby Dale Official Guide, 1972
Heath, Chris, *Denby & District – From Pre-history to the Present*, Wharncliffe Books 2001
Heath, Chris, *A History of the Denby Dale Pies*, J R Nicholls 1998
Heath, Chris, *Denebi – Farmstead of the Danes*, Richard Netherwood 1997
Hey, David, *A History of Penistone & District*, Wharncliffe Books 2002
Hudds. Archives, Jonas Kenyon & Co. collection
Hudds. Archives, Norton collection
Hunter, Rev. Joseph, *South Yorkshire VII*, E P Publishing 1974 r/p
John Goodchild Collection, Court Rolls – Denby etc. (1344–1501)
Penistone Almanac, 1953
Penistone Almanac, 1954
Penistone WEA Group, *A Further History of Penistone*
Nottingham Archives, Savile collection – particularly: DDSR1/2/32, DDSR1/2/11, DDSR1/2/24, DDSR1/14/10a, DDSR1/2/18, DDSR1/2/16, DDSR1/2/7, DDFS10/13/14, DDSR1/2/19, DDSR1/2/28, DDSR1/2/20
Hoyle Eli, *History of Barnsley & Surrounding Area*, Barnsley Chronicle 1904/5
Umpleby, Tom, *Water Mills & Furnaces on the Yorkshire Dearne*, Wakefield Historical Publications 2000
Various Editors, *The Oxford Surnames Companion*, Oxford University Press 2002
West Yorkshire Federation of Women's Institutes, *The South & West Yorkshire Village Book*, Countryside Books 1991
Waters, Colin, *A Dictionary of Old Trades, Titles & Occupations*, Countryside Books 2000
Williams, Thomas, *A Memoir of Mr James Wood*, 1883
Wilkinson, Joseph, *Worthies of Barnsley*, Barnsley Chronicle c.1880

The information taken from the documents I have utilised is in most cases only representative of the document as a whole. Local and family historians should be very aware of this and would be well advised to obtain a copy of the document in question for further research. It should also be noted that ancient handwriting is notoriously difficult to transcribe, as such, the information in this work is only that which the author has been able to extract from the documents to the best of his ability. Nottingham Archives and the Borthwick Institute both operate a copying service (for items which are suitable) at a very cost effective rate. They also house hundreds of other records for the Denby area and are a must for any budding enthusiast. They can be contacted at the following addresses:

Nottingham Archives: County House, Castle Meadow Road, Nottingham, NG2 1AG.
Borthwick Institute: St Anthony's Hall, Peasholme Green, York, YO1 2PW

Index

Purely for reasons of space this index is very highly selective. It is impossible to include all the personal and place names included within and is designed to help the reader around the book rather than be fully comprehensive. Entries regarding individuals relate to the most specific passages in the text about them, they do appear in other areas of the book, though in a more supporting roll.